Auguste Comte and the Religion of Humanity
The Post-Theistic Program of French Social Theory

This book offers an exciting reinterpretation of Auguste Comte, the founder of French sociology. Following the development of his philosophy of positivism, Comte later focussed on the importance of the emotions in his philosophy, resulting in the creation of a new religious system, the Religion of Humanity. Andrew Wernick provides the first in-depth critique of Comte's concept of religion and its place in his thinking on politics, sociology and philosophy of science. He places Comte's ideas in the context of post-1789 French political and intellectual history, and of modern philosophy, especially post-modernism. Wernick relates Comte to Marx and Nietzsche as seminal figures of modernity and examines key features of modern and postmodern French social theory, tracing the inherent flaws and disintegration of Comte's system. Wernick offers original and fascinating insights in this rich study which will attract a wide audience from sociologists and philosophers to cultural theorists and historians.

ANDREW WERNICK is Professor of Cultural Studies and Sociology at Trent University, Ontario, Canada. He is director of the Center for the Study of Theory, Culture and Politics, and Director of the Graduate Program in Methodologies for the Study of Western History and Culture. His publications include *Promotional Culture* (1991), *Shadow of Spirit: Religion and Postmodernism* (with P. Berry, 1993) and *Images of Ageing* (with M. Featherstone, 1994).

Auguste Comte and the Religion of Humanity

The Post-Theistic Program of French Social Theory

Andrew Wernick

CAMBRIDGE UNIVERSITY PRESS

PUBLISHED BY THE PRESS SYNDICATE OF THE UNIVERSITY OF CAMBRIDGE
The Pitt Building, Trumpington Street, Cambridge, United Kingdom

CAMBRIDGE UNIVERSITY PRESS
The Edinburgh Building, Cambridge CB2 2RU, UK   www.cup.cam.ac.uk
40 West 20th Street, New York, NY 10011–4211, USA   www.cup.org
10 Stamford Road, Oakleigh, Melbourne 3166, Australia
Ruiz de Alarcón 13, 28014 Madrid, Spain

First published 2001

Printed in the United Kingdom at the University Press, Cambridge

Typeface Plantin 10/12 pt   *System* 3b2   [CE]

A catalogue record for this book is available from the British Library

ISBN 0 521 66272 9 hardback

In memory of my father, Abram Joseph Wernick

The story is told of an automaton constructed in such a way that it could play a winning game of chess, answering each move of an opponent with a countermove . . . One can imagine a philosophical counterpart to this device. The puppet called 'historical materialism' is to win all the time. It can easily be a match for anyone if it enlists the services of theology, which today, as we know, is wizened and has to keep out of sight.

Walter Benjamin, 'Theses on the Philosophy of History'

Contents

Acknowledgments

My interest in French social theory had its distant origin in a conversation with Jonathan Bordo. Other friends and colleagues at Trent who have helped shape and enrich this interest include John Fekete, John Hillman, Zsuzsa Baross, Constantin Boundas and Peter Kulchyski. Interchanges with Philippa Berry, Phillip Blond, Mike Featherstone, Mike Gane, Gad Horowitz, Arthur Kroker and Heather Jon Maroney have also been of great benefit over the years. I thank Gad Horowitz for his help and encouragement with the manuscript, an earlier version of which was accepted as a doctoral thesis at the University of Toronto. My thanks also to Mike Gane for his valuable comments, the two anonymous reviewers at Cambridge University Press who saved me from many errors, and Jean Gauthier and Heather Jon Maroney for pointing me towards some key references. My intellectual, as well as every other kind of, debt to the latter is incalculable.

Introduction: rethinking Comte

At the heart of Auguste Comte's program for resolving the 'crisis' of (early) industrial society – and explicitly so with the publication, in 1851, of *Système de politique positive ou Traité de sociologie* – was a project for 'positivising' religion by instituting (as its subtitle announced) *la religion de l'Humanité*. My aim in this inquiry is to interrogate that project, together with the wider conceptualisation to which it was linked.

Today, no doubt, to suggest that Comte's labyrinthine synthesis of philosophy, science, sociology, politics and religion is *worth* reexamining, let alone from its religious side, will meet with scepticism. We have learnt very well to mistrust all systematisers, and we are bored with the shibboleths of the nineteenth century. Who cares, any more, about Comte's totalising scientism, or about the organised idolatry of *la société* which it underwrote? Why dig up Positivism, only (presumably) to bury it again? One answer, I mean to show, stems from Comte's crucial but underrecognised place in the formation of modern, and postmodern, French thought. Another concerns the continuing (or renewed) pertinence of fundamental thinking about the social itself as a topic for reflection. Yet another would argue the value of grappling with Comte as a way to clarify problems in the vantage point (political, reflexive, emancipatory) from which, in the first place, these considerations press into view.

This will already make clear that the interrogation I have in mind is not only the hard questioning of a suspect caught near the scene of a crime. Even those, I will suggest, for whom Comte is the intellectual progenitor of an odiously self-enclosed corporatism may learn something from his thinking. What I propose is an engagement with Comte, not just against and about him. The themes of such an engagement, and its angle of approach, require more comment. But before elaborating, it may be useful to set the stage by recalling first, in Comte's own terms, what he actually meant to establish. What was, or was to be, 'positive' religion?

The project of Positive Religion

Based on a 'demonstrable faith', but otherwise homologous with the Catholic form of Christianity it was 'destined' to replace, the religion of Humanity was to be a triple institution.[1] Its full establishment required a doctrine (*dogme*), a moral rule (*régime*) and a system of worship (*culte*), all organised and coordinated through a Positivist Church. The first of these, the doctrine, could be considered established in Comte's own writings, though not yet in complete form. The 'objective synthesis' of the *Philosophie positive* needed to be complemented by a 'subjective synthesis', for which the *Politique positive* was to provide the groundwork. As well, though he never got beyond a sketch-plan, there was to be a summarising and integrating *science de la morale*.[2] Taken as a whole, the Positivist System would provide the scientific–humanist equivalent to what systematic theology had been in the high Middle Ages: it would serve as the intellectually unifying basis of the new industrial order.

Of course, Positivism would be without effect if not disseminated. Hence the need for an educational reform, which in turn was part of a broader pattern of institutional changes designed to provide industrial society with an entire *régime* of cooperative purpose and order.[3] What this entailed for the individual was a lifelong process of moral education.[4] It would begin at home with Mother, continue in the schools with a revamped curriculum under (male) teacher-priests,[5] and persist in the sermons and ceremonies which Positive Religion would install in a systematic and pervasive ritual round. Prominent among the latter were the sacraments (*présentation, initiation, admission, destination, mariage, maturité, retraite, transformation, incorporation*)[6] which were to accompany each stage of the life course, and through which each servant of

---

[1] Comte provides a detailed account of Positive Religion in volume IV of *Politique positive*. Its three parts, moving from *culte* to *dogme* to *régime*, are outlined in chapters 2–4. See x:9–248.

[2] In the still fuller version of the doctrine, 'First Philosophy' would summarise the methodological principles of Positivism, 'Second Philosophy' would consist of the Subjective Synthesis, including the theoretical part of *la Morale*, and 'Third Philosophy' would systematise *l'action totale de l'Humanité sur son Planète* (x:246–7).

[3] 'Quand la discipline inspirée par l'amour se trouve ainsi fondée sur la foi, le régime la complète et la consolide en développant une activité d'où résulte la réaction, à la fois directrice et répressive, de l'ensemble envers les parties' (x:167).

[4] Besides the direct inculcation of *altruisme*, the formula for recalcitrant impulses was that 'in the name of happiness and duty' the *instinct nutritif* should be restrained, the sexual instinct severely so, and that envy and vanity should be weakened (x:344).

[5] From ages 7 to 14, with one year being devoted to each of seven courses of study, corresponding to the seven branches of knowledge (x:250–2).

[6] The last sacrament, *incorporation* (into le Grand-Être) would come after death, following a favourable judgment for those deemed worthy of remembrance (x:130).

Humanity would solemnly rededicate himself (or herself)[7] to a life of service.

But it was not only individuals who were to be 'rallied' and 'regulated'. The *régime* governed the form and functioning of the 'tissues' and 'organs' which made up the social body as a whole. Hence a mass of prescriptions for the harmonious (re)ordering of every major institution. The family: role-divided, chivalric, extended, replete with children, servants and animals (x:292–6). The sphere of production: cooperative, functionally ordered, justly meritocratic (x:338–42). The polity: reduced to the humanly manageable scale of a small republic,[8] oriented to production not war, and linked to others in an ultimately global confederation. Overarching direction would be provided by a complementary leadership of temporal and spiritual authorities. The former (*les patriciens*) was to consist of bankers, industrialists and engineers from whom, in each republic, a committee of thirty, topped by a triumvirate, would be selected to direct the state (x:345). The new 'Spirituals', on the other hand, would be the scientists–philosophers–teachers–pastors encadred in the Positivist priesthood itself.[9]

As with Positivism's feudal–Catholic predecessor, the two leading powers of industrial society were to be not only functionally distinct: each was to have its own form of rule. The lay elites who coordinated production (and distribution) would control the repressive organs of the state. The officers of the Positivist Church, commanding neither wealth nor force, were to exercise a purely moral suasion (VII:504). But there were also differences. The priests of Humanity would have not only care of souls, but also – having regard to their integrated expertise in all the sciences of Man – of bodies too (x:281). As well, their spiritual authority – i.e. their capacity to mobilise public opinion, whether against incorrigible displays of egoism and immorality, or against destructive social conflict over the distribution of social wealth[10] – would be rooted not only in the prestige of their office as representatives of Humanity and mediators of its grace, but also in the ties 'spontaneously developed' between themselves and their natural allies. Positivism would draw the support of *les prolétaires* as industrialism's indispensable, but excluded,

---

[7] For women, destined for marriage and motherhood, and excluded from external careers, there would be three fewer sacraments – i.e. no *destination* independent of *mariage*, and correspondingly no *maturité* or *retrait* (x:123).

[8] The world, with an estimated population of 140 million, would be divided into 70 republics with 300,000 family households and 1–3 million inhabitants each (x:309–10).

[9] For the triple function of *le pouvoir spirituel* ('conseiller, consacrer, et régler'), see x:9. For its guiding role within the wider industrial intelligentsia, see x:253–5.

[10] Salaries would be fixed according to a just scale and dispensed centrally through the employer-based civic authority (x:340).

class.[11] It would also forge links to women, finding in *la femme* a powerful moralising influence hitherto confined within the familial household, for which Positive Religion would provide, at last, due place and recognition.[12]

The third element of positive religion was its cult: the organised yet 'effusive' worship of Humanity. Under the guidance of the new priest-hood, this was to be conducted through public festivals (calibrated with the Positivist Calendar in 'appreciations' for the greatest aspects and benefactors of the Grand-Être),[13] through worship at the family hearth and ancestral tomb, and through thrice-daily private devotions (x:131). If the doctrine was designed to *synthesise* the understanding, and the regime to *synergise* action, the cult was to mobilise and canalise that benevolent harmonisation of the instincts Comte called *sympathie*, as the proper inspiration for the other two.

The living centre of Positive Religion was, indeed, precisely here: in the feelings of venerative, identificatory and devotional love towards Humanity which the liturgy and teaching of its Church were designed continually to engender. As with Feuerbach (1957), Positivism took sentiments, especially those of the most elevated forms of love, to be the essence of religion.[14] In Comte's general formula: feeling guides action in line with practical knowledge supplied by the intellect. The worship of Humanity was to fix in its adherents a lively impression of such harmonious coordination of the whole human being. The effusions of its rituals would also strengthen the altruistic impulses seen as vital for the correct orientation of thinking and acting. To which there was a corollary. If the cult of Humanity 'consecrated feeling over intellect', it also, in the Romantic vocabulary of gender dimorphism, elevated the symbolic role of women, identified by Comte as a sex naturally predisposed to express and embody the finest (and least grossly physical) sentiments of all. From medieval chivalry and Maryolatry, Positive

[11] Strictly speaking, *les prolétaires* were not to be considered a 'class' at all, but the 'nutritive' function's 'moral milieu' (x:332–3).

[12] Within the spiritual power, nonetheless, even the saintliest women were subordinate to (exclusively male) priests. 'Le caractère propre au sacerdoce ressort naturellement de sa comparaison générale avec celui qui convient à la femme. Plus sympathiques et plus synthétiques que le milieu pratique qu'ils doivent discipliner, les deux éléments de la spiritualité ne diffèrent que par la proportion des deux qualités, dont la première est plus féminine et la seconde plus sacerdotable' (x:72).

[13] The Festivals are discussed throughout the *Politique positive*. The *Calendrier* itself, subtitled 'Tableau concret de la préparation humaine', with its thirteen lunar months and prescribed daily festivals, is appended to the *Catéchisme positiviste* (XI:334).

[14] 'Destinée surtout à nous apprendre à vivre pour l'autrui, la religion doit essentiellement consister à régulariser la culture direct des instincts sympathétiques.' This would 'healthily' reverse the priority which Christianity (in traditional form) had given to doctrine over worship (x:85).

Religion would distil guardian angels and subcults of Clotilde ('ma sainte ange')[15] and the *Vierge-Mère*. Not to mention the sacred icon of *l'Humanité* itself: in the statuary of its Temples, a thirty-year-old woman cradling a boy-child in her tender arms (XI:127).

Looking back over the period of his first synthesis (1826–42) Comte liked to think of himself as the Aristotle of Positivism. With the religious program, announced in the second, he aspired to be its St Paul – not only as an evangelist for the new faith, but above all as the organiser of its Church. Besides congregations, there were literal churches to be built, surrounded by elaborate cemeteries, and Positivist priests to be recruited, trained and set to work. The religion of Humanity was to have two hundred residential presbyteries in France alone, with one priest per 6,000 inhabitants.[16] Beyond that, beginning with the most advanced societies of Western Europe, then spreading from the 'white races' to the 'less advanced' regions of Asia and Africa, it was to expand into a global organisation. Coordinated by national and regional councils, under the overall guidance of seven 'metropolitans', this would culminate in the primacy of the *sacerdoce* in Paris (x:323–7). Not merely St Paul; in fact, Comte was to be Positivism's St Peter as well, inaugurating the office of *Grand-prêtre de l'Humanité* in his own august person.[17]

Comte, Nietzsche, Marx

In practical terms, Comte's founding religious project was a complete, even preposterous, failure.[18] It was, like Comte himself, an easy-to-satirise victim of its own rigidities, archaisms and inflated ambition. Nevertheless, the thinking *behind* that project is worth reflecting on because in two important respects the problems with which Comte was grappling in the aftermath of the French Revolution have not only endured but belong, I would argue, within the still unsurpassed horizons of our epoch.

---

[15] As he called 'Mon éternelle amie, Madame Clotilde de Vaux (née Marie), morte, sous mes yeux, au commencement de sa trente-deuxième année', in the *dédicace* which prefaced the first volume of *Politique positive*.

[16] Each to house 7 vicars and 3 fully fledged priests, plus lay workers and any number of trainees. Altogether, there were to be 100,000 fully qualified Positivist priests worldwide. The master plan is outlined in *Catéchisme positive* (XI:272).

[17] 'Toute la hiérarchie théorie subit immédiatement l'impulsion continue du Grand-Prêtre, qui nomme, déplace, suspend, et même révoque, sous sa seule responsabilité, ses membres quelconques' (x:325–6).

[18] For a first-hand account of the Positivist Society and its aims, see Littré, 1864:592–603. As a curious residue of the Society's Latin American influence, the official state motto of Brazil, where Positivists were active within the modernising elite at the end of the nineteenth century, is to this day *Ordem e progresso*.

To be noted first is Comte's (anticipatory) relation to Nietzsche as a pioneering but troubled champion of the post-Enlightenment break with theism. For all its dogmatic and ecclesiastical airs, Comte's positive faith in Humanity is suspended over the abyss which Nietzsche inscribed with 'the death of God', to which it can be interpreted as both a panic reaction and a strategic response. Like Nietzsche's madman in the marketplace, Comte was 'seeking God'; yet he was doing so, in the endless turmoil of post-Napoleonic France, in the very midst of God's cultural demise. For Comte, too, the waning of theism in the dawn of positivity entailed, at the limit, not just the decay of belief in an external yet ineffable super-being,[19] nor indeed just the delegitimising moral and political consequences of this. It entailed a shattering epistemic break. The rise of a scientific world-view spelt the end of all supernaturalist ontologies, however attenuated, and their displacement by an immanentist materialism, grasped as the primacy of experienced actuality behind and beyond which we cannot go. At the same time, partly through the discoveries of empirical science itself, this same shift induced a profound decentring. After Copernicus, Kepler, Galileo and Newton, the human species upon whose reason and experience the new science was based, was discovered not to be the centre of anything.

[T]he discovery, or rather the proof, of the double movement of the earth constitutes the most important revolution in science belonging to the preliminary stage of human reason . . . it is by virtue of the earth's motion that the Positive doctrine has come to be directly incompatible with all theological doctrine by making our largest speculations relative, whereas previously they had an absolute character. (XI:190-1)

The 'this-sided' disintegration of a shadowy beyond implied the valorisation of human actuality. Yet the Copernican turn undermined the naive anthropocentrism on which the old theism had depended. To make humankind the measure and source of all moral and epistemological value might still be the indicated path. However, if we were to be true to our knowledge, it was a path that could only be taken with the clear recognition that for the human subject to take itself as a foundation was a *relative* standpoint which could only be ratified as such. In any case, a return to innocent illusion was barred. If the humanity pitched into an a-centric universe was to provide itself with a new map and compass, this could only be done in full awareness of the perspectival relativity of all human constructions, and with no guarantees concerning their Truth.[20]

---

[19] The historical course of the *décadence de Dieu* is traced in the third volume of *Politique positive* (IX:507 et seq.).

[20] Macherey (1989:31-3, 121-2) also notes the similarity between Comte's relativism and

The striking affinities between Comte's and Nietzsche's understandings of the paradoxical implications of the scientific break from theism are not accidental. Nietzsche cites or alludes to Comte in several of the texts[21] in which he discusses what it would mean to become contemporary with, and take responsibility for, the enhanced scientific and technological power of the species, and the this-sided grasp of the world on which such knowledge depends. But the relation is two-way. If Nietzsche, in a certain measure, appropriated Comte, Comte can also be read in the light of Nietzsche. That is: his entire reconstructive effort can be seen as an attempt to grapple with the vertiginous disorientation – and nihilism – which Nietzsche was to place at the foreground of attention. Of course it is a different response. Rather than pushing perspectivalism or nihilism all the way, Comte strenuously reacts, in the medium of a traumatised ex-Catholic sensibility, against the threat of 'anarchy', both social and interior to the individual subject. And where Nietzsche, allergic to 'moralic acid', embraced Dionysus (as a figure for the divine but amoral procreativity of Life) against the Crucified, Comte followed the 'secularising' path of those who sought, contrariwise, to extract from Christianity – indeed from all religions – Love as the rational kernel of its ethic, and Humanity as the truth of its God.

The stormy passage, from Hegel to Nietzsche via the Young Hegelians, of the immanent critique of religion in nineteenth-century German thought was examined by Löwith in a celebrated debate with Blumenberg about 'secularisation'.[22] A comparison with the corresponding French narrative would be instructive. In general terms, the German development proceeds from the cultural and subjective grounding of 'spirit', an interiorisation of the divine principle that had already been personalised and desacerdotalised through Protestantism; whereas the French, in the current that runs through the *idéologues*,

Nietzsche's perspectivism, though without reference to the 'Copernicanism' that is a recurrent theme in Comte (e.g.VII:46 and IX:349).

[21] Besides the reference to 'positivism' in the 'History of an Error' section of *Twilight of the Idols* (Nietzsche, 1990:50), two passages in *Daybreak* explicitly comment on Comte (Nietzsche, 1982:82, 215–16). I discuss these in chapter 7 below.

[22] Löwith's *From Hegel to Nietzsche* (1967) argues the continuity of modern German philosophy with Protestant theology, particularly in those moves which proclaimed a break from, or supersession of, the latter. The general framework is laid out in *Meaning in History* (1949), and it is this text which Blumenberg addresses in *Legitimacy of the Modern Age* (1985:27–9). For Löwith, modern thought in repudiating God only secularised the Christian theme of salvation in/through history and so did not involve a fundamental break. The real break was Christianity's own turning away from the cosmos to history as the ground of meaning in the first place. Blumenberg attacks this view as 'substantialist', and insists that intellectual modernity is indeed discontinuous, particularly with regard to its changed grounds for the legitimacy of knowledge and judgment.

Saint-Simonians and sociologists, generated a civic humanism saturated with the corporatism and religious externalism of the unreconstructedly Catholic. Thus the divinisation of Man implicit, for example, in Feuerbach's ambition to translate theology into anthropology, focussed on the generic essence of the human individual. For Saint-Simon, Comte and Durkheim, on the other hand, divine predicates were shifted onto a metaindividual *topos* constituted by the human collectivity in a strong and organic sense.

Nietzsche, it can be said, broke from any version of this neo-Christian schema, while Comte clearly did not. Indeed, Comte's religion of Humanity can be regarded as just a stopgap, or detour, in the 'self-devaluating of the highest values hitherto' (Nietzsche, 1968:9) which Nietzsche, drawing more radical conclusions, wished to push through to a 'transvaluation of all values'. As such, it would be a case of what Heidegger called 'incomplete nihilism',[23] a critique of metaphysics that takes fright at the abyss of evacuated faith and tries to staunch the wound with debris from the shattered idols. It can even be read as not a real rupture at all. As John Milbank observes, '"society is God" can always be deconstructed to read "society is God's presence"' (1993:52).

It can nevertheless be argued that Comte still belongs to a Nietzschian problematic because, in his effort to reconstruct subjectivity in light of the scientific transformation of knowledge, he aimed to root out not only supernaturalism but any absolutely fixed truth, and even – notwithstanding any worshipful way *La Déesse* was to be imagined – any essentialist mysticism about Humanity itself. Against readings of Comte, then, that primarily emphasise his continuity with the ideology[24] (Nisbet, 1973) and theology (Milbank, 1993) of the Catholic reactionaries, I would like to insist that his religiosity is *also* marked by the deeply reflected tension of a thought which is, so to speak, becoming post-theistic. As such, its lines of flight intersect with contemporary discussions which, via Heidegger, Bataille and the postmoderns, have revived Nietzsche's scenario of dying gods and twilight idols as the

---

[23] 'Incomplete nihilism does indeed replace the former values with others, but it still posits the latter always in the old position of authority that is, as it were, gratuitously maintained and the ideal realm of the supersensory. Completed nihilism however must do away even with the place of value itself, with the supersensory as a realm' (1977a:69). For Heidegger, Nietzsche's own 'positivist' enmeshment in a vocabulary of values and valuation left him still within the modern philosophy of the subject, so that his own transvaluation was itself only 'incompletely nihilist' (ibid.:104–9).

[24] Nisbet's emphasis on the influence of conservative religious thought on French sociology (e.g. 1973:238–41) leads him to misread some aspects of the latter. Speaking of Durkheim, he observes, 'His positivism has little to do with Comte's brand' (1965:28).

groundless ground on which to construct an understanding of our own discontents and possibilities.

Comte's contradictory position as an anti-metaphysician who sacralises a socio-historical conception of the human also holds a special interest for those trying to think through what it means, at millennium's end, to be of (or on) the left. As an eccentric outrider of the Saint-Simonians, Comte belongs to the ideological preformation of modern socialism.[25] As such, his work may be dismissed as a historical footnote to the founders. What is worth highlighting, though, is precisely what was entailed by this preformative role.

Comte not only espoused, but deeply probed the rationale for, a cooperative form of society; a rationale which he linked on the one hand to the fundamental (and historically developing) nature of social being, and on the other to the problems of developing a non-transcendentalist religious perspective in tune with the scientific age. Considering that the deepest presuppositions of the transformist impulse – for so long 'wizened and out of sight' both in the Marxism that has prevailed on its radical side and in the moralism (manifest today in identity politics and the 'equity agenda') that has prevailed on its reformist side – became fragile and exposed in the unravelling of the socialist project in the last decades of the twentieth century, we can see here a second order of contemporary significance. As displayed, for example, in Habermas's reflection on communicative rationality (1987), in Derrida's spectrological meditations on justice as the 'messianic' element in Marx (1993), in Levinas's phenomenology of the Other (1969), and (at a less exalted theoretical level) in Lerner's 'politics of meaning' (1996), a reconsideration of the ideological, even religious, roots of socialism has moved (back) on to the agenda. Re-examining earlier figures like Comte, then, can become part of a renewed effort to clarify, and soberly rethink, what most deeply defines a progressive, emancipatory or – to use the maligned word – communist commitment.

Comte, to be sure, is a strange mirror to hold up. His political relation to the socialist tradition is ambiguous, to say the least. A top-down reformist who eschewed the collectivisation of private property in favour of measures to ensure its morally responsive stewardship,[26] his politics

---

[25] For Comte's place in the larger contemporary Parisian constellation of prophetic and utopian thinkers, see Manuel, 1962:249–96.

[26] These measures included: the establishment of a fixed scale of salaries (x:340–3), the institution of local *salons* for mingling and instruction, which would bring *patriciens* and *prolétaires* together in the same moral milieu (x:314–15), and a succession process in which the passage of property to heirs would be vetted, and eventually, through artificial conception (x:278), separated from heredity as such. The total intended effect was to create a moral atmosphere in which *occupations personnelles* would be converted

had much in common with the Saint-Simonian current, in whose direct orbit he was from 1817 to 1825.[27] His political objective, which never changed, was to complete the work of 1789 by developing an institutional framework (including a 'terrestrial morality') within which science-based knowledge and production could become systematic, harmonious and predominant, to the benefit of society as a whole. Remnants of the *ancien régime* were at first the main target. 'It is on the revolutionary school alone', he noted in *Philosophie positive*, 'that we can expect that the positive polity can experience a predominant influence, because this is the only one that is always open to new action on behalf of progress.'[28] In that spirit, he was an anti-monarchist during the Bourbon restoration, while under Louis-Philippe he urged a cross-class alliance of workers and 'patriciens' to press for the reforms that would permit the new industrial/positive system fully to emerge. At the same time, and increasingly, Comte was a partisan of order as well as progress. He was hostile to any form of popular insurrection, or indeed democratising project. With the rise of a radical workers' movement in the watershed decade of the 1840s, he began, accordingly, to seek alliances on the right. In the upheavals of 1848–51, he detached himself from the republicans, argued for a 'dictatorship' (as under Danton), then gave cautious welcome to Louis Bonaparte, whose regime he tried to win to the cause.[29] When that came to nothing, he was again pushed into

into *fonctions civiques*, and in which all would be cooperating in a collective and, above all, future-oriented task (IX:491).

[27] In 1817 Comte became Saint-Simon's personal secretary and editor of his house journal, *L'Industrie*. The master's refusal to acknowledge Comte's authorship of key articles, and arguments about who was stealing ideas from whom, led to a bitter break. On Saint-Simon's death in 1825, Comte nonetheless agreed to contribute an essay to the founding issue of *Le Producteur*, which his closest followers put together a bare three weeks after the old man was gone. For a detailed account of Comte's break with Saint-Simon, see Gouhier (1965:95–109) and Pickering (1993:192–244). The essay at the centre of their final dispute (which Comte wrote in 1922 but which Saint-Simon published, with a disclaimer, only in 1824) was 'Plan des travaux scientifiques nécessaires pour réorganiser la société'. He always referred to it as 'mon opuscule fondamental'. He republished it, with five other early essays, as an appendix to the last volume of *Politique positive*.

[28] Martineau, 1853, II:437. A critical but 'appreciative' assessment of the 'époque critique, ou âge de transition révolutionnaire' is laid out in the 55th *leçon* of *Le cours de philosophie positive* (V:394–623).

[29] For Comte's political trajectory, see Pickering, 1993:chs. 2 and 10, and Gouhier, 1965:144–8. Comte's critique of the Bourbon Restoration for its 'retrograde' alliance with remnants of the *ancien régime* continued into the Orleanist regime of Louis-Philippe. Unlike other moderate Republicans, though, he equally opposed Parliamentarism, as he made clear in a letter (with other signatories) he sent to Louis-Philippe in 1840 (Pickering, 1993:432). After seeking the support of women and workers in the *Catéchisme positiviste* of 1852, he sought those of *les hommes d'état* in his *Appel aux conservateurs*, which appealed for subsidies to support (his own) *sacerdoce*. Its tone may

opposition, where, till his death in 1857, he confined his attention to appealing for money, developing a core of acolytes, and propagandising for Positivism and its Church.[30]

The limitations of nineteenth-century French 'socialism', in the non-Marxist stream that runs from the Saint-Simonians to the social democracy of Jean Jaurès and the solidarism (with which Durkheim was briefly associated) of Léon Bourgeois,[31] are easy enough to state. It reduced to a moral plane both the problem of and solution to the contradictions of industrial capitalism. These contradictions it also defined as transitional rather than inherent, resulting from the incompleteness of industrialism's emancipation from pre-industrial ways of seeing, feeling, thinking and acting. Correlative with this conflation, which was carried into the heart of Comtean, and Durkheimian, sociology, there is no conceptual room for the economic as such, either as the basis of class relations or as the moulder of social structures and processes through the logic of capital and commodities. Such phenomena are assimilated instead to technical realities (production, industry) on the one side, and to social-moral ones (distribution, coordination) on the other. Therewith, the conflictual and disintegrative effects of the free market are defined as a kind of cultural pathology which can be cured by institutional reforms designed to harmonise, solidarise, ethicise etc. the whole sphere of production and exchange. Anarchists, libertarians and Critical Theorists will add that, faulty social analysis aside, there are serious weaknesses of vision in this form of socialism too. Enthusiasm for *l'industrie* was the watchword for a bad utopia: society as a vast workshop, productivist, technocratic and held together as a managed harmony of useful functions by a centrally directed state. It is a vision which hovers at the edges of the *Communist Manifesto*'s transitional program,[32] and one that, for all of Marx's own horizon of freedom beyond the realm of necessity, the ideologues of the Second and Third Internationals never submitted to much critical scrutiny.

Once such a critique is admitted, however, there remains a residue of

---

be gathered from the new slogan that appears in its frontispiece: *La Famille, la Patrie, l'Humanité.*

[30] After Comte's death, the Positivist Society, under Pierre Laffitte, continued to propagate Comte's ideas. Its last major public involvement was a campaign, in alliance with the Parisian Catholic hierarchy, to prevent the city authorities from relocating the main Paris cemetery outside the city limits. See Ariès (1981:541–5). The cult of the dead was a central feature of religious Positivism.

[31] Léon Bourgeois expounded his social philosophy in *La solidarité* (1896). For Durkheim's involvement with *solidarisme*, see Lukes, 1972:350–4.

[32] In points 6 ('centralisation of all means of communication and transportation in the hands of the state') and 8 ('establishment of industrial armies, especially for agriculture') (Feuer, 1959:28).

considerations that have not been entirely dispelled. One set of issues concerns the constitution and axiological status of the collective subject. 'The standpoint of the old type of materialism', wrote Marx in his 'Theses on Feuerbach', 'is civil society. The standpoint of the new materialism is social humanity or human society' (Marx and Engels, 1947:199). The dictum applies to the ideological as well as the theoretical plane. In all its variants, and however qualified by individualism, socialism's sacral term is always some version of the first person plural. This 'we' forms both the ground and horizon of progressive political activity. The transformist aim is to autonomise and finally heal it, so that the organised collectivity of society is no longer coercive, no longer masks the domination structure of a pseudo-community, and does not stand in contradiction to the 'I's that make it up. But how is such a collectivity – Bloch's 'not-yet community'?[33] Bernstein's (and Habermas's) community-as-regulative-ideal? Blanchot's (1986) *communité invouable?* – to be conceived? How is it to be thought with respect to social, psychological and historical categories? How, with respect to agency? How, if we are to avoid dogmatism or idealism, can 'social humanity', or a guiding 'we', be grounded? What meaning can be ascribed to it within a critical, demythologised, socio-historical self-understanding?

I do not want to suggest that Comte provides a satisfactory answer to these questions. Nonetheless, what he projected into the category of *l'Humanité* arose from a persevering attempt both to provide one, and in the context of a world-view which aimed to make theory practical, and return it to earth. Comte's elaboration of that term, then, including his attempt to ground it in an analysis of 'the social tie', might usefully be revisited as part of a wider inquiry into the social problematics of transformist thought.

Comte's treatment, however, is connected to a less digestible point. The worship of *l'Humanité* was not just designed to inspire us all forward. Its institution, as concept and cult, was tied, within a program of social reconstruction, to the perspective of unity and order. Progress itself, Comte insisted, is 'the progress of order'. And what secures order, as the complex of practices that bind individuals together in a society, and binds together this binding, is 'religion'. In so far as Comte confounds, under the technicist rubric of industrial society, the problem of capitalist order with that of social order as such, we may dismiss both his analysis and his prescriptions as a misrecognition of the problem. Given the social antagonisms and cultural corrosion that are endemic to

---

[33] For the 'not-yet' as a dialectical utopian category, see Bloch, 1995:310–11.

the dynamics of capitalist industrialisation, it is no wonder he proposes such a vast apparatus of *régulation* and *ralliement* to hold it all together. Has he not, in fact, simply mistaken the ideological superstructure for the base of the social formation he would religiously unify?

These objections may be granted, yet it may still be possible to learn from what Comte was aiming to do. Colletti, dismissive of determinist and economistic forms of Marxism, but equally opposed to the inflated role of will and subjectivity in counter-strains, suggested a policy, in such matters, of constructive engagement. The split between Kautsky and Plekhanov on the one side, and 'Austro-Marxists' on the other, he notes, 'can be traced to the basic orientations into which bourgeois culture was split in the second half of the nineteenth century' (1972:18). That split, between equally one-sided approaches to the relation between social consciousness and social being, had persisted in orthodox Marxism's attitude to its 'bourgeois' sociological rival. Classical sociology may be judged idealist, subjectivist etc. in so far as it takes consciousness (the *conscience collective* for Durkheim, the intentionality of social action for Weber) to be the key for explaining social structure. But criticising this should not lead us to forget, first, that ideology is also consciousness which, as mental appropriation, changes both subject and object, and, second, that 'ideological social relations' are an independently effective part of the social whole.[34]

Colletti implies the possibility of a critical appropriation in which one form of one-sidedness might correct another. Althusser, thinking more especially of French classical sociology, though less open about the appropriation he is recommending, goes further. Ideology – as the sphere in which individuals are 'interpellated' as subjects and in which, as a crucial element of that interpellation and its cognitive consequences, individuals bear an 'imaginary relation to their real conditions of existence' (1971:152–5) – is irreducible. It is not, as some passages in the early Marx appeared to suggest,[35] destined to disappear as an

---

[34] 'The term "socio-economic formation" is a vivid expression of the fact that the object of *Capital* has the character of a "whole" . . . i.e. something including in its scope both social *being* and social *consciousness*, or rather both conditions *a parte objecti* and conditions *a parte subjecti* . . . Both subject and object are part of an *objective* subject-object process. The superstructure is itself an aspect and articulation of the structure . . . it is however equally true that the superstructural or ideological level, though it may be *part* of the structure and of social being, nonetheless is so as *consciousness*, i.e. it has a specific role *vis-à-vis* other parts of the structure' (Colletti, 1972:10–11). It may be noted that Colletti follows Rickert in including Comte (as a small-'p' positivist) among those who do not recognise this. However, as I suggest (chapter 4 below), such a characterisation misses the mark.

[35] Althusser discusses Marx's treatment of 'philosophy', and the status of his own, in *For Marx* (1969). See especially 28–30 and chap. 2, 'On the Young Marx'.

expression or epiphenomenon of class domination, or after 'real knowledge' has replaced empty 'speculation' (Marx and Engels, 1947:15). In
effect, what Comte calls 'religion' is what Althusser calls 'ideology';
from which angle, the way to understand what the Comte/Durkheim
tradition defined as the problem of religion and social order would be to
recast it (and the mechanistic metaphor of the 'superstructure') in terms
of the structures and processes through which the prevailing complex of
social relations is *reproduced*.

Comte and the canon

So far I have suggested that there are substantive reasons why re-
examining Comte's thought might be worth while. But as the reference
to Althusser implies, there is also another reason. This has to do with a
further set of issues concerning misimpressions – affecting other figures
beside Comte himself – which have arisen because of Comte's place, or
rather non-place, in the canon of modern western thought.

Talcott Parsons opened *The Social System* with the rhetorical question
(from Crane Brinton) 'Who now reads Spencer?' (1968:3). With more
than equal force we could ask the same about Comte. Since the early
studies by John Stuart Mill (1961) and Caird (1885), and writings by
Harrison (1975) and other partisans of the Positivist Society, there have
been, until very recently (Pickering, 1993; Scharff, 1995), no serious
full-length studies of his thought in English.[36] In the history of socialism,
Comte's place has been eclipsed by Saint-Simon (whom few read
either), and in that of French sociology (with more justification) by
Durkheim. Comte's reputation in France has fared little better. He may
have been, in the century before Sartre, 'the only mind worthy of
interest which French philosophy produced' (Althusser, 1969:25); but
after the initial flurry of controversy, and Lévy-Bruhl's sympathetic
explication (1903), Comte's work was largely ignored – buried, as
Althusser puts it, under a 'relentless hostility'.[37]

---

[36] Mary Pickering's intellectual biography of Comte – the first volume of which (up to
1842) was published in 1993 – significantly updates Gouhier (1933–41, 1965) and is an
important historiographic resource. Robert Scharff's *Comte after Positivism* (1995), a
finely argued rescue of Comte's philosophy of science from Mill's appropriation, treats
Comte in the 'post-positivist' context of Anglo-American philosophical discussion
about 'historical sensitivity and ahistorical objectivism'. These books, published since
this study was begun, suggest that an interest in Comte is beginning to revive.

[37] Partly, perhaps, as a result of Althusser's own influence, there was some revival of
interest in Comte in France during the 1970s. Particularly noteworthy is the work of
Angèle Krémer-Marietti (1980, 1982), which reexamines Comte's notion of representation, language and sentiments, and of Kofman (1978) which (psycho)analyses the
gender dimension. The cursory treatment that Foucault gives Comte in *The Order of*

Comte's obscurity would be unremarkable if he had been a merely minor and transient figure. However, and leaving aside his British influence through John Stuart Mill, Comte's influence on French thought, and so, these days, on Anglophone thought as well, has been profound.[38] Somewhat like Hegel, that other grand historicist totaliser of his epoch, his system broke into pieces among his legatees.[39] But elements of that system entered many discourses, academic and non-academic,[40] some with a powerful posthumous career. This is evident in biology[41] and even more in sociology, a word he coined. In the quest for a positive 'science of science', a Comtean imprint is also palpable in the field of historical epistemology: that is, in the project of developing a theoretical history of knowledge, pursued in different ways by Bachelard, Koyré, Canguilhem and, more latterly, Foucault.[42]

There have also been periodic attempts to amend and reformulate Comte's larger project, including its political and religious dimensions. Though he cited Montesquieu, Rousseau and Saint-Simon as the main precursors of his relaunched sociology,[43] Durkheim's wider program

Things (1970), even in a work that focuses on the hinge period to which Comte belonged, is indicative however of the marginalised position Comte more generally continued to hold.

[38] Comte's thought also had an (unacknowledged) impact in Germany. Husserl's diagnosis of the 'spiritual crisis', with its attack on the ascendancy of a 'negative' rationality, and its championing of 'philosophy-science', differs from Comte in urging a return to pre-Socratic Greek philosophical roots, but its starting point (and its language) is almost identical. '(O)ur age is according to its vocation a great age – only it suffers from the skepticism that has disintegrated the old, unclarified ideals. And for that reason it suffers from the too negligible development and force of philosophy, which has not yet progressed enough to overcome skeptical negativism (which calls itself positivism) by means of true positivism' (Husserl, 1965:145). The allusion in the last line is unmistakable.

[39] For a first-hand account of splits in the Positivist Society itself, see Littré (1864). For the decline of the Positivist movement in Britain, see Wright (1986:240–72).

[40] Among those influenced by Comte were Charles Maurras, founder of Action Française (Nolte, 1965:52 et seq.), and Pierre de Coubertin, founder of the modern Olympic Movement.

[41] For the influence of Positivism on biology in nineteenth-century France, both through _La Société de Biologie_ (founded in 1848 by Robin and Segond) and through Émile Littré, see Canguilhem (1994:251–60).

[42] In his introduction to the English edition of Canguilhem's _The Normal and the Pathological_, Foucault surveys this development, highlighting the fact that 'for a century and a half (after 1789) the history of science carried with it in France philosophical stakes' (Canguilhem, 1991:11). For him, though, Comte is less central than a more general contrast between the French and German engagements with the 'question of Enlightenment'. The German case involved philosophy 'in a historical and political reflection on society . . . In France it is the history of science which has above all served to support the philosophical question of the Enlightenment: after all, the positivism of Comte and his successors was one way of taking up again the questioning by Mendelssohn and Kant on the scale of a general history of societies' (10).

[43] Durkheim's essay on Montesquieu, 'Quid Secondatus politicae scientiae instituendae

can certainly be understood that way; as too, though the disguise is heavier, can the early Althusser. With the reception of linguistic theory and phenomenology, and with the rise of structuralism and poststructuralism, the Positivist matrix which had shadowed, and partly shaped, the *sciences humaines* during the first half of this century was certainly dislocated and displaced. Even here, though, Comtean themes have often been close to the surface, as for example in that chapter of *De la grammatologie* where Derrida asks whether grammatology can be 'a positive science'.[44]

In France, the background presence of the Comtean inheritance has been real, but of little mainstream interest. In the Anglophone vogue for new French thought, lack of acknowledgment has been reinforced by lack of knowledge. Deconstruction, received into American thinking through literary studies, and taken up by a political interest in 'decentring' the (western, white, male, heterosexual etc.) subject, popularly gave itself a pedigree that ran almost in a straight line from Nietzsche to Heidegger to Derrida.[45] A sideshoot went from Saussure and Peirce to Barthes, discourse analysis and Foucault. In such a truncated account, the fuller intellectual history sedimented within (post)structuralism understandably got lost in translation.

The British case was less straightforward. There, as Anthony Easthope (1991:1–33) has detailed, the initial reception of new French thought went mainly through Althusser, in the context of a far-reaching 1970s debate within and about Marxism.[46] What came out of that moment was a reworked neo-Gramscian theory of hegemony (Hall, 1984), a theory of ideology which took critical social and cultural theory towards a problematisation of subjectivity and discourse,[47] and was a

cotulerit', written as the Latin thesis requirement for his *agrégation*, and his essay on Rousseau's *Contrat social*, posthumously published in 1918, were published together in English in 1965 (Durkheim, 1965). Durkheim's Bordeaux lectures on socialism and Saint-Simon credit the latter, much more than Comte, with the scientific–diagnostic science of society he aimed to develop (Durkheim, 1962).

[44] In part I, chap. 3. Not surprisingly, since Derrida takes writing to be the undoing of any *logos*, Derrida's answer is more than negative. 'On what condition is grammatology possible? Its fundamental condition is certainly the undoing [*solicitation*] of logocentrism. But this condition of possibility turns into a condition of impossibility. In fact it risks ruining the principle of science as well. Graphematics or grammatology ought no longer to be presented as sciences; their goal should be exorbitant compared to *grammatological* language' (Derrida, 1974:74).

[45] Mark Taylor's *Altarity* (1987), which sketches out the genealogy for a 'postmodern a/ theology' from Hegel, Kierkegaard, Nietzsche and Heidegger to Derrida (and so reads the latter through the prism of the former), is a case in point.

[46] Ioan Davies (1995:10–62) has examined this debate, which prominently pitted E. P. Thompson against Perry Anderson and the dominant group in the *New Left Review*, in the course of a wider examination of the rise of a British 'cultural Marxism'.

[47] The intermediary figures here were Ernesto Laclau and Chantal Mouffe (1985).

pathway towards the galaxy of Parisian postmoderns. Paul Hirst's (1975) Althusserian study of Durkheim implied a corrective, and so also continuous, relation between them; but neither he nor anyone else was concerned to explore Althusser's larger debt to Comte. When Althusser recanted the 'theoreticist' positions advanced in *For Marx* and *Reading Capital*, he confessed that 'Nous avons été Spinozistes' (1974:65). Some, looking for elaboration, went back to Spinoza himself;[48] but debate focussed on issues of theory and practice,[49] and none were disposed to challenge this characterisation as the proper name for Althusser's deviation. The price of ignorance was a missed opportunity. Had Althusser been understood against the background of what was distinctive in the modern French sociological tradition as a whole, it might have been possible to see that Hegel – and Stalin – were not the only ghosts at the table of contemporary Marxist theory. It might also have been possible to see that the Althusserian intervention invited critical reflection not just on socialist *science*, but on socialist *ideology* – using that term 'positively' – as well.

Whitehead observed that 'a science that omits to forget its founders is lost'. But this only holds in the domain of what Horkheimer called 'traditional theory' (1972:188–243) – that is, where knowledge accumulates in some objectifiable way, and where the results can be conceptually separated from the process of thought which produced it. Neither condition obtains in social, political and cultural theory where theory, having to grapple with the inherence of the subject in the object, must eschew a false detachment and strive instead for critical reflexivity. Nor are these conditions satisfied where the aim is to develop, not simply the one best theorisation, but an entire repertoire of modes of thinking, and thinking about thinking, which might optimally help to generate a multidimensional understanding of a multiplex world. Under such circumstances, founding figures are certainly not to be fetishised. But neither are they to be forgotten, at least as mnemonic markers for the themes, concepts and framing devices carried by their thought, together with the other names that mark its subsequent development and dissemination.

The question of canons – what they include and exclude, how they

---

[48] 'For Althusser, ideology is best understood as a concept precisely equivalent to Spinoza's "knowledge of imagination" . . . In fact it is no exaggeration to say that the entire project of Althusserianism comes down to the issue of Spinoza *versus* Hegel, or the claims of a Marxist theoretical "science" as opposed to a subject-centred dialectics of class-consciousness, alienation, "expressive causality" and other such Hegelian residues' (Norris, 1991:34–5). Althusser's relation to Spinoza is also an important feature of Eliot (1987).

[49] See especially the title essay in E. P. Thompson's *The Poverty of Theory* (1978).

are formed, and what to make of them – has become controversial with respect to literature and the arts, as well as in the domain of theory (Guillory, 1993). The very notion has become suspect, implying (in the medieval manner) pregiven Authorities whose lead we must follow and to whom we must defer. But in a more pluralistic and less dogmatic sense what one might call, if not a canon, then a shifting canonical assemblage of the intellectual tradition, is indispensable for theorising in the human domain. Within such an assemblage, carrying forward the themes, categories and metatheory of even major thinkers now passé, can provide both a principle of intelligibility vis-à-vis related, or opposed, forms of theoretical approach, and an ongoing resource, at least as a kind of second-order software, if no longer with respect to their 'effects of truth'. This is not to say that the intellectual canon is always what it should be; nor – though it is never fixed, and always contested – that it can be altered at will. It is just that we tend to construct our organon for thinking with the aid of what, and whom, the current canon foregrounds. To which extent, the relation to it of past thinkers, paradigms and traditions is always worth reconsidering.

Comte's posthumous disregard can be blamed on his own idiosyncratic and sectarian deficiencies. However, recalled now as neither a real philosopher nor a real sociologist, we can also interpret his being forgotten as an effect of the very process of intellectual fragmentation which he strove in vain to overcome. In this respect, he belongs to a larger tradition of reflecting and theorising about the grand themes of society and human nature which, for most of this century, has fitted poorly into the established disciplinary grid, and has been marginalised as a result. One does not have to claim Comte's genius to have been equal to that of those great German thinkers whose philosophical reputation (deservedly) outstrips his, and whose *speculations orgueilleuses* he despised, in order to argue that this disregard is unwarranted. What makes it so is the strategic place Comte occupies in modern European intellectual history. Indeed, it is plausible to argue that that history, and its informing effects on the present, are unintelligible if we take no account of the project and metanarrative Comte tried to synthesise, the influence it came to have in the (French) development of the human sciences, and, by way of postmodern theory, the more recent impact, and implications, of its disarticulation and collapse.

A better understanding of Comte can help illuminate, more particularly, two developments in the larger complex of European thought. The first, originating with Bacon's *Great Instauration*, is traceable through the *Encyclopédistes*, to Condorcet, Destutt de Tracy and the *idéologues*, and thence to Saint-Simon, Comte and their derivatives. The guiding aim of this current was to develop a grand synthesis of scientific knowledge through systematically mapping its results and principles. This in turn would provide a basis both for a naturalistic understanding of humanity's place in the cosmos, and for forging an intellectual instrument for extending human (self-)control. In historical terms, the project presented itself as a correction of Aristotle – particularly the Aristotle of the Scholastics – in light of the rise of the natural sciences. If the initial target was Aristotelianism, however, the principal thought-opponent was Plato, and by extension all a prioristic, idealist, in short 'metaphysical', forms of reason. Comte's contribution was to apply this critique to the rationalist political and moral theory of the *philosophes* so that, by means of a real 'science of Man', the Baconian matrix could be fully positivised as the subject and object of its own gaze.

The second sub-genealogy we have already come to. More particularly French, it pertains to the theoretical career of that idea for a post-theistic religion which, after 1789,[50] reconstructive reformers sought to install as the historically proper replacement for the Catholicism of the *ancien régime*. At the centre of this story is the rise and fall of the social – *qua* Humanity and Society – as a sacred absolute, and of sociology as the *logos* of that god. This itself, though, may be regarded as a (perhaps closing) chapter of a much longer French adventure with reason and faith – an adventure which issued from patristic Christianity's attempt to reconcile the mysteries of faith with Greek philosophy, and whose opening storms go back to medieval theology and controversies over rationalism and natural philosophy at the University of Paris in the twelfth and thirteenth centuries (Pieper, 1960). In its classically constructive moment, and with a neo-Kantian amendment,[51] the (modern) narrative runs from Saint-Simon's *Nouveau christianisme* and Comte's *Religion positive*, to Durkheim's civic religion. The project's disintegration can be traced through the structuralist, phenomenological (and Bataillian) break-up of the Society-subject, and thence to all the 'death of . . .' pronouncements which returned thought to a black hole in which reason and faith had both disappeared.

---

[50] Beginning with the Jacobins' *culte de la Raison* in 1793, and *culte de l'Être suprême* in 1794. At the inauguration of the latter in the Champs de Mars, 'Robespierre set fire, with a torch handed to him by David, to a huge cardboard figure of atheism, which went up in flames, exposing to view a rather smoky statue of Wisdom, after which the whole Convention, and delegates from the sections, ascended an artificial mountain where appropriate ceremonies were performed' (Cobban, 1982:232). Gouhier suggests that Comte's religion of Humanity can be understood as 'une survivance de l'époche révolutionnaire' (Gouhier, 1933–41, I:5–7).

[51] Durkheim's 'neo-naturalist' reconciliation of positivism and Kantian idealism is examined by Wallwork in *Durkheim: Morality and Milieu*. The immediate linking figure is Charles Renouvier (Lukes, 1972:54–7).

Comte offers an illuminating vantage point from which to examine both of these developments. His Positivism was fashioned *both* as a scientific systematisation of science *and* as humanistically demystified religion. To be sure, Comte was not the only cross-over point. Bacon's House of Salomon prefigured the Positivist priesthood. Appeals to 'natural religion', as an alternative to the prescientific reliance on Authority and Revelation, were a common coin among freethinkers in the century preceding Comte. De Tracy's *Elémens d'idéologie* and Saint-Simon's writings *before* he met Comte – indicating the need for a science of Man and, on that basis, a new synthesis of knowledge to complete the scientific revolution as the industrial-age basis for a moral renovation[52] – show clearly enough that these themes were not original with him. But Comte was the first to think out, systematically and self-consciously, the integration of both projects. Hence, in the intellectual tradition of modernity, the importance his thought holds both as a strategic reference point and as an event with its own continuing effects.

Order of exposition

Against the background of these considerations, I propose to investigate the themes, structure and movement of the Comtean system with particular attention to the relation between its religious and social-theoretical elements. I focus on the religious side for two reasons. First, because this is crucial to understanding Comte's project as a whole; secondly, as a way to broach more contemporary issues concerning transcendence, politics and the social, particularly as these touch on the problem of critically rethinking what Comte formulated as Humanist faith.

To that end, I propose to explore Comte's religious and theoretical position – in his terms, the doctrine of Positive Religion – at four levels. The first (chapters 2 and 3) will consider the overall schematics of his attempt to produce a totalisation of human knowledge and consciousness. The next (chapter 4), will consider his proto-sociological analysis of the contemporary 'religious crisis' to which that totalisation, and its associated program of reforms, was conceived as a response. Chapters 5 and 6 examine his theory of social being, in both its 'static' and 'dynamic' aspects, highlighting that being's complex dual status (as subject/object for both science and religion) and its transcending significance as the self-perfecting incarnation of Love. This, finally

---

[52] The need for a philosophical synthesis of the sciences is laid out in Saint-Simon's 1807 essay, *Introduction aux travaux scientifiques du XIXème siècle*. His *Mémoire sur la science de l'homme* was written in 1813. See Pickering, 1993:70–85.

(chapter 7), will bring us to Comte's reflection on the nature of the Positivist godhead, which figured *l'Humanité* as *le Grand-Être*, and whose dedicated *serviteurs* he enjoined us all to be.

Comte's thought, I mean to show, was radically flawed, not only as science and as a socio-political program, but at its fideistic core, that is, as a religious position that would sublate the old gods. At the same time, it opened up a complex of issues concerning what is theoretically, ideologically and politically implied by a thoroughgoingly 'social outlook' that cannot be lightly dismissed. In that spirit, the study will conclude (chapter 8) with a consideration of what might be retrieved from the ruins. After Durkheim, the secularising attempt to conceive, and institute, the human collectivity as a divine ensemble irrevocably collapsed. Nevertheless, the work of Bataille, Althusser, Baudrillard and Nancy is adduced to show that drawing the non-catastrophic consequences of this collapse has enabled revised versions of (what I will call) socio-theology to generate a new (or renewed) field of questions still pertinent to a politically charged manner of thinking about the social.

In explicating Comte himself, the order of inquiry could no doubt have been different. Comte's system of systems, somewhat like Hegel's 'circle of circles', is complexly interrelated, indeed to the point of a baffling self-referentiality. It can be entered anywhere or nowhere. But for the same reason, at whatever level we enter it, we cannot avoid encountering the totalising systematicity which characterised every aspect of his thinking. To begin with a reflection on its abstract schematics at least has the advantage of underlining that point. Such a starting point will also introduce us to that 'mania for unity' which John Stuart Mill (1961) and many others have found indigestible in the temper and movement of Comte's thought. As we shall see, Comte's synthesising zeal not only symptomatises a horror for the hell of non-closure. It also self-consciously expressed what he took to be a divine impulse, *l'amour universel* – an impulse which lies at the heart of his religious project, and whose misrecognition, and implicit violence, can be diagnosed, religiously as well as conceptually, as its original sin.

The system and its logic (1): from positive
philosophy to social science

The two Comtes

Any attempt to think through the coherence (or non-coherence) of
Comte's work as a whole is faced with a difficulty that has attended its
reception from the outset. The world religion he aimed to found, and
whose *Grand-prêtre* he proclaimed himself to be, was never more than a
marginal sect. The Positivist catechism, calendar, liturgy, sacraments
etc. are of interest today only as an example of the kind of ideological
exotica that flourished in the radical period that culminated, politically,
in the upheavals of 1848.[1] At the same time, Comte's entire oeuvre
consisted of tracts designed to establish the intellectual basis of that
religion, to train its clergy,[2] or to evangelise on its behalf. To take Comte
seriously, then, has always required some strategy for separating what
Durkheim and others called 'the absurdities' into which Comte's religious mission led him[3] from those aspects of his work (conventionally,

---

[1] Besides the projects and social experiments associated with Manuel's 'prophets of Paris'
– Fourier, Proudhon, Saint-Simon, Enfantin and Comte himself – the period from the
1830s to the 1860s also saw the rise, throughout Europe and North America, of a
multitude of movements, from Chartism, cooperativism, socialism, neo-Malthusianism,
feminism and abolitionism, to nationalism and folkloric and feudal-aristocratic revivals;
to which must be added, in the New World, an apocalyptic frontier revivalism (Bloom,
1993) and the flowering of a host of intentional communities.

[2] The need for a new 'spiritual power', which would control education and whose overall
function would be 'le gouvernement de l'opinion, c'est à dire l'établissement et le
maintient des principes qui doivent présider aux divers rapports sociaux' (xa:193), was
already clear to Comte when he began his *Cours de philosophie positive* in April 1826. In
its 'live' version, the *cours* was a cadre-training exercise, as well as a way to earn money.
Though he was still hazy about the Positivist clergy's specific form of organisation
(xa:214–15), the general argument for establishing one is laid out in *Considérations sur le
pouvoir spirituel* (ibid.). Note also his comment in the opening pages of *Politique positive*
that since that 'decisive work' in 1826 he had dedicated his life 'à fonder une autorité
théorique vraiment digne de dériger l'entière régénération des opinions et des moeurs,
en remplaçant définitivement le monothéisme épuisé' (VII:2).

[3] Durkheim's discussion of the classical Positivists in *Socialism and Saint-Simon* makes the
latter the real founder of 'social physics' and treats the later Comte (whose 'law of three
stages' he also dismisses) as a religious sectarian (1962).

his philosophy of science, and the methodological reflections under-pinning his premature founding of sociology) deemed to have a more enduring intellectual relevance.[4]

Among the eccentricities which found their way into his texts, and which, outside the coterie of true believers, have particularly held him up to ridicule, were a numerology (which dubbed the first three cardinal numerals sacred, held the number seven, and generally all primes, in high regard, and provided classificatory principles for his profusion of systems and *tableaux générales*)[5] and an extreme version of the Romantic *culte de la Femme*. Comte's gynolatry was combined, moreover, with an almost parodic puritanism. This turned women into *anges gardiennes*, complete with an ideal of 'chaste marriage', a sub-cult of the *Vierge-Mère*, and a *utopie* of female parthenogenesis held out before biology as an inspiration to produce the technical means for making the sexual instincts physically obsolete (x:240–1).

Such motifs are particularly evident in the works of Comte's later years. On this basis, and following the lead of Littré (1845, 1864) and Mill,[6] the leading contemporaries through whom Comte was dissemi-nated as a respectable figure, it became conventional to distinguish between these and his earlier writings. Chief among the latter, after the *opuscules* of Comte's formative but troubled period of employment, tutelage and collaboration with Saint-Simon (1817–24),[7] was his first, and in his terms 'fundamental', synthesis: the six-volume *Cours de philosophie positive*, first presented in lecture form during the late 1820s[8] and published between 1830 and 1842. It was this which gained Comte

---

[4] The only serious and non-sectarian commentator who tried to relate Comte's philosophy of science and attempted founding of sociology to his religious project was Lévy-Bruhl (1903). See however my comment on Lévy-Bruhl in chap. 7 below.

[5] On primes and the number seven, see IX:130. Concerning the 'sacred numbers' one, two and three: 'On voit, en effet . . . que le premier, symbole de synthèse, représente aussi la sympathie; tandis que le second indique l'ordre, défini par l'arrangement, toujours binaire; et le dernier, propre à tout évolution, exprime naturellement le progrès' (x:101).

[6] 'It is precisely because I consider M. Comte to have been a great thinker, that I regard it as a duty to balance the strong & deeply felt admiration which I express for what I deem the fundamental parts of his philosophy by an equally emphatic expression of the opposite feeling I entertain towards other parts. It is M. Comte himself, who, in my judgement, has thrown ridicule on his own philosophy by the extravagance of his later writings' (letter of Mill to Richard Congreve, 8 Aug. 1865, cited in Pickering, 1993:697).

[7] Appended to the fourth volume of *Politique positive*, in *Appendice général du système de politique positive*. These essays consist of: 'Séparation générale entre les opinions et les désirs' (1819); 'Sommaire appréciation de l'ensemble du passé moderne' (1820); and – 'l'opuscule fondamental' – 'Plan des travaux scientifiques nécessaires pour réorganiser la société' (1822). The *Appendice* is rounded out with three further essays written after 1824: 'Considérations philosophiques sur les sciences et les savants' (1825); 'Considéra-tions sur le pouvoir spirituel' (1826); and 'Examen du traité de Broussais sur l'irritation' (1828).

[8] The initial attempt, held at his home in the spring of 1826, was interrupted by mental

a position of intellectual prominence far beyond the circle of his immediate admirers, and indeed made him one of the nineteenth century's most influential thinkers. To the later and more dubious corpus, belong the four volumes of *Système de politique positive; ou traité de sociologie instituant la religion de l'Humanité* (1851–4), the *Catéchisme positiviste; ou sommaire exposition de la religion universelle* (1852), and *La synthèse subjective, ou système universel des conceptions propres à l'état normal de l'Humanité*, of whose projected four volumes Comte was only able to complete the first, *Système de logique positive*, before his death in 1857. If the *Philosophie positive*, with its encyclopedic theory/history of the sciences and its sketch-plan for a science of society and history, was deemed worthy of serious attention, these subsequent works, with their dottily punctilious prescriptions for Positivist discipline and worship, were to be prudently set aside.

There is certainly biographical warrant for positing a break in Comte's thought following his first major work, and, indeed, for suspecting what followed to be the ramblings of a ruined mind.[9] Between 1844 and 1846 came the extraordinary episode of Comte's brief, passionate but 'morally pure' affair with the ineligible Clotilde de Vaux (both were unhappily separated from their former spouses). The experience converted him to the principle of the primacy of sentiment over intellect.[10] It was at that point too, immediately following Clotilde's rapid descent into illness and death, and his memorialising transfiguration of her into *ma sainte ange*, that Comte explicitly assumed the role, and persona, of Pope of Humanity.[11] Those, including Comte's estranged wife Caroline Massin, who had morally and financially supported him in his losing battles to gain a permanent teaching post at the École Polytechnique,[12] were henceforth no longer seen as friends but backsliding congregants who had a duty to support *le sacerdoce*. By the end of the decade, his disabling mood swings between depression and mania had been replaced by an impersonal calm. Overall, as Henri Gouhier pithily remarks (1965:175), 'Le système avait dévoré l'homme.'

illness. After his recovery he gave an abridged but public version of the *cours* at the Athénée (Pickering, 1993:365–71, 429–30).

9 Comte had suffered a full psychotic breakdown in 1826. For an account see Pickering (1993:380–404) and Gouhier (1965:121–32).

10 See the *dédicace* to Clotilde which prefaces *Politique positive* (VII:iv et seq.).

11 In the spring of 1849, according to Gouhier. For the 1846–9 course of Comte's conversion, see Gouhier, 1965:211–13.

12 The *Préface personnelle* to vol. VI of the *Cours*, published in 1842, details Comte's side of the story and appeals for support against his 'persecuteurs'. The title page of the volume notes his part-time (and annually renewable) post at the École Polytechnique as *répétiteur d'analyse* and *examinateur*. That was to remain his only formal connection. For his battles with the École, see Pickering, 1993:429–76.

Psycho-biographical questions aside, however, it would be a mistake to overstate the extent of real theoretical rupture that attended these developments. Comte had been working on his *Système de politique positive* throughout the period of writing and publishing the *Cours*. The two were always seen as complementary works, the one providing 'the base' and the other 'the goal' of the 'same universal system, where intelligence and sociability are intimately combined' (x:2). The fact that Comte saw fit to append his six early 'opuscules' – which already sketched out most of the major themes of Positive Religion, including its scientific humanist doctrine and its neo-medieval division of spiritual and temporal powers – to the final volume of the *Politique positive* further indicates his sense of continuity with regard to a project that had been developing over three decades. To be sure, between the preliminary account of 'social physics' given in the *Philosophie positive* and the fuller treatise on 'sociology' provided in the *Politique positive*, something new had been introduced. But the overarching elements of this turn in Comte's thinking – the 'primacy of sentiment', the refiguring of *l'Humanité* as *le Grand-Être*, the 'direct institution' of *la religion de l'Humanité* – are not simply reducible to manic symptoms. They are presented as necessary adjuncts to Comte's first synthesis which seek to address what would otherwise be an insufficiency in the systematics of *le système*.

Philosophie positive had culminated in a discussion of the methodo-logical prerequisites for establishing 'social physics' (volume IV), and a general sketch of its findings (volumes V–VI). What *Politique positive* claimed to display was the transformed condition of this science resulting from the impact back on to itself of the 'subjective' movement in thought which positive sociology's own unveiling of *l'Humanité* as *le Grand-Être* had necessarily provoked. It was a transformation destined to affect all the other positivised sciences in their turn. Comte makes this clear both in the conclusion to *Politique positive* (XI:529–40) and in the introduction to *La synthèse subjective*. Of the latter's projected four volumes,[13] the one he completed, on mathematics (*Système de logique positive*), was itself conceived as belonging to a larger series dedicated to the 'subjective synthesis' of each of the fundamental branches making up *l'échelle encyclopédique*. (A new distinction drawn between sociology proper and the *science de morale* increased the number of these from six to seven.) After his own subjective synthesis of mathematics/logic, that

---

[13] Volume IV of *Politique positive*, published in 1854, specifies that *Le système de logique positive* would appear in 1856, *Le système de morale positive* (two volumes) in 1859, and *Le système de l'industrie positive* in 1861. This plan, it should be noted, would correspond, in the tenth seven-year period of his life, to his *retraite normale*, envisaged as *une dernière période septénaire de pleine activité théorique* (x:542).

of the next four branches of knowledge, devoted to an equivalent revamping of astronomy, physics, chemistry and biology, would be left for his successors. The subjective synthesis of sociology, on the other hand, was to be regarded as effectively accomplished by the *Politique positive*. As for what was now the 'final science', *la morale*, which focussed on the (laws governing the socially inserted) human individual, this was to be expounded in volumes 2 and 3. The fourth and final volume, *Système d'industrie positive*, was projected to crown the 'subjective synthesis' with yet another. Moving from the synthesis of the intellect (in *Philosophie positive*) and the synthesis of sentiment (in *Politique positive* and beyond) to the synthesis of action, its aim would be to manifest the harmony among the differentiated practices of science-based production – material, political and moral – which, in the industrial stage of social development, would 'normally' prevail.[14]

If we are to grasp the overall logic of Comte's attempted totalisation, then, his later work cannot be ignored. Neither completely continuous, nor completely discontinuous, with positions previously taken, its main interpretative, indeed substantive, challenge to the critical reader concerns neither the extravagant self-identification of the author nor the detail of his cultic prescriptions. These, at this distance, can be waved aside. The deeper problem concerns the necessity it claims for the project of 'subjective synthesis' itself – including the all-embracing worship of *l'Humanité* which underlies it – in furthering that total harmonisation of thought, sentiment and action which Comte had aimed at all along.[15]

To pursue that issue we must examine in more detail the movement of Comte's thinking from the first synthesis to the second. The remainder of this chapter will be taken up with the initial systematics of Positive Philosophy, central to which was the notion of completing positivisation through the establishment of social science. After that, we can consider what happened to his system when the effort was made to take full

---

[14] The full ground plan for the 'subjective synthesis', and how Comte's projected four-volume series relates to it, is sketched out in XII:6–26.

[15] For Littré this was the nub of the matter. 'De la méthode objective, sur laquelle est fondée tout l'édifice de la philosophie positive, il passe à la méthode subjective, qui lui inspire la Politique positive et la Synthèse subjective' (1864:517). In upholding the former against the latter, he notes: 'Dans la méthode subjective, les conséquences sont métaphysiques comme le point de départ, n'ont besoin que de satisfaire à la condition d'être logiques, et ne trouvent ni ne requièrent les confirmations a priori de l'expérience' (532). For contemporaries, the consistency between the two halves of Comte's work was only evident to those like Pierre Laffitte who already accepted the religious standpoint presupposed and expounded in the second. Littré's intellectual biography is especially valuable for its first-hand account of the sectarian atmosphere in which these initial controversies unfolded.

account of the implications of having made that would-be completing move.

Positive philosophy and social science

The order in which Comte's first synthesis, the *Système* (or *Cours*) *de philosophie positive*, presents its materials is deceptively linear. It unfolds a compendium of contemporary scientific knowledge, divided into what he determined to be its six fundamental branches: mathematics, astronomy, physics, chemistry, biology and 'social physics'.[16] Each is treated historically, as a process of cumulative development, and arranged in an order which moves through the sciences according to the decreasing degree of generality, and increasing degrees of complexity and specificity, of the range of phenomena with which they deal (1:47–95). The sixth science is an innovation. Indeed, its founding *as* a science, through the establishment of an appropriate methodology and definition of the field, is the climax of the work, as of the larger cognitive transformation it recounts and reflects.[17]

At first sight, the flow of the argument, and sociology's place in it, seems clear enough. There are three steps: (1) from the history of the preceding sciences (including the histories of how they *became* sciences) is distilled a conception of scientificity (*positivité*) which (2) is then applied to the founding of a new, and in point of fact the only remaining, branch of science.[18] This new science, sociology, in turn (3), forms the theoretical basis for a transformation of the practice corresponding to it: politics. Elaborating the results of this latter operation, Comte concludes by telling us (IV:842–3), will be the subject of a further opus, *Politique positive*, whose purpose will be to detail the program of reforms the

---

[16] The term *sociologie*, which replaces *physique sociale* in later works, is first introduced in *leçon* 47 of the *Cours*, in the course of reviewing the formative contributions to it of Montesquieu and Condorcet (1:200–1). About the Greek–Roman hybridity of this coinage, to which he adds the terms *sociocratie* (for the Positive polity) and *sociolatrie* (for Positive Religion), he later comments: 'J'ai d'abord regretté la composition hybride de ces trois termes indispensables, quoiqu'elle soit évidemment motivée par l'insuffisance spéciale des racines purement grecques. Mais j'ai ensuite reconnu que cette imperfection grammaticale trouve une heureux compensation dans l'aptitude directe d'une telle structure à rappeler toujours le concours historique des deux sources antiques, l'une sociale, l'autre mentale, de la civilisation moderne' (VII:403n). See also Pickering, 1993:615.

[17] '. . . la science sociale n'est pas seulement la plus importante de toutes; mais elle fournit surtout l'unique lien, à la fois logique et scientifique, que comporte désormais l'ensemble de nos réelles contemplations' (VII:2).

[18] In fact, the positivisation of social science required both the development of the preceding five positive branches of knowledge and the development of society itself to the point where the law of social as well as intellectual progress could be empirically derived. The (double) relation of sociology to history was unique among the sciences in this respect (IV:179 et seq.).

Cours had only sketched out for resolving, definitively, the 'great social crisis' by which contemporary Europe is beset.

Each of these points deserves careful scrutiny. But two peculiarities of the linking argument should be noted.

The first concerns the movement from theory to practice. In the opening chapter of the *Cours* Comte tells us that the construction of Positivism as an all-embracing philosophy is intended not just as an intellectual contribution but as directly useful to the establishment of social order and the furtherance of progress (1:43). Indeed, Positive Philosophy is presented as the very cornerstone of social reconstruction, 'the only solid basis for social organisation able to end the state of crisis in which the most civilised nations have so long found themselves' (1:339). Yet by the end of the *Cours* that assertion is presented as a practical conclusion validly drawn from a sociological analysis produced by a new science which issues from the application of principles given by Positivism itself (VI:376 and 788). No doubt the second thesis, concerning the practical mission of Positivism, obeys the prescription concerning knowledge formation given in the first. If the advocacy of Positive Philosophy as a cure for the present crisis of post-Revolutionary French, and European, society is to be consistent with the spirit of that same philosophy, that advocacy must itself have a positive basis. But there is a circularity. The programmatic necessity for the system is made to derive from the conclusions to which its crowning moment, the founding of sociology, leads.[19] For the logic to cohere, the oracle of sociology must have been constructed in such a way that it is guaranteed, retroactively, to deliver the right message. We may suspect that the conceptual violence of ensuring this left detectable scars. As we move closer to Comte's sociology proper, that suspicion can be tested. For the moment I will observe just that the marks left by Comte's operation of fashioning his science in light of its intended conclusions are well hidden because of the completeness with which the leaps of faith that constitute his 'science' of the 'social' are integrated, seamlessly, into the proliferating systematics of his system.

This begins to be apparent when we turn to the second peculiarity in

---

[19] Other commentators have noted the circularity. Sylvain Pérignon, in the introduction to the edition of Comte's works from which I have been citing, puts it this way: 'La philosophie positive ... apparaît donc, d'une pointe de vue logique, comme le corollaire immédiat de la création de la physique sociale, qu'elle contribue cependant à réaliser. Autrement dit: *la philosophie positive fonde méthodologiquement ce qui la fonde logiquement*' (1:xvi; emphasis in original). Pickering comments that 'In using universal sociological laws to verify sociology, Comte was making sociology legitimize itself' (1993:564). To clarify the nature of this circle, which such formulations view as singular, I am suggesting here that it is better regarded as *two* circles, the one logical and epistemological, the other practical and historical.

the argument, which displays the same circularity between the philosophical system and its sociology at the level of the *theoretical* relations between them as it does at the level of their *programmatic* import. It is asserted that the founding of sociology comes about by applying principles of scientificity established through the system of Positive Philosophy. Indeed, sociological method requires the positivist synthesis of knowledge as its starting point (IV:230). But it is also asserted that this system depends for its own conceptual existence on that same scientific advance.[20] There is not a linear relation, then, between step one in his argument, establishing the principles of scientificity, and step two, applying them in the founding of a new science.

To appreciate the logic that flows the other way – i.e. the dependence of Positive Philosophy on positivised knowledge about the social – we have only to consider what, for Comte, is the nature of the scientific principles the former establishes, and whence they derive. These principles are not arrived at *a priori*, by rational intuition. They are induced from what at least purports to be the actual history of human knowledge. The epistemological, ontological and methodological generalisations of which these principles consist are themselves presented, accordingly, as empirical rather than purely ideational statements.[21] Together, these generalisations make up what Comte, following Francis Bacon's 'confused attempt' to provide the natural sciences with a unifying capstone, calls 'first philosophy', which, 'being destined to serve henceforth as a permanent basis for all human speculations, should be carefully reduced to the simplest possible expression' (I:61). Comte later (in *Politique positive* – X:176–80) summarises his 'first philosophy' in fifteen rules, which are divided into three subgroups.[22] The first, 'equally objective and subjective', concerns the search for natural laws; the second, 'mainly subjective and relating to the understanding', gives the 'statical' and 'dynamical' laws of cognition; the third, 'mainly objective', summarises what the positive sciences have

---

[20] 'En effet, la fondation de la physique sociale complétant enfin le système de sciences naturelles, il devient possible et même nécessaire de résumer les diverses connaissances acquises, parvenu alors à un état fixe et homogène, pour les coordonner en les présentant comme autant de branches d'un tronc unique, au lieu de continuer à les concevoir seulement comme autant de corps isolés' (I:19).

[21] 'Regardant toutes les théories scientifiques comme autant de grands faits logiques, c'est uniquement par l'observation approfondie de ces faits qu'on peut s'élever à la connaissance des lois logiques' (I:18). The same point recurs throughout the *Politique positive*: 'C'est donc uniquement par l'étude positive de la grand évolution humaine que l'on peut découvrir les lois réelles de l'intelligence' (IX:46).

[22] A 'Tableau des quinze grandes lois de philosophie première', putting the material of X:176–80 in point form, was appended by Pierre Laffitte to the second edition of the *Catéchisme positiviste* (XI:388).

discovered to be the most general laws of motion and order in the material universe.

Needless to say, the Positivist version of 'first philosophy' was intended to displace rather than expand upon what Aristotle meant by that term, i.e. inquiry into 'the nature of being, as being'. The project of fundamental ontology had been relaunched by Descartes and the great metaphysicians of the seventeenth century (Woolhouse, 1993). From these thinkers Comte extracted a conception of the relation between mathematics and *l'ordre universel* – moving equilibrium as the key to understanding both motion and natural existence (x:178) – but he objected to their a prioristic approach and to their starting point in individual reason. Bacon's *Novum Organum*, on the other hand, had envisaged a non-metaphysical 'first philosophy', dedicated rather to summarising what science induced to be the most general laws of Nature.[23] Comte rejected as chimerical any search for a single Law of Laws, opting instead for a methodological unification of the sciences; but in general orientation it was Bacon's lead he followed.

For Comte, accordingly, at the highest level of abstraction the principles of correct understanding are those developed in the *practice* of science, whose own validity hinges on whatever testable knowledge that practice has produced. Of course, there is no science in general. In the real world of scientific practice the sciences are particular and plural, and their methods, like the hypothesised phenomenal regularities they seek to discover, are relative to distinct fields of knowledge. Thus the question of what it means to be scientific cannot be answered in the abstract, but only on the basis of the disparate methods which have actually been developed. Astronomy developed the method of observation, the physical–chemical sciences that of experiment, and biology the method of comparison. To which, as Comte explains in *leçon* 48, sociology is now obliged by *its* subject matter to add *la méthode historique*. 'Science' is to be understood, then, as a developing ensemble of theoretical practices, differentiated into phenomenal domains, each with its own protocols and forms of legitimacy-by-results.[24] To which must be added that the course of this complex occurrence comprises an order

---

[23] '[By] 'first philosophy' . . . what we mean is . . . to design some general science, for the reception of axioms, not peculiar to any one science, but common to a number of them' (Bacon, 1901:138).

[24] 'Isolément d'aucune application effective, les plus justes notions sur la méthode se réduisent nécessairement à quelques généralités incontestables mais très vague . . . Il est donc sensible que, en sociologie comme ailleurs, et même plus qu'ailleurs, la méthode positive ne saurait être essentiellement appréciée que d'après la considération rationelle de ses principaux emplois, à mesure que de leur accomplissement graduel' (IV:229–30).

of factuality in itself. Hence *Philosophie positive*, grounded in a systematic reconstruction of the history of the sciences, and which Comte's subsequent fifteen principles of First Philosophy aimed to summarise.

Comte's empirical and historical approach to the derivation of the principles of science could hardly be otherwise. At the widest level what he is attempting is not just the theorisation of positivity, but the positivisation of theory. That is what *Philosophie positive* means. But we must then ask: upon which of the six fundamental branches of knowledge does this revamped philosophy – philosophy as the positive science of knowledge, having as its object the historically revealed laws of collective mentality – itself depend? The answer can only be: the science of the social. Just as the development of each science is affected by the development of all the others, so too is the progress of the sciences interdependent with that of the practical arts, and this entire complex 'is strictly tied to the general development of human society' (1:66). Indeed, since 'the static analysis of our social organism shows that it rests ultimately, and necessarily, on a certain system of fundamental opinions' (IV:518), it transpires that, in its 'dynamical part', the most important set of sociological laws concerns precisely the history of knowledge.[25] These laws dictate not only the 'general history of philosophy' and thus of social evolution, but also both the cognitive stages through which every branch of knowledge is destined to pass (from the 'theological' to the 'positive' by way of the 'metaphysical') and the chronological order (e.g. astronomy before physics, chemistry before biology) in which each successively less general, more complex, and more dependent science must undergo this process.

This, though, is not the only respect in which establishing a positive science of society is the precondition for establishing positive philosophy. Sociology also enters into the latter as part of its *own* knowledge domain. The laws of human knowledge can only be empirically derived from a consideration of the full range of phenomena to which they pertain. And that range is only available for study when the whole narrative of the positive sciences, with their distinct objects and approaches, can retrospectively be told. Only, that is, when the series made up of the fundamental branches of knowledge has already been completed by the actual emergence into positivity of its final term – sociology.

---

[25] 'C'est donc l'appréciation successive du système fondamental des opinions humaines relatives à l'ensemble des phénomènes quelconques, en un mot, l'histoire générale de la *philosophie*, quel que soit d'ailleurs son caractère effectif, théologique, métaphysique, ou positif, qui devra nécessairement présider à la coordination rationnelle de notre analyse historique' (IV:518–20; emphasis in original).

The fact that it was necessary, however, to positivise the study of society in order to positivise philosophy does not negate the importance to Comte of the converse proposition. Grasping the general principles of positivity, by way of the synthesised history of knowledge, was also crucial for the founding of sociology. The reasons were not only methodological (first generate the principles, then apply them to the social domain). They were also, in the widest sense, practical. Positivising philosophy brings about a revolution in that overarching branch of theory/knowledge which deals with theory/knowledge as such, while success in that revolution was itself necessary for establishing the institutional and cultural conditions in which sociology could firmly emerge as a science. To be sure, other sciences were able to launch themselves and develop without any prior need for a wholesale transformation in the prevailing system of knowledge – albeit, for example in the controversies surrounding Galileo's defence of Copernicus, that a sometimes furious epistemological resistance had to be overcome.[26] But for Comte the case of sociology is exceptional, and for precisely the same reason: that it is, in every sense, *la science finale*.

What distinguishes sociology from other sciences is that it brings the subject of knowledge itself, finally, into the scientific frame. Even the recognition that the social *can* be constituted as an object for knowledge is difficult because of the inextricably subjective implication of human beings in it. A particularly strenuous effort is needed, then, to escape from the coils of the commonsensical, interest- and affect-laden, in short prescientific, ideas which cling to the sociological object. This is so, indeed, not only at the point of the new science's founding, but long thereafter. Furthermore, as the Galileo episode attested (v:564), even sciences which deal with realities remote from the substance of human reality can find their advance blocked by *social* investments in the non-science they must displace.[27] What exacerbates this in the case of sociology is that the very substance of the theological and metaphysical speculation getting in the way is uniquely and directly tied to the social itself. To study the patterning of current beliefs and institutions with an eye to what they have been, could be and are elsewhere, engages political

[26] In physics, the primary opponent had been the metaphysical 'théorie des entités'. Comte took it as a fundamental principle that 'entities' were not phenomenally given, and that the sciences could only study produced effects. See vi:240–2.

[27] 'On voit par là comment l'admirable mouvement astronomique du seizième siècle doit nécessairement y conduire enfin la science à une opposition directe envers la métaphysique, succédant partout . . . à la théologie proprement dite, dont elle tendait dès lors à construire, à son profit, l'antique domination, à la fois mentale et sociale' (vi:240–1).

issues and interests *immediately*. Controversy and conflict are inevitable.[28]

What raises the stakes all the way, however, is sociology's pivotal and climactic position with respect to the progress of the 'scientific series'. Not only is the shift that positivisation implies in the mode of social theorising generally indexed to the long-term rise of a positivist outlook, in contest with the receding grip of the theologico-metaphysical. This entanglement in the broader politics of social belief, it shares with the difficult births of all preceding sciences. What profoundly complicates the gestation of sociology is that, with *its* birth, the whole positivisation of knowledge moves to completion. Science has no more worlds to conquer. The human subject itself is taken. Therewith was wrecked the uneasy dualism of natural and moral philosophy which, throughout the long period during which the physical sciences had struggled to emerge, had provided a compromise form in which the old 'theological synthesis' had been able, in league with a military–monarchical polity, to maintain its intellectual and social rule (IV:244–8). To found sociology as a positive science, in other words, would necessarily bring to a head the crisis in thought that had been brewing since the revival of natural science in medieval Europe, a crisis that could only be resolved by positivising, completely and coherently, the prevailing mode of theorising as such.

Given the stakes, resistance was inevitable. Thus, at least, could Comte console himself during the cold silence that greeted the volume-by-volume publication of *Positive Philosophy* until Littré's laudatory review in 1844.[29] Establishing positivity in the social domain went to the heart, as he saw it, of what was most passionately at stake in the conflicts that were paralysing contemporary society (I:41). The feudal–Catholic hegemony had been destroyed in the great revolutions of the past two centuries. But completion of the intellectual reorganisation needed to establish a new order was blocked by the way in which these same conflicts interfered with the emergence of that *science finale* which held its key. In the absence of such reorganisation, the terrain of post-1789 social and political theory had come to be monopolised and fought over by rival

---

[28] This was doubtless the truth in Bacon's deadpan remark that 'Anticipations are a ground sufficiently firm for consent, for even if men went mad all after the same fashion, they might agree with one another well enough . . . whereas interpretations . . . cannot suddenly strike the understanding; and therefore . . . must needs, in respect of the opinions of the time, seem harsh and out of tune, much as the mysteries of faith do' (1960:45).

[29] Littré, an eminent translator and liberal journalist, wrote six articles on Comte in *Le National* at the end of 1844. It was these which first gave Comte a respectful hearing in France outside the circle of his immediate admirers. See Gouhier, 1965:177.

partisans of equally prescientific philosophies. On one side was the alliance of *légistes et littérateurs* who had triumphed in the first stages of the Revolution, and who subscribed to a metaphysical belief that individuals could spin workable utopias out of their individual brains (v:453 et seq.). On the other was the 'retrograde party' of royalist counter-revolutionaries attached to the illusory absolutisms of Catholic dogma. Divided by a one-sided attachment either to reason and progress, or to faith and order, both camps were equally doctrinaire and equally incapable of thinking the reconstruction of the shattered social order in line with its actual laws and requirements (IV:8–9). Clearing a theoretical path for a science of society, then, necessitated the establishment of a third camp, free from the sterile antagonism between metaphysicians of progress and theologians of order: a camp, Comte argued, which could only arise – and in the Comtean project was actually doing so – from the emerging episteme of science itself. 'This general revolution of the human spirit is today entirely accomplished: it only remains . . . to complete positive philosophy by including in it the study of social phenomena, and then to summarise it in a single body of homogeneous doctrine. When this double task is sufficiently advanced, the definitive triumph of positive philosophy. . . will reestablish order in society' (I:41–2).

To situate the rise of sociology in such terms, of course, is already to be in its register. Indeed, to complete the circle, the diagnosis of the 'crisis' which Comte proffers – centring on the social instability produced by unresolved theoretico-ideological conflict – is not only already sociological. It issues in a *politique positive* which prescribes the installation of sociology itself as a scientific guide for a self-correcting path of 'normal' social development.[30] As a crucial component of that path, sociology, in turn, prescribes the institution (via an elaborate and universal system of education) of *Philosophie positive*. For, sociology tells us, only through a shared belief system intellectually based on such a philosophy will it be possible to achieve social consensus in the emerging scientific–industrial order, and so end the strife.[31]

---

[30] The 46th *leçon* (IV:1–176), which opens the section of the *Cours* establishing 'social physics', provides beforehand, and in just such terms, a sociological account of its necessity and timeliness (*opportunité*). It should be added that Comte never considered that after the 'positive state' had been socially achieved sociology would have any further theoretical development. In *Politique positive* it becomes fixed as a doctrine in the training of Positivist clergy, and its practical intervention is restricted to providing reasons for sustaining society in its now perfected form.

[31] The unifying effects of this philosophy, indeed, will be more complete than ever before. 'La principale propriété intellectuelle de l'état positif consistera certainement en son aptitude spontanée à déterminer et maintenir une entière cohérence mentale, qui n'a pu encore exister jamais à un pareil degré, même chez les esprits les mieux organisés et les plus avancés' (VI:789).

We can summarise by saying that if establishing a science of society is, *in theory*, essential for establishing a positive synthesis of human knowledge, the latter is also, *in practice*, essential for the former; while the conjoint establishment of both is conceived as *socio-historically* necessary by sociology itself. It is one tangle of roots. The complex interdependency of the perspectival shifts involved – the one launching sociology as a science, the other placing philosophy, as the unified/unifying theory of knowledge, on a positive basis – makes it impossible to completely separate them out. Nor, in reconstructing the logic of what Comte was trying to do, is there any need to. In effect, the theoretical *prise de position* which inaugurated Comte's *positivisme* was understood by him as a single, if complex, event: an irruption (in the name) of positivity that occurs simultaneously, and with both theoretical and political effects, on two interlocking planes. To employ a concept which Althusser (via Bachelard) later applied to Marx, but which he surely modelled on the prior structure of the Comtean operation itself, Comte's *Philosophie positive* aimed to effect a *double* 'epistemological break', a *coupure* which would have brought into being, all at once, Positive Philosophy and a Positive science of society.[32]

But what, as a mode of cognition, was *positivité*?[33] And what happens to it when it is (re)conceived from a sociological standpoint, i.e. when a positivist approach is taken towards understanding *positivité* itself? Pursuing these questions will lead us to see how, in trying to complete the objective synthesis of knowledge through establishing a science of society,

---

[32] 'I borrow . . . the concept of "epistemological break" from Gaston Bachelard to designate the mutation in the theoretical problematic contemporary with the foundation of a scientific discipline . . . There is an unequivocal "epistemological break" in Marx's work . . . [It] concerns conjointly *two distinct theoretical disciplines*. By founding the theory of history (historical materialism), Marx simultaneously broke with his erstwhile ideological philosophy and established a new philosophy (dialectical materialism)' (Althusser, 1969: 32–3).

[33] It need hardly be said that Comte's 'positivism' should be confused neither with 'logical positivism' nor with various more general scientistic or obectivist tendencies often referred to as 'positivist'. Some of these tendencies were criticised by Comte himself for their alienated *sécheresse* or disintegrative *esprit de détail*, or for a *matérialisme* that would reduce higher-order phenomena to lower-order ones. But the relation between Comte and these trends is complex. Comte's *positivisme* shared such features of the (narrowly scientistic) *positivismus* periodically debated in Germany as the epistemological privileging of scientific knowledge, the conception of the latter as empirically based and predictive, and the appropriateness of absorbing the human fully into the realm of the scientifically knowable. But as 'positive' and its derivatives acquired a general significance as a label for the whole system, its meaning also considerably expanded. In *Discours sur l'esprit positif* in 1844 Comte distinguishes at least six elements in its definition – realism, usefulness, certainty, precision, constructiveness and relativity (xia:41–4). To avoid some of the confusion, I have capitalised 'positive' and its derivatives, where appropriate, to indicate that it is Comte's doctrinal or expanded meaning of the word that is intended.

Comte was led by the very movement of his thought to complete that completion through the subjective synthesis attempted in his later work.

Positivity from Bacon to Comte

The eleventh month in the Positivist Calendar,[34] Descartes, is devoted to the celebration of 'modern philosophy', beginning with the thirteenth-century rise of neo-Aristotelianism and ending with Hume. Its second week, on the rise of the scientific outlook, ends by honouring Francis Bacon. It may be argued that Comte's Calendar honoured Bacon too little. Through Saint-Simon, and before him the *Encyclopédistes*, Bacon's influence on the formation of Positivism was immense. The Elizabethan courtier's vision, in *The New Atlantis*, of a society centred on science, presided over by a priestly caste of scientists and industrialists, and unified by a new religion dedicated to philanthropy and the expansion of human power, was of great attraction to the post-Revolutionary reformers grouped around *L'Industrie* and *Le Producteur*,[35] and was shared by Comte from the start.

The same can be said of Comte's basic conception of scientific knowledge. While Descartes' analytic geometry is held to provide the better account of the nature of scientific reasoning (and showed how mathematics itself could be synthesised), and Bacon's 'new organon' of induction is criticised for 'floating so often between empiricism and metaphysics', it is Bacon's at-the-time revolutionary proposal for organising 'natural philosophy' that Comte, most proximately, takes over and reworks.[36]

For both thinkers, science is an observationally based cognitive activity which links a human subject, suitably purged of illusory preconceptions, and a natural object, commonsensically regarded as being 'out there', in the systematically conducted pursuit of useful knowledge.

---

[34] The Calendar is included in *Catéchisme positiviste* (XI:facing 334).

[35] According to Manuel, Condorcet's commentary on *The New Atlantis* was included in the 1804 edition of Condorcet's *Esquisse* and 'exerted a profound influence on Saint-Simon and Comte' (Manuel, 1962:62).

[36] In the 57th *leçon* of the *Cours*, Bacon, Galileo and Descartes are singled out as 'les premiers fondateurs immédiats de la philosophie positive'. Galileo's contribution was judged to belong 'essentiellement à l'évolution scientifique' (VI:242). As for the other two, whereas Descartes 'aussi grand géomètre que profond philosophe, appréciant la positivité à sa vraie source initiale, en pose avec bien plus de fermeté et de précision les conditions essentielles . . . qu'ant à l'étude de l'homme et de la société, Bacon présent . . . une incontestable supériorité sur Descartes'. The latter had been content to abandon the moral and social domain to the 'ancient method', whereas Bacon 'a surtout en vue l'indispensable rénovation de cette seconde moitié du système philosophique, qu'il ose même concevoir comme déjà finalement destinée à la régénération totale de l'humanité' (VI:243).

For both, too, that knowledge takes the form of the discovery and interconnecting of laws by which the invariant order of nature makes its ineluctable presence felt.[37] Mastering the human environment depends, in fact, on recognising and utilising those laws, whose predictive power is at once the sign of their scientificity and of their utility as the basis for rational action. On such an account, what characterises scientific knowledge is that it is at once phenomenalist, nomothetic, predictive and instrumental, elements which are elegantly blended together in the third aphorism of Bacon's *Novum Organum*: 'Human knowledge and power meet in one; for where the cause is not known the effect cannot be produced. Nature to be commanded must be obeyed; and that which in contemplation is as the cause is in operation as the rule' (1960:39).

The same formula guides Comte's attempt to launch a *social* science whose scientificity would guarantee its human usefulness. Here, though, Comte went beyond Bacon. For while Bacon certainly regarded the study of 'Man' as a branch of natural philosophy, and even divided it into 'human and civil philosophy, as it considers man separately or joined in society' (1901:176), the social part was purely practical – it consisted of prudential maxims[38] – and the final ends of action belonged not to natural but to divine philosophy, whose absolute character and revealed source in God were unquestioned. Knowledge of the human, moreover, whether *qua* individual or 'as joined in society', was of a less certain sort than that which pertained to external nature. The latter 'strikes the human intellect with a direct ray', while the former, as man 'exhibited to himself', does so 'with a reflected ray'.[39] For Comte, on the other hand, society, including the ends it sets itself, was fully to be considered a scientifically cognisable domain of nature. In the social practice of politics, then, the same principle applied as in the industrial arts. Effective intervention to improve the human lot presupposed a scientific knowledge of the laws in operation. As the Comtean slogan puts it, *induire pour déduire, afin de construire.*

---

[37] 'Nous voyons . . . que le caractère fondamental de la philosophie positive est de regarder tous les phénomènes comme assujettis à des *lois* naturelles invariables, dont la découverte prise et la réduction au moindre possible nombre sont le but de tous nos efforts' (1:11–12; emphasis in original).

[38] 'Civil knowledge has three parts, suitable to the three principal acts of society; viz., 1. Conversation; 2. Business; 3. Government. For there are three kinds of good that men desire to procure by civil society; viz., 1. Refuge from solitude; 2. Assistance in the affairs of life; 3. Protection against injuries. And thus there are three kinds of prudence . . . viz., 1. Prudence in conversation; 2. Prudence in business; 3. Prudence in government' (Bacon, 1901:337).

[39] Bacon 1901:137–8. With divine knowledge, the least clearly present to the mind, 'God strikes [the human intellect] with a refracted ray, from the inequality of the medium between the Creator and his creatures' (138).

The transposition of the scientific idea from its home in what had traditionally been called 'natural philosophy' to 'moral philosophy' was not without its difficulties. Bacon's point about the 'reflected ray' had to be taken into account. The social domain was not just given to the senses *de l'extérieur*. We are in society, just as it is within us, so that its phenomenal boundaries are indistinct. Even more than in other phenomenal domains, then, that of the social has to be conceptually defined before it can become the object of what Comte conceived to be a science. The inescapable need to thematise the social permitted Comte, with a sleight of hand, to ontologise it, which had profound consequences for his entire system. But before coming to this, the provisional formula I am suggesting – that Comte equals Bacon plus 'sociology' – needs to be qualified. For if Comte's 'positivity' built on Bacon's conception of science, it also modified that conception in the light of what were taken to be gaps and inconsistencies; some of which indeed could only be addressed by positivising the social domain itself, and revising the concept of scientific knowing in light of what that implied.

Comte's corrective moves can be summarised under three heads. These concern the relation of *positivité*, respectively, to truth, to non-science and to practice.

Science and truth

Regarding the first, Comte took as given that any positive science must rigorously proceed from sense data. But whereas for Bacon systematic observation and experiment were the royal road to epistemological certitude, and could get behind phenomena to their true nature and causes, Comte rejected as inconsistent with such phenomenalism any clinging to it of an epistemologically 'absolute' point of view. Thus, while scientific procedures were designed to engender knowledge about 'objective' reality, that reality could not be known or understood in its essence, but only from without, in the form of its phenomenal appearance. Similarly, the invariable 'laws' which the sciences sought to discover had the status of hypotheses. The principle that there *are* natural laws, i.e. regularities which are immutable, Comte's second rule of 'first philosophy', is itself formulated as a hypothesis, albeit one which is the axiomatic precondition for all scientific inquiry.[40] What scientific laws represented, in any case, were not real causes – which we could

---

[40] 'Malgré le caractère exclusivement objectif qu'on attribue à ce dogme, je n'ai plus besoin de démontrer sa subjectivité, moins contestable au fond que l'objectivité. Car, celle-ci résultera toujours d'une induction purement empirique, quoique devenue, depuis longtemps, irrésistible . . .' (x:174).

never know, even supposing that the very notion of 'cause' was not itself metaphysical[41] – but observable and predictable regularities. From Newton's celestial dynamics to Gall's phrenology, scientific laws were just *faits générales* which connected, with maximum economy, all the known facts in a domain by relations of resemblance, concomitance or succession (1:3–4; x:173–4). Aristotle had distinguished between what could be known absolutely and what could only be known 'to us'.[42] For Comte, similarly, the first was beyond us, and scientific knowledge could only be of the latter sort: *relative*, therefore, to the limited standpoint of the human subject[43] in the degree of its attainable truth.

Science and non-science

The risk of such a position, which repeated the Kantian distinction between *noumena* and *phenomena*, was that it might undercut the aim to use scientific verity as the basis for a 'demonstrable faith'. But the strict subordination of *le dedans* to *le dehors*, of *impressions internelles* to *impressions externelles*,[44] still remained a rock for Comte on which to build at least a relatively true kind of knowledge. With that principle in place, he could still hold fast to Bacon's insistence that a qualitative distinction could be drawn between those forms of knowing which were scientific and those which were not.

41 In the *Politique positive*, Hume, Diderot and Kant are hailed as the trio who made possible this break from the 'absolutist' notion of causality, though the Kantian outcome still failed to escape altogether from the metaphysical orbit. Of these, Hume's attack on causality was decisive. Kant instituted 'les formules les plus propres à caractériser le dualisme fondamental entre le spectateur et le spectacle, entrevu par Hume et saisi par Diderot . . . Mais pour devenir décisive, cette substitution exigeait la découvert des véritables lois de l'évolution mentale, c'est-à-dire la fondation de la science sociale, laquelle devait reposer sur la biologie . . .' (IX:588).

42 'We must be careful not to overlook the difference that it makes whether we argue *from* or *to* first principles . . . Of course we must begin from what is known. But that is an ambiguous expression, for things are known in two ways. Some are known "to us" and some are known absolutely. For members of the Lyceum there can be little doubt that we must start from what is known to us . . . For we begin with the *fact*, and if there is sufficient reason for accepting it as such, there will be no need to ascertain also the *why* of the fact' (Aristotle, 1970:29–30). Compare Comte's statement in the first chapter of the *Cours*: 'Enfin, dans l'état positif, l'esprit humain reconnaissant l'impossibilité d'obtenir des notions absolues, renonce à chercher l'origine et la destination de l'univers, et à connaître les causes intimes des phénomènes, pour s'attacher unique-ment à découvrir, par l'usage bien combiné du raisonnement et de l'observation, leur lois effectives, c'est-à-dire leurs relations invariables de succession et similitude' (1:4).

43 Relative, he specifies pithily in *L'esprit positif*, with regard to 'our organisation and situation'(XIa:13). This is evidently a multiple relativity, a truth-for-ourselves that takes into account the biological and sociological nature of the human mind, its given stage of development, and the relation of the human species to the terrestrial world and beyond on which it depends.

44 Rule 4 of 'first philosophy'. See x:176.

For Comte as for Bacon such a distinction had implications for the practice as well as the theory of knowledge. Non-scientific modes of knowing were not nullities. In Bacon's terms, 'anticipations of nature', instantiated in the 'four idols' (of the tribe, the cave, the marketplace and the theatre (1901:239–42)), actively obstructed the progress of knowledge. They had, then, to be actively overthrown, both in the preliminary ground-clearing needed before any major branch of science could get going, and continuously thereafter through the discipline of scientific method. Embryonically, we could say, Bacon's metatheory of science contained a theory both of the epistemological difference as such between science and non-science, and of that difference as itself phenomenal, and liable in turn therefore to become the object of scientific, and of non-scientific, knowledge. Comte was happy to take all of this over, but with two important modifications.

First, the epistemological distinction had itself to be clarified. For Bacon, it was sufficient to distinguish as sharply as possible between 'anticipations' and 'interpretations' of Nature – i.e. between deducing the nature of things from truths held *a priori*, and inducing causal laws *a posteriori* on the basis of controlled observation and repeatable experiments (1901:21–2). For Comte, however, the path of knowledge could never be purely inductive. To be sure, Baconian inductivism was not just the blind search for correspondences. It sought to firm up tentative generalisations by looking for 'proper rejections and exclusions' (1960:99). This already implied that induction could not operate without some prior conception of what it sought to discover, including, fundamentally, that there were laws, or at least regularities, to find.[45] Even for Bacon, then, it was not possible to eliminate 'anticipatory' theorising altogether. For Comte, this was as it should be. Conjectures, he argued, including quite abstract ones about the general nature of the field, were necessary to mentally organise (however wrongly) what was known, and to stimulate research into what was not. There could have

---

[45] It is in just this sense that Heidegger affirms the essentially 'mathematical' character of modern science. '*Ta mathemata* means for the Greeks that which man knows in advance in his observation of whatever is and in his intercourse with things' (1977a:118). '[P]hysical science does not first become research through experiment; rather, on the contrary, experiment first becomes possible where and only where the knowledge of nature has become transformed into research. Only because modern physics is a physics that is essentially mathematical can it be experimental' (120). This pre-known includes not only that which is held to obtain universally (mathematics in the narrow sense) but also what is specific to the nature of any given field of research. Indeed, establishing this field together with its pre-known properties is what founds each particular science. 'Every science is, as research, grounded upon the projection of a circumscribed object-sphere' (123). In these terms, Comte's whole approach to creating sociology could be characterised as an effort to specify its general and distinctive *mathemata*.

been no science in any field without a long preliminary period in which completely imaginary notions guided what empirical inquiry there was.[46]

It followed that for a science to mature and retain its scientificity, what mattered was not the mere existence of theoretical presuppositions, but their type, and the status they were granted. The latter was straightforward. Such pre-theory was always to be regarded as heuristic and hypothetical. As for its content, the distinction to be drawn at the most fundamental level was between the kind of preconceptions which mystified things in advance, and those which pictured the object of knowledge as, and in the form of, something which could in principle be scientifically known. However, in clarifying this further, Bacon's unalloyed empiricism, and his heteroclite list of 'idols' to be demolished, was of little help. Some 'positive' working conception of the knowledge domain in question was always needed; and in defining this we required criteria for distinguishing, even in the most general terms, between scientific and non-scientific modalities of picturing it.

Comte's aperçu was that the scientific revolution's displacement of the heritage of Greek metaphysics as a tyrannical rule of abstractions could be connected to the Enlightenment critique of theistic religion as anthropomorphic myth.[47] The shadowy categories of metaphysics – being, substance, quality, cause etc. – were but abstractly spiritual versions of the divine principle, just as the God of monotheism was an abstract synthesis of the ancient gods who once roamed the earth. The gods of polytheism could themselves be understood as concretely imagined embodiments of the spirits which our fetishistic ancestors imagined to inhabit all sensory beings.[48] What was to be avoided, then,

---

[46] The principle is stated at the outset of the *Cours*. In all branches of knowledge, there is always the need 'd'une théorie quelconque pour lier les faits'. This aside from 'l'impossibilité évidente, pour l'esprit humain à son origine, de se former des théories après les observations' (1:6). Indeed, 'si, en contemplant les phénomènes, nous ne les attachions point immédiatement à quelques principes non-seulement il nous serait impossible de combiner ces observations isolées, et, par conséquent, d'en tirer aucun fruit, mais nous serions même entièrement incapables de les retenir; et, le plus souvent, les faits resteraient inaperçus sous nos yeux' (1:7).

[47] An understanding that 'Enlightenment has always taken the basic principle of myth to be anthropomorphism, the projection onto nature of the subjective' and that 'the disenchantment of the world is the extirpation of animism' was a cornerstone of Horkheimer and Adorno's critique of (the) Enlightenment. For them, the underlying program was 'patriarchal: the human mind, which overcomes superstition, is to hold sway over a disenchanted nature'. See *Dialectic of Enlightenment* (1989:5–7). I examine in chap. 6 below whether Comte's view of the man/nature relation can be properly described and criticised in such terms.

[48] The notion that metaphysics, defined generally as explanation by essences, is an attenuated form of theism, and that the human mind passes through it on the way to a fully scientific attitude, was already to be found in Turgot's 1750 discourse, *Tableau*

was not only, in the metaphysical mode of the scholastics, *a priori* conceptions of reality as deducible from an idea of what it essentially was, but, in all its guises, *théologisme*. Indeed, they were intimately related. To conceive the knowledge project as a search for the real nature and ultimate causes of being – which Comte called *ontologie* (VII:47) – could only lead to a mystical quest. It would be mystical, moreover, not just because it would be to imagine 'fictive beings' as the hidden truth of the phenomenal world (I:3); but because to do so would be to confuse that world with misrecognised representations of ourselves. Such representations were at the core of all metaphysics, whether explicitly theistic or not. They arose through an unconscious process of identification and projection through which the knowing subject spontaneously closed the gap of the unknown by supplying causes, by analogy with what was very close at hand, for its otherwise inexplicable character.[49] 'When one wants to penetrate the inexplicable mystery of the essential production of phenomena, nothing more satisfying may ever be supposed than to attribute them to internal or external wills, since one then assimilates them to the everyday effects of the feelings which animate us' (VII:47).

Negatively, then, the emancipation and proper functioning of a science required that we eschew projective anthropomorphism, not just in its most obvious forms but also in such still vaguely personified categories as 'Nature' (I:4). Phenomena were only to be explained in terms of other phenomena. And explanation should confine itself to the search for laws expressing observable regularities. A modest procedure. Yet it rested on one crucial presupposition, namely that such regularities exist. Nature is orderly existence. This was indeed the ontological assumption made by any science whatever. Beginning in ignorance, the sciences were engaged in filling in the blanks, proper to each domain, of what they all projected to be *l'ordre universel*.

For Comte, be it noted, whether at the level of the totality or of the partial realities dealt with by the 'fundamental sciences', that order was itself always abstract. Indeed, while it was the source of data, concrete

---

philosophique des progrès successifs de l'esprit humain. For the possible influence of this on Comte, see Pickering, 1993:200n.

49 'Car le principe théologique qui consiste à tout expliquer par des *volontés*, ne peut être pleinement écarté que quand, ayant reconnu inaccessible toute recherche des *causes*, on se borne a connaître les *lois* . . . Quand on veut pénétrer le mystère inaccessible de la production essentielle des phénomènes, on ne peut plus rien supposer de plus satisfaisant que de les attribuer à des volontés intérieurs ou extérieurs, puis qu'on les assimule ainsi aux effets journaliers des affections qui nous animent' (VII:47; emphasis in original). Nietzsche shared this understanding but extended it into a consideration of the metaphysics built, as the deposit of 'the oldest and longest lived psychology', into language itself (1990:59).

actuality was not *per se* the knowledge object of any 'fundamental' science.[50] There were of course sciences of the concrete, which were descriptive and mediated between theory and its real-world application. But these should not be confused with the abstract sciences on which they were based, and with which alone *philosophie positive* was concerned (1:58). Their boundaries were also quite different. The concrete is always a complex site wherein several quasi-distinct planes of existence (mechanical, chemical, organic etc.) intersect. Knowledge of these specific sites called for a composite and interdisciplinary approach, as for example in the relation of mineralogy to physics, chemistry and even, via geology, astronomy (1:59). In contrast, what *les sciences fondamentales* (mathematics, astronomy, physics, chemistry, biology and sociology) aimed to produce was a purely theoretical map of each basic order of phenomenal reality, with its specific body of laws and logical place in the 'ladder' of knowledge.

Once these sciences were all established, a coherent hierarchy of basic knowledges would come into being, organising the 'fundamental sciences' according to the relative generality, complexity and dependence of their respective domains. It was that prospect that for the first time made a positive classification of the sciences itself finally possible.[51] Positive indeed at two levels: for 'it is according to the mutual dependence that effectively exists among the various positive sciences that we ought to proceed when classifying them; and this dependence should result only from that of the corresponding phenomena' (1:59). The resulting system might seem a purely specular construct,[52] in which the forms of knowledge and forms of the known endlessly reflect one another. And so it would be if the facts and laws that figured there were not disciplined by evidential rigour. In practical terms, besides, the developing corpus of abstract knowledge was not, for Positivism, any

[50] 'Il faut distinguer, par rapport à tous les ordres de phénomènes, deux genres de sciences naturelles: les unes abstraites, générales, ont pour objet la découverte des lois qui régissent les diverses classes de phénomènes, en considérant tous les cas qu'on peut concevoir; les autres, particulières, descriptives . . . consistent dans l'application de ces lois à l'histoire effective des différents êtres existants. Les premières sont donc fondamentales . . .' (1:57-8).

[51] As against vain attempts, 'comme celles de Bacon et D'Alembert', to classify the sciences 'd'après une distinction quelconque des diverses facultés de l'esprit humain', or against others which invent categories *a priori*, or which confuse theoretical and practical knowledge, Comte singles out contemporary botanists and zoologists as those who have pointed the way to 'une théorie générale de classifications' (1:47-9).

[52] 'Alors, on reconnaît directement que le but le plus difficile et le plus important de notre existence consiste à transformer le cerveau humain en un miroir exact de l'ordre extérieur. C'est seulement ainsi qu'elle peut devenir la source directe de notre unité totale, en liant la vie affective et la vie active à leur commune destination' (VIII:382).

more than in Bacon's *New Organon*, an end in itself. In relation to the organised work of modifying nature to meet human needs – *l'industrie* – the system of fundamental sciences was simply a theoretical instrument, produced at one remove from the plenum of the real; an instrument which on the one hand would help humankind to make concrete interventions into its world, and on the other – the supreme point of the exercise – would provide the synthesising philosophy needed to restore, and perfect, social order.

But to ascend to this view of things, a second limitation in Bacon's conception of the relation between science and non-science would have to be overcome. The theologico-metaphysical blockages to scientific understanding (Bacon's 'anticipations' and 'idols') had not arisen, a scientific mind would presume, arbitrarily. Nor was the progress of science just a matter of individual intelligence and will. Otherwise, why had it taken two millennia since Thales for a properly scientific astronomy and physics to arise? To pose such a question *positively* involved more than maxims about method, more indeed than a science of individual mind such as Bacon metaphysically and incoherently tried to sketch out in *The Advancement of Learning*. If the distinction between science and non-science was to be understood not just theoretically as epistemological difference, but as a practical antagonism surrounding knowledge production on the plane of the actual, it must be grounded in a scientific understanding of all the orders of existence there in play. For Comte, this pointed across a boundary whose crossing Bacon was not able to contemplate. It meant completing *l'échelle encyclopédique* by bringing the knowing subject itself into full scientific purview, not only in terms of the intrinsic mechanisms of mental formation and development, but also of the contextual, i.e. social and historical, conditions in which these occurred.

Science and practice

A final set of problems Comte had to confront in appropriating the Baconian notion of positive science concerned its instrumentalism. For Bacon, 'experiments of fruit' were at once a verification principle and the point of the exercise.[53] Being able to predict the results of a deliberate manipulation of the tangible world was the mark of scientific knowledge. At the same time, knowledge in that form was the only knowledge that mattered; for only on its basis could we alter the world

[53] 'Of all signs there is none more certain or more noble than that taken from fruits. For fruits and works are as it were sponsors and sureties for the truth of philosophies' (Bacon, 1960:71).

to human advantage. Thus far, again, Comte was with Bacon. But two questions arose.

The first concerned the picture of reality presupposed by a positivity conceived as the handmaiden of practice. The problem here was how to square the idea of a rule-bound universal order with that of its human modifiability. Bacon, repeating a line that goes back to the Greek atomists, asserted that 'Towards the effecting of works, all that man can do is put together or put asunder natural bodies. The rest is done by nature working within' (Bacon, 1960:39). Thus it is bodies and not laws that are modified. Bacon's purview was confined to the physico-chemical sciences. But Comte needed a formula wide enough to embrace the life sciences, including those of Man and society, as well. Living matter could not be taken apart and put back together without destroying it, so Bacon's rule for the scope and limits of technological power could not apply across the board. Comte found what he was looking for in the proto-structuralist principle of what he called 'arrangement'. It is summarised in the third rule of Comte's 'first philosophy', which states that 'All modifications of the universal order are limited to the degree of intensity of the phenomena, their arrangement not admitting of alteration.'[54]

The principle of *arrangement* made it possible to present the issue that had played out in the absolutist and mechanicist thinking of the eighteenth century as determinism versus free will in more tractable terms, for it implied a form of lawfulness which contains limited degrees of what structuralists would call free play. But what determines this 'modifiability', and what prescribes its limits? Comte's general answer was that the overall (*cosmique*) *arrangement* was complex, with degrees of determinacy varying with the phenomenal order of reality where they occurred. Modifiability, in fact, was a matter of the relation between orders. Each order of existence had the limited power to modify the one on which it depended, and the more so the further up the scale we go.[55] Thus each 'successive order in the hierarchy is dependent on the one beneath it and is modified by the one succeeding' (x:175). Applied to life-forms and their conditions of existence, Comte's principle implied, within limits fixed by the orders of being thus connected, an interactive relation between agent and object. By Comte's time, biologists were beginning to conceptualise the latter through the category of *milieu*, and

[54] 'Les modifications quelconques de l'ordre universel s'y trouvent bornées à l'intensité des phénomènes, dont l'arrangement demeure inaltérable' (x:176).

[55] These secondary modifications 'deviennent plus profondes et plus multipliées à mesure que la complication croissante des phénomènes permet notre faible intervention de mieux altérer des résultats dus au concours d'influences plus diverses et plus accessibles' (VII:79).

for Comte this notion belonged to 'the first elementary basis of true biological philosophy'.[56] The physiologist Bernard employed the same notion to account for the relations and dependencies between cells, tissues and organs in an individual organism.[57] It could equally be extended outwards: the whole habitable planet as the human *milieu*. What the concept emphasised was the two-way relation (dependent–adaptive, appropriative–modifying) between life forms and the environment in and from which they lived. If humanity depended on the totality of material conditions that constituted its biological and physical milieu, that order, and especially for it, was *une fatalité modifiable*.

Comte's approach squared the immediate circle. However, it raised further questions even more perplexing. If humanity is the highest, because most complex, level of being, how is the order of dependency and modification to be conceived there, at the top of the scale? How are we to understand the transformation wherein humanity, with the aid of positive science, has qualitatively changed and enhanced its own modifying power? And suppose, finally, that we take scientific cognisance of the fact that the animals imperfectly banded together as humanity are *themselves* part of their – and our – *own* object world. How, then, are we to think humanity's capacity for *self-conscious* self-modification? Such questions could only be pursued through scientific study of precisely that being. If so, however, it would have to be recognised that such a science was like no other: not only because its theory and practice belongs to that science's own field of inquiry, but because they belong to that feature of it which, as self-transformation, elevates Humanity above all other forms of being in the known universe.

The second problem raised by a positivity designed in its very essence to be practical concerns its axiological grounding. If the capacity to manipulate the phenomenal world so as to produce predictable results supplants the discovery of Truth as the validating criterion for knowledge, the epistemological question becomes mingled with a moral one. For the activity of science could not then be justified even cognitively with reference to pure values of contemplation, but only in relation to its

[56] In his treatment of biology in *Philosophie positive*, Comte offers as an amendment to de Bainville's philosophical definition of life as 'composition et décomposition' that 'l'état vivant' also entails, as 'deux conditions fondamentales correlatives . . . un *organisme* déterminé et un *milieu* convenable' (III:230; emphasis in original). For Comte's relation to contemporary biological theory, see Pickering (1993:588–604) and Canguilhem (1994:237–60). The latter notes: 'Comte's conception of the milieu justified his belief that biology could not be a separate science. And his conception of the organism justified his belief that biology must be an autonomous science. The originality and force of his position lies in the correlation – or some would say, dialectical relation – between these two concepts' (1994:241).
[57] For a discussion of Bernard's notion of *milieu intérieur* see Hirst, 1975:63–7.

performativity. But we must then ask: Performativity for the sake of what? Bacon's answer would seem to be clear. What valorises science is its human utility. *The New Atlantis* presents an inspiring picture of what the 'great instauration' could do to improve the human condition. Above the gates of its most august building, the temple of Salomon, our travellers find the motto 'The end of our foundation is the knowledge of causes and secret causes of things; and the enlarging of the bounds of human empire, to the effecting of all things possible' (White, 1981:240). All around, the application of this program has led to a world where, helped by all manner of wonderful contrivances, the necessities of life are abundant, energy supplies are inexhaustible, and citizens are healthier and more comfortable than Bacon's contemporaries could have imagined.

Examined more closely, however, Bacon's orienting ideal for scientific progress rested on two indispensable principles. The first was an assertion of human entitlement to dominion over nature. The second was a moral imperative to use the fruits of that dominion for the benefit of all. With the triumph of liberal technological values, these principles would come to seem commonsensical. But for Bacon, given the ruling (still Christian) discourse, they required careful justification: a justification that could only be supplied by the biblical narrative read as, and in the light of, Revelation. Particularly damning was the argument that the advancement of knowledge 'has somewhat of the serpent, and puffeth up'. Bacon countered by reworking the meaning of the Paradise story in Genesis. Against those divines who 'pretend that knowledge is to be received with great limitation, as the aspiring to it was the original sin and the cause of the fall', Bacon insisted that the right to dominion over nature derived from God's commission to Adam, and the rise of natural science would put Man finally in the way of making it possible (1901:40).[58] Harnessing the hidden powers of nature represented, in fact, an earthly way to regain at least the original abundance, if not the innocence and felicity, of Paradise itself.[59]

[58] 'Only let the human race recover that right over nature which belongs to it by divine bequest, and let power be given it; the exercise thereof will be governed by sound reason and true religion' (1960:119). For a discussion of Bacon's relation to the Adamic commission, see Leiss, 1972:48–57.

[59] Against the theological argument that aspiring to knowledge of the divine powers in Creation led to Adam's fall, Bacon replies: 'It was not the pure knowledge of nature, by the light whereof man gave names to all the creatures in Paradise, agreeable to their natures, that occasioned the fall; but the proud knowledge of good and evil, with an intent in man to give law to himself, and depend no more upon God' (1901:40). For Bacon's account of the progress of knowledge in relation to the growth and beneficent effect ('in remedying the inconveniences arising from man to man' and 'relieving human necessities') of the practical arts, see pp. 67–85.

Whether that happened, however, would depend on the social use to which knowledge-based power was put. Hence, to take the second principle, Bacon's insistence on an ethic of philanthropy: those with control over the nature-dominating power were obliged to use that control not for themselves but for the common benefit. That ethic likewise had transcendent guarantees. The priests of Atlantis held daily services thanking 'God for his marvellous works . . . and imploring his aid and blessing' so that their labours could be turned to 'good and holy uses' (White, 1981:250). 'It is', Bacon notes in *The Advancement of Learning*, 'merely from its quality when taken without the true corrective that knowledge has somewhat of venom or malignity. The corrective which renders it sovereign is charity, for according to St Paul, "Knowledge puffeth up, but charity buildeth"' (1901:41). Baconian science, then, was to obey the Gospel injunction to 'love one another'. Given Man's fallen state, how could it be otherwise? Without a redeeming commitment to Christian *caritas*, dominion over nature would degenerate into vanity, pride and the domination of men by men.

There is no need to determine whether or not Bacon himself was pious or prudent 'behind' the Christian framework he invokes. The point is just that, if truly believed in, the biblical myths, or those which substitute for them in *The New Atlantis*, place the instrumentalism of science – its *telos* as technology – within a fixed, cosmic and moral frame of reference. Without some such mooring, on the other hand, Bacon's construction would fall apart. This was indeed bound to happen, for the Baconian appeal to Revelation was vulnerable to the demythologising spirit of science itself. By the eighteenth century the legitimacy problem (knowledge for what?) had become open. From Spinoza to La Mettrie, a fully atheist materialism had begun to raise its head. With the declining credibility of revealed religion, techno-progressive thinking faced a dilemma. Either the moral grounding of a world-mastering science would have to be left unsecured – letting the enterprise float, in principle and *de facto*, among the powers of the world, or some non-supernatural way would have to be found to legitimate the philanthropic ethic which had been shored up, in the old religion, by the word of God.

To take the first path would let the domination of nature become a master principle in itself. This however would contradict the ethical principle, especially if humanity itself became an object for science and thus also for domination. On the other hand, to take the second path, and address the problem head on, raised questions about what human ends *should* direct scientific–technological advance, as well as how, if not somehow scientifically, these ends could themselves be justified.

Once more, but this time with respect to goal-setting and *la morale*,

Comte's drive to secure positive science as a relative but *réaliste* form of knowing indicated the need to extend it to the human world. Suppose, the thought ran, that we turned a positivist eye towards what the metaphysical discourse of the seventeenth and eighteenth centuries called the problem of 'human nature'.[60] Suppose, that is, that we reformulated the issue of human goodness in terms of what scientific study tells us about the physical organism, its mental and moral faculties, and about its natural (but by the same token collective) history. It might then be possible to locate the instinct for human self-improvement and, even more important, the uniting, orienting and disciplining force of what Christianity called love, as law-bound features of the phenomenal world. If so, the implications would be as foundational as they could be from a positivist point of view. Reliers on fact would surely recognise such *faits moraux* as tantamount to a real Authority; and beyond this the search for axiological grounds would have no need to go.

[60] For an account of this development, and of Bichat and Gall's physiological researches into the relation between moral and intellectual faculties and the brain, see III:604 et seq.

3   The system and its logic (2): from sociology
     to the subjective synthesis

From every direction – epistemological, ontological, political, moral –
all roads along the path of securing the scientific outlook as an all-
encompassing system of thought led Comte to what he announced, in
Philosophie positive, as 'social physics' or 'sociology'.[1] A science of society
was required not just to complete the scientific revolution by including
all orders of phenomena in its range. It was also needed in order to
positivise our understanding of that, and thus to complete the positivisation of human thought about thought itself.

However, any such solution to the problems inhering in Bacon's
initial attempt to think through the implications of a world-view based
on the principles of a phenomenalist and instrumentalist practice of
science was bound to change the matrix. Foucault's account of how
'Man' (that 'strange being . . . whose nature is to know nature') was
'fabricated' by the 'demiurge of knowledge' makes a similar point
(1970:308–10). For Foucault there never was, nor could have been, a
single 'science of Man'.[2] Nevertheless, the emergence of *les sciences
humaines* into this giddily reflexive epistemic space was transforming. It
effected a decisive break from the 'classical' to the 'modern episteme',
in the course of which the transparent representationalism which governed
the former gave way to a more complex and would-be self-grounding
discursivity.

Foucault's account of this shift gives a pivotal role to Kant (1970:312
et seq.). He downplays, at the same time, the line of development which

---

[1] The last three volumes of *Philosophie positive*, which in the last replaces the earlier term
'social physics' with 'sociology', are devoted to the new science. A methodological
preamble and a section on statics (vol. IV) are followed by a treatise on dynamics (V) and
a final one on the current crisis and its predicted/prescribed resolution (VI). The four
volumes of *Politique positive* present the same material as 'subjectively' and religiously
transfigured.

[2] 'At first glance, one could say that the domain of the human sciences is covered by three
"sciences" – or rather by three epistemological regions, all subdivided among
themselves, and all interlocking with one another; these regions are defined by the triple
relation of the human sciences in general to biology, economics, and philology'
(Foucault, 1970:355).

led from Bacon, through Montesquieu and the *Encyclopédistes*, to Comte
– not to mention the tangled lineage which connects French sociology
and structural anthropology to Foucault himself. Comte appears only as
an exemplar of the attempt to develop a science of Man from the side of
biology.[3] To be sure, as even Comte acknowledged, Kant had been the
first to formulate 'the fundamental dualism between spectator and
spectacle' (IX:588), a dualism which carried over, as *le dehors* and *le
dedans*, the objective and the subjective, into his own system. It was
Comte himself, however – and, in this, critical of Kant[4] – who had first
thought through the implications of bringing Man *collectively* into the
episteme of modern science; and Comte, more particularly, who had
reflected from that angle on Man's distinctively dual mode of being, i.e.
as the one who is 'at the same time the foundation of all positivities and
present, in a way that cannot even be termed privileged, in the element
of empirical things' (Foucault, 1970:344).

How Comte brought Man into the scientific picture, and why, for
him, the full positivisation of human thought then entailed a *subjective*
and indeed *religious* turn, are questions we must now take up.

Sociology and its object

For Comte, the prerequisite for generating scientific knowledge about
anything was to determine to what class or classes of natural phenomena
it belongs. Upon that depends what fundamental science or sciences
must be relied upon for its study. With regard to human phenomena,
one such pertinent science was biology, and a great deal, Comte
thought, was to be learnt from it. Especially valuable in pinning down
'human nature' were the contemporary advances being made in physiology by Cabanis, Gall, Broussais and others.[5] As opposed to spec-

---

[3] In Foucault's tripartite scheme, Comte exemplifies a science of Man conceived from the
side of *life*, Marx one conceived from that of *labour*, and Nietzsche – undermining the
modern episteme from within – exemplifies what happens when 'Man' is studied from
the side of 'language' (1970:359–69).

[4] See above, chap. 2 n. 41. Comte's relation to Kant is discussed by Pickering
(1993:292–6). In his personal library Comte had two works of Kant's, *Idea for a
Universal History of Cosmopolitan Intent*, and translated extracts from *The Critique of Pure
Reason*. His indebtedness to Kant was no doubt greater than he acknowledges,
embarrassing perhaps, given his wider distaste for things German. The 'Bibliothèque
positiviste' that prefaces the *Catéchisme positiviste* has, in its 'Synthèse' section (thirty
volumes) no German philosophy at all; the French are represented by Descartes,
Diderot, Condorcet and de Maistre, the British by Bacon and Hume (XI:38).

[5] Cabanis's *Les rapports du physique et du moral de l'homme* was 'le précurseur immédiat à
l'heureuse révolution philosophique que nous devons à la génie de Gall' (III:668). Franz
Joseph Gall's 'cerebral physiology' (he was the leading proponent of phrenology)
provided the basis for Comte's own mapping of faculties and instincts in relation to the

ulative and introspective approaches to what Cousin, leader of the 'eclectic' school, lauded as 'psychology' (xa:217), these promised to correlate regions of the brain with specific instincts and faculties, including the higher-order ones of reflective and calculative intelligence, moral conscience and philanthropic love (III:646–60).

The determinants and determinations of human reality were not, however, exhausted thereby. There was a remainder which, although it might in a wider sense be regarded as biological, was not reducible to, or intelligible in terms of, the individual body and soul. It consisted of phenomena like 'customs, languages . . . and monuments' (IV:341), which arose from the way in which, however splendid their imagined isolation, human beings were always – as members of a species, and indeed a 'social species' – associated together as a group. For Comte, indeed, human beings were doubly associated together: first, through all the ties of mutual reliance, direct and indirect, which connect them as living contemporaries; secondly, by being implicated in a temporal process wherein each generation lives off, works on and transmits to the next, the fund of wealth, knowledge and institutions it has inherited from the past. The human species was not the only one whose forms of life, in interchange with nature, are collective.[6] To that extent, Comte thought, sociology could and should study the social patterns exhibited by other animals (IV:350–2). However, in the case of *les animales inférieurs* such a study would be dimensionally reduced. For, in addition to the richer social forms developed by human primates in virtue of their capacity for symbolic communication, the human collectivity, uniquely, had the developmental capacity to transmit and accumulate knowledge from one generation to the next (VI:612–13).

The irreducibility to individual biology of what is social and historical in the human domain made it the proper object of a distinct branch of knowledge. To which there was an evident methodological correlate: eternal vigilance against all those positions – economic (IV:210–22), voluntarist (242–9), psychological (III:612 et seq.) etc.[7] – which refused to accord collective phenomena such recognition. Here, indeed, the critique of metaphysics *within* the sociological field merged with that of

---

brain. Broussais's *De l'irritation et de la folie* – which Comte hailed for its attack on introspectionist psychology in his essay of 1828 (xa:216–28) – had achieved for the study of *le système nutritif* what Gall had done for *le cerveau*.

[6] 'Tous les êtres vivants présentent deux ordres de phénomènes essentiellement distincts, ceux relatifs à l'individu, et ceux qui concernent l'espèce, surtout quand elle est sociale. C'est principalement par rapport à l'homme que cette distinction est fondamentale' (I:77).

[7] For Comte's critique of Cabanis for ignoring the social side of moral phenomena, see xa:124–5; see also the correspondence cited in Pickering, 1993:151–2.

metaphysics as such. It was the 'vain belief' that the truth of what is can be deduced from the 'lucubrations of the individual mind' which underpinned the abstract rationalism of the metaphysical viewpoint.[8] Metaphysics was the philosophy of *égoisme*. On its critical side, it was reducible to the absolute 'dogma of free inquiry' (v:515). Not only, therefore, would positivising our understanding of the social make it possible to understand in positive terms the very opposition between science and non-science which the positive outlook must negotiate if it was to establish its dominance, but the full emancipation of positivity from 'theology' and 'metaphysics' implied a break altogether 'from the individual to the social point of view' (vi:810).

Comte's second move in constituting his new science was to project into the space of the sociological object not just a general level of metaindividual human reality, but a distinct and integral entity: *l'organisme sociale* (iv:280). It must immediately be said that Comte made no distinction between the first move and the second. He did not even suspect that they were distinct. For him, the social was always to be understood in reference to 'society' as a kind of unified singularity, just as the latter, as *un phénomène composé*, was to be understood as 'homogeneous' with the individual organisms treated in biology (iv:340). Durkheim attempted to screen out Comte's preconceptions, particularly with regard to *progrès*, by linking an empirical definition of 'social facts' to the indexical criterion of 'constraint' (1964:1–4, 13). He also separated rules for observation from explanatory ones (1964:14–46). Even so, he manifested the same confusion as Comte when he similarly moved from a concept of social facts as 'collective ways of thinking, acting and feeling' to an assumption that this collective quality presupposed *'une société'* – an entity with, indeed, 'normal' and 'pathological' forms.[9]

For sociology, whether, and how, the social is to be conceived as a

---

[8] For Comte's critique of metaphysics as applied specifically to the social (which it refuses to recognise as such) see the 47th *leçon* of the *Cours* (iv:179–228). Durkheim develops a similar line of argument in *The Rules of Sociological Method*. Against bio-psychological reductionism he writes: 'If we begin with the individual, we shall be able to understand nothing of what takes place in the group . . . every time that a social phenomenon is directly explained by a psychological phenomenon, we may be sure that the explanation is false' (1964:104).

[9] The ontological priority of *la société* is assumed from the outset in Durkheim's *Rules*. A social phenomenon 'is general because it is collective (that is, more or less obligatory), and certainly not collective because it is general. It is a group condition repeated in the individual because imposed on him. *It is to be found in each part because it exists in the whole*' (1964:9; my emphasis). Durkheim's main difference from Comte, in this respect, is that whereas for Comte the group, at its furthest extension, is the whole human species, for Durkheim 'It is only the individual societies which are born, develop, and die that can be observed, and therefore have objective existence' (1964:19).

distinct order of reality have long been contested.[10] Weber denied the premise through a concept of 'social action' which was itself interindividual.[11] The same, but in more polemical a register, may be said of (at least some pronouncements by) Marx.[12] All that need be remarked here is that the existence of such amorphously collective phenomena as language, and such micronically operative ones as gift exchange and the rituals of civility, suggest that it might be possible to affirm the irreducibility of 'the social' without having to posit 'society' as a distinct and integral being. However, Comte's leap from regarding *l'homme* as *une espèce sociable* to regarding *l'humanité* as *un organisme social* made such a midway position unthinkable.

In developing his own concept of the social, Comte declared himself indebted to Condorcet (IV:200–9) and de Maistre,[13] whose radically opposed viewpoints – progress versus order – he set himself to reconcile. From the Catholic counter-Revolution came the notion of society with a capital 's': a reality embracing but transcending the individual, whose imperious demand for harmony, order and unity was not just a heavenly ideal but a natural law.[14] Whatever the perturbations to which it was subject, self-equilibrating social mechanisms (e.g. sacrifice) ensured that this law continually asserted itself, even in the rebellion of sinful individuals.[15] From Condorcet's *L'esquisse d'un tableau historique des progrès de l'esprit humain*, Comte derived a way to arrange the materials

[10] These issues were freshly discussed, in an attempt to reconcile a hermeneutic, action-oriented approach with a structuralist orientation to the 'production and reproduction of social life', in Giddens's *New Rules for Sociological Method* (1993). Giddens does not take up the question here, though, of 'society' as a distinct macro-unit of analysis.

[11] Whether in the setting of *Gemeinschaft* or *Gesellschaft*, as Weber's definitions make clear: 'Communal action refers to that action which is oriented to the feeling of the actors that they belong together. Societal action, on the other hand, is oriented to a rationally motivated adjustment of interests' (Gerth and Mills 1958:183).

[12] 'The first premise of all human history is, of course, the existence of living human individuals . . . They themselves begin to distinguish themselves from animals as soon as they begin to *produce* their means of subsistence' (Marx and Engels, 1947:7).

[13] For Comte's 'appreciation' of de Maistre in the *Cours*, see IV:20–4. Praise for de Maistre's contribution to social statics is emphasised throughout *Politique positive*. In its 'Discours préliminaire' Comte notes that 'l'énergique réaction philosophique, par l'éminent de Maistre, a profondément concouru à préparer la vraie théorie du progrès. Malgré l'intention évidemment rétrograde qui anima cette école passagère, ses travaux figueront toujours parmi les antécédants nécessaires du positivisme systématique' (VII:64).

[14] For Milbank (1993:54–61), de Bonald, even more than de Maistre, is a key source for Comte's transcendent but positive conception of *société*. This, though, is little acknowledged by Comte himself. De Bonald is honoured in the 'Calendrier' only as a leap-year alternate to de Maistre on the 27th day of Descartes.

[15] 'It cannot be too often repeated that men do not at all guide the Revolution; it is the Revolution that uses men. It is well said that it has its own impetus. This phrase shows that never has the Divinity revealed itself so clearly in any human event. If it employs the most vile instruments, it is to regenerate by punishment' (de Maistre, 1971:50).

of human history so as to derive therefrom a picture of the laws which drove and regulated its 'continuous progress' (IV:201–9).[16] This picture, in turn, built on Pascal's image of Man (IV:186) as like an ever-developing individual being, in which each successive generation begins its own efforts at the higher place where the one before left off.[17]

What Comte called *l'humanité* was the totality – at once solidary and continuous, cohesive and developmental – which combined and unified these two concepts and aspects of our collective being.[18] 'The new science', he tells us,

will represent . . . the mass of the human species, whether present, past, or even future, as increasingly constituting in every respect, whether in the order of space or time, an immense and eternal social unity, whose various individual or national organs, ceaselessly united by an intimate and universal solidarity, inevitably contribute, each according to a determined mode and degree, to the fundamental evolution of humanity. (1:326–7)

What made it possible to recognise in such a vast and well-nigh ungraspable figure the distinct object of a science was that sociology's placement 'above' and after biology in the 'scientific series' invited a convenient analogical move. If sociology was a life science, Humanity could be regarded as a kind of organism. This implied that methods could be applied in its positive study which derived from (but also expanded on) those of the life sciences more generally.[19] Thus conceived, sociology would have two departments.[20] The 'statical' part, building on the biological theory of (an organism's) 'vital consensus', would consider what integrates humanity at any moment as a self-reproducing form of collective life (IV:277–9). Here the procedure would be to classify and compare societies with respect to their institutional constants and variations (institutions being understood as the

---

[16] Comte credits Montesquieu with being the first to suppose that there *were* laws of the social, and that these connected the polity to the prevailing moral and intellectual ideas; but criticises him for relying on climate to account for differences between social types and for having no theory of social development. See IV:193–202.

[17] 'Pour fixer plus convenablement les idées, il importe d'établir préalablement, par une indispensable abstraction scientifique, suivant l'heureux artifice judicieusement institué par Condorcet, l'hypothèse nécessaire d'un peuple unique auquel seraient idéalement rapportées toutes les modifications sociales consécutives effectivement observées chez les populations distinctes' (IV:291).

[18] For a discussion of the relation between the dimensions of 'solidarity' and 'continuity' in defining *l'humanité* as sociology's knowledge object, see IV: 291–311.

[19] '. . . la physique sociale doit être certainement conçue comme une science parfaitement distincte, directement fondée sur des bases qui lui sont propres, mais profondement ratachée, soit dans son point de départ, soit dans son développement continu, au système entier de la philosophie biologique' (IV:391).

[20] Comte credits Blainville, in his introduction to *Principes généraux d'anatomie comparée*, for having 'systématisé' the distinction between statics and dynamics for biology (1:27).

equivalents of organs, tissues, cells etc.) in order to derive the 'laws of solidarity'. The 'dynamical' part would search for society's 'laws of movement', understood as a process in which, as a result of the accretions of intellectual and moral progress, the collectivity shifts through successive, and relatively unified, phases of intellectual–religious, political and socio-technical development. Such study was again classificatory–comparative, but with the difference that it involved a time dimension. Building on the series of inductive methods developed by preceding sciences (IV:229 et seq.), sociology would extrapolate from biology the comparative search for co-variance, and, with regard to the developmentalism that was peculiar to the human, would add the 'historical' method of *filiation*, a step that would positivise (the study of) knowledge itself.[21]

Besides being comparative and historical, Comte's sociology was macronic. Given his understanding of the social as that which pertains to 'society', and his integral conception of the latter, it could hardly have been otherwise. The procedure was to compare whole societies, both at the same and at different stages of development, regarding as the latter both the same (national) society observed at different historical points and different societies which, though existing contemporaneously, exemplified those different stages among themselves (IV:353). Following Condorcet, as modified by Leibniz's dictum that 'the present is big with the future' (IV:292), the final scientific aim, abstracting from the myriad messy complexities of concrete history, would be to induce from both operations the laws of orderly progress as if they unfolded within one single society.

As a result of adopting this model, however, an ambiguity is introduced into what Comte's macro-unit of analysis actually is. To be sure, it was always some kind of *société*, a strongly defined human group characterised by its boundedness and bondedness as a unified and unifying association. But this category included both *les grands sociétés* (especially those of Western Europe) and the smaller groupings (family, tribe, polis) into which Humanity was organised at an earlier phase.[22] But what of the latter as sub-*sociétés* within the former? And what, more

---

[21] 'La comparaison historique des divers états consécutifs de l'humanité ne constitue pas seulement le principe artifice scientifique de la nouvelle philosophie politique: son développement rationnel formera directement aussi le fond même de la science' (IV:360).

[22] Comte's idea of *la série sociale* is developed in the 50th *leçon* of the *Cours*. The series runs from the family, regarded as 'le véritable germe nécessaire des diverses dispositions essentielles qui caractérisent l'organisme social' (IV:448), to 'la société proprement dite, dont la notion, parvenu à son entière extension scientifique, tend à embrasser la totalité de l'espèce humaine, et principalement l'ensemble de la race blanche' (IV:431).

generally, of all those cases in which the various boundaries of language, religion, intellectual culture, kinship, production and exchange, and 'political society' did not coincide? Comte could pass over these questions because the paramount entity to be grasped was the grand totality comprising *l'humanité* as a whole. But then is the sociological object a multiplicity (a comparative science of societies) or a singularity (the science of humanity as a whole)? And what in any case 'is' the latter? On the one hand, *l'humanité* was to be conceived as *la masse de l'espèce humaine* regarded in its entire geographical and historical extension, including into the future. On the other, and more narrowly, it named the concretely operative human community – but only and specifically at the globalised point at which its always expanding sociality had finally united the species in a single world society. Humanity in the second sense was the self-realisation of Humanity in the first. As such, indeed, it only came into existence during the 'industrial' stage of development, when it completed the series of partial social totalities that had begun with *la Famille, la Cité* and *la Patrie*. As we shall see, the fuzziness surrounding Comte's concepts of *humanité* and *société* was important to the working, and unworking, of his whole system, including at the religious level.

The final move in Comte's positivisation of the social field was the link it aimed to forge between predictive theory and prescriptive practice. Given the conceptual shape imparted to the sociological object, the step was made to seem obviousness itself. If society is an organism, sociology provides a scientific understanding of the conditions for its health. 'Positive politics', then, could follow a medical model of diagnosis and cure, modified by the relativity introduced into the criterion of healthy normality by the social organism's phase-shift path of growth and development. The laws of statics would provide functionalist rules for the 'normal' achievement of social unity; those of dynamics would specify the particular ordering requirements appropriate to the given level of social development.[23] For Comte, the pressing issue was how to move the polity forward at a time of transitional crisis between one social stage and another. The party of order could only envisage 'social health' on a restored feudal model. It was just here that discovering the laws of dynamics was crucial. For, in conjunction with a knowledge of statics, they would make it possible to predict the 'normal' outcome of

---

[23] Present 'political facts' could thus be considered in the same dispassionate scientific light as any other sociological phenomena: 'Sans admirer ni maudire les faits politiques, et en y voyant essentiellement, comme en toute autre science, la physique sociale considère donc chaque phénomène sous le double point de vue élémentaire de son harmonie avec l'état antérieur et l'état postérieur du développement humain' (IV:326).

the present phase-shift – to industrial society – on the basis of tendential laws extrapolated from the 'encyclopedic series' of human history (IV:249–50).

From the past to the future, and back to the present. *Voilà*, a scientific way to diagnose and, at least projectively, resolve health crises that arise in the social organism before they become disabling or worse. The current need was apparently chronic. But even under less turbulent conditions, social science would serve continually to clarify the necessary path of normal (because integrative and socially self-sustaining) progress.[24] Either way, we should note, the crises to be obviated were generated from within. Natural disasters were outside the scope of the sociological field. The possibility of endogenous crises itself testified to the potential for imperfection in the unfolding of the complex.[25] Such potential was clearly at its maximum in the flux and conflict which accompanied changes from one form of society to another. By the same token, however, the solution presented by the diagnostic and predictive powers of social science was endogenously produced, too – part and parcel of the transition to industrialism and positivity whose disintegrative turmoil it providentially functioned to resolve.

What is clear, in the practical role Comte accords sociology, is the difference between *its* instrumentalism and that obtaining in the physical sciences. The utility of the latter was morally indeterminate, but Comte's 'sociology' was not available for just any end. Nor, indeed, with its holistic focus, was it fine-tuned enough to be of much service to the multiplicity of particular interests which might benefit from a knowledge which promised them, over others, enhanced mastery of the social. The supreme end which sociology took as empirically given – the durable wellbeing of human society as a whole – it also prescribed. This was hardly incidental, of course, to Comte's purposes. Sociology needed to be goal-determining, not just means-determining, if it was to provide a *de jure*, as well as *de facto*, anchor for all the sciences and technical practices that reached their summit in the social. This was just the beauty of the bio-medical model. In 'health', it provided a univocal criterion for helpful practice; one that was presumably compelling when the organism concerned included ourselves.[26]

---

[24] The 'previsions' concerning humanity's final *état normal* are destined, Comte says in *Politique positive* (x:6) 'à fonder une politique capable de systématiser la marche spontanée de chaque population vers l'état normal'.

[25] 'Dans l'organisme social, en vertu de sa complication supérieure, les maladies et les crises sont nécessairement encore plus inévitables . . . que dans l'organisme individuel' (IV:325).

[26] Cf Durkheim: 'One may say, if science foresees, it does not command. That is true. Science tells us simply what is necessary to life. But obviously *the supposition, man wishes*

The paradox of Comte's socio-historical relativisation of moral and political values was that it created a *shifting* reality principle in terms of which they could still, in context, be 'objectively' judged. By treating norms and ideals as facts for a nomothetic science – a science which comprehended them as part of a developing and normally integrated whole – their 'correct' present form could be predicted according to empirically established *invariables lois* (IV:249 et seq.). This prediction provided a scientific basis for evaluating current tendencies and strategically intervening in the process. Yet there is no disguising that in normatising the 'healthy' state of society a questionable move was being made. Even if we accept the scientific credentials of Comte's bio-social schematics, why should we actually care about social health, or, for that matter, about the future of 'Humanity'? An answer in terms of the merely factual interconnectedness of individual and collective survival would take no account of the existential remoteness of the latter from the former. With a fictive 'God' out of the picture, who indeed was to say – for the group or the individual – that recklessness, even suicide, was wrong?

The transcendence of the social

The self-valorising character of Comte's sociology lies in its being able to approach such religio-moral questions from within its own discourse by the way it constructs its knowledge object as a positivity with both the right and the power to morally command. The human collectivity, apprehended as *société* and *humanité*, confronts the knowing subject as that which is always, already and inescapably the origin and terminus of his/her highest ends. In its towering moral authority over each individual member, it has the quality of the sacred, and objectively so.

That the transcendence of the social has the character, in Comte's sociology, not only of a fact but also of a *moral* fact, i.e. one that imposes a duty which can be wilfully disregarded,[27] arises from the relation between his superorganismic concept of society/humanity and his theory of the social tie. The latter, as the generalised affection and mental consensus which bind individuals together in a group, is the irreplaceable foundation for the former. This foundation, indeed, makes it the peculiar kind of being it is. A society is nothing outside the

---

to live, a very simple speculation, immediately transforms the laws science establishes into imperative rules of conduct' (1968a:34–5).

[27] 'Cet immense et éternel organisme se distingue surtout des autres êtres comme étant formé d'éléments séparables, dont chacun peut sentir sa propre coopération, et par suite la vouloir, ou même la refuser, du moins tant qu'elle demeure directe' (VIII:599–600).

association of the individuals of which it is composed. The converse, however, is not necessarily so. It is biologically possible for disaggregated elements – hermits and parasites, for example – to live apart without being morally fused into the body of the host.[28] Thus the unity of the social has none of the automaticity to be found among lower life forms. Humanity was not just 'a sort of giant polyp extending itself over the whole globe', for this would be to confuse 'a voluntary and optional association with a form of participation that was involuntary and indissoluble' (IV:351–2n).

Unlike in the symbiotic relation between cell and organism, then, Comte's 'social organism' has the contradictory character of being both a unity in itself and what Aristotelians would call a unity *per accidens*. It was within the psychic tension generated by that difference that the conversion of human collectivity into a moral authority took shape. In the finally realised stage of *l'état positif*, the whole human collectivity comes to present itself, in the self-conscious altruism of its members, as a transcendent Other with claims on obedience, loyalty and affection. In actively and lovingly responding to this claim, subjects become agents of society and of Humanity in their turn, showing that the commanding presence of the Good Other is also within.

For society to be experienced as transcendent to the individual in the first place presupposes, of course, that it already exists; and in a strong sense, not just as an easily disassembled aggregate of self-interested egos. At this primordial level, for Comte, the bond which constituted individuals as a collectivity was an affective force which manifested itself, even before 'societies properly so-called', as an 'essentially spontaneous *sociabilité*' (IV:431). This force rested – physiologically, according to contemporary phrenology – on an instinctual base; though within the individual topography of the human brain, egoistic instincts were stronger than altruistic ones. That *les penchants bienveillants* were nevertheless able not only to prevail but to stretch beyond the immediacy of the family to embrace the non-present others (geographically and temporally) of an entire society, was an effect of their own strengthening through the habits and ties of sociality itself. The wider and depersonalised extension of *altruisme* also involved a transfer, and refocussing, of affect. Its object becomes the generalised Other in whose singular image, as family, city, homeland, nation-state or Humanity, a given

---

[28] That human society 'as an *ensemble*' only includes participating individuals is made clear in the introduction to the *Catéchisme positiviste*: ' . . . vous devez définir . . . l'Humanité comme l'*ensemble* des êtres humains, passés, futurs, et présents. Ce mot *ensemble* vous indique assez qu'il n'y faut pas comprendre tous les hommes, ceux-là qui sont réellement assimilables, d'après une vraie coopération à l'existence commune' (XI:66; emphasis in original).

société offers itself to be cherished or revered. In the theatre of Comtean sociology, then, it is love – expressed in the supreme principle of *Vivre pour autrui* – which finally has the starring role. Altruistic affection not only glues individuals together in a collectivity but also effects a seam between the ontologically distinct planes of bio-individual and social reality. Without it there would be no properly social existence. Positivistically translated, St Paul's 'God is Love' expressed no more or less than this exultant, but fragile, moral–instinctual truth at the heart of the social.

The sacral quality that inhered in human society by virtue of both its immanent/transcendent relation to each of us and the loving sentiments it incarnates, was reinforced by a further feature on its dynamic side. The law of three stages recapitulates in grand historical terms what all persons 'under their eyes' could verify for themselves: that we are theologians in our childhood, metaphysicians in adolescence and 'scientific or positive' in adulthood (1:3). Comte's matter-of-fact presumption that the mental/moral development of the individual provides a model for that of the 'collective individual' comprising Humanity as a whole, enabled him to smuggle in a telos of self-realisation which further enhanced its transcending majesty. Maturity, which potentiates the individual being, brings realism, integration, self-possession and insight. It also brings the subordination of egoistic to social instincts (IV:502–3, 532–5). It was the same with *l'Humanité*. Completion of the long revolution which was bringing science and industry to power in the most advanced regions would break down national borders, establish international peace, and usher in a (confederally) unified world society. At which point, too, the collective achievement of a fully cooperative order would bring collective knowledge of itself. The coming into being of Humanity as a social, cultural and political fact would enable it to be recognised, universally, as the finally unveiled Grand-Être, the truth behind the fiction of all the false divinities that came before.[29]

In the giddy utopianism engendered by the great bourgeois revolutions of the eighteenth and nineteenth centuries, such humanist eschatologies were hardly uncommon.[30] In Comte's case, however, the

---

[29] 'Si l'existence du Grand-Être restait sérieusement contestable son règne ne serait prochain. Ainsi son développement actuel dispense de démontrer sa réalité, profondément surgie dans toutes les productions, morales, intellectuelles, et mêmes matérielles, dont l'analyse positive indique toujours le concours universel des temps et des lieux' (X:27). For the objective and subjective formation of *l'Humanité* as Grand-Être, see X:24–33.

[30] Carl Becker's *Heavenly City of the Eighteenth Century Philosophers* examines this strain in French thought; Manuel's *Prophets of Paris* continues the story into the nineteenth. The

combination of this with an ostensibly *inductive* scientism is so strikingly inconsistent that the suturing manoeuvre needs to be highlighted. To do so we must recall an aspect of Comte's intended improvement on Baconian inductivism. In Comte's refined conception, the phenomenal object-world confronting the knowing subject merely provided data from which, in the synthetic space of the 'fundamental' sciences, the laws that constitute scientific theory proper are derived. It was that theory itself, conversely, which made possible the scientific understanding of the concrete. Comte's approach – which might be described as a theoreticist instrumentalism – had the intended merit of avoiding *empiricisme* on the one side and *mysticisme* on the other.[31] But when it came to investigating the social he simplified the issue and effectively fell into both. By switching back and forth between *l'humanité* as the highest level of rule-bound order within *l'ordre universel* and the *particular* societies confronting the sociological observer, he confounded the distinction he otherwise insisted upon in fundamental sciences between their abstract knowledge-object and its 'real' referent. The merger was hidden in the 'rational fiction' (IV:291) that prearranged the mosaic of ever-existing societies into a developmental series. The abstract universal that resulted – *l'humanité* – served to designate at once an unfolding actuality, a higher reality to be served, and the conceptual object of his new science.[32]

translation of French revolutionary theory into German idealist philosophy was extensively criticised by Marx (e.g. in *The Communist Manifesto*, and *The German Ideology*), though the humanist consummation associated with communism in his early writings clearly sprang from the same soil. In recent years, however, Christopher Lasch has joined Blumenberg in querying the importance of the eschatological element in Enlightenment progressivism, a tradition Lasch wishes to resuscitate: 'Once we recognize the profound difference between the Christian view of history, prophetic or millenarian, and the modern conception of progress, we can understand what was so original about the latter: not the promise of a secular utopia that would bring history to a happy ending but the promise of steady improvement with no foreseeable ending at all' (Lasch, 1991:47).

[31] 'La vraie culture positive évite également les deux écueils opposés, le mysticisme et l'empiricisme, entre lesquels flotte nécessairement toute étude où la déduction et l'induction ne sont pas sagement combinées' (VII:518). Althusser was to make great play with Comte's distinction between the theoretical object of knowledge and its 'real' referent in his own critique of the twin errors of 'idealism' and 'empiricism'. He attributed the distinction to Spinoza, who 'warned us that the *object* of knowledge or essence was in itself absolutely distinct from the *real object*' (Althusser, 1970:40).

[32] In *Politique positive* (X:30), the distinctions are blurred in a further way. After defining 'Humanity' as 'l'ensemble des êtres, passés, futurs, et présents, qui concourrent librement à perfectionner l'ordre universel', he adds: it is superfluous to mention 'sa nature spécifique', since 'toute espèce sociable tend naturellement vers une telle convergence. Mais l'unité collective ne peut se réaliser, sur chaque planète, que chez la race prépondérante'.

Besides its circularity – the 'facts' are preorganised by the theory they are meant to validate – the appeal to historical data which legitimised this construction[33] glossed over the conceptually constructed character of *les faits* in any domain. In the case of sociology, the difficulty of pinning down phenomena was radical, and not only for the reasons of complexity Comte advanced (IV:335–6). Positive sociology posited as its largest *concretum* the socio-historical totality comprised by the species in all its actual spatio-temporal reach. Such an object exceeded presence, and could only ever be captured abstractly, through being imagined, reconstructed and conceptually condensed. The same, indeed, applied to sub-totalities within it, such as the national societies of Western Europe that allegedly represented the vanguard of the whole. No wonder, then, that Comte's discussion of sociological method insists that in this domain more than in all others 'one is obliged . . . to observe and create laws simultaneously' (IV:335). But even this formulation did not recognise the independent role of conceptualisation in constructing macro-sociological facts. Nor did it recognise the difficulty which the entanglement of the ideographic with the nomothetic in the very constitution of the knowledge-object placed in the way of sociology's becoming, in his sense, 'positive' at all.[34] All along the line, Comte could square the *idea* of Humanity's transcendence with that of its *actual* transcendence only in a figure which systematically blurred the difference between the abstract and concrete totalities it purported, 'scientifically', to grasp.

This blurring is most evident with regard to time. Sociology could not have positivised sooner, Comte argued, because it would have lacked the requisite historical data (X:139). But what of the future? As a *concretum*, the 'development' of Humanity extends forward into the unknown. To assume, even in principle, that the relevant facts of sociology were now all before us was precisely an assumption. Only at dusk – but then how would we know it *was* dusk? – could sociology's owl of Minerva take flight. That being so, both the 'laws of statics', based on such forms of society as had existed hitherto, and the 'laws of dynamics', induced from time-series data, could only ever be regarded as provisional. Comte covers himself in an extraordinary way. The blank of the unknowable future is filled in by *deducing* industrial society's perfected *état normal*, a feat which takes up the entire six hundred pages of *Politique*

---

[33] See especially the successive *appréciations* of the fetishistic/familial, polytheistic/civic, monotheistic/theological/military, and metaphysical/transitional stages that make up the four chapters of book v of the *Cours*.

[34] For a discussion of the relation between the abstract and concrete in the context of Comte's 'revolutionary' substitution of sociology for mathematics as a unifying foundation for the sciences, see Krémer-Marietti (1982:17–26).

positive's fourth volume.[35] In the immediately following first volume of *Synthèse subjective*, the speculative status of this deduction is underlined by a literary conceit. The 'normal future' which Comte constructs for industrial society is projected, a lifetime forward, into the year 1927.[36] Comte's acknowledgment of the ideal–imaginary character of his deduced projection did not prevent him from incorporating it into sociology's knowledge domain as a kind of fact. Not only, moreover, was this incorporation illicit, it had the added convenience of positing a developmental limit. Once the great transformation to industrial–Positivist order had been achieved, the whole progressive metamorphosis wrought by History would have come to an end. And after that? Perfect tranquillity and no more story.

On the side of abstract social knowledge, accepting the destiny of this closure eliminated the indeterminacy which would otherwise have marked its domain. On the side of the concrete, the predicted future merged with the program being urgently advanced. Programmatically, it served both as a tendential guide for assessing and analysing the contradictions and fluidities of the present, and as a practical ideal to be realised.[37] Just as with Marx's 'Theses on Feuerbach', in fact, practice is what closes the gap. In actually being realised, which Positivism as a movement aimed to speed up,[38] the Positive Polity's hypothetical status (as what would happen if/when the 'present crisis' were resolved) would be superseded. The shakiness (for a positivism that wants empirical certitude) of this whole manoeuvre – whose truth depends on bringing it about – is presumably why Comte ensconced himself safely in the future. From there, the laws governing collective human development from start to finish could be imagined as having already been empirically confirmed.

As Comte recognised, however, construing the sociological object as transcendent to the individual did not automatically convert the care for

[35] 'L'impossibilité d'y recourir à l'observation directe se trouve compensée par la prépondérance plus complète des conceptions statiques et la succession plus étendue des appréciations dynamiques' (x:4–5).

[36] '. . . l'artifice général qui préside [in this treatise] . . . consiste à supposer que je l'écris dans l'année 1927, qui doit, en mes yeux, constituer la septante-troisième année de l'état normal, d'après l'opinion établie par mon principal ouvrage sur la nature et la marche de la transition finale' (xi:vii). By writing as if in the future, Comte also writes as if already dead, citing the testament he had written the year before (1855): 'Habitant une tombe anticipée, je dois désormais tenir aux vivants un langage posthume, qui sera mieux affranchi des divers préjugés, surtout théoriques, dont nos descendants se trouveront préservées' (xii:ix).

[37] Comte's analysis of the future, in its very words, aimed to be performative: '. . . cette détermination décisif . . . d'après sa nature, inaugure déjà l'état qu'elle décrit' (x:6).

[38] '. . . l'évolution fondamentale de l'humanité devra être ainsi conçue comme seulement modifiable, à certains degrés déterminés, quant à sa simple vitesse' (iv:316).

its welfare into an overriding moral imperative. The historically evolving relation between a self-transcending Humanity and the altruistic love of the sociated individual may be graspable as a general fact. Yet to be regarded as a principle, indeed as the finally grounding principle, for human theory and practice, something more was required. The elevated ontological status of *l'humanité* relative to individual members must also be embraced and affirmed. Such an affirmation is made emotionally possible by the individual altruism that linkage in society presupposes and elicits. As an epistemic and axiological resting point for the Positivist world-view, though, feelings are not enough. To fix ends so as to discipline practice it was necessary that love for the higher organism that englobes us, together with the very positing of such a category, be completed, and hardened, by an act of will. In the language of Christianity, from which Comte explicitly drew, it required *faith*.

In *Philosophie positive*, the assumption is that such a faith, together with *le pouvoir spirituel* which fosters it (VI:483 et seq.), will spontaneously arise. With 'the direct institution of Positive religion', however, it ceases to be so taken for granted and its propagation becomes an urgent concern. A year before Comte's death, the frontispiece of *Synthèse subjective* added to previous Positivist mottoes an extract from *De Imitatio Christi*: 'Omnis ratio et naturalis investigatio fidem sequire debet, non praecedere, nec infringere' (Every exercise of reason, and natural inquiry, should follow faith, not precede or infringe upon it).[39] In the works of the 1850s, in fact, faith in and towards Humanity becomes the indispensable attitudinal decision at the centre of the system. It was given primacy not only as a general moral rule (the basis for morality itself), but as a rule for thinking. It was especially a rule for that thinking which was Positivism itself. Upon it depended, within Comte's totalisation, the entire union of theory and practice.[40] Only thus could thought be directed to complete the positivisation of knowledge by linking that process, through the reflexive diagnostics of sociology, to the social reconstruction which it both provoked and made possible.

At the end of the road, then, it would seem that Comte had just regressed to the arbitrary fideism his entire effort was aiming to surpass. Yet this would be too simple. The faith which Comte explicitly, after 1847, took to be at the irreducible core of his project was by no means conceived as the kind of blind leap it represented for, say, Pascal or certain of the patristics. The sacred being with which Positivist faith

---

[39] The dictum is first introduced in book III of *Politique positive* (IX:439).
[40] 'Dirigée par l'amour et réglée par la foi, l'activité consolide leur concours en développant l'industrie collective' (X:361).

aligned the individual was not, from a sociological perspective, immaterial, but a real *dehors*. Unlike the ineffable God of theology, moreover, *le* Grand-Être was neither outside the laws of nature nor able to suspend them. The fact that Humanity was elevated above us not just objectively, for the intellect, but subjectively, for our 'highest' sentiments, was itself scientifically graspable in terms of the 'normal' individual/group relation posited by social statics, and perfected according to *les lois du progrès*. Faith in Humanity, then, could take itself to be *une foi démontrable*: one that was both really religious, in the socially and individually effective sense, yet positive, demystified and entirely rational.[41]

There was, in addition, an equally consequential difference between the faiths of Christianity and Positivism on the side of the believing subject. Approaching religion sociologically enabled Comte to grasp his own lonely, but 'inaugurating', process of Positivist conversion as more than an individual act.[42] In historical terms, while the innovative labour of synthesising the scientific–industrial episteme was inevitably accomplished in an individual brain, the Positivist embrace of Humanity with which it was bound up could be scientifically comprehended as a determinate moment in a larger social shift.[43] If we combined the laws of progress with the laws of statics, we could further infer that this new faith, like its predecessor, would have to be consolidated *institutionally*, so as to become a continuing social fact.

And so to the final step. After putting faith in charge of a sociologised reason, Positivism's religious *prise de position* secured itself the only way it ultimately could: in a system of ongoing practices designed to

[41] 'La foi théologique, toujours liée à une révélation quelconque . . . est assurément d'une tout autre espèce que la foi positive, toujours subordonée à une véritable démonstration, dont l'examen est permis à chaqu'un sous des conditions déterminées.' However, both kinds of faith 'résultent également de cette universelle aptitude à la confiance, sans laquelle aucune société réelle ne saurait jamais subsister' (VI:504).

[42] The 'Préface personnelle' to the last volume of *Philosophie positive* (VI:vi–xl) was at pains to show 'la correlation nécessaire qui lie aujourd'hui ma position privée à la situation fondamentale du monde intellectuel'. Besides elaborating on the particular family and educational background which marked him out to be the philosopher of *la doctrine régénératrice*, he explains the persistent opposition he faced in trying to get a permanent academic position at l'École Polytechnique as having 'nothing essentially personal or fortuitous' about it. It was the 'spontaneous resistance' of an intellectual milieu still suffering the effects of 'the artificially prolonged interregnum' of the metaphysical spirit (VI:xxxiv). For their part, his opponents found him rancorous and argumentative, and the preface itself – which appealed to 'public opinion' throughout Europe – only stiffened the resolve to keep Comte out. It was also the last straw in Comte's relationship with Caroline Massin (Pickering, 1993:547–51).

[43] 'Il suffit alors qu'une angélique impulsion vînt oralement régénérer le fondateur de la sociologie . . . Alors surgit, au centre de l'anarchie occidentale, le type systématique de l'existence normale, personnifiée chez le penseur que son initiation dispose le plus à l'essor révolutionnaire, dont sa jeunesse ne fut préservée que par la vénération' (XII:44–5).

reproduce both the moral subjectivity in question and the mental categories requisite for conceiving this whole self-confirming complex as a naturally produced socio-historical necessity. Therewith, Comte's synthesising ardor, speaking through a positivism become sociological, is at last able to find a stable home. It takes its bearings, at first in imagination but increasingly as an instituted reality,[44] not just from Humanity as a consciously affirmed transcendental reality, but from within the prayerful and liturgical round of a newly organised religion, whose function it would be to perpetuate and extend the sociolatric faith. The basis and necessity for such an ecclesiastical and ritual institution is a discovery of sociology itself. But in accepting responsibility for the consequences, by working to reproduce the sacral quality it binds itself to in its object, positive sociology becomes part of the religion whose social and intellectual rationale it bespeaks. Just as '*theocracy* and *theolatry* rested on *theology*, *sociology* constitutes the systematic basis of *sociocracy* and *sociolatry*' (VII:403).

The subjective synthesis

In addition to its practical implications, the theoretical consequences, for Comte, of normatising sociology by sacralising its object in a faith ramified by a new would-be world religion were profound. Sociology's double register, as science and socio-theology, at the top of the encyclopedic scale of abstract knowledge, introduced a crucial complication into the system. A subjective supplement – the sentiments of love, altruism, veneration, attachment etc. associated with the shift 'from an individual to a social point of view' – had been precipitated from within the science dealing with the highest object. This object depended for its existence on all the other levels of *l'ordre universel*. By asserting the (practically necessary) 'primacy of feeling over intellect' within theory itself, then, Comte's religious turn could not but reverberate back down the system of sciences that sociology capped. Hence the impetus and necessity for initiating what he called in the conclusion to *Politique positive* (X:542–3) the third, and final, part of his system: *la synthèse subjective*.[45]

---

[44] Some milestones: in 1828 Comte begins to train cadres for the new Spiritual Power; in 1838 he begins his regimen of 'cerebral hygiene'; in 1846 he begins the cult of Clotilde; in 1850, by now self-proclaimed as *Grand-prêtre de l'Humanité*, he initiates the three most important of his seven sacraments, regarding birth, marriage and death (VII:19). He later defines 1847 as the pivotal year, marking 'l'irrévocable avènement du positivisme religieux en condensant nos sentiments, nos pensées et nos actions autour de l'Humanité définitivement substituée à Dieu' (IX:618).

[45] The basic idea was already outlined in the concluding chapter of *Philosophie positive*.

That project was never completed, but the sketch-plan for it in *Politique positive* (X:197–233),[46] together with the one extant volume (on mathematics and logic), makes clear the general features of its design. To be emphasised first is its appellation as 'subjective'. It was to be subjective in a double sense. On the one hand, what was to be systematically unified was human subjectivity itself. In this regard, it continued the process begun, but only at the level of the intellect, in the synthesis of objective knowledge which Comte claimed to have accomplished in the *Philosophie positive*. On the other hand, 'subjective' also qualified the *mode* of synthesis. What was to be understood *about* the subject was to be understood as occurring *within* the subject, in harmony therefore with all its faculties, including, especially, the affects.[47] Overall, by adopting the standpoint of 'subjective synthesis' Comte repudiated the thought, still lingering in *Philosophie positive*, that for society as well as for the individual, subjective harmony depended primarily on systematising the intellect, and that in the epoch of science and industry the intellect could be systematised solely on the basis of 'objective' knowledge (VII:3–4).

To discover the 'most general axioms' (Bacon, 1960:43) had been the ultimate ambition of Baconian science. That aim was given renewed impetus by post-Newtonian advances in mathematical physics, and in more primitive form was seized on by Saint-Simon in his postulation of gravity itself as the 'sole cause of all physical and moral phenomena' (cited in Pickering, 1993:72). Comte's point of departure in *Philosophie politique* had been to break from this 'algebraic' mode, by socio-historically relativising the phenomenon of science, yet in this very relativity finding, in the formation of science itself, a principle of mental unity. By displaying the linkage among the sciences from the vantage point of sociology (with its law of three stages, and deduction of the sciences' 'normal' coordination), Comte had been able to disavow any 'metaphysical' pretensions to epistemological absolutism, while retaining an anchor in scientific objectivity.

With that same move, however, the project of developing an *objective*

Speaking of the social science now established, he remarks: 'La nature du sujet, où la solidarité est beaucoup plus complète que partout ailleurs, lui assure spontanément, dès sa naissance, en compensation nécessaire de sa complication plus grande, une rationalité supérieure à celle de toutes les sciences préliminaires . . . en y établissant aussitôt l'ascendant normal de l'esprit d'ensemble, qui, d'une telle source, doit bientôt se répandre sur toutes les parties antérieures de la philosophie abstraite' (VI:783).

[46] Arranged in an *Encyclopédie abstraite* which comprised (naturally) seven volumes of seven chapters each (X:197).

[47] 'Devenant à la fois plus sympathétique, plus synergique, et plus sympathique, la nature humaine tend ainsi vers la systématisation résulté de l'ascendant croissant de l'altruise sur l'égoïsme' (X:177).

synthesis became entangled with the need to demonstrate – and in so doing, to enact – the grounds of its own underpinning by a committedly human and social point of view. Once over this brink, Comte was brought to recognise that scientificity alone, even at the one-removed level of method, could not provide a unifying principle for consciousness unless complemented by that same commitment. In a phrase which recalls Aquinas on grace (*gratia non tollit naturam, sed perficit*: grace does not abolish nature, but perfects it) Comte affirmed that:

> *To complete the laws there must be wills.* Subjectively appreciated, this complement suits the speculative life as much as the active life, given the common insufficiency of legal motives. The lack of precision of social laws as a guide for human practice finds its equivalent in the helplessness of theoretical explanations with regard to the concrete spectacle. Commandment must assist arrangement for order to be complete. (XII:25; emphasis in original)

From which it followed, also, that the task of intellectual coordination positive philosophy had set itself was not a purely intellectual matter. Such coordination engaged the whole person, including the sentiments. It was also purposive, implying a moral orientation of the knowing subject towards altruistic practice. From this angle, Comte concluded, the 'objective' synthesis attempted in *Philosophie positive* had been necessary but insufficient (VII:443–4). Its insufficiency was both performative, as appealing only to the head and not the heart, and theoretical, as not reflecting on the relationship between the intellectual and the other faculties in its systematisation of the laws of the individual and collective mind.

The explicit introduction of sentiments into the Positivist totalisation, together with the importance of thematising these in terms of individual moral psychology, was linked to a second distinguishing feature of the *synthèse subjective*. While the first synthesis was inscribed within the master science of society, the second derived its organising principles from the science of *la morale* (X:195). Unlike sociology, this new *science finale* was not, strictly, a branch of science in its own right. It was a composite of two others: human biology (as this bore on a physiological theory of affects and faculties) and sociology. Moreover, as the domain 'where we study our nature in order to rule our existence' (X:181), it combined theory and practice. Indeed, it was the preeminent site of their union. As both practical and concrete, then, *la Morale* had no place in the initial scientific series. For just these reasons, however, its independent articulation in the second, 'subjective', series was essential. *La Morale* treated the constitution of the human being whose subjective condition was to be actually, and 'healthily', synthesised. It thus provided the organising principle for the entire subjective synthesis, because in *la science de Morale* the knowing subject ascends to itself, as both the summary of the totality (all sciences meet in Man)[48] and as the being whose mental/moral framework is embodied in that totality's conceptual construction.

According to the outline we have (x:230–8),[49] *la Morale* was to consist of two parts. The first, 'instituting the knowledge of human nature', would provide a synthesised theory of bio-psychological and socially mediated psychic integration; the second, 'instituting the improvement of human nature', a system of education which aimed to perfect the inner harmony of the individual soul.[50] As with sociology and social unity, functional integration at the individual level was made normative by its linkage to an ideal of health – an ideal rendered complex at both levels by their inextricable interrelation (x:233–6). A society of complete egoists was impossible; but the 'normal' state of individual subjective harmony was also unthinkable outside the moralising effects of the group. If the first was a sociological law, the second was biological, and followed from Gall and Bastiat's mapping of the brain and its functions (x:222). For the isolated individual the psychic preponderance of feelings over cognitive functions, and the 'dispersive' tendencies of the former, implied both the absence of, and the need for, a controlling psychic centre. This could only be provided by an 'external' mental force capable of disciplining the lower drives and rallying the weaker but nobler ones to an orienting Good outside the organism.[51] *La science de Morale* had, of course, a historical dimension as well. The more Humanity developed its forms and powers, the more the social tie was pacific, voluntary and founded on the socialised preponderance of *altruisme*; and the more, correspondingly, was the inner harmony of the individual itself perfected. At both levels, in the 'final' state of a fully positivised industrial society a fully equilibrated condition of mental and emotional organisation would have been achieved. In that happy condition, love would provide the motive for activity, while the intellect –

---

48 'Il ne peut, en effet, exister aucun phénomène appréciable qui ne soit vraiment humain, non-seulement d'après son examen subjectif, mais aussi dans sa nature objective; car l'homme résume en lui toutes les lois du monde, comme les anciens l'avaient dignement senti' (x:181).

49 See also the chapter-by-chapter plan of *la Morale* appended to the English edition of *Catéchisme positiviste* (Comte, 1973).

50 The theoretical first part was to be the seventh and culminating part of the *Encyclopédie abstraite*. The second part, on moral education, was reserved for educating the priesthood (x:230–1). The first and second parts of *la Morale* were intended to be volumes three and four of the work *Synthèse subjective*, described in the last pages of *Politique positive* (x:532).

51 For an account of the interplay between the evolution of the 'social organism' and the rise of instinctual sociability, see VII:91 et seq.

highly developed but knowing its proper station – would supply knowledge for its means (x:525). The result, indeed, would be a unity of unities.
For besides resting on the proper relation among sentiment, intellect and
action, each of these general faculties was itself the site of a special
coordination, respectively termed *synthèse*, *sympathie* and *synergie*.[52]

It is from this vantage point that the resystematisation of knowledge
projected for the *synthèse subjective* unfolds. Its intent was to provide a
'universal system of conceptions proper to the normal (i.e. perfected)
state of Humanity'.[53] The sciences, now deemed complete, were to be
coordinated not only among themselves' but also with the sentiments
and actions to which, in the 'normal' state of sociocracy and sociolatry,
the intellect whose evolution they represented was intrinsically linked.
The resulting *encyclopédie*, organised into courses, was to provide the
basis for the school curriculum for all 14–21-year-olds (x:251). It would
also provide the religion of Humanity with its central body of doctrine –
complemented on the methodological side by 'first philosophy' and the
initial system of *philosophie positive*, and on the side of synergising action
by the second part of *la Morale* (on moral education), together with the
still more 'final' theory of social practice contained in the never-written
Système de l'industrie positive (x:246).

To fulfil this office, and with the grandly synthetic addition of *la
Morale*, each branch of scientific knowledge was to be systematically
summarised so as to show its inner coherence, its integration within the
ascending scientific series, and its role in building up an attitude of
service and worship towards the Great Being of Humanity. With *l'amour
pour principe*, altruistic sentiments would in fact be given a *triple* field of
play. First, love of Humanity would orient and valorise the practices
which the sciences make possible. More abstractly, that same love would
animate the will to unity underlying the whole synthesising movement
itself.[54] This was partly because an auto-affected humanity would be
serving itself in the practical results; but also because, when freed of *les
instincts grossiers*, the impulse to join things together in perfect harmony
is precisely what love is.[55] As against the dissociated *sécheresse* of modern

---

[52] 'Écartant tous les préjugés théoriques, tant scientifiques que théologiques ou
métaphysiques, propres à l'initiation humaine, la sagesse finale institue la synergie
d'après une synthèse fondée sur la sympathie, en concevant toute activité dirigée par
l'amour vers l'harmonie universelle' (XII:9). See also x:162–4.

[53] The subtitle given *Synthèse subjective* on the title page of its first and only published
volume in 1856.

[54] A religion 'fondée sur l'amour de l'Humanité . . . peut seul systématiser à la fois toutes
nos constructions spéculatives, tant esthétiques que scientifiques, en instituant l'unique
lien durable que comportent nos pensées et nos sentiments' (VII:352).

[55] 'Moralement envisagée . . . [l]e sentiment s'y montre plus propre à régler l'intelligence,
et même l'activité . . . Toutes les spéculations y tendent à consolider l'amour universel,

scientific culture, finally, the love which courses through subjectively synthesised knowledge would be encouraged to flow towards the object to be known. That is, towards the world we are in, and of which we are intrinsically a part.[56]

Within a positivised self-understanding, the subjective synthesis would thus draw together worship and knowledge, and so replicate the affect-laden register of Christian theology itself. Indeed, by transposing what is to be venerated from the suprasensible realm of 'God' to the phenomenal one apprehended by the various branches of science, the subjective synthesis went one better. The medieval 'God', already an abstraction from the nature spirits which preceded it, had become ever more hidden behind, and beyond, the world investigated by secular knowledge.[57] That withdrawal of affect from the realm of the senses was what the subjective synthesis would be able to correct. Radiating with the *altruisme, bienveillance* and *vénération* which it receives from, and directs towards, a positively apprehended *Humanité*, the subjectively synthesised knowledge would reinvest the exterior human milieu with love. As a result, all the sciences, even those that do not deal with Humanity as such, would be drawn – through a mechanism which replicated the effects of a much more archaic *fétichisme* – into the spirit of the Positivist cult (VII:438–42).

Comte's treatise on mathematics – *Système de logique positive ou traité de philosophie mathématique* – meant to exemplify this subjective make-over of knowledge, as well as to set it on its way. Taking a lead from Descartes and Leibniz,[58] it displays *la science fondamentale* as covering the most general attributes of phenomenal existence: number (*calcul*), extension (*géométrie*) and motion (*mécanique*) (XII:70). So conceived, mathematical laws are rooted in a comprehension of *le dehors*, focussing on the laws that traverse all orders of being. At the same time, however, the mental coordination of these laws was a subjective matter. The logic in which mathematical philosophy expressed itself, therefore, had to be

seul capable de les systématiser, de les consacrer, et de les discipliner . . . Ainsi devenue le régulateur général, non-seulement du culte, mais aussi du dogme et du régime, l'instinct sympathique a pleinement constaté son aptitude synthétique' (X:525).
[56] In the subjective synthesis, 'l'idée relative du *monde*' would substitute for 'l'idée absolue de *l'univers*' (VII:438; emphasis in original). In amplifying, Comte refers to 'notre monde proprement dit, c'est-à-dire l'ensemble des existences inorganiques qui intéressent l'Humanité' (VII:457).
[57] Comte often comments that Paul, regarded as Christianity's real founder, 'opposed grace to nature'. See for example IX:429.
[58] These two were considered to have laid the basis for a positive philosophy of mathematics through establishing a general geometry translatable into algebraic terms: 'Après que le principe cartésien eut institué la géométrie générale, la conception leibnitzienne devint bientôt nécessaire pour la constituer' (XII:417).

shaped with both material and psycho-social realities in mind. Hence, not only is the progression from number, to spatiality, to movement narrated as the general logic of the complexification of substance; this abstract cosmogenesis also serves as a mirror in which to reflect the *human* progression, through higher and higher states of order, towards the self-perfection of its own 'total equilibrium'. From the side of that same equilibrated subject, meanwhile, the harmonious and altruistic mode of thinking required to grasp mathematics in terms of this religiously convenient teleology is self-reflected, with reference to sociology and the *science de la morale*, as subjectively necessary for that equilibrium itself.[59] Put in such terms, Comte's philosophy of mathematics can be described as an attempt to combine, at the most abstract level of thought and most sublimated level of feeling, a *cognitively* driven logic of the object with an *affectively* driven logic of the subject. Hence its suitability to furnish the subjective synthesis with a basis of what he called Positive Logic. This first volume, with its subtitle's promise to furnish the 'normal' principles of human understanding, would provide the mental principles for all the rest.

The dual status of *logique positive* – which both analyses and exemplifies, for the active intelligence, the mental harmony that will/should 'normally' prevail – is evident enough. It is offered, in the usual Comtean manner, as a scientific prescription. More striking is the way in which this harmony was conceived through a reflection on the relation among feeling, thought and language, a model then applied to the ordering of mathematics itself. Much as in Romantic language philosophy,[60] Comte was troubled by the abstract quality of (conventional) signs.[61] In contrast to the direct (and musical) affectivity developed

---

[59] Hence the need for a subjective law that, via the principle of inertia, subordinates the laws of dynamics to those of statics. As the subjective basis for the theory of general mechanics, the principle is propounded that: 'Graduellement neutralisés sous les conditions convenables de direction et intensité, les divers moteurs peuvent se combiner de manière à ne produire qu'un équilibre total, où leurs efforts respectifs ne sont directement jugeables que d'après leurs pressions mutuelles' (XII:601).

[60] Comte's theory of language combined a biological understanding of natural language with a Rousseauesque picture of how that natural language evolved, in the human case, out of the sonic and mimetic expression of affective body states. Hence the close relation between Comte's conception of the aesthetic arts and the need to reemphasise and reintegrate them into the positive state. 'Nos facultés quelconques d'expression sont toujours d'origine esthétique ... La biologie explique aisément cette loi, en rappelant que la réaction musculaire, vocale ou mimique, d'où résulte l'expression, est surtout commandé par la partie affective du cerveau' (VII:290).

[61] Comte's 'Théorie positive du langage humain' is outlined in chap. 40 of *Politique positive*. After distinguishing between 'involuntary' (gestural) and 'voluntary' or 'artificial' signs ('toujours de véritables institutions sociales' (VIII:221)), Comte there defines the sign as 'la liaison constante entre une influence objective et une impression subjective' (VIII:222).

under the aegis of *fétichisme* and the (poetic) language of *images* developed by polytheism, the rise of signs (and 'prosaic' discursivity), attributed to the monotheistic phase, permitted ideas to be directly attached to signifiers without the intermediary of sentiments (VIII:233–4). This enabled thought to become analytic and deductive, and was indispensable both for the rise of positive science and for the work of intellectual synthesis, which monotheism was the first to undertake. As valuable as this was, however, the 'healthy' and 'normal' integration of the human soul required that the head not be severed from the heart.[62] It required, therefore, both a recovery of the primal language of sentiments (the *effusions* which always accompanied Positivist prayers (X:114–15)) and a linguistic way to bridge the gap between such expressive immediacy and the affectless employment of *signes*. Hence the great mental – and religious – importance of *images*, a category which we can take to include the entire class of iconic and indexical signs. The crucial intermediary role of these, and more generally of the poetic and visual arts,[63] flowed from their dual role in psychic life. Images are the stuff both of dreams and fantasy, *and* of storable experience from *le dehors*. Instantly apprehensible through the way they mime inner and outer reality, they were much better suited than purely abstract or verbal signs to invest a charge of feeling in the meanings they convey. They were also sufficiently objectifiable and repeatable that they could become conventionally coded with associated ideas. Images, then, were apt for attaching sentiments to signs and vice versa. 'Just as the image, recalled under the sign, will strengthen thought through the awakening of sentiment, so, conversely, an outpouring of sentiment will give rise to the image in order to clarify the notion.'

In the 'final' form of language, where 'signs properly speaking would combine with the power of sentiments helped by images' (XII:29), all three modes would be harmonised. From that vantage point, Positive Logic would adduce the principles of mental unity, both internally and with regard to the 'healthy' interchange between 'movement and sensation', of *l'image intérieure* and *l'image extérieure*. Overall, then, it would comprise a kind of practical logic of logic, centred on language, whose

---

[62] 'Ni l'esprit ni le coeur ne peuvent développer une paisible activité sans ce concours continu, instinctif ou systématique, entre la logique du sentiment et celle de la raison' (VII:450).

[63] Vigorously defending himself against the charge that Positivism is 'anti-aesthetic' – which was a vice only of the sciences during their dispersively overspecialised period – Comte notes in *Politique positive*: 'Parvenu jusqu'aux spéculations sociales, qui constituent sa vraie destination finale, sa réalité caractéristique l'oblige d'embrasser les conceptions esthétiques, comme les considérations affectives, afin de représenter le véritable ensemble des phénomènes humains, même individuels, et surtout collectifs' (VII:275).

aim would be to theorise 'the normal concurrence of feelings, images and signs, in order to inspire us with the conceptions suited to our moral, intellectual and physical needs' (XII:27).

The privileged role of language in Comte's overall synthesis came from its providing the subjective condition for the human organism's linkage to *le dehors*.[64] The specific problem for mathematics concerned the establishment of happy and integrated relations between modes of representation advanced by sub-regions of its own field. In its presently disorganised condition, Comte argued, order was continually threatened by rival imperialising claims, especially by those of the *algébristes* (VII:471). Yet, correctly understood, the historical divisions in the field itself provided the answer. The key bridging role (which it must modestly learn to see itself as having) was played by geometry (XII:72). Its capacity, since Descartes, to spatialise even non-spatial dimensions of material existence facilitated the requisite interplay between images (with their attendant sentiments) and signs (with their abstract meanings). It did so, moreover, not only in geometry proper, where physical extension provided a material point of reference, but everywhere a metaphorics of quantifiable space could be employed. The very rise of geometry in this role made mathematics a first-order paradigm for the three-logics model of mental order, provided only that it be combined, subjectively, with that world of sentiment which *les images* opened the mind to receive.[65]

Hence, indeed, a further aspect of Positive Logic's foundational role in inducting trainee priests into Positivist doctrine. Besides processing mental materials in a form most able to connect ideas with feelings, geometry provided an image of the reality mathematics deals with which enabled even this most abstract of object-fields to receive and focus our highest affects. In so doing, it was able to awaken a form of *fétichisme* that would strengthen Positive Religion itself. The subjectively synthesised philosophy of mathematics enjoins us, in effect, to make a deliberately 'fictive' move. We are to imagine as the source of everything, as that which makes both thought and reality possible, the blank ground

---

[64] For a detailed analysis of Comte's theory of language, and its relation to *Logique positive*, see Krémer-Marietti, 1982: 210–51. Krémer-Marietti is particularly concerned to explore the points of contact between Comte's theory of language and Freud's unconscious, Nietzsche's understanding of art, and Saussure's notion of the sign.

[65] The subjective appreciation of mathematics would convert all of its signifying materials into *images*, including number. Hence the symbolic schema in which, for example, 1 stood for *l'harmonie sympathique*, 2 for *l'ordre synthétique*, 3 for *le progrès synergique* (XII:108), and 7 for two of the third plus one of the first. This symbolic logic of numbers provided the organising frame for all Comte's writing and planned *cours*, including the organisation of paragraphs.

against which geometrical figures, and whatever they represent, are pictorially inscribed: *l'Espace*.[66]

L'Espace differs from the object of primitive fetishism in not being a material thing, but a way to represent 'la siège' of phenomenal reality as such. It is the subjective representation of that which makes possible both externally and internally originating *impressions*. A further difference is that *l'Espace* is not imagined to have the *full* attributes of life. It fictively represents only sentiment – *l'amour universel* – without having the capacity for willed action or thought.[67] The attitude towards *l'Espace* which Positive Logic proposes is *fétichiste*, nonetheless, by virtue of the way in which it lives out a directly emotive and identificatory relation between subject and object; a relation that is enjoined not only religiously but cognitively in that it allows us to fill the inevitable gap between the concrete plenitude of phenomenal reality and our capacity to apply even a complete body of abstract science to the complete and previsionary understanding of any specific case (XII:7).

Overall, indeed, there was a greater degree of continuity between fetishism and positivism than between the latter and more 'mature' forms of theologism (VIII:84–5). Primitive fetishism confounded the orders of the living and the dead; but at least it did not retire agency from the phenomenal world entirely, to the greater glory of God. In the context of overcoming the intellectual crisis perpetuated by the persistence of metaphysics, Comte's proposed fetishisation of space also had a strategic significance. As he was at pains to point out, it pre-empted the older, and anarchic, 'consecration of chaos' (XII:51). Unlike Chaos, the image of *l'Espace* projects into the originary process of becoming, not strife and the dissolution of all order, but *l'amour universel*, figured as the precondition for order of any kind. By this means, in effect, we are emotionally drawn to submit voluntarily to the most general laws of existence, *la suprême fatalité*, because these laws are imagined to be identical with both the source and destination of our highest impulses. Fate, love and order are condensed together in the same symbol.[68]

---

[66] Comte realised of course that the 'space' of Cartesian geometry and Newtonian astrophysics had a long history, antecedent indeed to all science. In his definition of *l'espace* (here lower case and unfetishised) in *Politique positive*, he notes: 'on n'y doit voir qu'un fluide universel, spontanément imaginé, dans l'enfance du génie humain, pour permettre de concevoir l'étendu, et même le mouvement, indépendamment des corps réels. Faute d'un tel milieu, des signes sans images deviendraient notre unique ressource envers l'essor abstrait des spéculations géométriques et mécaniques extension' (X:53–4).

[67] 'Il faut donc conserver à l'Espace l'existence purement passive, où le type humain se trouve réduit au sentiment, dont la suprématie constitue ainsi le seul attribut pleinement universel' (XII:51).

[68] 'Faute d'un tel joug, le problème humain resterait insoluble, parce que l'altruisme ne

Comte intended that a similar fetishism would envelop the middle portions of the *synthèse subjective* devoted to the physical sciences. Here, though, the fetish-object – *la Terre* – was one stage less abstract. To the Earth we could impute not just sentiments, but activity; and we could imagine it as being driven along a path of self-perfection by something akin to a good will (XII:50). By worshipping, venerating and serving the planet as the material source, support, and abode for human life, biology, chemistry, physics and even astronomy, would be inhibited from wandering into 'puerile and incoherent research' (VII:456). With such an orientation, a practical eye would be kept turned toward what it was useful to know about our terrestrial milieu; not just to satisfy material needs, but the better to perfect ourselves as its noblest product.

Hence, to complete the model, the Comtean trinity: *l'Espace* as *le Grand-Milieu*; *la Terre* as *le Grand-Fétiche*; and both sanctified as the cosmic foundation from which arises *l'Humanité* as *le* Grand-Être (XII:51–2). It is following this movement that the seven sciences of the subjective synthesis are arranged in their ascending scale (XII:63–4). At the base, mathematics cognitively inducts us into the worship of Space. In the middle ranges, astronomy, physics, chemistry and non-human biology prepare worship of the Earth. At the top, human biology, sociology and *la morale* compose (in the extended sense) *la science sacrée*. Here, finally, *le* Grand-Être, through its scientifically educated agents, comes worshipfully and caringly to study itself[69].

The logic of the system

From the *Philosophie positive* and *Politique positive* to the final system of systems inaugurated by the *Synthèse subjective*, we see the same figure continually repeated: a politically and religiously engaged totalisation of scientifically transformed knowledge which seeks to ground, scientifically, its own engagement. That such grounding could not be apodictic, or absolute, was acknowledged from the start. The system could only be systematised on a 'relative' basis, i.e. from the self-centred and self-interested side of a humanity which had recognised that its self-placement at the centre of things was, in an infinite Newtonian universe, a pure, if humanly necessary, fiction.

Such a vantage point, by being rooted in a pervasive sense of each

pourrait jamais surmonter l'égoisme. Assisté par la suprême fatalité, l'amour universel peut habituellement obtenir que la personnalité se subordonne à la sociabilité' (XII:16).
[69] 'Tant que le culte positif s'adresse directement à l'Humanité, nul artifice n'y devient obligé, puisque le sujet y coïncide avec l'obect, d'après une saine appréciation de l'homme comme serviteur actuel et futur organe du Grand-Être' (XII:18).

human being's belonging in, and dependency on, the collective being of society and, ultimately, of Humanity as a whole, was less arbitrary than that of the isolated individual. But only relatively. Between the 'ought' of (Humanist) commitment and the 'is' of (Positivist) reason there is always a gap which can only be closed by an act of theoretical or emotional force. The positive philosophy of science could only be systematised through the invention of sociology. The objective (but non-absolute) unification of the sciences required a subjective synthesis of the knowing mind. The whole system required and presupposed reso-cialisation through educational reform and the establishment of a religion. In face of this, Comte's continual drive nevertheless to complete his system in a final synthesis that would fully ground his faith in Humanity in the 'positive' truths it led us to discover betrayed, not so much bad faith as the personal and political anxiety that was pushing him to resolve the contemporary 'crisis'. Whatever the motive, the results were bound to remain unsatisfactory. Whether in the medium of an intellectualist sociologism, a religio-sentimental sociologism or a bio-sociologically composite *science de morale*, a leap of faith – finally to a mode of consciousness conceived as 'normal', and itself ramified by a self-instituted religious pressure to conform – was always needed to make the system cohere.

Against this background, the history of Comte's systematising efforts, from the *Philosophie positive* and *Politique positive* to the *Synthèse subjective* and the further systems of *la Morale* and *L'industrie* which he never lived to write, can be read as the history of his system's attempted closures. I have noted several dubious manoeuvres through which these attempts were made: the conflation of the abstract and the concrete, the collapse of 'the social' into 'society', the bio-medical model of the latter, according evidential status to a predictive teleology, proof-by-future-actualisation and, buttressed by the hyperorganised practices of a new religion, the 'normal preponderance' of altruism and Humanist faith. The last two, by frankly placing the issue of validation outside the realm of scientific reason, are less objectionable, perhaps, than the others. But this did not prevent Comte from continuing his ultimately futile effort of closure by referring, in the one case, practice, and in the other, faith, to a criterion of normality given by his crowning 'moral science'. The same problem of grounding the ungroundable is thus reproduced at every stage of his unfolding totalisation, and in an ever more elaborate fashion. Its consequences are legible in the Comtean trail of false or dogmatic endings which, at every crucial stage in the argument, stop further reflection – be it sociological, religious or metatheoretical – by occlusion or decree.

There is, though, a more sympathetic way to understand Comte's dilemma. We can look at it, so to speak, in reverse. Not, that is, as a scientific, or metascientific, discourse whose necessary open-endedness is thwarted and foreclosed by the specious effort to demonstrate what is already fervently believed; but as a *fides quaerens intellectum*, i.e. as a faith *seeking* (the term to be emphasised) an understanding. To do so admittedly breaks with Comte's own formula from the *Imitatio Christi* about the need to *subordinate* reason to faith. It reaches instead to the more supple and dialectical formulation of the faith–reason problem given in a less brittle and defensive stage of medieval theology. This is the one proposed in the Boethian slogan *fidem si poteris rationemque conjunge* (join faith, if you can, and reason) which was advanced by Anselm and others in the moderate (i.e. anti-Abelardian) scholastic party of the late twelfth century.[70] To be sure, went the argument, faith is primary. *Credo ut intelligo* – I believe in order to understand. At the same time, my efforts at understanding are guided by the desire, at the end of the journey, to have rationally illuminated the mysteries of faith. In this two-way relationship of faith to reason there is always a tension. I have faith that reason can grasp the grounds of what I believe, just as I also believe that believing will illuminate the understanding so that the world as it really is can be lucidly grasped. But all that faith – in reason, in the intelligibility of the world, in God, in faith itself – is needed precisely because the unity of knowledge and self-knowledge escapes me. It gives the intellectual project the strength to proceed; and to do so without the stress of having to imagine that the faith–reason gap is already closed, or that the religious *mysterium* is yet – or ever could be – fully cleared up.[71]

To reframe Comte's project in such terms would make it possible to reopen, from within, issues surrounding his *intellectum* that are dogmatically suppressed; and to do this not by bracketing his faith as – of course, and despite his best efforts – *undemonstrable*, but by making it focal, and bracketing instead the pretensions to scientificity that achieve the false, and self-deluded, closures of his system.[72] The point of such a

[70] Boethius' principle was enunciated as the last line of a letter from him to Pope John I. For an account of this, and its subsequent influence on scholastic theology, see Pieper, 1960: 37–8.

[71] As Anselm put it: 'I do not attempt, O Lord, to penetrate Thy profundity, for I deem my intellect in no way sufficient thereto, but I desire to understand in some degree Thy truth, which my heart believes and loves. For I do not seek to understand, in order that I may believe; but I believe, that I may understand. For I believe this too, that unless I believed, I could not understand' (cited in Coppleston, 1962:177).

[72] It should be emphasised that Comte's *foi démontrable* was not *une foi démontrée*, though the assumption was that it always *could* be demonstrated. This corresponded 'à la maturité de la raison humaine, destinée à développer les conséquences sans délibérer

procedure – the opposite approach to that taken by those like Simpson (1969) who primarily stress Comte's role in the ancestry of academic sociology – is not only, it should be made clear, to save Comte, as a religious thinker, from a reduced, i.e. non-religious, interpretation. Still less is it to save Comtean religion itself from criticism. To the contrary, by taking his faith seriously as the basis, impulse and horizon of his thought, it can be subjected to critical scrutiny in its own terms, together with his related construction of the modern 'religious crisis' and its Positive resolution.

sur les principes' (x:267). Comte's phrase opens the *intellectum* of his faith only immediately to close it, hiding the faith that sustains the demonstrability of that faith in a morally pragmatist aversion to idle speculation.

As his every page proclaims, Comte's effort to resynthesise contemporary thought by (simultaneously) securing the moorings for his Humanist faith was practically intended. It was driven, indeed, by a pressing sense of urgency – an urgency proportional to the scale and gravity of the historical problem he took himself to have been called upon to address. With monarchical absolutism swept away, the conditions existed for a decisive advance. But for two centuries the old order had shielded society from a growing spiritual anarchy which threatened 'modern societies' with 'universal dismemberment' (v:485). Unless the requisite new fundamental consensus could be established, the 'great moral and political crisis of present societies' (1:40) would be insurmountable.

Of course, for the correct solution to be prescribed, and for the Positivist system to legitimise *itself* as intrinsic to that solution, it was necessary that the problem itself be properly diagnosed. And properly, in this context, could only mean in accord with the findings of the human–social science that completed the positivising of knowledge. It is not hard to show, at the least, that this 'science' is prematurely deployed. Not just its data, but its categorical framework, produce an all-too-convenient fit between what its author already experienced as the problem and what he believed to be the solution. Nevertheless Comte's analysis of (early) industrialism's travails need not be dismissed out of hand. To say that he misperceived the social, or religious, problems posed by the rise of industrial capitalism is not necessarily to say that his anxieties, and hopes, lack any historical reference. The hundred years of industrialism in Europe *after* Comte were even more turbulent, sanguinary and, at times, disintegrative than the century before. What reasonable analysis of 'modern western society' could deny that its history of prodigious techno-economic development has been punctuated by an unresolved (perhaps unresolvable) stability problem?[1] Or

---

[1] At a time when conventional wisdom (again) has it that history is over (Fukuyama, 1992), or that fundamental sources of socio-economic conflict have been structurally contained (Baudrillard as the postmodern Marcuse), or that henceforth the explosive

that an element of this instability has been cultural or even, in a diffuse sense, 'religious' – sometimes, as in the totalitarian catastrophes of the 1930s and 40s, with dramatically regressive results?

The *form* of Comte's analysis also deserves attention. At first sight, its scientistic insistence exhibits the one-sidedness of that objectivising rationalism which Hegel criticised in the (non-Protestant) Enlightenment.[2] Without recourse to any phenomenology or philosophy of the subject, Comte certainly had no developed metalanguage with which to reflect on the structure of a reflexive rationality. This is not to deny that Comte has a host of classificatory categories on which he conceptually reflects. But unlike Kant and Hegel he has no terminology with which to reflect on the structure of reflection as such.[3] Indeed, he was averse to the very notion of reflexivity, not only because of his phenomenalism – thought could only be known through its exterior manifestations in the body or in its social objectifications – but also in principle. 'The thinking individual cannot divide himself in two, the one reasoning while the other watches him do so' (1:29). Thus if the self could come to know itself at all, it certainly could not do so directly, in the form of *observation intérieure*.

Yet a reflexive rationality is just what he was trying to develop; not, to be sure, through abandoning objectivism, but by pushing it all the way. The arrival of sociological thinking, particularly of a holistic and historicising kind, in any case forced the issue. To take full account of social mediations expands and complicates any project of self-understanding. It does so not only by relating the subject of knowledge to his/her socio-historical circumstances, themselves understood as socio-historically conditioned, but also by inviting reflection on this viewpoint as itself determined by a form of understanding which needs to be socio-

issues are now largely exterior to western societies in the form of intercivilisational conflicts (Huntington, 1996), it may be salutary to recall the 'convergence theory' and 'end of ideology' thinking that were prevalent in the late fifties and early sixties.

[2] For Hegel, French rationalism, from Descartes to the *philosophes*, was restricted to a merely external 'understanding'. 'Instead of making its way into the inherent content of the matter at hand, understanding always takes a survey of the whole, and assumes a position above the particular existence where it is speaking, i.e. it does not see it at all' (Hegel, 1967: 112).

[3] Whether there is an *implicit* metatheory that would be able to meet German Idealist philosophy on its own ground is a different issue. Pickering's archival research turned up references to lost translations of extracts from Kant, Fichte and Hegel that Comte apparently kept in his private files. This contradicts his claim never to have read any of them 'in any language' (Pickering, 1993:278). It also suggests an at least competitive awareness that his was not the only serious current attempt to develop a 'subjective synthesis'. A trace of acknowledgment is perhaps to be found in the reference to the 'superior spirit' and 'precious disposition for general meditations' of German philosophy at the end of the 57th *leçon* of the *Cours*.

historically explained. Comte's analysis of his historical situation – wherein not only the Positivist faith and synthesis, but his own Positivist intervention, were part of the Positivist *demonstrandum* – was indeed not just reflexive, but multidimensionally so.

One *sociological* feature of this complexity should be underlined straight away. This is Comte's recognition that, by virtue of the thinking, feeling and acting subject's inherence in the object of sociological knowledge, that object has, objectively speaking, a dual character. To grasp the social as belonging to the order of the *dehors* is to grasp it as having an irreducibly subjective dimension. In the case of *la société*, as in the case of the individual within it, *le dehors* includes *le dedans*. That same duality, moreover, of inside and outside, of subjective and objective, applies to that element of social reality which is sociology itself. Whence the rationale for combining an objective investigation of the social with a subjective engagement with it, which the *Politique positive* exemplifies as the inauguration of a more general movement to rethink positivised knowledge from the perspective of its 'subjective synthesis'.

If we follow Comte in taking the intrusion of the subjective into the objective in the social domain to be one of its defining characteristics, we may well, and for precisely that reason, deny his claim that 'the collective development of the human species' can become, in theory or in practice, the object of a science at all.[4] But the idea, in some form or another, of developing a perspective on the social, and of our place in it, which combines an understanding 'from within' with one 'from without', remains fundamental. It points, indeed, to what might be a more appropriate way to conceive a (humanly useful) sociology: not as a 'positive science', but as a critically reflexive discourse that at every level combines, and oscillates between, the viewpoints of subject and object, in all the ways in which this dichotomy might be conceived.

A *totalising* reflexivity, however, such as Comte attempted, runs risks. One arises from the temptation of socio-historical reduction. This would be to think of all thinking as no more than expressing a particular constellation of social and historical circumstances. Late Enlightenment tendencies in that direction were denounced by Husserl not only for

---

[4] 'There is . . . no theory of society, even that of the sociologists concerned with general laws, that does not contain political motivations, and the truth of these must be decided not in supposedly neutral reflection but in personal thought and action, in concrete historical activity' (Horkheimer, 1972: 222). Comte, we may note, would disagree with this statement in only one respect. For him, the truth of the political motivation underlying his sociology could itself be scientifically validated – though (the endless circle) only from the perspective of a science which had already adopted the 'social point of view'. Horkheimer's 'critical theory' is more straightforward in acknowledging the non-apodictic nature of its founding socio-political assumptions.

their relativisation of all validity claims, but also as not allowing for the *epoche* which theory in the Greek sense requires (1965:122 et seq.). Nietzsche's critique of the 'mania for history' and Benjamin's (1969:261–3) critique of social democracy's 'historicism' made similar points with regard to action. If the first danger is an ultra-relativism that submerges thought wholly within the historical flow, a second danger is of pretending to integrate the 'within' of the social with its 'without', but effecting a false closure which actually structures itself around an experience and a wish. Both the subjective and objective sides of analysis then become absorbed into a vast rationalisation, and the attempt at reflexive socio-historical understanding relapses, misrecognised, into ideologising pure and simple. This danger, too, was high with Comte: both because of his too close analogy between *la société* and the individual subject and because, in reflecting on the foundations of his thinking, he made little distinction between himself and his publicly assumed role. He imagined himself to be just a functionary of Humanity whom accidents of birth and biography had uniquely fitted for an already prepared world-historical task. As with Hegel, and given what his mind had worked over, and become, the ratiocination of finite being could thus take itself to have an immediately universal significance.

The self-confirming character of an ideological circle may certainly be suspected in the relation Comte draws among his faith, his religious program and his sociological diagnosis. Ostensibly, the conceptual and evidential link between his analysis of the 'current crisis' and his proposed solution is provided, independently of both, by an inductive–predictive science. However, the organic–functional categories of the latter, which naturalise Comte's own subjectivity as paradigmatic of what was besetting (and could save) industrial society at large, themselves arise through what is given to us as a merely analogical intuition – that the social crisis is like an individual one, and that both are to be understood as the *désorganisation* of an organism.[5] Thus his understanding of that crisis, and his religious solution to it, endlessly reflect one another, blinding him to what is contingent, and unconsciously projective, in the subjectivity in play. In which case, and if the pain came first, could we not say that Comte's solution, and the entire philanthropic will to unity it incarnates, is to be read symptomatically, indeed as a reactive response?

To entertain this possibility would seem to negate Comte's analysis

[5] For Comte's discussion of *la manie* as an example of Broussais's principle that 'l'état pathologique' must always be considered as 'un simple prolongement des phénomènes de l'état normal, exagérés ou atténués au delà leurs limites ordinaires de variations', see III:658–9.

before we have begun. Such a flaw would not be fatal, though, to its interest value. Indeed, it carries an interpretative suggestion. If the Positivist program simply presents in reverse image what Comte already apprehended as a crisis (his own, generalised as *our* own), then examining his sociological account of that crisis would provide an illuminating point of entry for critically exploring his faith. What, then, was *la crise moderne*? How had it arisen? And what, as signalled by Comte's understanding of it as ultimately 'religious', did he take to be socially and humanly at stake?

The troubles of industrialism

Comte was born, four years after Thermidor, into a petit-bourgeois provincial Catholic royalist family, against which, in all respects, he rebelled.[6] He continued to be a rebel at the elite École Polytechnique, a hotbed of Republicanism, where, in 1815–16, he was prominently involved in protests against an 'insolent' teacher which led to the Restoration authorities delicensing the school.[7] Comte's refusal of the school's offer to enter him for the higher civil service exams in return for good behaviour (Pickering, 1993:40) prevented resumption of his formal studies when the school reopened a year later. This began a pattern of self-righteous quarrelsomeness which was always to block his never-abandoned ambitions for an academic career in that same institution. The product of a dysfunctional family, and chronically incapable of sustaining intimate friendships, the same self-defeating dynamic marked his private existence.[8] It no doubt exacerbated the psychosomatic

---

[6] He was already a Republican anticlerical in *lycée*. As a student, besides his public activism, he adopted Auguste instead of Isidore as his first name, refused his family-approved and -supported career future as an engineer, and defiantly married the socially unsuitable Caroline Massin (whose marriage enabled her to get off the local prefecture's health registry of prostitutes). For a detailed account of Comte's family in Montpellier, and his relations with them, see Gouhier, 1933, 1:32–61.

[7] Pickering (1993:29–30) attributes a somewhat more leading role to Comte in these events than does Gouhier (1933, 1:116–22). Comte was, though, one of the fifteen in his class to be formally expelled.

[8] The family drama would be worthy of a full-scale study. It seems that Comte, the eldest son, despised his father, disliked but was emotionally dependent on his religiously devout mother (older by 12 years and effectively head of the household), and had quarrelsome relations with Alix, his devotedly self-sacrificing stay-at-home sister. The latter he blamed for their brother Adolphe's death, in Martinique at the age of 19, pursued by scandal and bad debts. All suffered chronic ill health, and all (except the devotedly indolent Adolphe, but perhaps him too) oriented their lives through forms of faith and duty that involved personal sacrifice. Under the circumstances, Comte's later account of himself as not, until Clotilde, being capable of love is unsurprising, as is his subsequent idealisation of an impersonal *amour désintéressé* (Pickering, 1993:9–17; Gouhier, 1933, 1:50–61). Comte's 20-year relationship with Caroline Massin, by all

ailments that were to afflict him all his life.[9] But through it all the precocious and rebellious first son thirsted to be an intellectual and moral leader – the *fondateur*, no less, of the post-Absolutist, post-Christian world struggling chaotically to be born.

It was from this crucible of contradictions that Comte's life-project took shape. Trained in mathematics and biology,[10] and self-taught in everything else, the remoteness of a highly specialised scientific culture from the burning political and social issues of his day repelled him; yet he found in its rising intellectual prestige a potential authority substitute for the older one that he, in microcosm, and France as a whole, had overthrown. Here might be the basis for a healing regeneration and a post-Revolutionary new order.[11]

After abandoning the radical Republicanism of his student days[12] for this more reconstructionist perspective, what became Comte's firm understanding of the historical situation crystallised in his early to mid twenties, during his years with Saint-Simon. Drawing at once from Condorcet's progressivist vision in *L'Esquisse*, and from de Maistre's denunciatory critique of the negative forces unleashed in the Revolution, it was first sketched out in the *opuscule fondamental* of 1822 (xa:47–81)[13] and elaborated in the last two volumes of *Philosophie positive*. While it was not until after 1847 that Comte's account of the contemporary 'crisis' acquired a fully religious cast, in basic outline it remained the same throughout his career.

accounts a free spirit with a mind of her own, was always beset by the problem that he thought he was 'saving' her, and that this mission and its social cost to him were unappreciated.

[9] Gouhier (1933, 1:60) observes: 'Dès 1820, Comte se plaint de son estomac et c'est d'une tumeur de l'estomac qui l'enlévera en 1857. Ses crises nerveuses coïncident toujours avec les troubles digestifs et l'unité de sa vie physiologique paraît aussi remarquable que l'unité de sa vie intellectuelle.'

[10] He studied biology for one term, at l'École de Médecine in his home town of Montpellier, following his expulsion from the École Polytechnique. The school was 'vitalist' in outlook. For Comte's relation to the Montpellier school of biology, see Canguilhem, 1994:237–61.

[11] Comte's notion that the scientific intelligentsia could be forged into a new *pouvoir spirituel* was already well formed before he began work on the *Cours* in 1826. See his essays 'Considérations philosophiques sur les sciences et les savants' (1825), and 'Considérations sur le pouvoir spirituel' (1826), appended to the last volume of *Politique positive* (x:137–215).

[12] For Comte's political perspective during his *lycée* and École Polytechnique period, see Pickering, 1993:20–30. His early guides were Rousseau and Voltaire, and (within the Revolution) Danton and the Convention. He supported Napoleon (in the streets) during 1815, but this was in the context of a struggle against the threat of a Bourbon restoration.

[13] 'La seule manière de mettre un terme à cette orageuse situation . . . c'est de déterminer les nations civilisées à quitter la direction critique pour la direction organique, à porter tous leurs efforts vers la formation du nouveau système social' (xa:48).

Comte's point of departure was the ongoing and extreme political turbulence of post-Revolutionary France, with its dizzying parade of republican, monarchical and dictatorial regimes, and its intense antagonisms between partisans of restoration and of the ideals of 1789. For Comte, what all this turmoil manifested, at root, was the failure of a newly emergent form of civilisation to establish, as yet, the requisite social framework for its stable development, particularly in the ideational sphere. This was exacerbated by the way in which the process of dissolving the old form of social organisation to make way for the new had acquired a momentum of its own. Thus the crisis had a two-fold character:

Two, naturally different, movements disturb contemporary society: one is a movement of disorganisation, the other one of reorganisation. By the first, society is led towards a deep moral and political anarchy which seems to threaten its incipient and inevitable dissolution. By the second it is led to the definitive social state of the species, the most suited to its nature . . . The great crisis undergone by the most civilised nations consists in the coexistence of these two opposed tendencies. (xa:46)

The crisis pitted against one another particular social interests. In the Bourbon restoration, and in the continual intrigue after it was again overthrown, defeated remnants of the court, the church and the aristocracy sought a restoration of their own wealth and power. Champions of liberty and reason, for their part, were drawn from rising social forces which had benefited from destroying the old regime.[14] But foregrounded, for Comte, was the conflict over ideas in which the conflict between classes, to use Marx's words, was 'lived and fought out' (Feuer, 1959:44). Here, over the whole range of issues from property law and state form, to education, the principles of morality, and the true nature of Man, raged a war between incompatible philosophies,[15] one basing

---

[14] However, the two key forces in the 'critical' movement of struggle, the *légistes* and *métaphysiciens scolastiques* (succeeded in the seventeenth and eighteenth centuries by the *philosophes* and *littérateurs*), were of transitional importance only, since scientists and industrialists, not they, were destined to build and direct the ruling 'organs' of the new industrial order (v:446–52). This disjuncture enabled Comte to think of himself as ideally positioned to begin organising, against the 'metaphysicians' of Revolution, that new leadership's intellectual wing. Whence, despite all the rebuffs, his obsessive pursuit of a professorship at l'École Polytechnique. He no doubt imagined himself transforming this leading school for science and engineering into the cadre-building centre for the new *pouvoir spirituel*.

[15] Comte clarifies his use of the term philosophy in the opening preface of *Philosophie positive*: 'Je regrette . . . d'avoir été obligé d'adopter, à défaut de tout autre, un terme comme *philosophie*, qui a été si abusivement employé dans une multiplicité d'acceptations diverses . . . Je ne bornerai donc, dans cet avertissement, à déclarer que j'emploie le mot *philosophie*, dans l'acceptation que lui donnaient les Anciens, et particulièrement Aristote, comme désignant le système général des conceptions humaines' (i:xii).

itself on Reason, the other on Faith, both seeking ascendancy within society as a whole.

Besides the immediate difficulty this presented for establishing any stable political regime, the continued dissensus symptomatised, in something like a medical sense, a deep disorder in the social organism. Since life forms existed only by virtue of their 'vital consensus' (IV:439), and since it was an axiom of social physics that 'the whole social mechanism depends on opinions', it followed that a fixed agreement 'relative to all the fundamental maxims . . . is the first condition for real social order'. Underlying the 'great political and moral crisis of contemporary societies', then, was an 'intellectual anarchy' which presented – 'first intellectually, then morally' – a potentially dissolvent social threat (1:40).

Neither of the two main warring theoretico-ideological camps, however, held the key to how the problem might be overcome. One represented an otherworldly religious viewpoint which had become obsolete; the other embodied an abstract and critical rationalism that had become entirely anarchic and 'did not know how to construct' (xa:45–56). The chronic conflict between 'theological' partisans of the *ancien régime* and 'metaphysical' partisans of liberty, fraternity, equality and progress[16] could only be resolved through the triumph of a synthesising third camp. This would be oriented to progress *and* order, and it would negotiate the split between faith and reason by basing itself on the unified philosophical spirit of the scientific revolution allied to a purely 'terrestrial' morality.

Both the possibility, and the necessity, of a 'really organic new doctrine' flowed from the very conditions that had undermined feudalism and begun to shape the emergence of something new. Considered in the sweep of history, what was coming to an end was a military form of society, ultimately based on conquest and plunder as the dominant mode of collective wealth acquisition, of which European feudalism was the 'defensive' second phase (v:395–6). What had rendered it obsolete and displaced its leading classes and institutions, was the rise, and increasing productivity, of organised work: *l'industrie*. The 'modifying power' of the latter expanded with modern science, as applied within an increasingly efficient division of labour. Industry, in turn, provided stimulus and support for scientific research. From the Renaissance onwards, the scientific and industrial revolutions had gone hand in hand, first helped, then hindered by the various *dictatures temporelles*

---

16 'L'une a tendu à dissoudre la morale, l'autre n'a pu la préserver, et sa vaine intervention même abouti qu'à rendre cette dissolution plus active, en faisant rejaillir sur la morale l'irrévocable discrédit mental de la théologie' (v:621).

whose development out of the medieval state was the political comple-ment of the Reformation (VI:117).

The temporal and spiritual powers of feudalism also decayed, however, because of internal contradictions (v:416–17). The rise of the monarchical state absorbed a decadent feudal nobility, undermined the headship of the papacy, and paved the way for the Reformation. The ('provisional') synthesis of the medieval church was itself only ever an incoherent mix of metaphysics and theology, of *égoisme* and *altruisme*. The tension generated a rogue rationalism from out of theology itself (v:454–62). The dialectical character of Comte's analysis of feudalism, in which a contradictory complex of dominant but declining forces engenders, through the civilisational advance it facilitates, a contra-dictory complex of rising forces, with which it then comes into increasing conflict, is striking. A key disagreement in nineteenth-century progressivism would come to be between those, like Marx and Engels, for whom industrial society, the free market and the liberal state were susceptible to the same dialectical treatment as feudalism, and those, like Comte and Hegel, who saw the great transformation to modernity out of post-feudal absolutism as now essentially accom-plished (save for stabilisation), so that no further radical upheavals need be contemplated.

For Comte, the transformation to a new form of society was furthest advanced in northwestern Europe, though not, as a fashionable anglo-philia would have it, in England, but in France.[17] In the former, a 'dictatorship of the nobility' had preserved retrograde elements from the feudal polity which the French monarchy had overwhelmed (v:487). English Protestantism also made 'the metaphysical philosophy' domi-nant, whereas in France there was no middle ground, the altruistic element of the Catholic *morale* was less disrupted, and isolated Versailles had been powerless to control the surging forces that eventually swept it away. In France uniquely (v:583–4), the historical way was open, after six centuries of turmoil, for the new order finally and fully to emerge. All that was required, in the aftermath of 1789–94, was a reconstructive reform. In this reform, with parasites and agitators pushed aside, *l'industrie* would finally move from the political margins to the centre, while on the spiritual–intellectual side the same revamped knowledge which had transformed productive practice would become the consen-

---

[17] The picture of England as the vanguard of modernity was of long standing among French reformers and went back at least to Montesquieu. It was strongly maintained by Saint-Simon (Manuel, 1962:108), whose *Lettres d'un habitant de Genève à ses contemporains* made great play with a contrast between the proud beef-eating English workers and their miserable French counterparts who starve and 'are beaten with sticks'.

sual basis for social, moral and philosophical thinking as well. As a further result, the 'moral anarchy' of production – whose 'material antagonism' pitted the 'contempt' of the bosses against the 'envy' of the workers in a spreading field of pure force – would also come to an end (v:549–50).

Thus far and in broad outline, we may say, Comte was still with Saint-Simon. Where he began to depart from his mentor was in his insistence, against the latter's speculative rush to solutions, that both the emergence of the new order and the crisis itself be analysed scientifically. Hence the need to establish, and not just call for, 'social physics'.[18] Indeed, as we have seen, not only was a science of society necessary to supply action with its reality principle, it was also necessary in order to complete the positivisation of knowledge and so make possible the philosophical synthesis required for the restoration of a stable, because epistemologically updated, consensus.

Up to a point, the schema for the new science which Comte sketches out in his 1822 'Plan des Travaux scientifiques' and elaborates in the last three volumes of *Philosophie positive* just fills in the Saint-Simonian blanks. Its 'statics' and 'dynamics', applied to the encyclopedic tableau of human history from earliest times, make social physics into a kind of knowledge machine which would enable us to predict both the theoretical–ideological basis of the new order and its 'normal' institutional form. But Comte was driven to go deeper. How, he asked, if a new order was destined to emerge, could the present disorder be accounted for? And how, if society was, like the rest of nature, a determinately lawful domain, could the intervention of a 'positive politics' even be conceived? Why, indeed, was it necessary?

For Saint-Simon, at the turn of the century the situation facing even the most ambitious reformers was fluid, and everything seemed possible. His analysis of industrialism's incomplete transition was sketchy, and he was more interested in immediate schemes and solutions.[19] Comte was

[18] While Saint-Simon's conception of 'social physics' was inchoate, and he was shifting in an 'organic' direction at the same time as Comte, it can be argued that Comte's break with Saint Simon also involved a theoretical divergence. Gouhier (1941, III:393–4) argues that Comte initially absorbed from Saint-Simon the importance of political economy to forming a real science of man. Comte's writings from 1822–4 and thereafter continue to identify the new temporal power with the industrial economy, and to see in the Smithian 'division of labour' a key concept, but there are two new elements in his thinking. First, that *les retrogrades* were right to denounce 'the ravages of egoism in modern society' (ibid.:333), and second, the 'law of three stages' (whatever its pedigree (ibid.:395 et seq.)), which enabled Comte to put in scientific order the entire *tableau historique*. These were combined in Comte's conception of social physics as a life science, and of society as the perfection of the organism.

[19] On Saint-Simon's 'picaresque' and 'mercurial' character, see Manuel, 1962:106–7.

of a different generation. He came of age after the revolutionary glow, chastened by life experiences under Napoleon, Louis XVIII and Louis-Philippe. For him, the unfolding situation was more akin to Greek *stasis*. The impasse seemed to be not passing but prolonged, especially measured against that longer arc of 'revolutionary transition' that went back at least to the late Middle Ages.[20] Bazard and Enfantin, rival carriers of the Saint-Simonian torch, carried forward Saint-Simon's notion of social development as an ascending spiral, alternating on the way up between 'critical' and 'organic' periods.[21] But this was too general a model in which to identify the specific features of the 'critical' period now, one hoped, unfolding towards its climax. Besides, not only did the necessity for this latter have to be explained. It was also important to know why, and with what consequences, there had been 'a vicious prolongation of the negative transition essentially accomplished in the eighteenth century' (v:623).

Comte's explanation was ingenious. The general necessity for transitional crises at key turning points in social development he derived from the law of three stages itself.[22] The co-presence of contradictory philosophical schools, which had similarly marked the transition to feudalism a millennium and a half before, reflected not only the clash of emerging and obsolete social forces, as tied to the visions animating the successive forms of society to which, structurally, they belonged. It also reflected the 'necessarily uneven (*inégal*) progress' of the whole positivising process (IV:21). Each domain of knowledge, starting with astronomy, had to undergo the shift from the theological to the positive (I:14–15). But their speeds of transition varied according to the relations of dependence among knowledge domains, as well as according to the relative complexity and specificity (or inverse generality) of each. The chronological order in which they had positivised – from astronomy to physics, chemistry, biology and now sociology – followed their logical order in 'the encyclopedic scale' (I:68–9). Throughout the whole devel-

---

[20] Comte's account of 'L'époque critique ou âge de transition révolutionnaire' is traced out in *leçon* 55 of the *Cours*. Against those who considered the sixteenth century to mark the beginnings of modernity, Comte insisted that it began at the end of the thirteenth century, for by then 'la constitution catholique et féodale avait suffisamment rempli . . . son office, indispensable mais passagère . . .' (v:407). This view is repeated in the *Politique positive* (IX:528–9).

[21] The motto of Saint-Simon's projected *nouvelle encyclopédie* had been 'The philosophy of the eighteenth century was critical and revolutionary, that of the nineteenth century will be inventive and organisational' (Manuel, 1962:118).

[22] Canguilhem (1994:250) detects in Comte's law of three stages an even more general law of biological motion, inspired by Richerand and Barthez's theory of the zigzag or wave-like nature of all animal movements. For Comte, in this light, 'the progress of civilisation does not march in one straight line' but through 'a series of oscillations, not unlike the oscillations we see in the mechanism of locomotion' (249).

opment, then, relatively backward and relatively advanced sectors of knowledge had always to coexist, creating the basis both for local, intra-knowledge, conflicts and for global conflicts among rival-based syntheses of general principle.

This same line of reasoning could also account for the particular virulence which such conflict had assumed in Comte's own day. Precisely because the whole process of intellectual development had a beginning (fetishism) and an end (positivity), transition points were not wholly symmetrical. In fact, the final transition involved the deepest conflicts, particularly at the intellectual level. Unlike previous shifts from one theological form to another, the move to positivity from theology as such involved a complete epistemological break. For that same reason it could not occur in one sudden leap. Not just for each branch of knowledge but in the progress of 'philosophy' overall, there was an intermediary phase in which the spirit world withdrew to the abstraction of essences, while the absolutism of the theological viewpoint combined with a deductivism based on the would-be sovereign power of human reason.[23]

In late-medieval Europe, the hybrid 'metaphysical stage' had restored the Aristotelian division between moral and natural philosophy, with the former ruled by theology and the latter (the world of 'the inert') incubating the sciences, themselves still invested with a largely metaphysical spirit (v:281–3). This provided a compromise in which the growing theoretico-ideological contradictions could be contained. But as the sciences advanced and as reason extended its claims in the moral and political realm, open conflict broke out. On the one side, beginning with Innocent III's establishment of the Inquisition, the church became repressive. On the other, beginning with the controversies over dialectic and natural philosophy, rationalism became rebellious. From Averroist querying Revelation to the virtual atheism of Hobbes and Spinoza, the anticlerical assault of Voltaire and the outright materialism of d'Holbach and other 'freethinkers', a human reason taken as its own foundation took increasingly polemical aim at the whole monotheistic synthesis – a system of thought which had governed mentalities in the West since Constantine. But this was just the problem. Without an anchor in *le dehors*, the intermediary philosophy could only clear the ground, its intellectual and political speculations built on sand, while its 'anarchic'

---

[23] 'La théologie et la physique sont si profondément incompatibles, leurs conceptions ont un caractère si radicalement opposé, qu'avant de renoncer aux unes pour employer exclusivement les autres, l'intelligence humaine a dû se servir de conceptions intermédiaires, d'un caractère bâtard, propres, par cela même, à opérer graduellement la transition' (1:10–11).

spirit – incarnate in the 'purely negative' Enlightenment principle of free individual inquiry (V:515) – increasingly became a blockage in the development of both constructive reform and a fully scientific understanding of the world.

Compounding the situation, knowledge of the social, as the most specific, complex and dependent order of reality, was the last to positivise. This meant that theological and metaphysical modes of thought continued to dominate the social field even after the positivisation of every other. But the dominance of that field by theism and metaphysics not only inhibited the development of sociology itself, and thus, too, the development of a fully positive philosophy, but the rivalry between them was also a source of disturbance in its own right. And the contradictions could condense. In France, during the culminating stage of the positivist transformation, that is exactly what had happened: the ideological friction generated by the clash of theological and metaphysical viewpoints had combined with the political friction generated by the same clash occurring directly on the plane of social ideas.

The historical results were revealing. Against the dogmatic obduracy of the *ancien régime*, what had taken to the field was a metaphysical social theory pushing for arbitrarily contrived programs of radical reform. For Comte, as for de Maistre whose critique of the *philosophes* he took over, Rousseau's *Social Contract* typified the worst of the genre.[24] At once individualist and voluntarist – as if an ideal political order could be simply legislated into existence – the metaphysicians of the Revolution failed to appreciate that the social had its own laws and modalities, and that these signally included the need for a coordinating centre. In the disastrous results that followed,[25] the only benefit of the endless constitution-making was the instructive value of a disconfirming experiment.[26]

At the same time, the fact that these experiments occurred at all indicated that the overall laws of the social were not those of an iron and mechanical determinism. De Maistre had seen in the Jacobin uprising a satanic force which had issued, through the inscrutable workings of Providence, in the punishment of the wicked in a Terror of their own

---

[24] For Comte's critique of Rousseau's reductive solution to the social question through 'mesures purement politiques, d'où une aveugle imitation de l'antiquité l'entraînait à faire violemment dépendre jusqu'à la discipline morale', see V:617 et seq.

[25] The one exception was the ten-month interlude of the Convention. This alone provided a suitable governmental model, because, 'entre l'expulsion nécessaire des discuteurs et le sanguinaire triomphe des fanatiques', it had wisely transferred responsibility for 'la défense nationale . . . [aux] chefs d'élite' (IX:599).

[26] This was, though, an important benefit. Pathology revealed the limits within which 'vital laws' operate. The observation of pathology gave sociology, like biology, a methodological equivalent to laboratory experiment (III:260–3).

devising. In that vein, and since he took God to be working through, not against, the laws of nature, he sketched a whole social theory of sacrifice to account for both the scandal of the Cross and the sanguinary dynamics of the revolutionary episode (de Maistre, 1971:292–4).[27] For Comte, on the other hand, the experiments and excesses of the period also indicated that there was a certain freedom to err. In so far, indeed, as the Revolution and its aftershocks were objectively making the transition to the new regime more difficult, and, at the least, slowing it down, it appeared that in-built tendencies towards order could be thwarted and that the *progress* of progress itself had an in-built margin of indeterminacy.

This indeterminacy was, in turn, a special case of a more general principle. The regularities of succession and concomitance specified in laws were to be understood only as the limits within which variance was possible. The more complex an order of phenomena, the greater the range of its possible variance, and the greater its susceptibility, therefore, both to pathology and to human intervention. Sociological laws were the most malleable of all (IV:314). It was in this domain, therefore, that 'the pathological state was most frequent and serious', and where too, for good and ill, there was most scope for action (VII:135). The political implications were evident. First, and against all voluntarist illusion, there were strict limits to what such intervention could achieve. The social forces actually in play were determined by the developmental conjuncture, not by political actors, who could affect only their relative *intensité* (IV:316). Nor could the general line of march be changed. It was inconceivable that industrial society could establish order and harmony on the basis of a restored Catholicism and idle land-owning aristocracy. However, what *was* modifiable in the 'fundamental evolution of humanity' was its 'simple speed', and thus, more particularly, the speed with which the final stage of positivisation itself could be accomplished (ibid.). On the one hand, then, even more than in the case of a lower biological organism, the developmental process of *l'humanité* was vulnerable to disturbance. On the other hand, with intelligent self-doctoring, and reinforcement of *les forces régénératrices*, pathologies could be treated, obstacles to development could be overcome, and the metamor-

---

[27] De Maistre held the necessity of sacrifice to derive from original sin; but upon that premise he develops a theory of the socially regenerative power of blood, of the sacrificees' necessary innocence, of sacrificial substitution, and of the reversion to slaughter pure and simple (as in the Terror and in the 'enlightened' Europeans' treatment of the northern Amerindians) when the sublimated sacrificial mechanism of Christianity is suspended and the 'holy laws of humanity' disavowed (de Maistre, 1971:296). The twentieth-century adventures of that idea can be traced through Hubert and Mauss (1964) to Bataille (1985) and Girard (1972, 1987).

phosis to a higher, more complex stage of sociality could even be accelerated.[28]

That same consideration, moreover, gave Comte a more englobing way to define the whole problem. The gradual advance of *l'industrie*[29] implied, both intellectually and in the sphere of production, an increasing division of labour. Such differentiation, including 'the wise separation of temporal and spiritual powers', was itself a developmental law of life.[30] However, growing differentiation would 'contradict existence if it were not always accompanied by a perfecting of general unity' (ix:9).[31] And so to the contemporary issue: as tasks had become more specialised, and as experience-based knowledge and reflective intelligence had supplanted the fixity of false (but useful) beliefs, both behaviour and consensus had become less instinctual, and society had become less automatic and military in its functioning.

This outcome was double-edged. From slavery to serfdom to free labour, growing individual liberty had been essential for the emergence of a higher, more flexible form of social unity. But liberty became anarchic if undirected, and egoistic if not imbued with a social outlook. At the climax of the process, then, a fully positivised will was required both to complete the metamorphosis and, once instituted, to sustain industrialism's 'normal' form of social organisation.[32] Viewed like this,

---

[28] As Canguilhem has noted (1991:47–64), Comte's appropriation of Broussais was crucial. From Broussais, Comte took both the general principle that diseases are disturbances of vital functions and the specific principle that diseases were to be understood as the 'excess of lack of excitation in the various tissues above or below the degree established as the norm' (47–8). With regard to Comte's linking of this to his political doctrine, Canguilhem observes: 'By stating in a general way that diseases do not change vital phenomena, Comte is justified in stating that the cure for political crises consists in bringing society back to its essential and permanent structure, and tolerating progress only within limits of variation of natural order defined by social statics' (1991:64).

[29] Comte follows the Scottish economists Robertson and Smith in tracing the rise of *l'industrie* back to the growth of towns and the rise of 'free' labour in the Middle Ages in Europe from the eleventh century onwards. See vi:29 et seq.

[30] Already in the 1822 *Travaux scientifiques*, the economists' division of labour is identified with a more general tendency of organic life towards complexity through functional specialisation (xa:198). The principle is flatly stated in *leçon* 50 of the *Cours*: 'Bien loin que la simplicité constitue la mesure principale de la perfection réelle, le système entier des études biologiques concourt à montrer, au contraire, que la perfection croissante de l'organisme animal consiste surtout dans la spécialité de plus en plus prononcée des diverses fonctions accomplies par les organes de plus en plus distincts, et néanmoins toujours exactement solidaires' (1:469).

[31] For Comte, this principle had been discovered by Aristotle, in his principle that the essential nature of collective organisation consisted in 'la séparation des offices et la combinaison des efforts' (viii:281). Aristotle's *Politics*, for Comte, was the founding text of sociological statics.

[32] For Comte, this implied the need for a revolutionary government, which (like the Convention under Danton) would exercise a temporary dictatorship in order to

the sociology and philosophy which provided intelligence for that will
was itself a 'normal' development (x:518). Nevertheless, the stakes were
high. For the same consideration raised the troubling thought that
without a supreme effort to develop that will, the conflict-laden impasse
of unresolved transition might persist, or even – the greatest danger –
that the whole locomotive of progress might go off the rails.

If we take stock of where Comte's analysis was taking him, one thing
is apparent. The more Comte elaborated his theory of the 'crisis', the
deeper and more dangerous it seemed to be. Because of the power and
energy of the 'negative forces' that had (necessarily) presided over the
Revolution, the Positivist reconstruction now needed to complete the
industrial transformation of society had not appeared on cue. Thus a
'normal intermediary crisis' had become abnormally 'prolonged'. This
prolongation, in turn, both worsened the dissolvent effects of a metaphysics become purely anarchical[33] and perpetuated a wider 'philosophical' conflict which was itself a deep cause of intellectual and moral
disorder (v:617). Whence, in fact, a tension that marked Comte's whole
account. On the one hand, he wanted to argue that the troubles of early
industrialism were strictly *passagères* – a friction of movement, tied to the
emergence of a final form of civilisation that had already arrived – and
not, as more radical thinkers were beginning to argue, endemic in the
system of private property and commodity production within which the
dynamic of industrialisation was unfolding. On the other hand, it
seemed that the current problems of transition risked becoming so
severe that they jeopardised both order and progress as such.

What Comte had done was to explain the 'crisis' as arising primarily
from a contradiction between the base (the differentiated, machinic and
market-mediated practices of *l'industrie*)[34] and the political–ideological
superstructure (not yet updated and rebuilt), exacerbated by (developmental) contradictions in the latter. Not just in Marxist terms but in
Comte's, this would be to define the crisis as merely transitional. Except

implement the necessary reforms. The call for a revolutionary triumvirate to direct the
final transition was part of the political program of the Positivist Society from its
founding in February 1848. See Gouhier, 1965:218–19.

[33] 'Il serait assurément superflu de s'arrêter ici à caractériser expressément les ravages
qu'a dû une métaphysique qui, détruisant toutes les bases antérieures de la morale
publique et même privée . . . livrait désormais toutes les règles de conduite à
l'appréciation superficielle et partiale des consciences individuelles' (v:617). Comte's
subsequent reference to 'aberrations morales fort analogues à celles de l'école
d'Épicure' (v:620) makes clear that this final unravelling entails the unbridled
resurgence of fleshly desires, made worse by 'aberrant' calls (e.g. of the Saint-
Simonians) for sexual freedom.

[34] The medieval (spontaneous), early modern (politically utilised) and modern (goal-
defining) evolution of *l'industrie* is outlined, and 'appreciated', in *leçon* 57 of the *Cours*
(VI:29–122).

for two crucial riders: first, one element of that superstructure – human knowledge, its development and applications – was taken to be also part of the base; secondly, because of the importance of vital 'consensus' to the maintenance of (social) life, the contradictions provoked by ideational conflict across the whole range of social relations were taken as having the capacity, at the limit, to menace society as such.

Comte's stress on the ideological dimension of the 'crisis' can be questioned, as can the wider explanatory frame. If the autonomising power of capital were introduced into Comte's picture of industrialism, we would have to say that he both underestimated the structural intractability of the social problems he was seeking to understand and overestimated the place of consciousness in them. Whence the growing desperation that accompanied what Comte insisted, despite the profundity of the 'crisis', was a project not for industrial society's radical transformation, but for corrective reform. At the same time, if Comte had been able to define the latter as not the end of the civilisational line, and as contradictory in itself, there might have been a better balance between his *explanans* (a problem of consciousness) and his *explanandum* (incipient social breakdown). Nor would he have had to place so much weight on the positivised faith and will of a lonely vanguard as the heroically indispensable means for further human advance.

That the task, nonetheless, was not wholly chimerical was indicated to Comte by the fact that the twin pillars of the new order were already, almost, in place. On the spiritual side, the way was prepared for a replacement faith and church by the positivisation of knowledge and the rising authority of science. On the temporal side, an accumulation of developments from the emancipation of *les communes*, the dissolution of serfdom and hereditary castes, and the spread of meritocratic values in a culture of thrift and work, to the rise of workshops, machine production and banks, had created the practical and experiential basis for an industrial form of organisation to prevail.[35] To be sure, in *un âge de spécialité*, what was lacking, throughout, was *l'esprit d'ensemble*. However, such a spirit could be secured, and the morphological development of industrialism completed, by pushing the division of labour one last step. This would be to establish a dual elite of scientific and industrial 'specialists in the general', with a division of labour between them (VI:462 et seq.). The latter would executively manage the (minimal) state, while the former, as coordinators of knowledge, would be responsible for education as well as for the overall supervision of industrial society's moral wellbeing. To which, too, would correspond a hierarch-

---

[35] The civilisational shift from *la vie militaire* to *la vie industrielle* is set forth in the 56th *leçon* of the *Cours*.

ical completion of the division of labour in theoretical practice. Here, at the apex of the sciences, there would be a distinctly organised coordinating philosophy, which, as transmitted by its cadres, would 'make *l'esprit d'ensemble* directly prevail' (VI:557).

But why priests? Why, after first advancing this program, did Comte feel the need to supplement the 'normal' institutional framework of industrialism with a full-scale *religion*?

The question of religion

The abstract answer we already know. What converts, via the projected final science of *la Morale*, the problematisation of the 'crisis' in the *Philosophie positive* into the explicitly religious one presented in the *Politique positive* is the opening of the binary schema – intellect/action, *l'esprit/coeur* – into a trinary one. This occurs through the introduction of *les sentiments*, objectively grasped through a physiological science of individual needs and instincts, as an irreducible third category.[36] To move into a religious register was to adopt a mode of thinking in which the highest sentiments – those of *l'amour* – were actively, and self-consciously, in command. 'The continuous preponderance of the sentiments over the intellect and activity becomes thus the fundamental law of human harmony' (X:45).[37]

To be sure, the sentiments had not previously been ignored. Besides the biological basis claimed in the *Cours* for the innateness of *altruisme* (III:634–41), for the efficacy of moral habit (644), and for the 'everyday

---

[36] In conceptual terms, he tells us in *Politique positive*, the change came through making a distinction with respect to the category of *le coeur*. In his initial *théorie de l'âme*, it had included 'tantôt l'affection qui dispose à agir et tantôt la force qui dirige l'action réelle'. This distinction was manifest 'surtout dans la comparaison moral des deux sexes où le mot *coeur* désigne alternativement tendresse et l'énergie'. The revised theory 'composée d'abord de coeur et *d'esprit* . . . nous offre maintentant la succession normale du coeur proprement dit, de l'esprit et du caractère'. The conception remains binary, he adds, 'tant qu'on n'y considère que l'économie totale, qui constitue alors une combinaison irréductible. Mais elle devient *ternaire* quand on veut s'y représenter la marche générale d'un tel ensemble' (VII:684; my emphasis). This attempt to show the logical consistency of his first position with his second relies, we may note, on the Positivist theory of numbers which assigns 2 to combination/arrangement and 3 to progress/development. It does not hide, at the same time, that it involves the admission of a 'female' principle, *la tendresse*.

[37] The mutually interacting forces of intellect and action continue, nonetheless, to drive affective development. This is because 'la région affective du cerveau n'a pas de relation directe avec le monde extérieur . . . Ainsi, l'influence mutuelle des familles et des générations ne peut point modifier directement nos penchants. Elle ne les affecte que par suite des changements qu'elle apporte dans nos pensées et nos actes' (IX:11). The progressive preponderance of higher sentiments – summarised in the law that 'l'homme devient de plus en plus religieux' (X:10) – is thus externally determined. This point is pursued further in chap. 6 below.

experience' that 'the affections, inclinations, passions, constitute the principal motives in human life' (618), Comte's analysis of *l'évolution esthétique* (VI:123–79) highlighted the coordination of affective life as a prominent element of the emerging 'positive state'.[38] As for the religious buttressing of *les penchants bienveillants*, we may also take at face value Comte's claim that he had always intended a two-part work. First he would establish the 'last domain of positive rationality'; then, 'on this unshakable base', he would 'build the new occidental faith, and institute its priesthood'. In this way, reversing the bad order of Christianity, a 'healthy philosophy' would 'be able at last to found the true religion' (VII:3). Be that as it may, there is no suggestion of cult or liturgy attached to the *pouvoir spirituelle* outlined in his 1828 essay or in the last volume of *Philosophie positive*. The full *subjective*, and consequently *sociological*, force of acknowledging the place of the sentiments in sociality only came to him during his *rénovation morale* of 1847.

What marks the caesura is that it was then, under the deeply affecting auspices of *ma sainte ange*,[39] that *le fondateur du philosophie positive* personally, and in the sublimest sense, discovered love.[40] With that, the

---

[38] In the *Cours*, poetry and the fine arts were always to be regarded as secondary to science/philosophy in stamping the mental character of an age. But their expressive role – 'destinées à l'idéal représentation sympathique des divers sentiments qui caractérisent la nature humaine' (VI:124) – made the arts a crucial intermediary between *la vie active* and *la vie contemplative* (VI:142). Stimulated by the rise of *la vie industrielle*, their role had decisively grown, especially in view of 'la grave lacune qui résulte provisoirement, à cet égard, de l'inévitable désuétude des usages religieux' (VI:145). In the second synthesis, where new *usages religieux* are proposed, the independent religious role of the arts is reduced, but their general importance as moral educator of the senses remains, and is even enhanced. In his *théorie positive du langage humain* (VIII:216–22), with its triple logic of sentiments, images and signs, poetic and mimetic expression mediate what mediates between the sensory within and without. Too simply regarded as having a merely propagandist view of the arts, Comte's aesthetic theory deserves much more attention than I am able to give it here.

[39] Comte's *dédicace* to Clotilde in the preface to *Politique positive* is much more than a personal testimonial to a tragically lost love. It records a moment of religious conversion and gives universal significance – with explanations – to a publicly confessed 'private cult' in her memory. A few lines from the concluding peroration will convey the general flavour: 'Adieu, mon immuable compagne. Adieu, ma sainte Clotilde, toi qui me tenais lieu à la fois d'épouse, de soeur, et de fille! Adieu, mon élève chérie, et ma digne collègue! Ton angélique inspiration dominera tout le reste de ma vie, tant publique que privée, pour présider encore a mon épuisable perfectionnement, en épurant mes sentiments, agrandissant mes pensées, et ennoblissant ma conduite ... Comme principale récompense personelle des nobles travaux qui me restent à accomplir sous ta puissante invocation, j'obtiendrai peut-être que ton nom devienne enfin inséparable du mien dans les plus lointains souvenirs de l'humanité reconnaissante' (VII:xx–xxi).

[40] Gouhier emphasises the experiential side of this discovery. Comte was already proposing to 'preach the love of Humanity; he knew what Humanity was, but not love' (1933, I:27). 'This love did not add a single idea to a system of ideas that was self-sufficient, but a living reality without which this system of ideas would have been a dead letter' (1933:29). This view is more perspicacious than one which would play down the

realisation dawned – with all its cultic and liturgical consequences – that the heart and not only the head had to be engaged if the saving grace of the spirit of the whole was to unite the scattered elements of a divided and fragmented society. For *le dehors* to anchor the mental and active life of each individual, and to supply the motive force for the subordination of each to a common purpose, that *dehors* had to be loved and not just cognitively known. Borrowing from the best insights of the previous monotheism, but suitably relativised and humanised, what was needed was not merely *une nouvelle foi*, as he had previously proclaimed, but one which combined, as fully as the old faith had done, the doctrinal moment of *belief* with a sublimely disinterested *love* for its object (VIII:46–9).

However, love could not just grow out of belief. The forces pushing for a positivisation of the intellect were quite distinct from those – for example the moral and domestic elevation of women – which socially fostered the growth of love. Hence, for Comte, both 'the difficulty and the importance of combining' these 'two religious conditions', 'whether naturally or artificially' (VIII:47). By 'naturally' he meant in marriage, with his own union of head and heart, with Clotilde, as a prototype. By 'artificially' he meant the establishment of a wider institution, to harmonise society as a whole. Just as the scientific cultivation and dissemination of *la foi démontrable* required teachers and an educational apparatus, so there also needed to be a system of worship and prayer to vivify the sentiments without which the *altruisme* guiding it would be arid and without deep moral force. Recognising the need to 'incorporate the sentiments into the positivist synthesis' had as its practical counterpart, then, Positivism's transformation into a fully articulated religion.[41]

In these categorically expanded terms, the crisis of industrialism which persisted in the absence of such an institution was itself to be understood as 'religious'. Concomitant with intellectual disorder (the unresolved and unresolvable war of opinion between theological and metaphysical viewpoints) and with institutional disorder (dysfunctions associated with an incomplete division of labour), there had come to be disorder as well at the level of sentiments. Despite its 'essentially intellectual character', the 'alteration' of sentiments had in fact become 'the gravest aspect of the modern anarchy' (X:370–1). In the absence of an authoritative, because consensual, centre around which to rally the

religious continuity of Comte's 'grande mission' before and after Clotilde. But Gouhier goes too far in ignoring the theoretical impact of Comte's religio-affective epiphany on both his sociological analysis and on his system as a whole.

[41] The argument is developed in the first chapter of the second volume of *Politique positive* (VIII), 'Théorie générale de religion, ou théorie positive de l'unité humaine'.

higher sentiments of love, the lower, egoistic instincts – 'nutritive', sexual, power-oriented and full of vanity/ambition – were insufficiently restrained.[42] This both produced chronic interindividual conflict (the Hobbesian problem) and, at the intra-individual level, by permitting the egoistic instincts to dominate the altruistic ones, undermined the indispensable psychological basis for social cooperation. As a cumulative result, the social crisis with which France, and the wider industrialising world, had come to be afflicted was total. And, indeed, in a double sense. On the one hand it was at once a disorder of thought, action and feeling, a crisis affecting, that is, all three fundamental aspects of human existence.[43] On the other hand, it was a crisis for human being as such, a crisis in which *l'organisme social*, as a reality transcending the aggregation of self-interested individuals composing it, was itself ultimately at stake.

I would make three observations about this diagnosis.

The first is to note that, in the course of elaborating it, Comte's understanding of 'religion' undergoes a change. In his earlier works, religion is not a key category.[44] If used at all (e.g. to designate Christianity), it is just a descriptive label, understood with reference to belief in some form of the supernatural, and applied only to the various forms of 'theology', from fetishism to monotheism. His more inclusive term is 'philosophy', which focusses on the intellectual side, so that the whole series, from theology through metaphysics to positivism itself, can be presented in its continuity as a succession of systems of general ideas. As for the differentiation in the governmental function between *le pouvoir spirituel* and *le pouvoir temporel*, this is explained primarily with reference to the theory of the *répartition des travaux* (IV:481–4). The retention of

---

[42] The interrelated control processes of *ralliement* and *règlement* – which were to have a prominent Durkheimian future – are introduced, in *Politique positive*, as a cornerstone of *la théorie positive de religion*. 'Quoique toujours liés de plus en plus, ces deux modes ne seront jamais confondus, et chacun d'eux suscite une attribution correspondante de la religion. Cet état synthétique consiste ainsi, tantôt à *régler* chaque existence personelle, tantôt à *rallier* les diverses individualités' (VIII:9; emphasis in original).

[43] The full extent of the dissolvent trend seen under this triple perspective is neatly summarised in *Politique positive*: 'À mesure que la foi se dissout, les esprits s'isolent et se rétrécissent, les notions de détail prévalent sur les vues d'ensemble. En même temps, l'anarchie mentale altère graduellement les préceptes moraux, d'abord dans la vie publique, puis envers les relations domestiques, et même enfin quant à l'existence personelle. Un égoïsme croissant tend à détruire les meilleures traditions du moyen âge, en surmontant de plus en plus la résistance féminine, sous les impulsions avouées de l'orgueil et de la vanité, qui laissent souvent apercevoir celles de la cupidité. L'usurpation temporelle dissipant toute trace de la séparation normale entre les deux pouvoirs, la politique se matérialise, et partout on demande aux lois de régler ce qui dépend seulement sur les mœurs' (IX:533).

[44] In *leçon* 50 of the *Cours*, devoted to the general principles of social statics 'ou théorie générale de l'ordre spontané des sociétés humaines' (IV:430), there is no discussion of religion as such, and, so far as I can see, the word religion does not even occur.

this principle in the Positivist program explicitly acknowledges the example of developed (i.e. 'Catholic') monotheism, but the principle itself is not linked to any more general conception of religion as a form or level of social organisation.

Against this background, the category of 'religion' makes its sociological appearance in the *Politique positive* as a kind of missing ingredient, an x factor, to supplement the conceptual lack in the social statics presented in the earlier system of Positive Philosophy. Religion, triply articulated as cult, doctrine and regime (VIII:1920), is that dimension of social life which 'rallies and regulates' the sentiments in harmony with thought and action. Through it, a being is 'bound from within to without by the complete convergence of sentiments and thoughts towards the superior power which determines its acts' (VIII:18). This definition, it will be noted, is not tied to the particularities of belief: different religions posit different identities for that external power. It is related instead to a special social function, and to the organs instituted to carry it out. The term, then, has a generalisable, yet restricted, range of sociological application. Empirically, Comte's 'religion' would consist of all the organised practices and representations which pertain to the cultivation of the highest instincts and their harmonious integration into collective life. However, because of the supreme importance of the sentiments in achieving intellectual and political–institutional harmony, this conception of religion necessarily expands, so that it comes to include all that is practically involved in harmonising social, and indeed individual, life as such. 'In this treatise', Comte intones at the beginning of volume two of *Politique positive*,

religion will always be characterised by the state of complete harmony proper to human existence, whether collective or individual, when all its parts whatever are properly coordinated. This definition . . . concerns equally the heart and the mind whose concourse is indispensable to such a unity. Religion thus constitutes, for the soul, a normal consensus exactly comparable to that of health with regard to the body. (VIII:8)

A little further on, and again in the *Catechism of Positive Religion*, Comte's enlarged characterisation is given an etymological justification.[45] The word religion 'is so constructed as to express a twofold connection which . . . is sufficient to summarise the whole abstract theory of our unity. To constitute a complete and durable harmony, what is really wanted is to *bind together* [*lier*] the within by love and to

---

[45] The same etymological play is made with the word *humanité*, as we shall see in chap. 7. That words should have deposited within their multiple senses an extractable insight about real connections was part of Comte's general theory of language. See chap. 4 of the second volume of *Politique positive* (VIII:216–62).

bind it again [*relier*] to the without by faith' (XI:46). As conceptually
clarifying as this seems to be, however, it amounts to a sleight of hand.
For, in keeping with the slide from religion as an instance of the social
totality to religion as that which constitutes it as such, there is a
conflation between social unity and the maintenance of that unity, or, to
put it in Durkheimian and Althusserian terms, between the social tie
and its reproduction.

'Religion' is simultaneously characterised, in other words, as what
primordially composes disparate individuals into *un organisme social* and
as whatever process may be involved in this primordial composition's
ongoing practical accomplishment. It is, then, both the first-order unity
of the social, and also its second-order, or reduplicative, unity. What
Comte's commentary on the 're' of religion enables him to overlook is
the questions that might arise if these were distinguished. For example:
is the 'community' that we might posit as underlying all social relations
the same as a communing that takes place with respect to some unifying
Other? If not, might there be a contradiction between the (pattern-
maintaining and integrative) requirements of reproducing *institutionalised* social relations and the letting be of such 'community'? (Nancy,
1991:141). But again, does that question admit of different answers
depending on the *modality* of those already-instituted relations – for
instance, with regard to their degree of coerciveness or exploitativeness,
or to their implication in various kinds of exchange?

The second point is more obvious. Comte's definition of religion,
which ultimately assimilates society and religion to one another, rests on
a particular theory of social being. It presupposes 'societies' as integral
entities. And it assumes that the integrity of such entities – particularly
as we ascend from the 'direct unity' of the family to the 'indirect' and
'associational' character of society in the extended sense (IV:448–9) – is
a problematic, disturbable function of the cognitive/emotional binding
of individuals together into groups. The social-psychological (and
moral) character of this binding, and of the articulation of individuals to
the collectivities so formed, will be taken up in the next chapter. What
needs to be highlighted here is the import of this social ontology for
what, in Comte's formulation of the religion question, was practically at
stake. Societies, like all organisms, like all complex orderings of matter,
could break up, dissolve into their constituent elements. Life depends
on a balance between 'absorption and exhalation'. Under the influence
of this law, 'The Great Being finds itself as subjected as lower ones to
the permanent necessity of an elementary renewal' (VII:590). In the
'positive theory of death', death is a contingent consequence of disturbed harmony whose constant active renewal constitutes life (VIII:586

et seq.). The inference was clear. In securing the spiritual and institutional unity of the social, religion obviated not just (individual and collective) disorders in the plural, but disorder as such. In its absence, in a full-scale *crise morale*, society could die.

Thirdly, Comte's determination of religion as the health, *qua* 'normal harmony' and unity, of the social rests on an absolute dichotomy between order and disorder, without any sustainable possibilities in between. Order is full and complete, or else it risks degenerating into chaos. Order itself, this implies, is necessarily repressive. It restrains an entropic tendency to disorder which is perpetually present.[46] Its achievement in any complex organism, correspondingly, requires a functional subordination of the parts to the whole, which itself can only be secured through their subordination to a common centre.

In effect, Comte combines the second law of thermodynamics with the transfer, on to his fundamental conception of *société*, of the functionally hierarchised notion of structure that characterised traditional Catholic social doctrine.[47] That same doctrine had provided a conceptual basis for de Bonald and de Maistre's defence of centred unity – sovereignty – as represented, in the church, by the headship of God, Christ and pope, and in the polity by theocratic monarchy.[48] In industrial society the content of such sovereignty must be brought up to date, but the form stays the same. Hence, in the schema of Positive Religion, the singular and supreme focus for love, belief and action represented by the Great Being of Humanity. Hence, too, the application of this schema to figuring the 'divine constitution' of the individual psyche. Unless embedded in an interpsychic structure which directs the ego towards, and organises its whole psychological apparatus around, a fixed point in *le dehors* (in Christianity, a purely imaginary Big Other), the individual psyche would lack an organising centre and dissolve into an internal chaos of warring impulses. It was in just such terms that Comte criticised philosophies, from Descartes onwards, which attempted to base themselves on 'the famous theory of the I' (III:621) as a coherent

---

[46] 'Dans la nature inerte, l'activité d'un système quelconque tend à détruire sa structure, même en mécanique' (VIII:340).

[47] '[T]oute société . . . suppose, par une évidente nécessité, non seulement des diversités, mais aussi des inégalités quelconques: car il ne saurait y avoir de véritable société sans le concours permanent à une opération générale, poursuivie par des moyens distincts, convenablement subordonnés les uns aux autres' (IV:449). For the indissociability of *gouvernement* from *société*, see VIII:226.

[48] As a 'sovereign power . . . Christianity . . . is monarchical, as everyone knows, and this must be so, since, by the very nature of things, monarchy becomes the more necessary as the association becomes more numerous' (de Maistre, 1971:155). Comte's dictum that 'il n'existe pas davantage de société sans gouvernement que de gouvernement sans société' (VIII:267) derives from de Maistre in its very intonation.

and self-sufficient starting point for knowledge, or for understanding Man.

Comte's tenacious assumption concerning the natural necessity of centred and hierarchical unity for the existence and persistence of complex being determined ideals of social and individual life that were as opposed to the heterogeneous and the carnivalesque as to egalitarian utopias of *communitas*. A headless community, as championed by anarchists, from Fourier to Bataille, not to mention the generalised acentricity pursued, at the level of thinking itself, by Derrida,[49] was inconceivable. Freedom from order – whether social, psychological, aesthetic or philosophical – could only mean the destruction of being, and to champion it was wickedness itself. Nor could Comte conceive of being, social or otherwise, as a storm system of contending opposites. We could only burn in the Heraclitan fire. Following the post-structuralists, we could say, in fact, that Comte embodies the most tenacious, and abstract, feature of metaphysics itself. In every dimension of his systematising construct he was trapped in an unreflected schema of hierarchical binaries.[50]

This was a feature Comte shared with the prevailing thought-world of his time. But in his case it was also held in place by a psychobiographical factor which, indeed, he explicitly attempted to rationalise as an empirical reference point for his whole religious and sociological system. This was his terror of disorientation, a terror which he experienced at first hand during the manic collapse that disabled him in 1826,[51] and recurrently thereafter. That which he most feared he

---

49 For Derrida, decentring was an inevitable effect of a relativising self-consciousness that came about when 'language invaded the universal problematic . . . (and) in which everything became discourse'. This revealed 'a system where the central signified, the original or transcendental signifier is never absolutely present outside a system of differences. The absence of the transcendental signified extends the domain and interplay of signification indefinitely' (Macksey and Donato, 1972:249). The linguistic turn was preceded, he tells us, by a phase of contradictory thinking about language – roughly from Rousseau to Hegel – in which the dissolvent effects of language on 'the universal problematic' were, with detectable theoretical strain, contained. Comte's attempt to rein in the power of abstract signs belongs, it may be said, to that same moment.

50 Comte justified his constant appeal to the principle of 'one into two' by way of his theory of the universality of binariness as a feature of the 'combination' inherent in all *arrangement*. 'Toute combinaison, même physique, et surtout logique, devant être toujours binaire, comme l'indique assez l'etymologie. Cette règle s'étend nécessairement aux décompositions quelconques' (XI:74). In Comte's numerological symbolism, 1 stands for synthesis, 2 for 'ordre, défini par l'arrangement', 3 for progress (X:101).

51 Comte's first serious attacks of *manie* – sleepless exultation for days on end – were in early 1826, and he had a full breakdown in April, which halted for three years his ability to publicly conduct his *Cours*. He was hospitalised till December, and nursed back to health by Massin. He never trusted doctors to help him, and evolved an elaborate dietary and mental regimen which aimed, whether through vegetarianism, sexual

externalised through the horrific names of chaos and anarchy. Hence his almost talismanic need for the certitude of a faith; and hence too, against the dread of inner dissolution, his extreme, moralised, insistence on that rigid, and brittle, conception of unity and order which was its abstractly negating mirror opposite.

The subjective dimension

Put bluntly, Comte's embrace of a Humanist religious conviction is haunted by madness. It represents an almost prototypical example of Freud's diagnosis of 'popular religion' (i.e. the solace of belief in a celestial Father) as an obsessional neurosis which defends the ego against psychotic breakdown.[52] The obsessive regularity of the ritual round he imposed on himself following the traumatic death of Clotilde, his flight into the future *'habitant une tombe anticipée'*,[53] are easily diagnosed in such terms. So is the overarching will to unity which pervades, and is idealised in, his system. We may only marvel at the thoroughness with which Comte sought to reorganise the whole world round him, from the private cocoon of his house on the rue Monsieur-le-Prince to France, Europe and beyond, so as to buttress his neurotic solution by providing it, in a fantasy-seeking realisation, with universal social support.

Yet a psychologistic reduction of Comte's thought would scarcely do it justice. It would bypass his effort to reflect on his own *crise cérébrale* as

abstinence or not reading newspapers, to reduce stressful stimuli. See Pickering, 1993:371–403 and Gouhier, 1965:127–37.

[52] 'One might venture to regard obsessional neurosis as a pathological counterpart of the formation of a religion and religion as a universal obsessional neurosis. The most essential similarity would seem to reside in the underlying renunciation of the activation of instincts that are constitutionally present; and the chief difference would lie in the nature of those instincts, which in the neurosis are exclusively sexual in their origin, while in religion they spring from egoistic sources' (Freud, 1990:40). Comte, in the year following the trauma of Clotilde's death, would appear to have exemplified both mechanisms at once. He converted a private set of rituals into the model for a form of worship (*le culte intime*) that could be generalised to all Positivist believers. The priest-type black clothing that he adopted in the mid 1820s paved the way for his now adopting the public persona of *Grand-prêtre de l'Humanité*. Sexual renunciation, originating perhaps, before Clotilde, as impotence, became a matter of religious principle. His abandoned wife Caroline had no hesitation in declaring that he had gone mad (again) and that he should seek medical help (Gouhier, 1965:207–8).

[53] 'Habitant une tombe anticipée, je dois désormais tenir aux vivants un langage posthume, qui sera meiux affranchi des divers préjugés, surtout théoriques, dont nos descendants se trouveront priés . . . Sans cesser de vivre avec nos meilleurs ancêtres, je vais surtout vivre avec nos descendants, jusqu'à ce que je revive dans eux et par eux après avoir vécu pour eux.' According to Gouhier (1965:221), Comte incorporated this passage from his testament of 1855 regularly into his morning prayers (from 5.30 to 6.30 a.m.) as their opening *évocation*.

source material for a scientific theory of human nature.[54] That he should refer to inner experience at all is at first surprising – until we remember that the subjective turn in his thinking grew from the realisation that *la société* had a lived inside as well as an observed outside, so that the properly social orientation to the social had to be doubly two-sided. To be sure, in approaching interiority, he dismissed theories of the psyche based solely on introspection, favouring instead the 'cerebral physiology' of Broussais and Gall, whence Positivism was to draw the proper, because objective, basis for its own psychology. But the latter, which connected drives and faculties to the hard wiring of brain and nervous system, was nevertheless indexed to the phenomena of individual subjectivity, starting and ending with himself.

In any case, the social crisis of industrialism – pathologies of conflict and disorder stemming from the persistence of archaisms, the unsettling effects of a transitional 'negative philosophy', and the failure of the newly configured 'normality' to fully emerge – had its counterpart at the level of individual subjectivity, to which it was intimately and reciprocally linked. Two components of this, concerning modern disruptions, respectively, to *solidarité* and *continuité*, need to be distinguished, though they merge in a more general consideration which Comte himself is never quite able to name. Conjured in the spectre of social dissolution, both presented threats to what a later discourse would call the 'ontological security'[55] of the individual.

Ego and solidarity

The first problem concerns psycho-pathologies caused by that subjective severance of the individual from the social which Comte calls *égoïsme*. In *Politique positive*, Comte describes himself as having regressed during his illness in a way which recapitulated, backwards and forwards, the 'normal' course of cognitive development (IX:75–6). At the height of his breakdown, he tells us, he was gripped uncontrollably by a kind of infantile animism, which gave him insight both into the subjective side of Humanity's cognitive development[56] and into the nature of 'healthy'

54 This effort begins with his review of Broussais's Essai sur l'irritation et la folie in 1828, where 'j'utilisais déjà philosophiquement les lumières personnelles que cette triste expérience venait de me procurer si chèrement envers ce grand sujet' (VI:xii).
55 'A man may have a sense of his presence in the world as a real, alive, whole, and in a temporal sense, continuous person. As such he can live out in the world and meet others: a world and others experienced as equally real, alive, whole, and continuous. Such a basically *ontologically* secure person will encounter all the hazards of life . . . from a centrally firm sense of his own and other people's reality and identity' (Laing, 1969:39; emphasis in original).
56 'En me procurant aussitôt une confirmation décisive de ma loi des trois états, et me

mental balance. This insight makes its way into the summarising rules of 'first philosophy'. The subordination of 'subjective constructions to objective materials' is 'the fundamental static law of human understanding'; it is therefore necessary that 'les images intérieures' be 'less clear and active than *les impressions externelles*' (X:176). As a rule for the intellect, the proposition is couched epistemologically. Converted into a maxim for *la morale*, the rider is advanced as a necessary condition for both social order and mental health, a condition that could only be secured, at either level, to the extent that the individual was firmly drawn outwards, and held there, by an emotionally cathected place outside. Hence, Comte insists, the psychological (and not only social) importance of religion, which 'to rule and rally us, should, above all, subordinate us to an indubitable external power' (VIII:12).

Fetishism, as the most archaic form of religion *and* of psycho-mental development, provided a paradigm for the working of that mechanism.[57] It erred, to be sure, in attributing 'affections and wills' to inert matter, and in systematically confounding 'life' and 'spontaneous activity' (IX:87–8). But it firmly externalised the drives of the psyche by fixing the latter in an attitude 'bordering on adoration' towards the imaginatively projected-upon *dehors* (IX:92). All the successive synthesising philosophies – through all the shades of theism, metaphysics and now positivity – had functioned psychologically in the same way. All, likewise, had been able to do so because of their socially established dominance in the developmental epochs to which they belong. In every harmoniously operating case, a religiously buttressed consensus presented social members with an emotionally charged centre outside themselves which served at once to 'rally' sentiments, to coordinate them with the objects of thought and action, and, reinforced by the discipline of a *régime*, to 'regulate' the lower instincts (VIII:20–1). Waning theistic belief, however, had weakened this mechanism, and the shattering of the church without replacement had weakened it further. In the ensuing moral crisis, the outer solidarity of society and the inner solidarity of the individual had simultaneously, and increasingly, come into question.[58]

In Comte's understanding of the impact of social disintegration on

faisant mieux sentir la relativité nécessaire de toutes nos conceptions, ce terrible épisode me permit ensuite de m'identifier davantage avec l'une quelconque des phases humaines, d'après ma propre expérience' (IX:75–6).

[57] 'Outre que l'histoire trouve toujours le fétichisme au début de chaque civilisation, l'évolution personnelle manifeste, avec une pleine évidence, ce point de départ nécessaire de toute intelligence, tant humaine qu'animale' (IX:82).

[58] It need hardly be said that Comte offers no empirical evidence whatever to substantiate his claim that the crisis was becoming worse, or that complete breakdown was imminent. Durkheim undertook this task fifty years later in *Suicide*, examining historical changes and social variances in the suicide rate in ten European countries

individual subjectivity we can see the outline of the two-by-two matrix which Durkheim was to elaborate in *Suicide*.[59] Comte's 'rallying' and 'regulating' dimensions of the internalised Big Real are recapitulated in Durkheim's distinction between 'ideals' and 'norms'. For Durkheim, the breakdown of moral consensus is similarly conceived as upsetting the subjective balance of the individual by uncorking both the instinctual as such, and within that the physical impulses that express themselves as limitless greed and desire. However, and leaving aside Durkheim's liberal–individualist modification of Comte's normative depiction of industrialism (and his added pathologies of *altruisme* and *fatalisme*), Comte collapses the distinction Durkheim also made between the disorders of *égoïsme* and *anomie*, i.e. between deficiencies of rallying (ideals) and of regulation (norms). He thereby included in the same omnibus category – *égoïsme* – disorders on the one hand of cognitive disorientation, and on the other of deficient impulse control. This conflation is itself occluded by the theory of internal and external impressions, the former driven by the affects, through which they are both, as confirmed by Comte's own manic episode, explained. This enabled him, in turn, both to formulate a (socially embedded) theory of madness – an excess of subjectivity – as well as to identify a polar-opposite disorder of *idiotisme* which results from 'too much submission to the external spectacle, with an insufficient internal reaction' (VIII:486). However, it did not cross his mind that, in balancing internal and external impressions, there can also be too much mental unity; nor indeed that overunification was itself a problem for any program that attempted to transpose on to the necessarily more individuated, and cyclonic, terrain of 'industrial society', the architectonics of an idealised medieval *harmonie*.

But Comte is not just an inferior (if formative) precursor of Durkheim. Classical French sociology, in freeing itself from Comte's theory

---

between 1841 and 1878 as the index of a similarly defined problem of social integration (1951:46–53).

[59] Durkheim's *Suicide* highlights three main pathologies: egoism, anomie and altruism. Under modern conditions, he says, these are the most important. But a footnote at the end of chap. 5 notes that 'there is a type of suicide the opposite of anomic suicide, just as egoistic and altruistic suicides are opposites. It is the suicide deriving from excessive regulation, that of persons with futures pitilessly blocked and passions violently choked by oppressive discipline. So, for completeness' sake, we should set up a fourth suicidal type . . . Do not the suicides of slaves belong to this type? . . . We might call it *fatalistic suicide*' (1951:276n). Durkheim plainly has in mind a matrix like this:

	Too low	Too high
Moral regulation (norms)	Anomie	Fatalism
Moral 'ralliement' (ideals)	Egoism	Altruism

of social dynamics, and especially from his formula for progress (Durkheim, 1964:18–20), also cut itself off from Comte's interest in time.[60] In so doing, it abandoned reflection on the second aspect of Comte's thematisation of the subjective aspect of the 'current crisis'. This concerned problems for individual orientation that flowed, not from a breakdown in consensus, but from disruptions that the birth of industrial society had brought with respect to *continuité*. Not the least of these concerned the need, in an unsettled post-Christian universe, to rethink the meaning of death.

Continuity and death

Comte had criticised (Catholic) Christianity not only for its obsolete belief in 'fictive beings' but also for the individualism of its salvation scheme.[61] In the old religion, each believer was encouraged, as a motivator for moral action, to focus on his/her own judged fate in the afterlife. The refocussing of moral affects and energies towards Humanity, and so towards the super-entity in which we *really* 'live, move and have our being', would remove this antisocial blemish. By the same token, however, a positivised world-view would remove the hope of personal immortality, together with the existentially orienting framework given by what was promised, or threatened, beyond the grave. It left, then, an evident lacuna. Without belief in heaven, hell and an immortal soul, how could individual life – let alone one dedicated to selfless abnegation – be subjectively harmonised in the face of its apprehended finitude?

As with other dimensions of Positive Religion, Comte's response to the mortality question draws its form from the Catholicism it aims to supersede.[62] An otherworldly heaven is declared a fiction. But the

---

[60] A decisive break was made by Lévi-Strauss in declaring that history was the domain of contingency, synchronic social structures alone were scientifically knowable, and attempts like Comte's to provide a model for history were themselves analysable as myth (1967:1–26).

[61] Monotheism, in fact, was the very fount of egoism: 'la théorie de l'égoïsme, bien que spéculativement propre . . . à la philosophie métaphysique, y émana surtout de la théologie elle-même, qui . . . aboutissait finalement, dans la pratique, à une équivalente consécration, par la prépondérance, aussi exorbitante qu'inévitable, que toute la morale religieuse accorde nécessairement . . . à la préoccupation du salut personnel' (v:577). Already in the *Philosophie positive*, then, we see Comte moving towards a modification in his theory of stages. Its first form is Theology–Metaphysics–Positivism, the middle as a hybridic bridge between the others. In its second form, metaphysics and monotheism are grouped *together* as the bad but necessary transitional stage between the spontaneous initial harmony of fetishism and the final harmony of Positivism. This, in the *Synthèse subjective*, becomes the dominant historical schema.

[62] In his 'appreciation' of monotheism in *Politique positive*, Comte notes that what had to

promise of a kind of immortality reappears through the process whereby faithful servants of Humanity are themselves posthumously incorporated into the immortal body of Humanity.[63] Individual existence is conceived of as having two stages, first 'objective' and then 'subjective'. The former is life itself, the latter a mode of existence, *la vie subjective*, which is purely imaginary and depends entirely on the memory that survives, and is perpetuated, in the consciousness of others (x:101–5). To achieve that blessed state – at best to be venerated in prayer, in the manner of the saints[64] – is to have a kind of perpetual life. Entry into a 'subjective' mode of existence parallels the Christian account in other respects too. Like the ascent of the soul into heaven, the passage from 'objective' to 'subjective' being entails a purification – not just in the sense that, upon dying, gross matter is transcended, but in the sublimer sense that the subjective being of one who persists in the mode of memory is idealised as the residue of a socially valued life (viii:61 et seq.).[65] As such, indeed, it transmutes into a pure and efficacious force for good. 'The noble existence which perpetuates us in others becomes . . . the worthy continuation of that by which we deserved this immortality' (xi:92). Nor, finally, is the 'subjective existence' of the deceased wholly inert.

Our dead are freed from material and vital necessities, and they leave us the memory of these only that we may represent them better as we knew them. But

perish in Catholicism 'était la doctrine, et non l'organisation, qui n'a été passagèrement ruinée que par son adhérence élémentaire à la philosophie théologique . . . tandis qu'une telle constitution, convenablement reconstruite sur des bases intellectuelles à la fois plus étendues et plus stables, devra finalement présider à l'indispensable réorganisation spirituelle des sociétés modernes' (v:392). Catholicism, on this reading, was beset by a contradiction between its (egoistic and abstract) theory and its (love-engendering) cultic practice and organisational structure. Positivism would save the form of the one by replacing the content of the other. With such an affirmation, Mill and others should not have been so surprised by the religious innovations of 1847 onwards.

[63] 'Chacun de ses vrais éléments comport deux existences successives: l'une objective, toujours passagère, où il sert directement le Grand-Être, d'après l'ensemble des préparations antérieures; l'autre subjective, naturellement perpétuelle, où son service prolonge indirectement, par les résultats qu'il laisse à ses successeurs. À proprement parler, chaque homme ne peut presque jamais devenir un organe de l'Humanité que dans cette seconde vie' (viii:60).

[64] For those deemed worthy, seven years after *la consécration suprême* in the final 'objective' sacrament of *transformation*, 'le sacrament subjectif complète la série des préparations objectives, en proclamant . . . une solennelle incorporation au Grand-Être' (x:130).

[65] The memorial service, in which the life of the deceased is publicly and selectively celebrated, has today become a social fixture. Comte's anticipatory variant was to give it a socially ontological status. The dead other, purged of negative associations, was to be not merely incorporated into the collective memory, but into the (subjective) being of Humanity itself. In medieval form, as Ariès has shown (1981:143–5), the eulogy was associated with public demonstrations of grief and mourning, and not at all with making assertions about the salvation of the departed soul.

they do not cease to love and even to think, in us and through us. The sweet exchange of feelings and ideas that passed between us and them, during their objective life, becomes at once closer and more continuous when they are detached from bodily existence. (XI:92)

Like medieval Catholicism's saints and angels, those who were true organs of Humanity during their lifetime can continue to be so, then, from beyond the grave. As for the 'damned', i.e. those whose bad deeds at the end of the day outweigh the good, the ennobled prolongation of subjective existence in Humanist heaven is justly denied. Hardened criminals will be buried in unmarked graves. The most wicked, besides being capitally punished by the Temporal Power, will be blotted out from public memory. Even their bodily remains will be symbolically unmarked, disappearing into the anatomical laboratories of medical science (X:75).

Comte's secular transposition of Catholicism's snakes-and-ladders schema of personal immortality rested, however, on a crucial assumption. This was that individuals actually would be remembered, both privately and, for the most worthy, through public perpetuation in the collective memory. But – and here was the deeper problem – this could not be at all guaranteed. Just as industrialisation had brought chronic problems concerning consensus and solidarity, so too, in the turbulent transition from feudalism, the maintenance of *continuité* had been disrupted, and appropriate mechanisms to restore it had signally failed to emerge. Care for the collective memory could certainly no longer be left to Christianity. Its own memorials, which praised saints and martyrs but ignored great thinkers, statesmen and artists, were egregiously selective. Also, as displayed by unattended church graveyards, the church's attitude to the more ordinary dead was affected by a mystical notion of resurrection that used fear of death to orient believers towards a wholly otherworldly salvation. In other ways, however, the metaphysical camp was worse. With its blind trust in Reason, it had been as unthinking about the prerequisites of social unity through time as it had of those in space. 'The living rise up against the dead, as witnessed by a blind hostility towards the whole of the Middle Ages, poorly compensated by an irrational admiration for antiquity' (IX:367). The deists had no sense of *filiation* at all.[66]

The crucial importance to Comte of (a morally selective) collective memory becomes even clearer when we realise that what was at stake in ensuring it was not only the proper edification of individuals and a

---

[66] 'En effet, l'anarchie occidentale consiste principalement dans l'altération de la continuité humaine, successivement violée par le catholicisme maudissant l'antiquité, le protestantisme réprouvant le moyen âge, et le déisme niant toute filiation' (IX:2).

socially ramified scaffolding of deep personal incentives to induce an altruistic commitment to the human good. What is re-membered in all the memorialising practices prescribed by Positivism is Humanity itself. Nor was this just in the metonymic sense that, in the cult, each person remembered symbolises the whole. The point concerns, rather, the kind of whole it is. No more than 'society' does 'Humanity' consist only of the synchronously interconnected body of the living. The space of its existence includes the fourth dimension of time. It is intergenerational. Humanity includes, then, not just those presently with us, but also the dead, who live on only in our minds (IX:66). It also includes those not yet born, who constitute a future horizon for our furthest aims. What is more, human history is entering its final, fully 'mature', stage. So the ratio between 'objectively' and 'subjectively' existent members (i.e. between the living and the dead) has tilted decisively towards the latter.[67] The larger part of Humanity is a memory trace in the subjectivity of that diminishing minority currently alive. Without memorialisation, then, not only would society lack the unifying ties of 'continuity' which help give it, in the Aristotelian sense, an identity as perduring. L'Humanité, as the now mostly imaginary and (in memory) morally transfigured object of faith and service, would cease to exist.

Overall, then, the disruption of continuité posed a further, and profound, problem of moral order. Indeed, since 'true sociability consists more in successive continuity than in present solidarity' (XI:68), the more developed l'espèce humaine, the more continuité became the primary question. Without a shared sense of historical participation, without the moral incentive of being at least well remembered, how could altruism prevail? But in posing the issue this way, Comte highlights only that aspect of it which concerns moral integration and social order. Beyond that, the 'great western crisis' linked to the loss of collective memory also raised an existential spectre. If not directly mentioned, this spectre is implicit in his diagnosis and, subjectively speaking, is more fundamental still.

Edith Wyschogrod's Spirit in Ashes explores the contemporary aporias of what she calls the 'authenticity paradigm' lying at the heart of classical strategies for absorbing the 'wound of death' in an epoch when the real continuity of the human species has come to be threatened by the onset of the total 'death-world' and 'man-made mass death' (1985:8). According to this paradigm, it is the worthiness of the life lived in a shared and ongoing life-world that sustains the mortal subject. But there can be no such ontological security, no larger moral or logotherapeutic frame-

---

[67] 'Les vivants sont toujours, et de plus en plus, gouvernés nécessairement par les morts: telle est la loi fondamentale de l'ordre humain' (XI:68).

work, if the everyday or world-historical continuity of time cannot be taken for granted. Wyschogrod's work concerns the undermining effects of the loss of a future horizon, and it addresses an absolute limit, since it raises the issue in the context of *objective* (i.e. physical) threats to standing. What Comte was confronting was a lesser problem, perhaps. It concerned the merely social breakdown of institutions surrounding the collective memory. What this threatened was the *subjective* continuity of social time. But it similarly put in question the referentiality, through meaningful deeds and thoughts, of individuals' lives for others, and thus their mental standing as self-consciously finite projective being. Such a breakdown, if it ever became complete, would just as surely annihilate Hegel's Absolute Spirit as it would Comte's Humanity, and would just as surely invalidate, therefore, what his desupernaturalised salvation scheme at once presupposes and aims to maintain: the classical moral response to the meaning of a transient life.

Comte signalled the extent of his concern through a drastic and thoroughgoing proposal: the mnemonic assembly and maintenance of the finest in the human tradition through the vast sepulchral and museal labour of a new church. The Church of Humanity was to be, indeed, one vast exercise in memorialisation: from its celebratory calendar of benefactors, culminating in a 'festival for all the dead' (VII:344), to its funeral shrines and parks, to the private prayers through which the faithful thrice daily rekindle their ardour for the Goddess by recalling the finest features of the finest dear departed they can effusively bring to mind.[68] No doubt if tradition, and still more the capacity for one, were wholly extinct, Positivism's syncretic embrace of all the memory cults surrounding family, country and humanity would have had nothing to build on. Unlike Burke, however, Comte can place no trust in the slowly baking cake of custom, nor in the healthy accretion of popular 'prejudices'.[69] That which holds together social time and social space has withered into a defensive clinging to pre-industrial forms against the nihilists of abstracted rationality. The spontaneous operations of collective memory, and the ability of these operations to adapt to new

[68] For the Positivist manner of prayer in *le culte personnel*, see Gouhier, 1965:221–2. Each session, carefully timed and subdivided, would consist of a *commémoration* followed by an *effusion*, for which the supplicant kneels before his/her private altar.

[69] While Comte railed against the insensitivity of contemporary 'metaphysicians' to 'the best of the medieval traditions' (IX:533), his own appropriation of them was more of an abduction, and allows Hayek, for example, to include Comte in his devil's gallery of totalitarian social engineers (1953:191–206). There is at the same time at least an abstract affinity between Comte's notion of Humanity as an intergenerational process and Burke's view that society is a 'partnership not only of those who are living, but between those who are living, those who are dead, and those who are not yet born' (1965:117).

scientific–technical conditions, has atrophied. Altogether, the continuist temporality of the organically social has hollowed out, leaving the pressing need for a rationally engineered substitute.

What made the situation increasingly urgent was that if the unravelling went too far, just as with the dissolving of solidarity, it might undermine the subjective capacity for society to overcome it. On both scores, the unspoken fear was that it might already be too late. In face of this, the sheer artifice of Comte's proffered antidote – which he instituted not least for himself – is striking. The totally encompassing regimen of Positive Religion, blueprinted down to the last detail, resembles nothing so much as the frantic attempt to resuscitate a corpse.

5 Love and the social body

The notion that the darkest night is just before dawn is a commonplace of western eschatology. In the secularised version of that trope,[1] which surfaced in the dream of a redemptive social transformation during the epoch of bourgeois revolution, the contrast was between a coming reign of reason and freedom and a darkening night of repression, corruption and stupidity, in which old monarchical–clerical regimes were blocking the path of progress. For Hegel, the Jacobin terror was itself the darkest moment.[2] Thereafter, in the disillusioned light of capitalist day, it was the ravages of primitive accumulation and early industrial production in the 'dark satanic mills' that provided the nadir of self-caused social misery against which to set the millenarian hope. Whence, via both Saint-Simonian and left–Hegelian translations, the figure made its way into the imaginary of all variants of modern socialism, framing a sense of time that has been, and remains, intrinsic to the very formation of the left as an ideological and political force. Picking a phrase of Rosa Luxemburg's that had been a rallying cry in the Spartacist uprising in 1919, a French neo-Trotskyist circle launched a journal in 1949 with the name *Socialisme ou Barbarisme*.[3] When Jean-François Lyotard, who had

---

[1] Norman Cohn's classic study *The Pursuit of the Millennium* (1971) argues the importance to this of medieval millenarianism. He especially emphasises the modern influence of the trinitarian historical schema (age of the Father, age of the Son, age of the Holy Ghost) developed by the thirteenth-century Franciscan mystic Joachim of Fiore. Whatever the import of this for Hegel, Comte's own historical model, for all its three stages, was more binary than trinitarian. In whatever version he presented it, two organic unities – e.g. the fetishist/spontaneous synthesis of humanity's childhood and the perfected order of Positivist maturity – are linked by a long transitional period of troubles corresponding to those of youth.

[2] In the Hegelian narrative, the Terror and the death of God intertwine. Robespierre's 'Republic of Virtue' coincides with absolute freedom negating itself in the Revolution's abstract veneration of a wholly insubstantial beyond, before its final sublation in the rise of 'the moral life of Spirit' (1967:610). 'The remote beyond that lies beyond this its actual reality, hovers over the corpse of the vanished independence of what is real or believed to be, and hovers there merely as an exhalation of stale gas, of the empty *être suprême*' (602).

[3] For the history of this journal and its role in May 1968, see Starr, 1995:24–30. For Lyotard's relations with it, which he left in 1964, see Smart, 1993: 35–6.

been a member of its editorial collective, associated himself with contemporary 'suspicion towards all meta-narratives' in *The Postmodern
Condition* he was distancing himself not only from totalising philosophies
of history that saw that process culminating in a realised and liberated
humanity, but also from the apocalyptic sense of time to which such
thought-grounding teleologies were linked.[4]

In all these cases, from the Book of Revelation to the contestative–
utopian gestures and happenings of May 1968, we see the same figure –
disaster turning to triumph, misery to bliss – being used, above all, to
provide a definition of the present. It is a definition that can at once
console, inspire and make sense of a fluid yet frustratingly intractable
historical situation. It has echoes, too, in the traditions of the radical
right, as for example in Heidegger's play with Hölderlin's line 'But
where danger grows / The saving power is also.'[5] The effect of linking
this experience of time with a teleological view of human history is to
determine the present as the last stage of a crisis of transition which will
usher in the wonderful, actualised and redeemed world in which the
whole process culminates. The present, then, is endowed with a transcendental meaning. It constitutes – with maximum perils and maximum
promise – the crucial, because *penultimate* moment in the human story.

Comte, in these terms, is clearly a 'penultimatist'. The present age
was racked by 'une grande crise', in which the very capacity of the
human collectivity to survive *as* a collectivity was mortally at stake.
Hence the pressing need for the emergency repair job of a new,
revitalising religious institution. At the same time, as against the metaphysicians of Revolution, the crisis was to be viewed calmly, through the
Olympian eyes of a predictive science. If the old society was at an end, 'a
new one was on the point of being constituted' (xa:47). The present
turbulence was *passagère*, a passing necessity in the longer arc of crisis
which reached back to the fourteenth century and was destined to usher
in Humanity's *final*, and finally '*normal*', state of order and realised

---

4 It may be said that Lyotard still repeats the same idea. The dreadful totalitarianisms of
   modernism coexist, in the present, with the promise of a new (unpresentable) sublime:
   'We have paid dearly for our nostalgia for the all and the one, for a reconciliation of the
   concept and the sensible, for a transparent and communicable experience. Beneath the
   general demand for relaxation and appeasement we hear murmurings of the desire to
   reinstitute terror and fulfill the phantasm of taking possession of reality. The answer is:
   war on totality. Let us attest to the unpresentable, let us activate the differends and save
   the honor of the name' (1992:24–5).
5 'The self-same danger is . . . the saving power . . . in as much as it brings the saving
   power out of its . . . concealed essence' (Heidegger, 1977a:42). And so it is with
   'modern technology': 'Will insight into that which is disclosingly near bring itself into
   being . . . Will we see the lightning flash of Being in the essence of technology?' (ibid.:
   29).

progress. All that was needed to bring the disorderly epoch of metaphysics, individualism and social anarchy to an end was the synthesising, synergising and sympathising reforms that Comte's own efforts were designed to bring in train. Humanity, unveiled to Comte as *le vrai Grand-Être*, was on the verge of revealing its true destination to all.

As with many such philosophies of history, Comte's telos – the good horizon beyond the bad present – is derivatively Christian. According to the laws of social development, 'Man becomes more and more loving', while 'Humanity becomes more and more religious' (IX:10). At the summit of that development is an apprehension that we really are, in St Paul's phrase, 'every one members of one another';[6] as if the human collectivity had itself become the *deus communis* which the Incarnationist doctrine of Christianity had foregrounded over the *deus absconditus* of an older monotheism. Altogether, Comte's perfected humanity is a society become universal, a world united and perpetually at peace; and one that has become so because, propelled by its objective yet redemptive logic, the human community has been transfigured into one large family bound together by love. Such images today are banalised in Coke and Benetton commercials. Yet their promotional use suggests their continuing ideological power. Some such notion of future community, founded on the saving power of human love, continues to subtend progressive impulses, whether liberal and meliorist or socialist and revolutionary. In postmodern intellectual circles one could say that it is the conscious withdrawal of this horizon – in disavowal as well as disappointment – which negatively lends force to the thinking of 'post-marxists' too.[7]

The scientific basis on which Comte tried to provide for the axial place of love in his scheme of things is now obsolete. However, Comte's 'positive theory of the soul' did represent a systematic attempt to cash out Saint-Simon's ambition to base moral and political principles on a science of man,[8] and in so doing to reflect 'positively' on the fundamental nature of what the western tradition has long regarded as its supreme ethical value. It did so moreover not only with respect to the relation between love and (a physicalist) psychology, but also with

---

[6] 'On voit déjà l'admirable saint Paul devancer, par le sentiment, la conception de l'Humanité, dans cette image touchante mais contradictoire: *nous sommes tous les membres les uns des autres*. Le principe positiviste devait seul révéler le tronc unique auquel appartiennent nécessairement tous ses membres spontanément confus' (XI:70; emphasis in original).

[7] For a powerful analysis of the 'logics of failed revolt' at work in the writings of the French post-structuralists, see Starr, 1995:15–34.

[8] A detailed account of the relation between Comte's and Saint-Simon's 'science of Man' is given in vol. III of Gouhier's *La jeunesse d'Auguste Comte*, especially 385–407.

reference to the anatomy of the social. Indeed, Comte's account of the
affective element in social relations represents a seminal effort to
delineate, at both the individual and social levels, the determinants of
what a Freudian tradition calls the libidinal economy.[9] In this context,
critical reflection on Comte's version of a love-centred social teleology
can serve two purposes. On one hand, the very fullness of Comte's
conceptualisation can aid in the development of a framework for assessing the logic and categories employed in all such thematisations. On
the other, Comte's eccentric blending of Catholic–conservative with
liberal–progressive visions of love and community provides an intriguing
reference point for interrogating other versions of that ideal, and
especially those, from communitarian to social-democratic, which are
more heavily weighted towards the latter. His combined championing of
social love and rejection of radical egalitarianism oppose him both to
Marx *and* to Nietzsche. His insistence that love and social unity be
thought through in relation not only to space, as solidarity, but in
relation to time, as continuity, also points to a dimension of the problem
of 'community' which – *pace* Innis's 'Plea for time'[10] – has largely
dropped out of sight.[11]

Whatever we make, then, of Comte's 'cerebral physiology' and his
grand narrative of progress, his characterisation of love in relation to
individual and social being is still, in certain respects, worth pondering.
In Comte's religion of love – and religion for him was always, whether it
knew it or not, the social organiser of love – we confront an eminently
challengeable, yet possibly instructive, variant of love itself as an ethical
and political ideal.

[9] But of course without any concept of the unconscious, and with *les penchants* and *les
sentiments* instead of desire. Comte used the paired terms *économie individuelle/économie
sociale* to speak of the ensemble of active/intellectual/affective forces in play.

[10] For Innis, a declining concern for time and a chronic 'presentism' had resulted from
the techno-economic movement of industrialism itself. 'Industrialism implies technology and the cutting of time into precise fragments suited to the needs of the engineer
and the accountant' (1982:140). Comte's point about *l'esprit de détail* is similar, except
that he considers its dissolvent effect mainly with regard to social space (solidarity),
while the modern rupture with *continuité* is taken, most proximately, to have religio-
ideological causes.

[11] The concern for 'roots' in contemporary ethno-cultural discussion (as for example in
Bernal's *Black Athena*), might be taken as a counter-example, though it is generally less
focussed on recovering continuity *per se* than in forging collective identities out of
rediscovered (or invented) origins. For a broad-ranging discussion of the revised place
of tradition in post-Cold War 'realignment' of left and right, see Giddens, 1994.
'Socialists', he observes, 'more often than not find themselves trying to conserve
existing institutions – most notably the welfare state – rather than to undermine them.
And who are the attackers, the radicals who wish to dismantle existing structures? Why,
quite often they are none other than the conservatives – who it seems wish to conserve
no longer' (22).

Individual and society

Comte's 'individual' and 'society' are evidently implicated in one another, yet he by no means reduced the psychological determinations of the individual to the overriding fact of this implication, any more than he reduced his understanding of the determinations of the social solely to that of a single human organism writ large.[12] In delineating his conception of love in relation to the constitution of human society, then, we must first disentangle its sociological and individual–psychological elements. After that, we can dynamise the model. That will enable us to see how Comte conceived of love as a growing force – a force destined, at once, to replace violence as the affective foundation of social unity, and to universalise itself into a generalised benevolence that would embrace not only the perfect wholeness achieved by the human species as it became at last pervasively *religious* and *aimant*, but even the planet and the 'universal order' beyond.

All begins, and ends, with the question of order. Progress is its perfecting.[13] In Comte's understanding of the 'general laws of life' there is more than a shadow of Aristotle's natural entelechies, and (perhaps through Leibniz) of the scholastics' appeal to a language of 'substantial forms'.[14] In positivist terms, though, there could be no final causes. So if nature behaved as if there were, this must be accounted for in some other way. Comte's accounting unfolded within a wider effort to square a conception of the biological organism – the phenomenal entities of the new life sciences of botany, biology and physiology – with the mechanistic principles which had proved so effective in scientifically mastering the non-life domains of astronomy and physics.[15] Differences of quality,

---

[12] 'Il serait . . . irrationel . . . de vouloir servilement conformer l'analyse fondamentale de l'organisme collectif à celle de l'organisme individuel . . . Toutefois, la similitude essentielle des deux cas statiques doit déterminer un certain correspondance . . .' (VIII:289).

[13] 'L'ordre devient alors la condition permanente du progrès, tandis que le progrès constitue le but continu de l'ordre. Enfin, par une plus profonde appréciation, le positivisme représente le progrès humain comme consistant toujours dans le simple développement de l'ordre fondamental, qui contient nécessairement le germe de tous les progrès possibles' (VII:105).

[14] For the importance of this notion for Spinoza and Leibniz, see Woolhouse, 1993:9–12. 'Substantial' forms are contrasted with secondary or 'accidental forms'. The latter can change without affecting the ongoing and defining essence of an entity, while the former define an entity's 'essential unity'. The principle that progress is always the progress of order can easily be translated into such terms. For Comte, organicity is the 'substantial form' of organisms as such. There is thus an essential continuity with respect to that form however it develops, both throughout human history and also throughout *la série animale*, from the most primitive unicellular creature to *l'Humanité* itself.

[15] See *leçon* 38 of the *Cours*, especially III:323–42. After disposing of the reductionist notion

Comte never tires of assuring us, including (as Broussais had apparently demonstrated) the difference between normality and pathology, can always be understood as differences in magnitude with respect to the limits of equilibrium (III:261–3). Whence the importance he ascribed to advances since the seventeenth century which had led mathematics, through Cartesian geometry and differential calculus, to a general theory of mechanics. These advances held the prospect, he believed, of describing the complex dynamics of life-forms and thereby grasping, if not the 'hidden causes' of life, then at least the mathematical properties of the regularities of concomitance and succession which life-forms exhibited in what we could observe of their 'events' (III:341).

From the three laws of motion, identified with Kepler (inertia), Galileo (co-variance of all elements in a system) and Newton (equivalence of action and reaction), and developed into a general theory by Lagrange and others, Comte derived a general equilibrium theory applicable to complex systems.[16] Within the given range of stability conditions, equilibrium is self-correcting, a principle that applies not only to static systems but also to dynamic ones, including those composed of *forces vivantes* (I:600–4). In this abstract but universally applicable sense, order dominates progress, and an entity's manner of organisation, and reorganisation, dominates its course of development. As the 13th Law of Positivism's 'first philosophy' puts it: 'Always subordinate the theory of motion to that of existence, by conceiving all progress as the development of the particular order in question, the conditions of such order, whatever they be, regulating the mutations which together make up its evolution' (XI:388).

But what about the order, and orderly progress through all the metamorphoses of its life cycle, of that life-form Comte called 'society'? If it was a life-form – and certainly, like other organisms, it actively maintained itself by modifying the milieu on which it was physically dependent (III:226–7) – then it should at least obey the general laws of life. These included that in-built tendency to dynamic equilibrium which he conceived as order-in-progress. However, as witnessed by the very crisis Comte was seeking to address, order in the social sphere

that the biological domain is calculable in the same way as lower domains, Comte excoriates 'l'absurde principale de la prétendue indépendance des êtres vivants à l'égard des lois universelles du monde matériel'. This has led 'les physiologistes à regarder ces êtres comme essentiellement soustraits à l'empire des théories fondamentales de l'équilibre et du mouvement; tandis que ces théories constituent, au contraire, la véritable base élémentaire de l'économie organique envisagée sous cet aspect' (III:331–2).

[16] Summarised in the 'mainly objective' laws, numbers 10–12, of first philosophy (XI:388). For an elaboration of Comte's understanding of the laws of static and dynamic mechanics as they pertain to the theory of equilibrium, see *leçon* 18 of the *Cours*, especially 567–89.

could hardly be regarded as automatic. It could readily, and deeply, be disturbed. This was indeed just the point. The question of order in relation to social development was a special case, and it was so because of the special kind of 'existence' society constituted.

What distinguished human society from all the other organisms studied by the life sciences was not just its unparalleled size and complexity, but the problematic manner in which the individual organisms of which it was composed combined into a vital system (VIII:288–30). Unlike cells in a physical body – whose existence Comte in any case doubted[17] – each individual in the human group is capable, if not of living entirely outside the social ensemble (as god or beast, noted Aristotle), then certainly of acting, thinking and feeling at variance with it. Each individual has its own conditions and imperatives of life; independently of social requirements, it has a mind and will of its own. The parallel between the systematic conception of the individual organism and the collective organism could not then be complete, 'since the composite nature of the one differs profoundly from the indivisible constitution of the other' (VIII:228). To be sure, for Comte it was not individuals but 'organs' and 'tissues' that formed the irreducible elements of *l'organisme universel*.[18] Nevertheless, without the cooperation of individuals these latter could not even exist. Thus the achievement of order in society involved not only a harmony of 'organs and functions' corresponding to the equilibrium conditions proper to its stage of development, it also required the successful combining of individual human organisms into a group that was sufficiently unified, in the first place, to have functions and organs capable of operating at a social level. Social operation, in other words, necessitated interindividual cooperation.

Comte conceded that the collective existence would be destroyed 'if agreement was ever able to extinguish independence. Human cooperation needs the separation of efforts as much as their convergence.' But this was not the main problem. The constant and imminent danger 'consists above all in an excess of independence' (X:34). So the question arises about the nature of cooperation itself. The possibility of this freely

---

17 Comte saw the concept of 'cell' as an illicit analogy from the molecule of chemistry (III:343). He also considered that the idea harboured a metaphysical search for the essential substance of 'life', as opposed to his own approach, which emphasised its overall mode of 'organisation' (III:228 et seq.). According to Pickering (1993:595), Comte's rejection of cellular theory (as well as vivisection and microscopic research) meant that 'Comte failed to put himself at the forefront of biological research' and 'proved embarrassing to some of his disciples'.

18 'Il faut surtout distinguer entre les éléments, immédiats ou médiats, propres à l'organisme universel, et les agents ou représentants qu'il exige . . . [L]'Humanité se décompose, d'abord en Cités, puis en Familles, mais jamais en individus' (X:31).

occurring implies the willingness of individuals to forgo individual interests in favour of collective ones, an attitude of unselfish sociality which Comte called *altruisme*. Put this way, the whole moral problem of society, indeed the moral secret of religion itself, was how to secure the preponderance of altruistic over egoistic instincts. This would not be an issue if, as with ants and bees, the requisite cooperative spirit (*l'esprit d'ensemble*) was instinctually dominant, and thus biologically guaranteed. On the other hand, however, if there were no instinctual basis for cooperation at all it could only ever be achieved coercively, that is through the forced unity of a group held in thrall by 'the right of the strongest' or by mutually exercised violence. This, though, could hardly be thought of as a real bonding between individuals, and would leave the social as such unexplained.

The human-nature debates that traversed early-modern political theory had pitted partisans of 'natural goodness', like Shaftesbury, against those, like Hobbes, who asserted, in conformity with the doctrine of original sin, the limitless egoism of human desire.[19] Between these positions Comte, in effect, steered a midway course, one not far indeed, in its dynamic and dialectical understanding of the human faculties, from that of Rousseau. Like the citizen of Geneva,[20] Comte held that human impulses were dichotomous, divided into a conflicting and mutually interacting set of self-regarding impulses on the one hand, and a set of other-regarding ones on the other, linked to natural sympathy for fellow creatures.[21]

But two things distinguished Comte's version of this position. One was his insistence that the understanding of instincts, including their relation to reason and the formation of will, be placed on a physiological basis.[22] Affective and intellectual functions were to be conceived as

[19] The relation of these positions to the 'idea of progress' is discussed in Bury, 1960:177 et seq.

[20] Comte of course would have denied the comparison. Among metaphysical thinkers, he judged this midway position to have been best developed by Hume, Smith and Ferguson, 'l'école écossaise, qui admettait la sympathie en même temps que l'égoïsme' (III:630). Comte's references to Rousseau, who developed just such a position in part one of his *Discourse on Inequality*, are invariably negative.

[21] In discussing this distinction in chap. 45 of the *Cours* (the ten components of the instinctual/phrenological 'series' are only systematised in vol. I, chap. 3, of *Politique positive*), Comte follows Gall in labelling the egoistic instincts as *penchants* and the altruistic ones as *sentiments* (III:640). In his later revision of Gall, however, he reserves the former term for 'the instincts when active' and the latter for 'the instincts when passive' (VII:680).

[22] The term 'instinct' was broadly defined so as to include all the classical 'faculties'. It included 'toute impulsion spontanée vers une direction déterminée, indépendamment d'aucune influence étrangère' (VII:622). This accorded with Comte's notion, again developed from Gall, that not only the 'affective motors' but also the 'intellectual functions' and 'practical qualities' (courage, prudence, perseverance) were 'interior

'interior phenomena proper to the cerebral ganglions' (III:609). The second, closely related, was that the two sets of instincts, altruistic and egoistic, were set into a larger natural hierarchy – a double one, in fact – in which the affective refinement and moral worth of an instinct was inversely proportional to its natural force (IV:440–2). This principle, in turn, explained the contradictory relation of the individual to the group. In the case of the individual psyche, the 'coarsest' instincts – which comprised the egoistic impulses of the body (hunger and sex) and its activity (the 'instinct for self-improvement') and of the soul (vanity and ambition) – were more energetic and powerful than the 'worthier' ones of social sympathy (III:619). Yet what was functionally important for *la société* was the preponderance of the latter over the former. Hence the perennial moral problem of ensuring, through some form of social intervention, that the biologically natural hierarchy of impulses in the individual was corrected, and indeed reversed (VII:692).

Comte's conception of the affective basis of the social tie was opposed, it will be clear, not only to any merely negative conception of sociality founded in fear and coercion, but to any version of contract theory. The objection that a situation in which individuals consciously combine, by a founding and implicitly repeated act of will, already presupposes the social state it would explain, had been formulated by many thinkers before Comte, including both Rousseau and de Maistre.[23] Comte similarly stressed the impossibility of a social bond resting solely on the exercise of the mind (III:618). For him, indeed, contract-based theories of the social were not just incorrect. They symptomatised a broader aspect of contemporary humanity's long metaphysical disorder: the linked rebellions of the individual against society, and of the head against the heart. Only a mind already impelled by needs welling up from benevolent, altruistic, instincts could think, in the first place, from the perspective of the social interest. The price of this not being the case was that the thought of individuals would be impelled by the asocial, not to say antisocial, instincts of egoism. Even, then, for the achievement of the *philosophical* consensus which Comte envisaged as the precondition for a restored social unity, a more

functions of the brain'. Comte's full classification is given in the *tableau systématique* appended to *Politique positive* (VII:727).

[23] Of course, while Rousseau and de Maistre both rejected the idea of an original compact, they differed sharply over whether the procedure of deriving society from a prior state of nature was itself admissible. For Rousseau, society was an increasingly non-natural result of solving problems caused, initially, by some originary disturbance in the state of nature. For de Maistre, 'to talk of a state of nature in opposition to the social state is to talk nonsense voluntarily' (1971:95). 'Man's *natural state* is . . . to be what he is today and what he has always been, that is to say, *sociable*' (98; emphasis in original).

primordial, affective, bonding between individuals was necessary. That it was possible at all, despite the spontaneous and driven selfishness of individuals, depended on the existence of an actual impulse for sociability. The totality of sub-instincts which made up this impulse – *attachement*, *vénération*, and *bonté* or *bienveillance* (VIII:16) – comprised what Comte called *l'amour*.[24]

Love and the social tie

'Love', it will be noted, is for Comte a plural force: *les sentiments sociaux*. This accorded with his version of Gall's 'cerebral physiology'.[25] But it also accorded with what he took to be the complexity of the social tie. In the case of a social group whose members are personally known to one another and whose interaction is face-to-face, the social tie can readily be conceived to consist in the direct bonds of affection that form directly and dyadically between pairs of individuals. The overall result, in that case, is that the group so formed is intensively bound together so that it assumes the form of a 'veritable union'.[26] But what of the case of larger groups in which encounter and interaction are more sporadic, or of national societies where interaction between more than subsets of individuals with one another is inconceivable? And, at the limit of globality, what sort of social tie is it, or could there possibly be, which binds all the people in the world together into the Ecumene of Humanity? At the very least we would have to say that the Other

[24] The first two forms of love were qualified as 'special', as having a circumscribed object of affection; the third was 'general' because its object was diffuse. This made *bienveillance* alone wholly disinterested. It was thus 'l'instinct suprême, ou l'amour universel, dont la *charité* des chrétiens constituait l'ébauche théologique' (VII:701; emphasis in original).

[25] 'Ces penchants supérieurs sont peu nombreux: mais on ne pourrait les réduire à un seul, sans retomber aussitôt dans la confusion métaphysique d'où Gall nous à retirés' (VII:701).

[26] '[I]l est incontestable que l'ensemble des relations domestiques ne correspond point à une association proprement dite, mais qu'il compose une véritable *union* . . . À raison de sa profonde intimité, la liaison domestique est donc d'une tout autre nature que la liaison sociale. Son vrai caractère est essentiellement moral . . . Fondée sur l'attachement et la reconnaisance, l'union domestique est surtout destinée à satisfaire directement, par sa seule existence, l'ensemble de nos instincts sympathiques, indépendamment de toute pensée de coopération active et continue à un but quelconque' (IV:472; emphasis in original). This passage makes clear that Comte, at least in the *Cours*, was working with Aristotle's definition of organised society as 'an association of persons formed with a view to some good purpose' (1962:25). Hence, of course, the importance of a consensus over ends. The theoretical problem this presented for Comte was how to square the voluntary character of such an 'association' with its ontological priority to the individual. The 'voluntary' character of *sociétés proprement dites* is sustained in *Politique positive*, but not the characterisation of a society as 'an association'.

(*l'autrui*) to whom loving sentiments are directed becomes more abstract as the group increases in scale and anonymity.

For Comte there were in fact (at least) two distinct modalities in which living individuals could, and did, bond with other living individuals in order to constitute, in the strong sense of the term, a social group. The first is the one already mentioned, that of directly emotive interindividual attachment. This was exemplified for Comte by the sentiments that bound together a family.[27] These sentiments themselves, be it noted, were conceived to be heterogeneous, both with respect to the social relations involved and with respect to the corresponding forms of love. The bonds of affection between husband and wife, parents and children, and indeed between siblings, had each their own specific character. 'The family', moreover, had pregiven structural asymmetries. Whatever its historical vicissitudes, it was always taken to be sharply age-graded and sexually differentiated.[28] This same unequal structure was, we might add, androcentrically, indeed patriarchally, defined from the vantage point of the mature married male who was its 'temporal' head. A profound consequence was that the matrix of affective bonds that Comte regarded as paradigmatic for an analysis of primary group attachments was always already hierarchically inscribed.

This is clear in his account of the two-way relation between children and parents. The love felt for parents, not only as Origin but as household rulers, providers and protectors, is mingled with awe and respect. The love from parents to children is bounteous from a position of power. The first is the case of what Comte calls *vénération*;[29] the second, where affection is mingled with protective magnanimity, is *bienveillance* or *bonté*.[30] Altogether, then, the affective relation between parents and

---

27 The affective dimension of the family is discussed in *leçon* 50 of the *Cours* (IV:447 et seq.), and in chap. 3 of vol. II of *Politique positive ou théorie positive de la famille humaine* (VIII:177–215). The latter dispenses with the former's distinction between *les instincts sympathiques* and *le sentiment de coopération*, working instead with the 'systematic' trichotomy among *attachement*, *vénération* and *bienveillance*.

28 '. . . la théorie sociologique de la famille peut être essentiellement réduite à l'examen rationnel de deux ordres fondamentaux de relations nécessaires, savoir: la subordination des sexes, et ensuite celle des âges, dont l'une institue la famille tandis que l'autre la maintient' (IV:452).

29 What distinguishes the two 'special' social instincts of *attachement* and *vénération* is that the first 'indique les instincts les plus circonstrites. Il ne lie profondément que deux êtres à la fois. Quant à la *vénération* . . . [l]a soumission volontaire constitue son caractère essentielle. C'est pourquoi elle s'applique toujours aux chefs, tandis que le penchant précédent préfère l'égalité' (VII:702; emphasis in original).

30 '[C]'est la paternité qui nous enseigne directement à aimer nos inférieurs. La bonté proprement dite suppose toujours une sorte de protection' (VIII:189). The phrase 'proprement dite' implies a distinction between *bonté* and *bienveillance* which Comte glosses over in constructing his instinctual 'series'. For him, in fact, there are *four* forms of love: *attachement* (towards an equal), *vénération* (towards a superior), *bonté* (towards

children, as generally between superiors and inferiors, entails the reciprocity of different, but similarly hierarchised, forms of love. But what of marriage? Here we might think that Comte had identified a form of love between equals, and the *attachement* which ordinarily designates 'the profound linking of two beings' (VII:702) is certainly positioned in his scale of loves as the locus of affective parity. However, the sexual division of labour – he deals with the world, she with household and children – which Comte took to be both socially necessary and biologically given (women were *le sexe affective*, men *le sexe intellectuel et actif* (VII:246)) complicated the picture. There was in fact a double asymmetry between spouses. The husband had material power and was head of the household. But in matters of feeling he was inferior to a wife who was consequently to be adored at the same time as regarded with the kind of *bienveillance* proper towards a child.[31] Thus even marital affection turns out to be less an *attachement* in Comte's sense than a double hybrid of the two unequal sorts of love.[32]

What is remarkable in Comte's account is his reluctance to place himself, and theorise from, within the one nexus of his family system wherein the power relations of gender and generation would be nullified: the affective relations between same-sex siblings. They are mentioned, only to be dismissed as 'of too little political importance to be specially dwelt on in this study' and, in any case, as attaching themselves, when they acquire any scope, 'to a notable inequality of age' (IV:466–7). Thus,

whenever fraternal coordination is strongly enough established to exercise any political influence, this is evidently, at root, because the older brothers, assuming a kind of paternal ascendancy, artificial or spontaneous, maintain domestic unity against individual differences . . . One cannot doubt, consequently, that absolute fraternal equality is transitory . . . destined later to dissolve under a new spontaneous organisation of the domestic hierarchy. (IV:467)[33]

an inferior), and *bienveillance* (general and diffuse). If he had been able to admit as fundamental the distinction between equal and unequal he would have had, at the least, to modify his instinctual schema.

[31] The affective superiority of women, and the natural superiority of men in every other respect, was both physiologically given and accentuated by social evolution. 'La biologie tend finalement à représenter le sexe féminin . . . comme nécessairement constitué . . . en une sorte de l'état d'enfance continue, qui l'éloigne davantage, sous les plus important rapports, du type idéal de la race' (IV:456). Lest it be thought that he has mistaken the cause (infantilisation) for the effect, Comte adds that no one today can seriously contest 'l'évident infériorité relative de la femme . . . soit en vertu du moindre force de son intelligence, soit à la raison de sa plus vive susceptibilité morale et physique, si antipathique à toute abstraction et à toute contention scientifique' (IV:457).

[32] 'Plus tendre que l'amitié fraternelle, l'union conjugale inspire une vénération plus pure et plus vive que le respect filial, et plus dévouée que la protection paternelle' (VIII:187).

[33] A similar argument is offered in *Politique positive* (VIII:185–6), although it is also conceded that sibling love is 'le mieux susceptible d'extension extérieur' and, at least

Comte's catalogue of interindividual forms of affection within the family, then, is starkly incomplete. *Fraternité* gets short shrift, *sororité* (at least as a solidary relation)[34] gets no attention at all. Not only, in consequence, does Comte deny the viability of *fraternité* as a political ethic, there is also no discussion of how an egalitarian sibling affection might extend its range informally as friendship[35] – an absence which can be read as allergic not only to the give-and-take of friendship itself, but also to the kind of solidarity that arises in the course of rebellious (and potentially anarchic) struggle against any and every dominant power.

The complex of emotional bonds uniting Comte's *famille* provided him with a model for thinking about social unity in a broader sense. The same three forms of love, *attachement, vénération, bienveillance,* parade all over his social stage. However, the mode of direct interindividual ties which the familial model exemplifies could only obtain within the restricted range of a primary group, at most the family extended into a tribe. For individuals to be mutually attached as anonymous members of a larger association required a different affective mechanism. This was a form of attachment mediated by common attachment to that transpersonal Other represented by the group itself. This *second* modality of the social tie still rested on the binding force of love. But the mechanism was indirect, and the resulting interindividual ties 'more extended' and 'less intense' (IX:190). In the first instance, and as an expression of *vénération* and *bonté* rather than *attachement,* the object of affection was not a person.[36] It was that entity constituted by all persons

among living contemporaries, 'fournit partout le type spontané de l'amour universel' (186). The reference (186) to the prevalence of fraternal bitterness – *amerture* – suggests that personal experience confirmed his depreciation of fraternity. Likewise his reference to the guiding role of *les aînés,* which recalls not only his literal place in the birth order but also his leadership role in the student movement at the École Polytechnique in 1815–16.

34 A man's sister, like his wife and daughter, could of course be venerated as an embodiment of *le type féminin.* For the (subordinate) place of sisterly adoration within *le culte intime,* see X:111.

35 The one place *l'amitié* enters (if implicitly) into his social theory is in his discussion of *fétichisme* in *Politique positive,* a kin-based mode whose 'limited relations' encourage *attachement.* 'Ce noble instinct avait dignement surgi sous le fétichisme, avec les deux autres affections sympathiques. Néanmoins, notre première enfance ne put vraiment suffire à notre initiation morale qu'envers l'attachement proprement dit, auquel des relations bornées conviennent davantage' (IX:235). The particularity of 'attachment' is its limit. It is therefore not this, but the 'veneration' fostered by polytheism and monotheism which eventually extends, with all its hierarchical quality, into *le bonté* which Positivism brings to the fore.

36 In the *Philosophie positive* the shift from the family to a wider form of association is presented as reversing the relation between 'special' and 'general' forms of sociability: 'Dans les combinaisons sociales proprement dites, l'économie élémentaire présente inévitablement un caractère inverse: le sentiment de coopération, jusqu'alors accessoire, devient, à son tour, prépondérant, et l'instinct sympathique, malgré son

in so far as they are similarly connected with one another through their common but separate love for this connecting Third. On that basis, and as a kind of secondary effect, an *attachement* could then form also between fellow group members. But it was necessarily weaker than the kind obtaining within a family, while the primary ingredient of the extended social tie was what tied each to the Other composed of them all.

The germ of such a mediated social attachment could already be found in the family. The solidarity that flowed from its members' common love for their particular family was symbolised in the name of the family 'house'.[37] Its role in the family, though, was secondary to that of 'the direct satisfaction of sympathetic instincts' (IV:472), and it was only in the more extended group identification which came about with the formation of *la cité* in the city-state of early antiquity that the solidarising role of this second mechanism became decisive. The symbolic focus of the *cité*, and of the national societies that came later, was the collectively occupied territory, *la patrie*. Adoption of this focus at once extended the group to its maximal range of familiarity, fixed activity in relation to the productive development of a given piece of *la terre*, and provided an affectively suffused image of the collectivity as a common object of non-personal love. Whence its crucial intermediary role between the family and humanity as a whole, 'where activity combines with veneration around a fixed hearth' (IX:363). Attaching a people to a physical territory made visible and social the dependence of humanity on an external milieu which it also loved as its own.[38] With an extension of scale, moreover, a remarkable property of this form of social tie came to the fore: its capacity to transcend the always potentially conflictual particularities of smaller-scale but more personally intense attachments, including the *égoïsme collectif* engendered by the family itself (VIII:212).

Viewed in global perspective, however, civic patriotisms were them-

---

indispensable persistence, ne peut plus former le lien *principal*' (IV:472; emphasis in original). The argument in *Politique positive* (IX:443 et seq.) is fundamentally the same, except for the key mediating role played by *vénération*. This is now included among the 'special' social sentiments, because its object can be a particular collectivity as well as a particular person.

[37] 'L'etymologie du mot *patrie*, et l'usage universel qui confond la famille avec la *maison*, suffiraient pour indiquer l'intime connexité entre la possession du sol et l'ensemble de l'existence domestique' (VIII:286–7; emphasis in original).

[38] For the crucial role played by the city-state in Comte's *théorie positive de la propriété*, see IX:362 et seq. For Comte, there was no 'right of first occupier,' collective property in land was antecedent to individual ownership, and pride in property was to be regarded above all as a moral force attaching the human collectivity actively and affectively to *le dehors*.

selves conflictually differential and limited by particularisms of people and place.[39] This was why the most elevated minds, from the Roman philosophers of *humanitas* (IX:348) to the eighteenth-century dreamers of 'universal peace', had always aspired to a sociality that could embrace the whole of humanity. This impulse had been nurtured contradictorily (both because of its 'intellectual egoism' and because of the persistent militarism of the countervailing system of states) by the now shattered Christian church. But in an age of massive industrial production and growing interconnectedness, such promptings appeared to be losing, at last, their wishful quality. For Comte, as for liberals and socialists, industrialism was creating the real conditions, both material and moral, for a worldwide order to be finally established. So the furthest possible extension of the social tie based on group, rather than individual, attachment could already be practically envisaged. A world federation was ready to come into being. Now that *la révolution occidentale* had prepared the ground, the situation only required (though it was a big only) that the sentiments spontaneously seeking to attach themselves to Humanity as a whole be provided with a suitable symbolic focus, buttressed by a socially reproductive apparatus of worship and belief.

Each successively more inclusive affective community – *la famille, la cité, l'Église, l'Humanité* – had its 'appreciated' place in *la série sociale* (VIII:304), a scale which simultaneously provided a historical, socio-logical and moral framework for grasping the significance of the final emergence of society's final term in Comte's own day.[40] The series schematised the rise, and ultimate universalisation, of the social. It also framed a synchronic account of the circles of sociality in which con-temporary members of the most advanced national societies were affectively embedded. At the same time it was a moral scale, describing a hierarchy of moral refinement in which each wider group attachment, while weaker (because more abstract) than the one below, was, by the same token, more elevated. As we move from love of family to love of country and ultimately to love of humanity, that love becomes ever more universal because ever less mired in the contradictions and imperfec-tions of particularity.

---

[39] 'Tous les groupes limités tend d'abord à des hostilités mutuelles . . . la patrie réellement mérite des reproches analogues' (VIII:212).

[40] In its elaborated form, this scale is incorporated into *le tableau socialatrique* (X:159). The latter divides the social field into 81 aspects (grouped into *liens fondamentaux, états préparatoires* and *fonctions normales*), and gives each one its own *fête*. Each lunar month is also dedicated to a principal social category (Humanité, Mariage, Paternité, Filiation, Fraternité, Domesticité, Fétichisme, Polythéisme, Monothéisme, Femme, Sacerdoce, Patriciat, Prolétariat).

The ascending scale of sociality also mirrored what Comte considered, both ontogenetically and phylogenetically, to be the logical and actual path of *individual* moral ascent. Thus, the family develops our sentiments, the city/state our active faculties, the church (theistic, then Humanist) our intelligence (VIII:341). At the same time, in the path from familial to patriotic to ecumenical–humanist attachments, progressively higher and purer modes of the social instinct are brought into play, distancing the embodied and situated individual more and more from its immediate egoistic interests and drives. But before turning to this, there is one more piece of Comte's construct to consider. I have mentioned that for Comte there were two modes of group attachment, immediate and mediate, and that each had its own distinctly structured instinctual base. In the first mode, what is brought into play is direct interindividual *attachement*. But what is the kind of 'love' mobilised in the individual's affective attachment to the social group as a whole?

Comte's answer is by no means straightforward. He sometimes used the term *attachement* generally to describe the ties which individuals have with one another within any sociated group. But such ties as form horizontally between group members are distinct from the affective relations which connect individuals to the group itself. Inasmuch as that object is necessarily larger and more elevated than any of the individuals of which it is composed, the sentiment of positive affect towards it would be defined in Comte's terms as *vénération*. It is a veneration, moreover, that is bound to heighten (but also etherealise) the further up the scale of social love-objects we go.[41] The pieties of respect for family can elicit a strong sense of honour and gratitude, but hardly a sense of abasement. The feelings of the patriot, however, were more elevated and could even transcend intense personal attachments. From which Comte extrapolated the possibility of a still higher level of veneration – a level at which veneration shakes off all particularity and transmutes, as a generalised *bienveillance*, into love's highest form.[42] Such a love had for its object Humanity as a whole – an entity whose majestic distance from, and eminence over, the individual properly called forth the kind of adoration which adherents of a fictive theism had become accustomed to pour out towards their God.[43]

[41] 'Depuis l'amour de la tribu ou de la peuplade, jusqu'au plus vaste patriotisme, et même jusqu'à la sympathie envers tous les êtres assimilables, le sentiment ne change pas sa nature. Seulement, il s'affaiblit et s'ennoblit à mesure qu'il s'étend' (VII:703).

[42] *Vénération* is the necessary mediation between *attachement* and *bienveillance*. 'On voit ainsi que, parmis les trois organes cérébraux des instincts altruistes, le sentiment religieux dépend principalement de l'organe moyen, consacré à la vénération' (VIII:15–16).

[43] Although Comte never examines the difference, in Christian worship, between the

This, though, is only a partial answer. For it does not yet take into account the complication introduced by Comte's insistence that a fully positivised understanding of *la société* should take into account (as rationalist theorists of the social had not) that it exists in time as well as space. The unity of the social had always to be explicated with respect to the dimension not just of *solidarité*, but also of *continuité* – without which, indeed, the capacity for cumulative (mental) development which distinguished *la société humaine* from that of other animals would be unintelligible.

Here, again, the paradigm was provided by the family with its three types of love and three types of social tie. Within Comte's *famille*, as I have noted, two structures of hierarchised relations and affections are set in play. One relates to gender and is centred on marriage. The second relates to age and articulates with generational difference. As with gender, the exchange of honour/respect and magnanimity between the generations elicits from each the asymmetrical form of love it is due. In Comte's Positively restored cult of the hearth, *attachement* (as between siblings) is the form of love proper towards age peers, *vénération* (as of children for parents) is the love due to elders, and *bonté* (as of parents for children) that due to the young (VIII:185–9). As with love and solidarity, but this time diachronically, particular bonds help unify the whole. Love among living generations binds the family together in its flow through time. In such relations, the family relates its present, affectively, to its future and its past.[44] But a family's generations are not just those now alive. There are ancestors, and children's children not yet born (X:32). The bondedness of a family through time, then, depends not only on direct intergenerational ties. It depends also on how strongly its members can cherish and draw strength from remembered predecessors while bountifully providing for those still to come.

The same considerations, but on larger scale, apply in the cases of love for country and love for humanity. The objects of patriotic and Humanist love are multigenerational. Accordingly, while that love, as from individual to *Maison, Patrie, Humanité*, is weighted towards the *venerative*, it nevertheless engages, as towards society present, past and

identificatory love for Christ the Mediator and the non-identificatory love for God the Father, it is clearly the former (as in the medieval *Imitatio Christi*) which provides the model for his love of Humanity. The latter is criticised as a kind of servile flattery. In worshipping the new *Déesse*, Comte explains in *Catéchisme positiviste*, 'Nous ne l'adorons pas comme l'ancien Dieu, pour la complimenter, ma fille, mais afin de la mieux servir, en nous améliorant' (XI:76).

44 'La constitution domestique fournit spontanément la première manifestation de cet attribut fondamental de toute existence composée; car les enfants représentent l'avenir, et les vieillards le passé, sous l'immédiate prépondérance de l'âge mûr' (X:35).

future, feelings of *attachment* and *benevolence* as well. In 'the healthy case', collective activity derives its inspiration from those who went before and its goal from those ahead: 'We always work for our descendants, but under the impulsion of our ancestors, whence derive both the elements and the procedures of all our operations' (x:34). Once more, then, we have a triply articulated form of social tie. In addition to (1) the immediate emotional attachment felt, with varying degrees of intensity, between current social members, there are also (2) the venerative love which keeps alive the finest works and personages in the national, or global, human tradition[45] and (3) the benevolent regard for future generations which keeps us pointed towards social progress and perfection.

Just as with the synchronic aspect of order, we may note, Comte's insistence on the continuous linkage of the present with past and future served both as a normative framework for describing/prescribing the temporal conditions for (both individual and collective) mental health and as an essential element of his social ontology. The combination of loves directed by individuals towards the big Other of the social not only makes possible a 'healthy' and harmonious integration of feeling, thought and action. It was also necessary to the actual existence of society, both in the present and as a being inherently extended through time. This, on the face of it, would imply an essential symmetry between solidarity and continuity as indispensable dimensions of social unity. However, two respects in which the cases are not symmetrical in Comte's construct should be underlined.

First, the mode of presence of society's past and future is clearly not the same as the mode of presence of its present, which has implications for the variant affective ties individuals form with it. For Comte the point is fundamental. The present society, though present only in its 'events', is apprehended objectively, as a phenomenal *dehors*, albeit as one we are also inside. Past generations, however, only exist in the mode of memory, imaginatively reconceived, and future ones in an imaginary which has not even second-hand phenomenal materials from which they might be conjured up. Love for *la société*, then, is one part 'objective' and two parts 'subjective'.[46] To the extent that it is the latter, such love is not directed towards an independently existing entity in the *dehors*, but

---

[45] In preliterate societies, tradition is maintained by the *double* venerative relation that (a) elicits respect for *les vieillards*, who themselves (b) veneratively perpetuate les traditions essentielles' (VIII:361).

[46] '[L]a vraie population humaine se compose . . . de deux masses toujours indispensables, dont la proportion varie sans cesse . . . Si l'action et le résultat dépend surtout de l'élément objectif, l'impulsion et la règle émanent principalement de l'élément subjectif. Libéralement dotés par nos prédécesseurs, nous transmettons gratuitement à

towards a being which is only constructed subjectively, and which therefore only now exists in the *dedans*. We can see here why Comte placed such stress at the outset of his *Synthèse subjective* on developing a logic of sentiments which would display the 'normal' harmony obtaining between the logics of sense, image and sign. The spontaneous evincing of affection for a being which lay mostly in the mind, and which preponderantly consisted, indeed, in memories of people and their achievements who had passed on, had already to have before it, in the mind's eye, something which had been built, as image and idea, out of the subjective materials of the mind itself. This was also, Comte explained, why Positivists pray with their eyes closed.[47]

The largely imaginary character of the collective object of Positivist love is linked, as we have seen, to the programmatic importance Comte placed on restoring a sense of collective memory. Indeed, Positivism would have us believe that the consecration of tradition is destined to become a more prominent feature of social organisation than ever before. More even than in the case of tribalism and ancestor-worship, 'the living' in industrial society 'will be governed by the dead' (XI:68). This points, though, to a second difference in Comte's treatment between solidarity and continuity, a difference which he did *not* reflect on, and which amounts, in fact, to an inconsistency in his overall design. As society becomes more extended, more differentiated and more voluntarily cooperative, the mode of *solidarité* shifts from direct emotional 'union' to a more attenuated and indirect form of linkage. But no similar or accompanying change in modality is projected with regard to *continuité*. On the contrary, the *de novo* character of first Christianity and then industrial modernity with respect to the thought and culture of previous epochs is defined purely as an 'aberration'.[48] Far from its heralding, for example, a more permanent shift in orientation towards the present and future, and away from the past, it contravenes the 'normal' path. The Positive Polity will not merely restore the lost continuity of historical tradition, but will amplify both the scale of that tradition and the social resources devoted to its transmission. To be sure, Comte justifies such an apparently retrogade effort (embodied in

nos successeurs l'ensemble du domaine humain, avec une extension de plus en plus faible en proportion de ce que nous reçûmes' (XI:69).

[47] 'Nos contemplations religieuses s'accompliront sciemment au dedans . . . Un signe familier indiquera bientôt cette distinction envers la majeure partie du culte privé. Car le positiviste ferme les yeux pendant ses effusions secrètes, afin de mieux voir l'image intérieure' (IX:83).

[48] For the pervasive significance of this term for Comte, which had the same general sense as the inversion metaphor mobilised by Marx in his concept of 'ideology', see Kofman, 1978:86–101.

the *Calendrier positive*) in terms of the world-uniting syncretism it might make possible. Appreciating the past facilitates the incorporation into the Positivist Church of peoples who *currently* represent the whole range of achieved developmental stages (VII:379–81). At the same time, though, this presupposes that the development of continuity, unlike that of solidarity, follows a linear course that merely intensifies, as society evolves, the form of temporal organisation proper to the family and *l'enfance humaine*.

The picture of Comte's conception of the social tie would now seem complete. However, a third modality can also be identified, albeit that, for him, it was so interwoven with the second that he never separately identified it. If the first form of social tie is that of direct interindividual mutual attachment, and the second that of a mediate attachment of individuals to one another through a transcendent Third, this final mode of attachment is a cooperativeness that operates immediately as a kind of second nature. It would arise in the case where – as a result of the final preponderance, in the fully Positivised Polity, of the highest form of love – each individual is so saturated with social feeling that his (and in the public realm, for Comte, it is always his)[49] *individuated* thought and action is immediately produced as *social* in sensibility and effect.

Saint-Simon's New Christian injunction to 'love one another as brothers' had arisen as a religious supplement to the main moral principle of industrialism, namely that all are to consider themselves workers in the common enterprise of improving life for all.[50] Against the background of an increasing differentiation of interrelated social tasks, Comte's *esprit de l'ensemble* pointed to the same harmonising need.[51] But

---

[49] 'Tel est donc le vrai sens général de la progression humaine: rendre la vie féminine de plus en plus domestique, et la dégager davantage de tout travail extérieur, afin de mieux assurer sa destination affective' (VII:249). The exclusion of women from economic and public life was to be compensated for by the systematic application of the rule – *la loi naturelle de notre espèce* – that *l'Homme doit nourrir la femme* (VII:248). This rule would extend to all women, including those without the direct support of a husband or family (249).

[50] Saint-Simon's principle that 'tous les hommes doivent se regarder comme frères' is set forth in 'l'Appel aux philanthropes' which (in 1821) closed the first part of his *Système industriel*. 'Les crétiens d'aujourd'hui sont appelés par Dieu à tirer les grandes conséquences politiques du principe général qui a été révés aux crétiens primitifs. Ces conséquences sont que le pouvoir temporel appartienne aux hommes utiles, laborieux et pacifiques; que le pouvoir spirituelle appartienne aux hommes qui possèdent les connaissances utiles à l'espèce humaine; en un mot, que le système industriel et scientifique se constitue' (cited in Gouhier, 1933–41, III:231).

[51] 'Toute la régénération pratique peut se réduire à systématiser dignement les tendances spontanées de l'industrie moderne vers le caractère collectif . . . Une existence où chacun travaille habituellement pour autrui devient mieux accessible au sentiment social que l'activité militaire' (X:57).

Comte took the argument one step further. The complex organisational structure of an advanced social organism implied not only differentiated tasks, but also differentiated skills, knowledge and even personalities.[52] In the end, therefore, in order to obviate the socially fragmenting effects of an intricate division of labour, what was needed was not so much a countervailing moral–affective unison as the achievement of a polyphonic harmony.[53] The machines of industry, and more especially the social machine of industrial society itself, would work harmoniously towards the common good only if each element of that machine took it upon itself to serve the social interest as an independently operating agent of the whole.

Of course the religion of Humanity had homogenising elements. Its cult and doctrine of Humanity were to be the same for all. But the *régime* was designed to moralise each particular *serviteur* with attention to the specific subjective requirements of serving the appointed office, given its particular place in the technical division of labour and the social chain of coordination and command. Altogether, then, through a combination of differential socialisation (confirmed, in career terms, at the point of *destination* (IV:123)) and all-suffusing *bienveillance*, Positive Religion was designed to produce and reproduce the subjectivity of that ideal synthetic subject: the fully social individual.

We may concur with Mill that the pervasively intrusive and obsessively systematised religious apparatus that Comte envisaged was at variance with the cultivation of independent thinking and action necessary for the perfectly *voluntary* cooperation that was its stated goal.[54] His second

---

[52] 'Les diverses aspirations qui résultent successivement de l'initiation humaine se trouvent ainsi réalisés simultanément, malgré leur apparente contradiction, due seulement à l'insuffisance de la synthèse provisoire. Toujours fondée sur l'ensemble de notre constitution, la discipline positive doit également seconder l'extension et l'harmonie de nos attributs quelconques' (x:46).

[53] It was on these grounds that Comte criticised the contemporary revolutionary left. Besides ignoring the need for *la continuité historique* (VII:160), it stressed a homogenising solidarity that would suppress individuality altogether. 'L'ignorance des lois réelles de la sociabilité se manifeste d'abord dans la dangereuse tendance du communisme à comprimer toute individualité. Outre qu'on oublie ainsi la prépondérance naturelle de l'instinct personnel, on méconnait l'un des deux caractères fondamentaux de l'organisme collectif, où la séparation des fonctions n'est pas moins nécessaire que leur concours . . . Le grand problème humaine consiste à concilier, autant que possible, cette libre division avec une convergence non moins urgente. Une préoccupation exclusive de cette dernière condition tendrait à détruire toute activité réelle, et même toute vraie dignité, en supprimant toute responsabilité' (VII:158).

[54] For Mill, Comte's attempt to theorise the conditions for voluntary cooperation within a spontaneous division of labour so emphasised *l'esprit de système* that it was invisible even as an aim. 'It never seems to enter into his conceptions that any one could object, *ab initio*, and ask, why this universal systematizing, systematizing, systematizing? Why is it necessary that all human life should point to one object, and be cultivated into a system of means to a single end?' (Mill, 1961:141).

mechanism of social unity, with its stress on doctrinal and cultic unity, is hard to square with the cultural exigencies of the third; yet both are supposed to operate at once. To which extent, there is indeed a contradiction in Comte's thinking. It should be noted, though, that the goal embodied in this third form of social tie – the achievement of an individuated community that would finally sublate entirely the antinomy of individual and society – is maximal. It is a limit case of sociality which, as an ideal for thought and practice, would be hard to exceed. In this respect, moreover, Comte is closer to the early Marx than to any kind of reforming liberalism. Marx's conception of the reconciliation of individual and society within 'human society or social humanity' (Marx and Engels, 1947:199), in which all will regard themselves immediately as social individuals ('the complete return of man to himself as a *social* (i.e. human) being' (1964:135)) and in which the 'free development of each is the condition for the free development of all' (Feuer, 1959:29), is echoed in the finally triumphant Humanity which Comte himself aimed to help make come to pass.

Marx's understanding of this ideal is doubtless more appealing than Comte's. He placed greater emphasis on the many-sided flowering of the individual. He also held to a considerably less directive notion of how such social individualism might arise. Marx (but not Stalin or Mao) saw no need for a *Kulturkampf* against 'bourgeois individualism', still less for the vast moralising and propagandistic apparatus represented by Comte's new *pouvoir spirituel*. By the same token, however, Marx could be said to have been one-sided in the other direction. In *The German Ideology*, the revolution itself serves as a once-and-for-all cleansing of 'the muck of ages' (Marx and Engels, 1947:69), and he has nothing to say about the reproduction, and vitalisation, of the moral culture that might be required for the 'free cooperation of free individuals' thereafter. Though Marx himself can hardly be held responsible, this left future socialists to that extent theoretically defenceless against the authoritarian and coercive strategies through which 'actually existing socialisms' attempted, this century, to close the gap.

Without arguing the need to abolish capitalism (the new order, in embryo, is already here), Durkheim's concern for 'moral education' and the restoration of 'professional associations' is preoccupied with just this issue. His *Division of Labour* aims to address Comte's inconsistency by drawing a sharp distinction between the two types of solidarity – the one founded in a unity of social sentiment and belief, the second in a functional interlock between differentiated and morally autonomous individuals – which Comte's perfected industrial order implausibly combines. Durkheim's disentanglement of organic from mechanical solidarity, and his assignment of them to historically successive social types, introduced a powerful corrective into the Comtean model. At the same time, Durkheim considerably abbreviated the Comtean problematic of the social tie, not only by dimensionally reducing its complicated mapping of the place of 'sentiments' in the cohesion and life of the social body, but also by ignoring (rather than, as was necessary, reformulating) its attention, in both respects, to the dimension of time.

Love and the psyche

Comte's 'treatise on theoretic morals', which he never lived to complete, was to be the second volume of the *Synthèse subjective*, 'instituant la connaissance de la nature humaine' (x:542). It was conceived as the summit of his system, a third system after those of Positive Philosophy and Positive Politics, which would unite theory with practice by placing the understanding of individual human subjectivity on a finally scientific basis. Just as his social theory was couched as a story of society's necessary progress towards perfect unity, his 'positive theory of the soul' (VII:731) unfolds a vision of its ideal but realisable perfection, with each perfection being assumed necessary for the achievement of the other. It is the broadly 'sociological' dimension of this theory which I have been considering so far. But to grasp more fully the character, and limitations, of Compte's conception of love and the social body, we must also scrutinise its psychological presuppositions. These were to be the topic of *La science de morale*'s first chapter, which aimed to advance a 'positive' framework for understanding the place of love in the economy of the individual psyche. While that chapter remained unwritten, its intended material, under the rubric of 'cerebral physiology', is already introduced in the *Système du politique positive* (VII:694–703) and summarised in *Catéchisme positiviste* (XI:231–41). The bare schema is presented in 'Tableau systématique de l'âme' (VII:facing 726).

In the nascent neuro-physiology of his day, three hypotheses, whose factuality he assumed to be demonstrated, caught Comte's attention. Together they promised to provide a scientific bridge between the physical and 'moral' study of *l'Homme*. The *first* was that the brain housed not only the mental faculties, but also those governing motor activity and, more significantly, the receptors and control switches for passions and impulses as well (VII:680). Understanding 'cerebral physiology', then, was key to breaking from a purely speculative (and introspective) approach to what had classically been called the problem of the soul, and in the eighteenth century of 'human nature'. The *second* was that these three sets of faculties were lodged in specifically locatable regions of the cerebral apparatus, and that this determined the commerce they had both with one another and with the organism's internal and external milieu (VII:682). The *third* was that the three cerebral functions, pertaining to sentiment, intellect and action, could be further subdivided into component functions. Each corresponded to a distinct feature or capacity of the 'moral personality' as classically understood, and each was similarly locatable, with its own neural sub-system and 'cerebral ganglion', in a specific region of the brain (VII:684).

What interests me here is not the empirical basis of these claims but the psychological assumptions which this schema, and particularly those aspects formulated under hypotheses two and three, permitted Comte to introduce as givens within his system.

From the second hypothesis (localisation of the three principal faculties), Comte derived an overall thesis about the relation between 'cerebral physiology' and the healthy, because harmonious, functioning of the psyche. 'The speculative and active regions of the brain have nervous communications with the senses and the muscles, so that they can perceive the outside world and modify it. In contrast, the affective region, which forms the principal mass, has no direct links at all with the outside, and only connects with it indirectly through its relations with (the faculties of) intelligence and activity' (XI:228). At the same time, the affective region of the brain is in the centre, and like the brain itself therefore has two symmetrical halves. Unlike the faculties of sensation/cognition and action/motion, then, which are 'intermittent' in their function, those pertaining to feelings and impulses are active all the time (VII:690). As a result, 'emotive life doubly constitutes the unity of the human or animal soul, whether as a principle of consensus or as a common source of its continuity' (ibid.).

The import of this topography in the context of the Comtean narrative about positivisation is dramatic. At the highest point of scientific development, when the human understanding of the human mind – and thus the very subject of scientific knowledge – itself becomes a topic for positive enquiry, what reason itself had deemed to be the self-sufficiency and psychic sovereignty of the rational ego is completely overthrown. In Comte's new picture – which effectively put Hume's anti-Cartesian scepticism on a 'scientific' basis – reason is not so much a slave to the passions as replaced by them at the directing (and literal) centre of the brain. Mental development itself, on this view, is driven by the need 'to clarify the action which some passion or other commanded' (VII:688). Not that passions alone would suffice. For the affective region is in every sense blind. It receives its impulses not through the senses, from the outside world, but from the body-world under the skin. Left to its own devices, its direction would be impractical and incoherent. For the human organism, then, to survive and thrive in its active relations with the world, the impulses that drive thought and action have continual need for the 'counsel' of the one and the externalising capacity of the other. Feeling impels action aided by thought. 'Act from feeling, think to act' (ibid.). The harmonious functioning of this tripartite system is, for Comte, the harmony of the soul itself.

However, given the asymmetry of the three principal regions of the brain, and of their respective relations with *le dedans* and *le dehors*, how is such harmony to be conceived? Neither thought nor will – those two shibboleths of radical Enlightenment reason – could serve as pivots around which an integrated subjectivity might form. This would fly in the face of the dominant role played in the mental apparatus by the affects, both within the apparatus as a whole and in the life of the other two mental faculties. The achievement of harmony, therefore, among feeling, thinking and acting must depend on the disposition of the affects themselves.

And so to Comte's third hypothesis. This was that each of the three main regions of the brain interrelated more specific capacities each of which had its own independently locatable cerebral basis. In his *tableau systématique*,[55] Comte classified eighteen such functions in all. Three of these, *Activité*, subdivided into *Courage* and *Prudence*, and *Firmeté*, *d'où prudence*, were classified as *qualités pratiques* or *résultats*. Five were classified as *fonctions intellectuelles* or *moyens*. These included four for *Conception*, subdivided into modes of thinking described as concrete–synthetic, abstract–analytic, inductive–generalising and deductive–systematising, plus one for *Expression*, which incorporated all forms of communication from the mimetic and oral to the written. It is the ten remaining functions, however, on which we need to focus. Gathered together under the abstract category of *Principe*, they composed what Comte called 'the affective motors: propensities when active; feelings when passive' (VII:726).

---

[55] Comte's 'Classification positive des dix-huit fonctions du cerveau humain ou tableau systématique de l'âme', which 'systematised' the 'cerebral physiology' he drew from Gall, was composed in November 1846 as part of his 'moral regeneration' (VII:679). It is reproduced at the end of the first volume of *Politique positive* (VII:facing 726) and again as an appendix to the *Catéchisme*. While he claimed therein to have mapped the brain's essential organs and functions, he frankly admitted to the incompleteness of its empirical basis. 'C'est pourqoui le nombre et le site des organes intellectuels et moraux s'y trouvent seuls indiqués, sans rien préciser même sur leur forme ou leur grandeur. Une étude objective, qui n'est pas encore instituée convenablement, peut seule compléter cette théorie subjective du cerveau, en déterminant la constitution propre de chacun d'eux' (IX:239).

As with every other aspect of Comte's taxonomies, the ten affects are arranged in a series with the logical property that each succeeding member of the series is dependent upon, but higher than, and therefore capable of modifying (within set limits), the one that comes before (VII:694–704). In ascending order, we have, first, the seven 'personal motors', sub-grouped into those of Interest and Ambition. The instincts of Interest were divided into those of Preservation, which comprised the nutritive, sexual and maternal impulses (these last two distinguished as interests of the 'race' rather than of the individual), and those of Improvement. These comprised the military instinct (improvement 'by destruction') and the industrial instinct (improvement 'by construction'). The *moteur* of Ambition, finally, was subdivided into the Temporal and the Spiritual, whence Pride, or 'the need for power', and Vanity, or 'the need for approbation'.

To complete the series – no surprise – the seven egoistic instincts are followed by the three social ones we have already encountered, i.e. the three species of Comtean love. First are the 'special' altruistic instincts of Attachment and Veneration. Then comes the 'general' one at the very top of the scale: 'Benevolence or Universal Love (sympathy), *humanity*'. The first two forms of love are 'special' because the immediate object of affection is particular individuals – companions and contemporaries in the case of *attachement*, the great and the dead in the case of *vénération* (VII:702–4). *Bienveillance*, on the other hand, initially cultivated in the form of parental love, is 'general' by virtue of the necessary vagueness of the future individuals it aims to benefit.[56] Christianity, of course, rendered the seven egoistic instincts as the seven deadly sins.[57] But it did not include at all these last three, 'social', instincts in its catalogue of innate human impulses. For believers, the disinterested love – *agape*, *charité* – that had the power to redeem fallen nature could only be conceived as coming into the soul from without. That is, through the mediating sacrifice of the Son, through priestly sacraments, and through the mysterious activity of the Spirit, all of which amounted to a free gift – the grace – of God. For Comte, on the other hand, while an external factor was still needed – society, in its march to perfection from family to

---

[56] This implied that *bienveillance* could not extend to the living. This is inconsistent, however, with Comte's characterisation of it as the same, in affectivity, as Christian charity (VII:701). The contradiction (already noted) arising from his reluctance to think out fully the distinction between *bonté* and *bienveillance* runs right through his account.

[57] It is noteworthy however that pride, the deadliest Christian sin, is for Comte the egoistic element closest (as number seven on the scale) to the social sentiments. For Comte the egoistic impulses were not evil *per se*, but only if in unbridled control of action and intelligence (VII:691–2).

country to Humanity – there were innate psychic materials upon which to build.[58]

Comte's series of propensities and sentiments is morally qualitative, running from the lowest and most vegetative of the base instincts to the highest and most angelic of the 'social' ones. But it exemplifies what Comte takes to be a physiological ordering as well. While the intellectual faculties are in the frontal lobe, and the active ones immediately behind (VII:684), the 'affective motors' are located in a kind of sphere that runs from the centre to the back of the cerebellum. They are so arranged, moreover, that the highest are towards the middle, with the lower ones fanning out in a nether region towards the lower back. The effect of this arrangement is that the outer and lower motors are closest to the direct ('vegetative') impulses flowing from the rest of the body. They are subject, therefore, to relatively higher and more continuous states of excitation than those located more deeply in the cerebral mass (ibid.). Hence, Comte believed, without any recourse to a doctrine of original sin, a physiological rationale could be given for what he took to be the principal practical problem of human community: the perennial conflict between *personnalité* (the egoistic instincts which 'alone motivate lower beings') and *sociabilité* (which 'in higher animals is joined with it' (VII:691)). The worthier and less selfish the component motive, the lower its degree of physical energy, and the lower its immediate capacity to influence conduct. However, the contiguity of the highest affects with the mental faculties gave it the greater power, when roused, to 'direct and stimulate the intelligence', just as, conversely, egoism had less need of intelligence to define the object of its own desire (VII:693). Overall, then, 'the imaginary conflict between nature and grace' is both explained and rendered soluble. For Positivism, it is 'replaced by the real opposition between the posterior mass of the brain, the seat of the personal instincts, and its interior region, where there are distinct organs for the sympathetic impulses and the intellectual functions' (XI:237).

Now, if we set the social question aside, this motivational regime does not, at first sight, present any special difficulty for the individual psyche. In complex beings, 'general harmony depends only on spontaneous impulses being subordinated to some single motor' (VII:700). A well-functioning interchange among sentiments, thought and action might well be imagined, then, on the basis of the spontaneous primacy of the

---

[58] 'Le grand saint Paul, en construisant sa doctrine générale de la lutte permanente entre la nature et la grâce, ébaucha réellement, à sa manière, l'ensemble du problème moral, non-seulement pratique mais aussi théorique. Car, cette précieuse fiction compensait provisoirement l'incompatibilité radicale du monothéisme avec l'existence naturelle des penchants bienveillants, qui poussent toutes les créatures à s'unir mutuellement au lieu de se vouer isolément à son créateur' (XI:225).

'lower' instincts. This indeed, argues Comte, is the typical condition of 'lower beings' (VII:691), just as it also characterised the situation of humanity during its long *état préparatoire*. In fact 'these lower exigencies [will] continue to dominate our own species, at least indirectly . . . when everyone is living for others. For if basic conservation did not arouse any personal needs, our collective direction would be as deprived of direction as each individual life' (VII:692). Two considerations suggested, however, that a psychological order organised around a pervasive *égoïsme* could not be *perfectly* harmonious. In the first place, the egoistic impulses are themselves a cacophony of inconsistent promptings (VIII:10). One psychological interest can clash with another. Gratifying the desire for power or approbation requires curbing more immediate appetites, while it is apt to provoke conflicts with others which might even place survival needs at risk. The instinct for improvement implies deferral of immediate consumption, while the latter may be at variance with the 'maternal instinct' and with species interest in successful biological reproduction. Overall, the egoistic self is intrinsically incoherent. In satisfying its appetites in relation to *le dedans*, it has an ongoing need for prudent psychological self-management. But on what basis? If instinct x is stronger, how can instinct y, at a higher but weaker level, direct the intelligence and the active character so as to regulate it and defer its lower gratifications? Such a personality is not, then, self-sufficiently stable.[59] Its stability and performative success depend on the growth of a self-disciplining force that is constantly at variance with the immediate promptings of impulse and that must nevertheless find some principle (but on what fixed basis?) in terms of which to regulate their fluctuating play.

This, though, is not the only difficulty. The assumption that the moral, spiritual or psychological nature of even the egoistic individual can be comprehended as if it were an asocial monad is impossible to sustain – not only in principle (Comte's human being, even *qua* biological organism, is always already socially implicated) but as soon as we take note of the fact that all three cerebral regions must be *developed* for there to be any organised personality at all. This assumes, *inter alia*, intelligence, ratiocination etc., and therefore (at the least) language, which is evidently a social product. Furthermore, with the possible exception of the instinct for physical survival – *l'instinct nutritif* – the very concept of egoistic instincts presupposes a social environment of some

---

[59] 'Les instincts inférieurs dirigent la conduite d'après des motifs purement internes, dont la multiplicité et la variation ne lui permettent aucune marche fixe, ni même aucun caractère habituel, sauf pendant les exigences périodiques des principaux appétits' (VII:700).

kind in which these instincts are deployed. Each succeeding egoistic impulse in Comte's 'positive classification' has, in fact, a higher social component than the one before.[60] The instinct for species survival follows that of individual survival. Instincts of improvement succeed those of interest, wherein the pacific conquest of nature follows the aggressive conquest of fellow Man. Beyond these, finally, the instincts of ambition – defined as crucial intermediaries in the ego's ascent to sociability (VII:698) – concern the articulation of individuals to the social orderings of power and status. In all these cases, and to an increasing extent, the play of self-interest already presupposes the implication of the egoistic individual in a social nexus entailing some degree of cooperation. Which in turn, on Comte's assumptions about the social tie, presupposes that the social instincts (in a similarly ascending scale of sociability) are themselves already actively in play.

But if even the dominance of egoistic instincts presupposes, at least indirectly, that the social ones are to some degree active, then the regulating function of the purely egoistic ego is significantly complicated. For, as the guiding principle for thought and action, it is placed in contradiction to these same social instincts (VII:692). Whence *le grand problème humain*: a split individual, part beast, part angel, in a continual state of internal civil war. That, indeed, is how Christian moralists from St Augustine to Kant had always seen the matter. But for Comte you cannot be just a little bit social. Once on the road to sociability, real harmony ('harder to realise than egoistic unity, but far superior in plenitude and stability' (VIII:9)) can only come into being when the altruistic instincts themselves become dominant within the affective apparatus; at which point it would be these, rather than self-interest, that would drive thought and action, and regulate the expression of all the other affects.

It is just here that the Comtean requisites of social and individual perfection converge. The higher instincts can only dominate the lower ones if they are strengthened through exercise (VII:92). And this could only be the case if the social tie had developed to the stage, beyond family and patriotism, where particular attachments had become subordinate to general ones.[61] But the exercise of altruistic instincts, and their enhanced power vis-à-vis the egoistic ones, and indeed the pre-

---

[60] '. . . il s'agit de décomposer peu à peu, d'abord la personnalité, puis la sociabilité, en penchants vraiment irréducibles . . . [E]ntre l'égoïsme complet et le pur altruisme, il faut intercaller les diverses affections intermédiaires, en procédant toujours dans la décomposition binaire' (VII:692–3).

[61] 'L'état social tend toujours vers cette inversion radicale de l'économie individuelle, parce qu'il développe nécessairement le plus faible instinct et comprime le plus énergique' (VII:692).

dominance of benevolence itself within the altruistic, could never be sufficiently guaranteed by the mere existence of society in its highest form – i.e. that formed by individuals out of their generous, selfless and voluntary cooperation. The system of instincts within the individual, like that of organs in society, is entropic. Without 'habitual exercise', they fade.[62] The highest instincts, because of their lowest bio-individual intensity, must be elicited and exercised all the time. Hence, once again, the supplementary need, implicit in the sociological ideal of perfection itself, for the organised social intervention of religion with all its strenuously demanding practices.

This still leaves us, though, with a puzzle. How, in practice, could the spontaneous relation of instinctual forces – *l'économie individuelle* – be harmoniously reversed? What happens to the lower instincts, and their force, when they are subordinated to higher ones? Even granted the muscular analogy according to which exercise can increase strength, where is the enhanced *energy* of the higher instincts to come from?

One possible answer to this last question is: from a common source. This would be the case in a model which conceived all the instincts as drawing from, and channelling, a common store of energy distributed throughout the body. Comte seems to be working with such a notion in his emphasis on the 'vegetative' as a basis for higher-order mental and affective functions (VII:594 et seq.) and in his implicit assumption that closing off one instinctual channel would make psychic energy available for active expression through another. Developing this further might have permitted him to formulate a theory of sublimation. However, he develops no such concept, holding rigorously to the hypothesis of a separate physiological locus for each of the ten instincts, and thus to a schema that bars the way to any suggestion that higher instincts are in some sense energetically derivative of lower ones. There is no theory of a larger Desire – nor for that matter of Lack – whose vicissitudes component instincts would all express.

Still less is there a Comtean theory of repression. Shutting down the valve on, let us say, the sexual instinct has no direct implication for the rise to power of 'benevolence'. Nor does its progressive diminution and displacement in the psychic economy of the sociated individual cause any distress or perverse secondary effects. If deprived of stimulus and opportunity, greed and lust simply atrophy, while the increasingly regular exercise of loving instincts can steadily enhance their own motivating power. For Comte, then, unlike Freud, the extreme altruistic

---

[62] This is stated as a general biological law, according to which 'tout appareil animal se développe par l'exercice habituel, et s'amoindrit, ou même s'atrophie, d'après la désuétude prolongée' (VII:608).

self-regulation of individuals in the 'normal' state of advanced industrial civilisation can in principle be perfectly harmonious, without any troubling rise of aggression or inner discontent.

I have already mentioned some instances of the institutional lengths to which Comte's social program would have gone in procuring and sustaining the requisite instinctual training. In the positive reinforcement of the best, private prayer would consume at least two hours a day in the schedule of each Humanist faithful,[63] and this is not to count the weekly, monthly and annual rituals of the 'public cult', nor the round of domestic 'consecrations' which were to accompany the sacraments of the life-course. In restraining the worst, a rich tapestry of images, beliefs and prohibitions would have ensured that the sexual instinct in particular was given the most minimal and disdainful play.[64] Priests, to be sure, in almost Lutheran fashion were commanded to marry. Marriage was obligatory for all.[65] But this was not just to prevent immorality by channelling sexual desire within the restraining responsibilities of marriage and parenthood. Still less was it a ratification of sexuality itself. Marriage was solely to bring a man under the uplifting influence of his wife. The ideal relationship would be one based entirely, indeed, on the loving sentiments of *attachement*, *vénération* and *bienveillance*, a marriage which would exclude lusts of the flesh altogether.[66]

As Comte proudly confesses in the dedicatory preface to the *Système*, this was precisely the height to which he had been led in his own relationship with the saintly Clotilde.[67] In the inspiring cult of her blessed memory, he had been happily able to sustain the sublime love she called forth, together with the coincident overcoming (or atrophying) of bodily desire.[68] An argument that Comte considered con-

---

[63] Regular prayers would take up one hour in the morning, half an hour at midday and fifteen minutes in bed while falling asleep (to be repeated in the event of waking up in the middle of the night) (XI:111). For Comte, the time spent on 'l'intime amélioration journalière' would substitute for time currently wasted in 'lectures vicieuses et les diversions inutiles ou funestes' (XI:112).

[64] 'Outre que l'éducation positive fera partout sentir les vices d'un tel instinct et suscitera l'espoir continu de sa désuétude, l'ensemble du régime final doit naturellement instituer, à son égard, un traitement révulsif plus efficace que les austérités catholiques' (X:286).

[65] 'Tous sont obligés au mariage, du moins subjectif, afin de subir dignement les influences affectives' (X:255).

[66] The 'superior perfection of a chaste relation' was to be celebrated in a special *fête* during each second month of the year, itself dedicated to *le lien conjugal dans tous ses modes* (X:138).

[67] The 'purity' and 'nobility' of such a relationship are stressed at every turn. It is summarily characterised as 'une sainte intimité, à la fois fraternelle et paternelle' (VII:iii).

[68] Pickering (1993:490–1) cites a letter from Comte to Clotilde in which he relates that his sexual relations with Massin came to an end as early as 1834, a year after another manic-depressive episode. Massin had complained in a letter to Blainville in 1839 of

firmed by personal experience we might prefer to decode as a rational-ised hysteria.[69] Be that as it may, what Comte's encomiums to Clotilde also dramatise is the crucial importance of *gender* to the ultimate coherence of his instinctual theory, and indeed of his social theory as well.

When we look at his scale of instincts we can see that the question of gender surfaces at just one small point. After the primal instinct for individual survival come two for the conservation of the species. All the other instincts are common to both sexes, but here the instinct divides into a male form, dominated by *l'instinct sexuel*, and a female form, dominated by *l'instinct maternel*. Of these, 'the first is more energetic and less noble than the second' (VII:696). In procreation, then, there is a fundamental, and innate, asymmetry with respect to the instincts drawn into play; which in turn provides a biological basis for asserting that men and women have an inherently different moral formation. The male desire for immediate self-gratification contrasts with a female desire for motherhood, a condition that demands self-sacrifice, family solidarity and a subordination of present to future needs. This pattern, moreover, is disjunctive. If men, 'dispersively' driven by sexual hunger, are natu-rally non-maternal, women, wanting only to love, can live without sex (VII:235). When Clotilde, the abandoned wife, insisted on a 'pure love' and a 'chaste union', she may have been restraining Comte, but she was not being *self*-restrained. Asexual *tendresse* and a devoted benevolence were supreme moral qualities she had just by virtue of being *une femme*.

Comte's dichotomy of male and female psychological character is hardly original. His importation of it into his instinct theory served only to buttress the emphatic support he gave to the high Romantic *culte de la femme*. In historical context we may only marvel at the extravagance, and revived medievalism, of his version.[70] A decade after libertarian

relational problems with 'physical causes that I would not dare to write or even say to a doctor'. Comte claimed to have conquered his strong sexual impulses at the age of thirty, as an act of moral will. Perhaps; but he likely also became impotent as a combined result of his mental illness and of anxiety provoked by Massin's open infidelities and general refusal of femininity as Comte defined it .

[69] Kofman's thesis is that Comte was defending himself against a female self-identifica-tion, and that the episode with Clotilde enabled him to switch from a 'male' scientific voice (that nonetheless masked a 'female' religious one) to the openly 'female' one assumed in his post-1847 priestly persona as *serviteur de l'Humanité*. From this angle, Comte's oeuvre and his personal–sexual difficulties were all of a piece: a phantasmatic effort to become the perfect woman in giving birth, virginally, to a perfect child. 'Ce qu'il craint (désire) ce n'est pas seulement d'être pris pour une femme, c'est d'être assimilé à une de ces femmes qui ne peuvent se montrer au grand jour, à une putain, comme l'était sa propre femme' (1978:29).

[70] The *culte de la femme* was to be the cornerstone of the private, as opposed to public, system of Positivist worship. It accorded with 'l'aptitude naturelle de chaque digne

Saint-Simonians were journeying east to make contact with the ancient cult of Isis and proclaiming 'the rehabilitation of the flesh' (Manuel 1862:151–7), and a decade after the founding of the American women's movement at Seneca Falls, Comte's contribution to thinking through what he, like others, called *l'émancipation de la Femme*,[71] was a retrograde attempt to synthesise the profane tradition of chivalry[72] with the sacred one of Maryolatry, improbably grasped through the twin lenses of contemporary science and the *Imitatio Christi*.

What needs to be emphasised, though, is not the curiosity value of Comte's gender theory, but its crucial place in his whole conceptualisation of moral–instinctual perfection. Woman appears in the story as a *dea ex machina*. She is the crucial 'intermediary between men and Humanity' (x:67). What permits Her to play this role is that for women the maternal instinct is, precisely, after hunger, the lowest and strongest. It includes, at the same time, a strong propensity for selfless nurturing. That is, for *bienveillance*, which is the highest instinct of all. In the case of women, then, the most altruistic impulse is directly stimulated[73] by a lower impulse built into their very egoism (xi:234). In the case of men,

femme à représenter l'Humanité . . . la meilleure personnification d'un ensemble fondé sur l'amour' (x:108–9). The 'normal' private female embodiments of *l'Humanité* were *les anges gardiennes* of mother, wife and sister. It should be noted, at the same time, that the public cult outlined in the *Calendrier* personified Humanity exclusively through male *serviteurs*. They alone (but only as *particular* men) were suitable to represent the march of intellectual, political and techno-economic progress (xi:143).

71 For Comte, 'emancipation' did not imply the 'anarchical dream' of gender equality, but the freedom of women to develop according to their own (essentially affective and domestic) nature (vii:244). The crucial development in this regard had been the late-medieval rise of chivalry and courtly love. 'Ainsi, le moyen âge, en émancipant la femme, fournit la base générale de l'organisation propre au mouvement moderne où cette influence radicale, qui, quoique passive, était universelle et continue, préserva l'ordre moral d'une entière dissolution' (ix:516).

72 Positivism would establish a new chivalric order, recruited from the patriciate. 'Ceux d'entre eux qui se sentiront animés d'une générosité équivalente à celle de leurs héroïques prédécesseurs, consacront, non leur épée, mais leur fortune, leur activité, et, au besoin, toute leur énergie, à la libre défense de tous les opprimés. De même qu'au moyen âge, cet office volontaire s'exercera surtout envers les classes spécialement exposées aux persécutions temporelles, c'est-à-dire les femmes, les philosophes, et les prolétaires' (vii:256–7). The protective function of the new chivalric order towards 'all the oppressed' parallels the principle that *l'homme doit nourrir la femme*, coupled with a similar obligation placed on *la classe actif* towards *la class contemplatif*. The gender coding is consistent throughout. The male principle (the temporal/active power) supports and protects the female principle (the spiritual/affective power) which transfigures the former through love.

73 The maternal instinct for Comte is nonetheless not to be confused with altruism itself. Each has its own distinct *siège* in the cerebral apparatus. In the least morally developed women motherhood can be entirely selfish. 'On reconnait que l'enfant peut constituer directement pour la mère, autant que le père, une simple possession personnelle, objet de domination, et souvent de cupidité, plus qu'une affection désintéressé' (xi:234). This can be read, perhaps, as a verdict on his own mother.

on the other hand, sexual desire is the 'most disruptive of egoistic impulses' (x:287) and is taken to have no redeeming moral feature at all. Nor, setting his face firmly against Plato's view, can eros sublimate into desire for transcarnal unity. Eros is immoral, not divine. Men, then, are morally inferior. To become benevolent they have to ascend the whole instinctual scale, while for women a raw form of benevolence is natural even in a socially rudimentary context.[74]

It follows that men learn to love (in the exalted sense) *through* women. In Positive Religion, it is through Woman that Man is saved. Hence the crucial mediating influence accorded to women in Comte's vision of a perfected social body – not only in the Humanist cult that pervades Positive Polity's final state, but also in day-to-day practice. 'Since the whole existence of the Great Being is founded on love . . . the affective sex is naturally its most perfect representative, and at the same time its principal ministry' (XI:105). Only women, restored and revered as a moral force, can counter the egoistic rebellion of head over heart that has characterised the metaphysical upheaval; only they, through the affective re-education of men, can make possible the constructive way out.[75]

Love and the other

Comte's model of the instincts leads him to identify as a supremely felicitous trend in industrialism the ever more sublimated, but also unhappy, course of *Kultur* depicted by Freud in *Civilisation and Its Discontents* (1949:121–2). For Comte, the advance of civilisation is likewise built on love and renunciation. But the former has no direct ties with sexuality, and the latter is a matter of affective training which can reduce *les penchants inférieurs* without remainder. Thus, in the final stage of human development, duty and happiness harmoniously combine in a moral perfection which, on the basis of bodily health, but also on the basis of vanquishing the body's socially superfluous demands, reveals the highest sentiments to be the true source of *le bonheur suprême*.[76]

[74] As Comte explains in the Catechism: 'La supériorité de votre sexe le dispense souvent d'une telle préparation, en le disposant à aimer aussitôt qu'il trouve des objets de l'amour, sans y cherchant aucune satisfaction personnelle. Mais la grossièreté masculine ne peut presque jamais passer de ce préambule indirecte' (XI:235).

[75] The regenerative role of women is discussed in chap. 3 of *Politique positive*, especially VII:205–13. Its twin pillars are marriage, where they are to play privately a morally moderating role, and the *culte de la Femme*, primarily private but also celebrated in leap years through a *fête générale des saintes Femmes*.

[76] 'Notre bonheur consistera surtout à aimer; et nous sentirons que l'amour, plus qu'aucune autre affection, se développe par un exercice qui, chez lui seul, peut également convenir à tous les individus à la fois, en s'accroissant avec un tel concours'

Today we would find implausible both the historical realism of Comte's model (advanced capitalism, if with ongoing cultural conflict, has become 'repressively desublimated' (Marcuse, 1966)) and its idealisation. Besides its neuroses, a Freudian would say, the psycho-social ideal Comte imagined as the apotheosis of Love would be disturbed in practice by undischarged aggression and the devitalising effects of hyper-repressively diverting libidinal energy from Love to Death. 'After sublimation, the erotic component no longer has the power to bind the whole of the destructive elements that were previously confined with it, and these are released in the form of inclinations to aggression and destruction' (Freud, 1950:80).

But this is not the only problem with Comte's conceptualisation of love and the social tie. There is a further flaw in his theory of affects, especially as it enters into an attempted synthesis between individual–organismic and social determinations. This is that the three species of love, like all the instincts, are figured, purely and exclusively, as forces which emanate outwards from psyche to world. Love, whether its object is personal or general, is like a beam from a lighthouse. Neither the direction nor the strength of the light is the slightest bit affected by the object it illuminates. There is no 'between', no mutual implication, which might connect, other than mechanically, the terms which it binds together. Curiously, then, Comtean love is not social in its substance but only in its effects.

This is why *attachement* occupies the lowest rung in his ladder of love. The mere liking of individuals for one another is conceived as the least altruistic social affect, and the weakest basis for the social tie. And so it is, considering what Comte's narrowly objectivising thematic of love as a one-way emotive force permits him to leave out. In his conception of the direct affection of one individual for another there is no taking the place of the other, no identification, no sympathy. The ego is neither pierced nor does it reach out in response to others' concrete, mortal existence. The Other for whom we live may always be represented (normally in memory) by an individual face; but it does not presence as 'face'.[77] Nor does it make any difference to the sentiment itself if affection is returned.

(VII:353). 'Confondant le devoir et le bonheur, la religion positive les fait irrévocablement consister dans le perfectionnement moral, source exclusive de la véritable unité' (X:324).

[77] This is to say, in Levinasian terms, that there is no (absolute) alterity in Comte's *autrui*. 'The face is present in its refusal to be contained. In this sense it cannot be comprehended, that is encompassed . . . The Other remains infinitely transcendent, infinitely foreign . . . [T]he ethical relationship which subtends discourse is not a species of consciousness whose ray emanates from the I; it puts the I in question. This putting in question emanates from the other' (Levinas, 1969:194–5). Comte's *autrui* is a thematised totality; Levinas's is an unthematisable infinity.

Mutual *attachement* has no intersubjective dimension; indeed, no interaction through which a bond of mutual sympathy might be forged, and
even grow. There is no dialectic of recognition. Not only, finally, is
Comte's analysis of attachment short on the subjective side of human
interactivity, it also lacks attention to the objective aspect of group
dynamics. If de Maistre's theory of sacrifice and substitution
(1971:291–8) pointed the way to an analysis of gifts and counter-gifts,
Comte's instinctualist conception of love and the social tie displaces any
lead he might have followed. *Attachement* cannot build or strengthen
through give and take. There is no symbolic exchange, no bonding
through (or conflictual politics of) *reciprocity*.

Attachement, then, is a weak affective tie, even in the most intensely
personal case. It has deep bonding power only in so far as it provides a
framework within which the two higher forms of love, veneration and
benevolence, might flourish. The male–female couple, when properly
role-divided, provides the paradigm for such a possibility. It is as if a
hydraulic principle is at work. To have higher social bonding power, love
must be drawn upwards, in worshipful respect and service, or else it
must flow down, as from parents to children, or from Humanity,
through her faithful servants, towards all her children. The altruism
Comte exalts is not only unilateral but thrives on the difference in
magnitude between the terms it connects.

From this, considered as an attempt to delineate a positively based
ideal of human community, two unfortunate consequences follow. First,
Comte's normative ideal of a perfected social–individual harmony
downplays both the instinctual basis for, and the strategic significance
of, direct individual ties with the living in favour of anonymous ties with
a general Other which projects into the future and gathers up the
memories of the dead. Within this generality of affection, the most
exalted ties to the social love-object are deflected away from the
present.[78] The gratitude for gifts received, which suffuses the sentiment
of benevolence, connects one generation with another, rather than this
generation with itself. To which extent, secondly, the gift, in Comte's
social ontology, is always one way. We can never repay Humanity for the
benefits of life, self and social milieu. In so far as we might aspire to do
so, by a life of service, the Humanity from whom we have received the
gift is already passed into subjectivity, while the Humanity our benevolence might benefit in future is in no position to give back. 'Thus
conceived, service to Humanity is essentially free. Each generation
should render freely to the next what it has freely received from the one

---

[78] 'Nous devons donc entrevoir avec les morts, et même les non-nées, un commerce plus
suivi, quoique moins spécial, qu'avec nos propres contemporains' (x:24).

before' (VIII:71). As a result, and however freely it flows, benevolence is all obligation. The highest form of love is expressed as an ethic and ethos of selfless service. As agents of the Humanity we cherish and revere, we have duties but can claim no rights.[79]

For all these reasons – the relatively weak instinctual basis for solidarity as against continuity, the privileging of the non-living Other, and the selflessness without reserve implied by the social debt – Comte's normative ideal of social–instinctual perfection is full of moral coercion. And it is so not only because of an instinctual theory which presupposes that the gratification of the lower impulses is at radical variance with gratification of the higher ones (it is a surplus-repressive model of a surplus-repressive economy),[80] but because of that theory's instinctually unidirectional character. The perfected social order which positive religion had to rebind, then, was not quite as perfect, even in Comtean terms, as he supposed. It was at once insufficiently solidary in itself – and so required the supplements of continual worship and sacerdotally supervised public opinion – and peopled by individuals so walled up in themselves that they were incapable of sympathy in anything like an intersubjective sense.

Comte was not wrong in imagining that industrialisation implied a deep transformation in the character of social relationships, that it rendered problematic pre-existing modes of group integration, and that thinking the good and bad possibilities of this required an understanding both of what Althusser called 'ideological reproduction' and of what Freudians call 'libidinal economy'. In this respect his thinking has an exemplary significance in the history of social thought. His intellectual madness, however, consisted in his attempt to rationalise as perfectly, and constitutively, 'social' an abstract benevolence which was split off both from desire and from any engagement with concrete–historical human beings.

---

[79] 'Dans l'état positif . . . l'idée de *droit* disparaît irrévocablement. Chacun a des devoirs, et envers tous; mais personne n'a aucun droit proprement dit' (VII:361; emphasis in original).

[80] Marcuse's *Eros and Civilisation* defines surplus repression as follows: '[W]hile any form of the reality principle demands a considerable degree and scope of repressive control over the instincts, the specific historical institutions of the reality principle and the specific interests of domination introduce *additional* controls over and above those indispensable for civilised human association. These additional controls arising from the specific institutions of domination are what we denote as *surplus–repressive*' (Marcuse, 1955:34). Gad Horowitz (1977) has considerably refined and developed this notion. The surplus–repressive character of Comte's social theory is hidden not only in his socio-morally reformed capitalism (an order in which domination is 'only' exercised by the whole over its parts), but also in a hierarchical conception of social and instinctual order which is irreducible at both levels, given the functional requirements of the bio-organism.

6   The path to perfection

For Comte, the coincidence of individual and collective perfection in the formation of a social body harmonised by love occurs only at the end of a long history. Nevertheless, this *summum bonum* is more than a regulative ideal, because, as in other grand narratives of progress, it finally *does* arrive, making visible, indeed, the logic of the process that had propelled it into being. Positivist principles, however, eschewed explanation in terms of final causes, and indeed explanation through causes at all. For Comte, then, demonstrating the necessary actualisation of social perfection required an inductive basis. It was a matter of 'instituting a true *liaison* between the historical facts' (v:8), together with the structural regularities by which these were always mediated.

This did not exempt Comte's construct from the charge by Durkheim, for example, that it was itself metaphysical, identifying 'historical development with an idea he already had of it', so that 'the facts seem to have reality only through the ideas which are their germ' (1964:19–20). At first sight, Comte's story about how *l'homme* becomes *l'Humanité* is metaphysical in an almost classic sense. It seems to unfold as an absolute idealism in which the logic of history is the logic of (the maturation and coming into self-possession of) mind itself. In his first version, in volume five of *Philosophie positive*, pride of place is given to the Law of Three Stages. Here the motor of social progress is the drive for knowledge as humanity's growing activity on, and in, 'the theatre of the terrestrial globe' (v:12) increasingly pushes the species to grasp and modify it as a law-ruled externality. In the second version, elaborated in the third volume of *Système de politique positive*, the logic of intellectual development is complemented by one of moral development.[1] Here the dominance of modal personality types by increasingly 'social' instincts correlates with social expansion and, with the passage from 'theologism' to positivity, similarly crosses a qualitative threshold in which altruism comes to prevail. If the first version tells the human story as essentially

---

[1] The new scheme is summarised in three 'fundamental laws' of social dynamics: 'nous devenons toujours plus intelligents, plus actifs, et plus aimants' (IX:72).

cognitive – the progress of knowledge – the second tells it as instinctual/ affective, as the awakening and elevation of the harmonising power of love. But in both cases the evolution dwelt on is inner. All proceeds as if subjectivity determines being and society is a supersubject, propelled towards an identity of essence and existence through the unfolding logic of its own mental and moral nature.

No doubt this is a metaphorics from which Comte never completely freed himself. Nevertheless, it is by no means his whole story. Intelligence may be constrained by its own static and dynamic laws to develop along a particular path, but the growth of knowledge was itself stimulated by, and always tended to harmonise with, the panoply of 'effective needs' (vi:634). These latter, moreover, were not simply given. They were generated in the interplay between physiological impulse and the external milieu. This interplay itself occurred as a social process. The prevailing mode of knowledge and related level of technical capacity shaped the prevailing institutional order, which provided a social medium (of advancing scale and complexity) for the moral/instinctual formation of individuals. The affects, likewise, had no independent logic of their own (ix:10–11). The prime mover of social and moral progress, in fact, was neither affect nor intellect, however crucial their conjoint transformation was to the final harmonic result. It was, rather, the third of Comte's categories of (human) existence, *l'activité*, 'which continually modifies the external world in accordance with the fundamental exigencies of our internal, corporeal and cerebral, constitution' (ix:55). From this angle, the key factor in the narrative of human perfection is the steady rise of organised, knowledge-based production – *l'industrie* – with its cumulating power to modify the physical milieu. The Positive transformation becomes possible, and necessary, when industry, made ever more powerful through natural science, becomes a predominant social power in its own right, thereby displacing military rule and promising the day when a united humanity will finally claim the wholly known earth for the satisfaction of its fully developed needs.[2]

Comte's ascent of Humanity, in sum, not only unfolds against the background of the limits and possibilities of a subjectivity shaped by the human brain. It is also determined, throughout, by a social logic, itself inscribed within a developing, and at root biologically prescribed, relationship between Man and Nature.[3] It is to these mediations, then,

---

[2] Or, in socio-theological terms: 'Voilà comment le Grand-Être, dans sa pleine maturité, prendra possession de son domaine planétaire, en y développant toutes les améliorations compatibles avec l'ordre universel' (x:61).

[3] '[L]'ordre moral de toute association humaine repose nécessairement sur son organisation intellectuelle, et celle-ci sur sa constitution matérielle. Or, cette dernière resterait, à son tour, sans fondement systématique, si elle était conçue isolément du milieu spécial

that we must turn if we wish to probe the a priorisms that deflect Comte's 'scientific' account of social development towards the good end he devoutly wished history to consummate.

Comte's account of how Man becomes Humanity is vulnerable on many scores. A centring of world history on its 'western' genealogy (Egypt, Greece, Rome, feudal and industrial Europe), with France at the pinnacle of that development and Paris as the spiritual capital of the perfected civilisation to come (x:373), will seem hopelessly parochial today.[4] Nor did Comte even suspect the labour of comparative civilisational analysis that Weber, for example, saw as necessary if such Eurocentrism was to be established as more than that.[5] However, the dubiousness of Comte's claim of universality for the western *série sociale* is not, here, my main concern. It is, rather, the *form* of his argument, particularly as that bears on his attempt to delineate a post-theistic moral ontology. In this respect, three linked features of his schema are especially worth examining. The first concerns the place of violence and *l'instinct déstructeur* (VII:697) in the development and perfecting of the social totality. The second concerns the implications of Humanity's growing *puissance modificatrice* for its destined place in the cosmos. The third concerns that wider order itself, as the object of Positive Religion's highest love. As we shall see, if Comte's analysis surrounding these points is enclosed within its guiding religious idea, that idea nonetheless goes through a remarkable mutation in his effort to bring it into consistency with what he took to be the reality principle actually at work.

qui lui correspond. Destinée surtout à le modifier continuellement pour satisfaire nos exigences végitatifs, elle doit d'abord s'y subordonne assez. Cette nécessité permanent devient ainsi la base de toute l'organisation sociale' (VIII:283).

[4] In his treatment of social dynamics in vol. v of *Philosophie positive*, Comte states as a primary 'logical restriction' that the analysis will concern 'exclusivement le développement effectif des populations les plus avancées, en écartant . . . toute vaine et irrationelle digression sur les divers autres centres de civilisation indépendante, dont l'évolution a été, par des causes quelconques, arrêtée jusqu'ici à un état plus imparfait . . . Notre exploration historique devra donc être presque uniquement réduite à l'avant-garde de l'humanité, comprenant la majeure partie de la race blanche ou les nations européennes, en nous bornant même . . . aux peuples de l'Europe occidentale' (IV:3).

[5] Whence the question that opens Weber's classic study of the relation between 'the Protestant ethic' and 'the spirit of capitalism': 'A product of modern European civilisation, studying any problem of universal history, is bound to ask himself to what combination of circumstances the fact should be attributed that in Western civilisation, and in Western civilisation only, cultural phenomena have appeared which (as we like to think) lie in a line of development having *universal* significance and value' (1958:1(a); emphasis in original).

The question of violence

Recorded history, as Comte well knew, has resounded with the clash of arms. For him, indeed, *la vie guerrière* is a primary fact, a self-evident starting point for tracing both the dynamics and the moral direction of progress (IX:59–60). From the very outset, the expansion of society from families to tribes, cities and empires, right through to the proto-Ecumene of Christendom and the modern system of nation-states, had been a military process. 'In fact', he notes, 'although human association cannot completely extend itself except through work, the initial development of this presupposes the existence of big societies [*grands sociétés*], which war alone can found' (IX:59–60).

This expansion was not just a quantitative matter. Because of what Comte assumed to be the initial prevalence of the most egoistic instincts, the coerced unity of military regimes had been necessary to ensure performance of the work required for collective material advance. It was thus an indispensable historical preparation for a mode of industry that could finally be motivated from within. The widening aggregations founded on force tended to create ever more universal circles of sociability, which themselves became transformed into moral institutions by the sentiments they elicited and strengthened. 'Even in a rudimentary state, reduced to simple brigandage . . . warfare cultivates mutual attachment, veneration of leaders, and even benevolence towards inferiors' (IX:56). That same movement also transmuted the terms of conquest, which for Comte was the normal aim of war (IX:59). The enslavement of prisoners replaced their execution (IX:187), and the abolition first of slavery, then of serfdom, encouraged 'industrial habits' preparing the way for a more pacific way of life based on divided tasks and free labour. With *la vie industrielle* now firmly established, all that remained was the 'civic incorporation' of the proletariat (IX:82–4), since the 'private morality proper to voluntary exchange tends to efface itself completely when the contrast between work and conquest seems reduced to the replacement of violence by fraud' (IX:58–9).

Intellectual development too, with its succeeding moments of religio-philosophical synthesis, had coincided with the development of society's military character. The period of fetishism, which culminated in an organised 'astrolatry' (VIII:88), saw intertribal warfare overtaken by that of the city-states, and then, as these extended their own range of conquest, by that of military empires. The polytheism that flourished with the latter expressed the reduction of fetishism's manifold of spirits to relatively ordered hierarchies of locally important cults, and the emergence, under the aegis of astronomy, of notions of fate and cosmic law.[6] Monotheism, as the logical culmination of the abstractive operation that had led from fetishism to polytheism, was associated with the full development of the latter's *sacerdoce* into an intellectual and moral power independent of the military state (VIII:89). Under monotheism too, the temporal power, increasingly preoccupied with the management of wealth, softened into a 'defensive' (i.e. feudal) form. It was this regime, finally, which had come into crisis with the rebellion of the urban 'communes', the disintegration of the monotheistic synthesis and the decisive rise of industry and science.

All told, then, there were three main phases in social development: active militarism, defensive militarism and industrialism.[7] With the onset of the latter, the conditions had been finally prepared for society to take the path of improvement through production rather than through plunder, so that the energy hitherto invested in conquering other peoples could be redirected into conquering the planet. The pacifying effects would extend to the entire animal kingdom.

Every animal species tends towards exclusive dominion on earth, just as each human population aims to dominate all the others. But these two struggles necessarily cease at one and the same time. When the true Great Being is sufficiently constituted, according to the mental and moral harmony of all its essential organs, its universal preponderance brings to an end the particular conquests of every other race. Animal unity thus tends to establish itself in the same way as human unity, by extending membership to those open to rallying themselves to the central organ, and by the extinction of those that are not. (VII:617)

One thing should already be clear. As the objective incarnation of the Good, *l'Humanité* is an emergent product of social history. At the same time, that history is propelled by war and subjugation, so that its *own* character is (at best) morally mixed. To be sure, all along the way, the social totality embodies at least a rudimentary form of love, just as it always bears a potential for the highest form of sociality, which is Humanity itself. But in preliminary stages of social development altruism was severely restricted in range, subordinated to an egoism and

---

[6] 'En effet, l'existence inaccessible des astres, leur régularité spéciale, et même l'universalité de leur spectacle, constituent autant de motifs d'y rattacher tous les phénomènes terrestres qui ne s'adaptent pas facilement aux personnifications polythéiques. Ainsi se forme graduellement la première astrologie, fille d'astrolâtrie et mère d'astronomie, en exagérant spontanément la subordination réelle de la terre envers le ciel' (IX:153).

[7] 'L'existence humaine commence, en effet, par être essentiellement militaire, pour devenir enfin complètement industrielle, en passant par une situation intermédiaire où la conquête se transforme en défense. Tels sont, évidemment les caractères respectifs de la civilisation ancienne, de la sociabilité moderne, et de la transition propre au moyen âge' (IX:331-2).

aggression it could only partially rein in. Humanity, then, in its actualised perfection, emerges through a process not just of cumulative improvement – as if whatever socially existed was already nascently good – but of purification, in which, once the requisite intellectual, practical and moral resources are historically assembled, a founding barbarity – the Hobbesian world of appetite channelled into warfare, conquest and slavery – is shaken off. But how is this shaking off to be understood? What happens – has happened – to the violence through which Humanity, in all its emergent perfection, had been born and grown up?

In part this is a sociological question, a matter of comprehending the real process in which a society based on force evolves into one based on positive social attachment and cooperation. But for Comte it is also a doctrinal question, one that contains moreover a great difficulty. If the Great Being of Humanity is to replace God as the true subject of divine predicates, as the real fount of our 'interior moral perfecting' (x:39), it must be wholly and sublimely good. To become wholly good, and worthy of being worshipped as such, the vitiating sources of the earlier violence must have disappeared. But if so, how? And what in any case was, and is, its ontological status in *l'ordre humain*?

At stake is the question of evil and the related one of original sin. *Ex hypothesi*, Comte was bound to reject both any notion that evil was a real force in nature – only a good cosmos could naturally evolve towards the good – and any version of original sin, whether that sin was social (as with Rousseau) or (as in Christian belief) lodged in the dark side of the human heart.[8] At the same time, however, Comte could not recuperate the cruel history of warfare and oppression simply through a privative concept of evil – violence as deprival or frustration – since this would have been at variance with his instinct theory and forced him to reconsider the coercion and repression hidden in his own ('systematic') idea of the Good. The question, then, could not be wholly evaded.

One kind of answer is given by the reconciliationism implicit in Comte's historical method itself.

The spontaneous tendency to comprehend and celebrate the whole of the past constitutes the most characteristic property of positive philosophy . . . Under

---

[8] Comte does not discuss the doctrine of original sin directly, but only as conveyed by the formula of grace versus nature, a doctrine whose chief error for him is its denial of the innateness of altruistic sentiments (VIII:115–16). By placing the weight of his critique on that point, however, he accepted its more general framework. Nature redeems itself through the self-perfection of Man. He thus avoided any consideration of the view that the species was inherently flawed in a sense that went beyond the irrepressibility of selfish motives, which themselves could be redeemed by altruism in an order of cooperative harmony and so were not inherently bad.

the Religion of Humanity, history becomes the sacred science, as devoted directly to the study of the Great Being's destiny. (IX:xxiv)

In that spirit, Positivist historiography, enlightened by love for Humanity, would retroactively refigure the miseries that the history of social violence has inflicted on its victims into necessary means of human advance.

Unlike in Condorcet's *Esquisse*, then, the barbarities of the past are not simply to be condemned from the moral heights of a later progress.[9] They are to be assessed for the advance they represent over what has gone before, and for what they 'prepare' in turn. Except for the fact that Comte treats as actual the historical path he can only predict – Minerva's owl flies in 1927 – his 'appreciative' account of the preparatory stages of history, and of the indispensable role played by conquest and coercion, is similar in spirit to Hegel's 'true theodicy'. Indeed, Comte's justificatory operation goes further. To be sure, in the industrial present, he excoriates such evils as colonial slavery.[10] But, with regard to prior horrors, there is no irrecoverable sense of loss, no shadow cast on the Positive by history's tragic dimension.[11] In venerating the Great Being that unfolds its potential through human history, the past, in all its salient moments, is simply to be celebrated in acts of grateful worship. In the Positivist Calendar, the fifth month is named after Julius Caesar

---

[9] 'Il [Condorcet] a condamné le passé au lieu de l'observer; et par suite son ouvrage n'a été qu'une longue et fatigante déclamation, dont il ne résulte réellement aucune instruction positive' (xa:114).

[10] While Comte 'appreciated' ancient slavery 'toujours normale tant que la production resta nécessairement subordonée à la conquête', modern slavery – *l'esclavage coloniale* – was worse than retrograde. 'Soumettant le travail à l'entrepreneur, il dégrade également l'un et l'autre. Il ne put jamais constituer qu'une monstruosité sociale, émanée de l'infâme oppression que la race intelligente exerce sur la race aimante, en abusant une puissance que l'humanité développa pour leur commun bonheur d'après leur digne concours' (IX:576).

[11] For a discussion of the tragic dimension in Hegel's philosophy of history, see Kaufmann, 1966:esp. 250–5. The following passage from Hegel's *Reason in History* might have been aimed at Comte himself: 'Without rhetorical exaggeration, a simple, truthful account of the miseries that have overwhelmed the most noble of nations and polities and the finest exemplars of private virtue forms a most fearful picture and excites emotions of the profoundest and most hopeless sadness, counterbalanced by no consoling result. We can endure it and strengthen ourselves against it only by thinking that this is the way it had to be – it is fate; nothing can be done. And at last, out of the boredom with which this sorrowful reflection threatens us, we draw back into the vitality of the present, into our aims and interests of the moment; we retreat, in short, into the selfishness that stands on the quiet shore and thence enjoys the distant spectacle of wreckage and confusion' (Hegel, 1953:26–7). In a quite different sense Macherey (1989:122) argues that Comte's thought can nonetheless be regarded as 'dans l'horizon d'une philosophie tragique'. This was because it evoked, beyond a self-imposed closure that equated the human world with the world as such, 'l'infini pascalien'.

and is dedicated to the commemoration of 'military civilisation' (XI:335).

But there is something more. Comte's refiguring of the past is not merely a collapse of history into veneration. History is *la science sacrée* not only because the sacred character of its subject attaches to the narrative itself. It is also sacred because Humanity exists in time as well as space, and the affective ties that bind the present to the past – its *continuité* – are an essential constituent of what it is. The past must be 'constructively' recuperated, then, for *l'Humanité* to exist at all. This recuperation is itself, moreover, a purifying process. Just as the post-humous incorporation of worthy individuals into Humanity purges their second life in memory of all but the exemplary qualities which they can represent and inspire, so too, in the sublimating selectivity of collective memory, the 'slaughter-bench' of history (Hegel, 1953:27) is put aside, collective miseries like slavery are transfigured by their place in the general advance, and, as concerns remembered individuals, only the good – *les vraiment assimilables* – survive.

Comte is thus able to sidestep the traditional issues of sin and evil by shifting their consideration to the subjective mode of being in which his 'Humanity' largely exists. Both in *la science sacrée* and in the 'normal' process of generational turnover, the bad is *really* purified away in the passage from what has happened to what is remembered – a transforma-tion which in the Positive Polity is to be systematised and presided over by the Positivist priesthood, with its special relation to the philosophy of history and its supervision of the cult of the dead. However, the 'subjective existence' of *l'Humanité* does not exhaust what it is. Humanity also exists objectively in the concatenation of social ties and sentiments whose rise to ascendancy within the social whole is the very condition for its having a subjective existence at all. So what – returning to the 'sociological' question – happens to evil on the plane of the *socius* itself?

Comte's account interweaves three logics. First, a dialectic of war and social development spirals towards love and harmony via the way conquest creates unities which engender psychic forces that transmute an egoistic economy into an altruistic one. Secondly, there is a dialectic of war and production in which *la vie guerrière* helps prepare the conditions for its supersession by *la vie industrielle*, so that the common goal of planetary modification comes to replace the divisive one of conquest as the self-consciously collective path of material self-improve-ment. To which, thirdly, there is an instinctual correlate. In the scale of egoistic instincts, affective motor number five ('improvement through construction, or industrial instinct') rises in exercised intensity at the expense of affective motor number four ('improvement through destruction, or military instinct').

The addendum is ingenious. For through it violence, at first sight given a leading role, is summoned on to the stage only to be conjured away and redefined as something else. On the one hand, that is to say, the path of war and the path of industry are distinguished, even motivationally, only with respect to the 'choice of means'(IX:239) with which they pursue the same reasonable aim of material self-improvement. On the other hand, both instinctually and functionally, destructiveness is never for its own sake. The force applied, and the will to apply it, is always instrumental, closely bound up indeed with a constructive intent. Thus Comte can equate the social violence of warfare, plunder, conquest and enslavement with the destructiveness involved, 'even for herbivores', in the universal impulse to remove 'obstacles' without which no animal 'would know how to subsist'.

To be sure, the motive of self-improvement is both egoistic in itself and, in preliminary stages of social development, colonised by a general preponderance of egoism, including the collective egoism of tribes, cities and nations (VII:69). In that context, whether industrial or military in form, *l'instinct du perfectionnement* was linked to greed, and bound to produce a struggle for dominance. Hence conflict and warfare. As well, even at a higher stage of development, the balance between the constructive and destructive components of 'improvement' always had to be watched, given the instinctually greater energy and universality of the latter.[12] With regard to political action, it was precisely such an imbalance, marked by the continuing dominance of 'metaphysics', which the constructive path of 'positive politics' set out to correct. However, *l'instinct déstructeur*, precisely by being assimilated to a wider *instinct du perfectionnement* (VII:727), is not subtended by any irreducible aggression or will to dominance *as such*.[13] There is no room for a purely malevolent impulse on Comte's entire cerebral map.

[12] The closest Comte comes to the thought that destructiveness can, in principle, become psychologically detached from its natural aim of *perfectionnement* is in a remark he makes while surveying the positive contribution of the various instincts to the perfecting of *l'existence active* (in chap. 4 of *Politique positive*'s last volume). 'Néanmoins, cet instinct exigera toujours une surveillance spéciale, parce qu'il ne cessera point de participer à nos opérations quelconques, même mentales, qui supposent la destruction continue des obstacles qu'éprouve la construction graduelle des moyens.' But he immediately adds that 'le penchant détruire, même quand il dégénère en médisance, peut être spontanément contenu, d'après l'ensemble des habitudes résultées de l'éducation positive' (x:287).

[13] A similar denial entered into Comte's 'positive theory of (material) property', which treated violent forms of 'material transmission' as imperfect means to attain constructive social ends. 'D'après leur dignité et leur efficacité décroissantes, nos quatre modes généraux de transmission matérielle doivent être rangés dans cet ordre

Even in these terms, though, the productive activity which militarism fosters through social pacification, and which ultimately replaces it as the path to self-improvement, has a curious ambiguity. *L'industrie* is touted as the basis for social peace. At the same time, *l'industrie* enables the Great Being to conquer the earth, and if it brings social peace it does so, in effect, by shifting the object of aggression from man to nature. The externalised violence of such a project had been foreshadowed in food production from earliest times. 'Without the vast destruction of animals accomplished by hunting peoples, and without the analogous ravages exercised by pastoral populations against vegetation, we would never have entered into possession of our planet' (IX:103). Thus the difference between *l'instinct déstructif* and *l'instinct conservateur* is not as great as it would seem. Correspondingly, as we follow humanity's shift from the one 'means of improvement' to the other, there turn out to be *two* aspects of continuity between warfare and industry. Not only do both aim at material betterment; both entail also the forceful subjugation (and where necessary, annihilation) of their object. Of these two traits, Comte emphasises only the former. In moving from divisive military warfare to the unifying scientific–industrial domination of the earth, the Baconian formula about obeying nature in order to command her is retained without comment, so self-evident does the necessity of such commanding seem.

In each of these ways – functionalist recuperation, selective memory, instinctual excision, assimilation into the instrumentalities of 'improvement' – the violence that Comte projects as having founded *les grands sociétés* and which is then diverted, by the beneficent unfolding of human capacity, into the collective exploitation of Humanity's milieu, loses its sting. In the march of progress, violence is finally superseded in a transformation that leaves no trace. What is saved thereby is the coherence of a historical model which purports to show the determinate possibility of collective self-perfection conceived, like the model itself, in the image of a frictionless harmony. Accordingly, while Comte's model resembles Hegel's in its desire to reconcile liberal and conservative viewpoints within an immanentist master framework that owes a great deal to Aristotle and Leibnitz, its logic is more dogmatic than dialectical. It is not so much that disharmony turns into harmony, and force into love, as that order imposes itself from the outset, while the violence that

normal, qui est aussi celui de leur introduction historique: le don, l'échange, l'héritage, et la conquête' (VII:155). He goes on to explain that private inheritance is a form of gift, and that conquest is effectively a 'forced' mode of exchange, in which the one party receives life and the other the property. Of course, free exchange is more morally advanced than forced exchange, but there is no allusion to the possibility that conquest may be driven by motives darker than the desire for material improvement.

persists into the Humanist heaven of industrialism is exnominated. There is no negation of the negation. Indeed, since violence is never taken to have any blindly inhuman side, there is no negation to negate.

Comte's bad other is not, in any case, violence, hatred or lust for power, but chaos and disorder. The negative pole is characterised by such terms as *dispersif, pertabateur, anarchiste.* To ward off such tendencies is the essential aim of *politique positive* itself. And how is this to be done? Not just by centrally applied force, since the perfection of order entails its becoming cooperative and voluntary. Required, rather, is a combination of 'rallying' and 'regulating' in which the force of the whole, imbued with *l'amour universel,* is exercised against its recalcitrant, egoistic parts. Thus, as *la vie militaire* gives way to *la vie industrielle,* state power becomes softened, legal sanctions become less brutal, and, in the fully Positive state, civic and domestic order are primarily maintained not by the coercive force of law but by moral pressure.[14] Of course, as under 'monotheism', a refashioned spiritual power will play a pervasive supervisory and counselling role. A penal code (with capital punishment for murder, duelling and suicide (VII:491)) will also be retained for the most obdurate and antisocial elements. But the principal mechanism for ensuring proper conduct will eschew the use or threat of force. It will be rooted, like Positive Religion itself, in the revamped 'moral order of domestic life'. Its key is mutual surveillance.

It is there that the fundamental maxim: Live for others (*vivre pour l'autrui*) receives its practical complement: live openly (*vivre au grand jour*), without which it would soon become insufficient, and often even illusory. Despite the self-interested precautions of metaphysical legislators, the western instinct should regard a normal publicity for private acts as the necessary guarantee for true citizenship [*civisme*] . . . All who would refuse to live openly [*au grand jour*] would justly be suspected of not really wanting to live for others. (x:312)

Comte's blend of panoptical[15] corporatism with a perfectionist repudiation of original sin exemplifies a certain form of modern totalitar-

---

[14] 'La répression temporelle devra plus fréquemment employer une autre classe de mesures matérielles, fondée sur l'institution civique de toute propriété réelle, et consistant dans la privation, temporaire ou définitive, des capitaux humains, quand leur dépositaires deviennent indignes. Mais envers les choses comme pour les personnes, quoiqu'à un moindre degré, le sacerdoce conseillera toujours au gouvernement de préferer les moyens positifs aux voies négatives, en récompensant les uns plutôt que punir les autres; ce qu'ignore entièrement notre brutale législation' (VIII:419).

[15] Comte makes no mention of Bentham, but his mechanism of everyday social control bears a striking similarity to the latter's *panopticon,* especially in Bentham's extension of this principle from prisons to 'work-houses, or manufactures, or mad-houses, or hospitals or schools'. 'In all these instances', Bentham notes, 'the more constantly the persons to be inspected are under the eyes of the persons who should inspect them, the more perfectly will the purpose of the establishment have been attained. Ideal

ianism. In which respect, Horkheimer and Adorno's stricture against Durkheimian sociology applies in full force to Comte. 'What is done to all by the few, always occurs as the subjection of individuals by the many: social repression always exhibits the masks of repression by a collective' (1989:22). The same mystification has a psychoanalytic dimension, too. In his obsession with the horrors of entropic tendencies to disorder – death itself – Comte paid no attention to the extroversion of the death wish in the form of aggression, a punishing superego and repetition compulsion. He therefore split it off from possible consideration as such, and blinded himself to its operation in his own mental activity.

Even if denied or reinterpreted, however, there is a remainder of violence in Comte's vision of a perfected human order which has not at all been purged away. In fact, there are two. First, there is the lingering project of domination that migrates from warfare into the conquest of nature; and, second, there is the social violence that remains in his system just by virtue of its being so emphatically a system. The latter symptomatises an irremediable weakness in his social thought, particularly in its effort to think human collectivity in the image of the divine. He is not able to think the first person plural as a non-repressive 'we'. More important, perhaps, he does not even suspect the possibility of the question. The sociological issue, moreover, discloses a theological one. For it touches both on the aptness of *l'Humanité* to fill the vacated place of the Judeo-Christian God, and on the character of the divinity at issue in the transfer.

These questions are difficult but can at least be posed. The first occlusion, however, i.e. of *l'industrie*'s external violence, is less clearcut. Comte offers, certainly, no reflection on the limitation of a viewpoint that identifies the way of peace with the project of 'possessing' and 'exploiting' the planet. Yet his elaboration of the Man/Nature relation, and of its positive–industrial transfiguration, stretches the Baconian paradigm to the limit. In so doing, a crucial, if contradictory, qualification is entered into its religiously constitutive anthropocentrism. Love culminates not in love for Humanity but for the 'universal order' to which Humanity must always submit and of which it is a dependent part (x:64). And this leads Comte – who had rediscovered the force of

perfection, if that were the object, would require that each person be in that predicament, during every instant of time. This being impossible, the next best thing to be wished for is, that, at every instant, seeing reason to believe as much, and not being able to satisfy himself to the contrary, he should conceive himself to be so' (from a letter of 1787, in Bentham, 1995:34). For Comte, the principle of *vivre au grand jour* entails not just that everyone is to play the role of 'inspector' for everyone else, but that even in the absence of such 'inspectors' everyone should live as if there were some.

fetishism in the regression of his *manie* – if not to a complete revision of the Adamic mandate as Lord of Creation, at least towards the Humanist incorporation of more ancient deities than 'God'.

Humanity and Nature

As I have been at pains to emphasise, despite the crucial place of ideas both for the formation of a cooperative consensus and for the 'consecration of authority' (IX:14), and despite the world-historical importance Comte attributed in that context to his own intellectual work, he by no means held to the sovereign autonomy of the intellect. 'Despite the abstract independence dreamed by the pride of theoreticians, all our mental revolutions emanate . . . from the successive exigencies of our practical situation. The activity which our instincts inspire, according to our needs, always rules the general exercise of our intelligence' (ibid.). Whether individual or collective, Comte makes clear, this action is to be understood as practically implicated in the world. Its object is always the modification of the milieu in line with experienced needs (XI:211). Theory itself is to be regarded as a form of action in that its results modify subjective existence just as material production modifies objective existence. Moreover, as the whole symphony of affective motors is successively brought into play, the needs which 'inspire activity' themselves change in line with socio-historical conditions. The species changes itself, then, by changing 'the material order which dominates it'.[16]

Again, there are striking parallels with Marx. This is not to say that Marx's pivotal notion of *praxis*, as elaborated in *The German Ideology* (Marx and Engels, 1947:6–15) and summarised in the 'Theses on Feuerbach', is identical with Comte's *pratique*. They are situated in different problematisations of the social. Comte's reference to 'our practical situation' assumes an inclusively collective historical subject whose hierarchical structure does not *per se* make its subjective unity into an illusory cover and justification for the partial and particular interests of a dominant class. This is related, as well, to a profound difference in their conception of what Marx calls the social relations of production. Hence their counterposed programs for the cooperative

---

[16] The interaction between organism and milieu is introduced as a general biological principle in the *Philosophie positive* (IV:230 et seq.). In *Politique positive*, the idea is considerably developed with regard both to the impact of the material order on individual and society, and to the human capacity to modify 'the modifiers'. See especially chap. 7 in vol. II, 'Théorie positive des limites générales de variations propres à l'ordre humain', on which much of the discussion in the present section is based.

reorganisation of industry itself. The social division of labour, including mental/manual, and as between managers and workers, is something that Comte would perfect by extending. Marx, at least in his early works, would break it down. Nor, finally, does Marx equate the progress of human needs with a de-emphasis on the physical ones to make room for the rise of an angelic love. He is anti-puritanical and emphasises, rather, the rich manifold of capacities and satisfactions which history reveals once the basic ones are served. Beyond necessity lies the realm of freedom,[17] at the furthest extension of which is the 'purposiveness without purpose' of art and play (Marcuse, 1955:162–3).

Nevertheless, in their valorisation of 'modern industry', Comte and Marx equally subscribe to the Enlightenment program of dominating nature through the application of science to serve human needs. Both see in this the key to overcoming the conflicts of scarcity and the establishment of social peace. Both regard the rise of the productive forces as the prime cause of other forms of progress. And both see a glorious destiny not only for Humanity as Lord of the Earth, but for the earth itself as humanly transformed. In *The Economic and Philosophic Manuscripts* Marx wrote:

This communism ['as the real appropriation of the human essence by and for man'], as fully developed naturalism, equals humanism, and as fully developed humanism equals naturalism; it is the *genuine* resolution of the conflict between man and nature and between man and man – the true resolution of the strife between man and man, between existence and essence, between objectification and self-confirmation, between freedom and necessity, between the individual and the species. Communism is the riddle of history solved, and it knows itself to be this solution. (1964:135)

Substitute positivism for communism, and *l'ordre universel* for nature, and we have a credo not inconsistent with that of Comte.

In Comte's formulation, the ever-enhancing modifying power of the human species puts it in a unique relation to nature. All forms of life carve out a niche and so modify (at the level of 'secondary phenomena') the immutable order around them. It is this activity which defines the

---

[17] 'With [man's] development the realm of natural necessity expands, because his wants increase; but at the same time, the forces of production, by which these wants are satisfied, also increase. Freedom in this field cannot consist of anything else but the fact that socialized mankind, the associated producers, regulate their interchange with Nature rationally, bring it under their common control, instead of being ruled by it as by some blind power . . . Nevertheless this always remains a realm of necessity. Beyond it begins that development of human potentiality for its own sake, the true realm of freedom, which however can only flourish on the basis of the realm of necessity as its basis' (from vol. III of *Capital*, cited/tr. in Bottomore and Rubel, 1963:260). Comte, by contrast, spiritualises Marx's 'realm of necessity' by making necessity itself, *le destin*, the object of *l'amour universel*.

essential difference between *l'ordre vital* and the rest of the cosmos (VII:586). But only in the hands of the human animal does that power have the capacity to increase, a capacity that begins to develop as soon as the ability to communicate and remember is aided by the production of signs. Linguistic capacity, in turn, enables know-how to be transmitted, and, through abstract reasoning, to accumulate from generation to generation.[18] In consequence, 'no other being can worthily work for itself except Humanity, whose objective servants return to the future part of its existence the products drawn from materials owing to that of its past' (X:327–8).

The first stage of terrestrial domination involved establishing the ascendancy of humankind as a life-form. Predators are killed. Edible prey are hunted down, before they and usable by-products are more systematically farmed. This, in turn, brings a fundamental shift in mode. As farming replaces hunter-gathering, we move from simple appropriation to cumulative modification (IX:104). In which respect, agriculture itself provides the model – after the long interval needed for the physical sciences to begin to uncover the secrets of the material universe – for the vastly expanded productive powers, beginning with energy sources, of modern industry. The horizons thereafter unceasingly expand. The vast engineering projects inspired by the Saint-Simonians, including the Suez Canal, are well known. Comte has his own list of techno-dreams. While silent about transport and unaware of the technological implications of contemporary advances in electricity, communications, photography etc., he envisages two other developments of breathtaking scope. The first is climate control. Here, beyond continuing measures 'to gradually diminish the influences accessible to our intervention' as well as to preserve us 'from those which remain inalterable' (VIII:461), he conceives – though just as an inspiring fiction – the fantastical project of 'correcting' the earth's elliptical orbit. The second, flowing from the rise of the life sciences, is bio-engineering, not just in food production, but in medicine, where his most ambitious scheme,

---

[18] In its social function, language, with its capacity to accumulate and transmit the results of collective work, is compared directly with the institution of material property. 'Sous cet aspect social, l'institution du langage doit être finalement comparée à celle de la propriété . . . Car la première accomplit, pour la vie spirituelle de l'Humanité, un office fondamental qui équivaut à celui qu'exerce la seconde envers la vie matérielle. Après avoir essentiellement facilité l'acquisition de toutes les connaissances humaines, théoriques ou pratiques, et dirigés par notre essor esthétique, le langage consacre cette double richesse, et la transmet à de nouveaux coopérateurs' (VIII:254).

[19] Comte offers other *utopies positives*, including the elevation of herbivores into carnivores. Their general rationale and place in the system is discussed in X:274–6. 'Cette théorie devient ici le complément de celle de la religion, en résumant l'unité réelle par une limite idéale, où viennent spécialement converger les voeux, les projets,

again presented as a fictive *utopie*,[19] was for artificial human reproduction. With such technical advances, we may note, a further line would have been crossed. Beyond mere dominion over plants and animals, the destiny of Humanity's *pouvoir matériel* would have become powerful enough to modify the biological and astronomical determinants of human life itself.

Even in the earliest days of the industrial revolution, the Baconian program – 'increase human knowledge to the achievement of all things possible' – had its detractors. Rousseau's counterblast against 'progress in the arts and sciences' identified the 'faculty of self-improvement' as the 'source of all human misfortunes' which makes man 'at length a tyrant over himself and nature' (1963:170–1). Over the next European century, the aesthetic pain evinced, in the souls of the sensitive, by Manchester-style urbanisation, the fouling of rivers and the industrialisation of green sites, is recorded in the cult of the pastoral, the folkloric, the medieval and the picturesque, as well as in the romanticism that reaches its musical heights in Beethoven, Brahms, Mendelssohn and Mahler.

The most far-reaching critiques of the domination of nature have come, however, in industrialism's later stages. One strand of thinking runs from German *Kultur-kritik* to the interwar preoccupation with mechanisation and 'technics', and enters classical sociology by way of Weber's analysis of the irrationality of rationalisation (Gerth and Mills, 1958:281 et seq.). This lamented the rise of formal and instrumental rationality at the expense of substantive reason and thematised the cultural and philosophical crisis that beckoned. For Lukács and the Frankfurt thinkers, such arguments, which resonated powerfully in the antimodernist right, were inflected towards the left. The reign of factuality, instrumentalism and (small-'p') positivism (Weber's 'iron cage') exemplified the reification effected by the 'fetishism of commodities' (Lukács, 1971:83–92). It also left a vacuum in transcending social aims which ideologically delivered science and technology over to the established (capitalist) order. As a result, humankind itself was becoming part of dominated nature. In the 'totally administered' societies

---

et les tentatives propres au perfectionnement continu de nos triple nature. Pour mieux instituer ce ralliement, il faut lui spécifier un seul but, sauf à le renouveler quand il se trouverait atteint; ce qui sera toujours possible, vu l'immense domaine de la providence humaine, à peine achevée jusqu'ici, même envers le milieu' (x:275). The setting and realisation of 'limit-ideals', which involves the interplay of poetic imagination and scientific–industrial advance, would make progress continue even beyond the attainment of the 'final state'. It clearly expresses the idea that Humanity, once fully existent as such, becomes the collective agent of its own history.

of the 1930s and 40s, 'the fully enlightened earth radiates disaster triumphant' (Horkheimer and Adorno, 1989:3).

These intellectual suspicions have been swelled, in our own times, by the nuclear threat, exponential population growth, the regression of biodiversity, and a soured love affair with automobiles, tower blocks, and the whole Le Corbusier vision of a modernist technotopia. In that context the focus has moved away from rationalisation, mechanisation and the 'disenchantment of the world' towards concerns about limits to growth and the gathering environmental crisis. Mainstream eco-critique (exemplified by the Brundtland Commission report (World Commission, 1987)) has concerned itself with 'sustainable development'. This proposes to moderate the industrial project by counselling attention to reproduction and time. Deep greenery, on the other hand, questions not only the human benefits of industrial modernity but anthropocentrism itself (Lovelock, 1979; Devall and Sessions, 1985). Heidegger, whose postmodern revival has hardly been dented by political exposure, bridges this latter tendency and the anti-instrumentalist critique. For him, the privilege of human being is to be the place where Being reveals itself. The demonic essence of *modernische Teknik* is to enframe thinking in a technological *Gestell* which makes such revealing inaccessible by turning all that is into mere raw materials, or 'standing reserve' (1977a:23).

The relation, in principle, of Comte's enthusiastic pro-industrialism to these gathering (and later) objections is complex. Moderate environmentalism, which insists on interconnectedness, correcting 'external effects', and the importance of material reproducibility through time, aims to enhance the prudential intelligence with which the technical exploitation of the planet is pursued. From a Comtean perspective, this could be considered just a friendly amendment. On the other hand, Comte's forthright insistence on a phenomenally based and instrumentalist practice of science, as well as on the legitimacy of extending such an approach to the human domain, leaves him vulnerable to the more fundamental challenges that can be generated from the side of Critical Theory. Horkheimer and Adorno's classic essay traces, from Odysseus to Bacon to mass culture and concentration camps, the dialectic of an enlightenment which turns the human domination of nature against humanity itself. An excursus on Comte would not have been out of place. Certainly, he does not shrink from the implication that the technological empowerment of the species can – indeed must – extend from control of its outer reality to social engineering and even to biological remaking.

However, as with so much of Comte's thinking, matters are less simple than they appear. His endorsement of cognitive instrumentalism and technological power is by no means unconditional. He condemns as 'idiotisme' an empiricism pursued in abstraction from sentiment and subjectivity (IX:20). Nor is his attachment to science-based power socially blind. As with Bacon himself, the techno-industrial project would be empty without a philanthropic spirit and 'the spice of religion'. Systematising what this might mean, and demonstrating its realisable character, is the whole burden of Comte's theoretical and practical effort.

From the vantage point of what he takes to be social science itself, most important, the predicted and advocated rise to ascendancy of the *puissance modifactrice* was inconceivable except in the context of a wider, socially perfecting, evolutionary step. For industrialism to triumph presupposed the completion of the scientific revolution, the fashioning of a new theoretical synthesis, and the establishment of a Positive Polity. Its very occurrence, then, was inextricably bound up with an institutionalised revolution in sentiments. The accompanying decisive passage from egoism to altruism would ensure that Northrop Frye's 'driverless train' of technology had not just a human driver, but one of matchless moral intent. There is a providential magic to this. The dangerously mighty power of modern industry gets placed in human hands just at the point where the impulse of individual and species self-improvement which it subserves is being transfigured by love. In hindsight, nothing of the sort has occurred. This does not address, though, what Positivism champions. This is not simply the utilitarian domination of nature, but that project as Positively – and therefore morally – transformed.

The distinction is crucial, for the social and spiritual transformation Comte envisages would qualitatively alter the means–end schema within which industrialisation proceeds. In contrast to the *égoïsme* which had deformed industrialism in its initial stages, the 'normal' form destined to emerge would be completely collective in spirit.[20] In the Positive Polity, production would lose its private character, and industrial benefits would be pursued for the common good. Pursuing that common good, moreover, would entail the improvement of the species not just materially, but in the highest moral sense. Altogether, then, the altruism that Comte envisages as the spiritual principle of a reconstructed industrialism is not just incompatible with the logic of effective demand

---

[20] 'Toute la régénération pratique peut se réduire à systématiser dignement les tendances spontanées de l'industrie vers le caractère collectif. La socratie doit, à cet égard, compléter la théocratie, en faisant sagement cesser une séparation provisoire, non moins irrationelle qu'immorale, entre les fonctions publiques et les offices publiques. Une existence où chacun travail pour l'autrui devient mieux accessible au sentiment social que l'activité militaire à la quelle seule il convient d'abord' (X:57).

as driven by market forces. The good at which it aims also goes beyond any utilitarian identification of the desirable with the desired, and of any project of merely Paretian optimisation with respect to the sum of individual utilities defined in terms of immediate needs. The good of all for whose sake human power is to be deployed, for example, includes obligations to the dead and the unborn.[21] As its paramount value, it also includes what is good for what makes us an all. Which is not to say that the will of each is destined always to conflict with the general will, since in the 'final state' individuals come to desire this higher good as an expression of their own (religiously cultivated) need.

Comte's affirmation of the industrial project is integrally connected, then, to the moral self-transcendence of the subject–object conceived to be at the centre of the process. To which extent, Positivism with a capital 'p' may be objectionable as a totalising utopia, but it would be a drastic simplification to understand it as just an early, and extreme, manifestation of one-dimensional, technicist thinking.

This still leaves, however, a 'deep green' objection. Does not Comte's glorification of scientific–industrial development *pro causa Humana* manifest hubris on behalf of the human species itself? Does it not uncritically arrogate to Humanity a kind of planetary right of the strongest? Worse: is it not idolatrous, revealing in the religious apotheosis of Humanity an absolutism that is utterly careless of particularity – whether of trees or people – and thus as oblivious to the call of beings as to that of Being? The questions would seem rhetorical, but we should not be too quick to respond.

In the first place, Comte repudiates entirely any spirit of arrogance with which the display of human technological power might be associated. 'It is to ameliorate our situation or our nature, not to vainly show off our power, that we ceaselessly tend to modify the universal economy' (VIII:465). In Comte's fully Positivised social order, then, the industrial effort would be pervasively moral, and it would be so because it was motivated by the selfless espousal of the highest interest of humanity as a whole. But what, for Comte, is this highest interest *itself*? Not happiness, certainly; although if moral wellbeing is the answer, happi-

---

[21] 'En écartant les parasites de plus en plus exceptionnels, tous les praticiens deviennent, dans l'état positif, des serviteurs directs du Grand-Être envers le trésor matériel que sa providence transmet à chaque génération pour la suivante' (IX:58).

[22] 'Dans toutes les classes, la principale félicité ressort de l'essor continu des instincts sympathiques, d'après une libre participation à l'activité sociale. Mais cette source commune du bonheur humain se modifie suivant les aptitudes et les situations, sous une sage application de l'éducation universelle. Car l'attachement et la bonté prévalent respectivement chez les inférieurs et les supérieurs, dont les destinations développent surtout la vie privée ou publique, tandis que la vénération devient mutuelle entre la

ness may providentially result from the ever more perfect harmonies achieved in its pursuit.[22] At the same time, this interest also exceeds that of present individuals and of the collective they temporarily make up. If the Humanity we venerate is mostly in the past, the Humanity we cherish as the final end of practice is projected towards the future. Humanity's highest interest lies, then, in the process of anthropological improvement itself. Hence the climactic place of progress in Comte's guiding motto – *l'amour pour principe, ordre pour base, progrès pour but*.

Improvement, of course, was always for Comte the improvement of order. One might suppose, then, that perfecting the *internal* harmony of the human order remains the ultimate end of the exercise. But the moral significance of rising human power over nature is not exhausted by the merely *social* transformation with which it is bound up. As we have seen, in seeking its ever more elevated definition of self-improvement, Humanity is driven not just to modify its milieu, but to change its very conditions of existence. What we must now add is that, for Comte, the increasing acquisition of such power brings Humanity to the point of a further moral advance – an advance which universalises the project of collective self-perfection itself. In being able to change its own material 'seat', Humanity is able to change – and for the morally better – aspects of that 'universal order' whose laws, scientists are bound to assume, rule the phenomenal world. Through an active, and not just resigned, submission to this order, 'humanity tends towards its normal attitude, as the supreme moderator of the natural economy, whose wise improvement becomes the continuous goal of its providential efforts, suitably helped by all the agents, organic and inorganic, which can cooperate' (VIII:42–3).[23]

Three examples of milieu–modification will clarify the meaning of what Comte takes to be the character of this extraordinary anthropological leap. The first is an archaic development that initiated, and foreshadowed, the transfigured relation between humankind and nature which Comte envisages. This is the domestication of animals (IX:140). Through it, humanity enters into a limitedly free, rather than hunting/hunted, relationship with those of its fellow-creatures (horses, oxen, dogs, cats etc.) which actively subserve human needs. The practical

richesse et le nombre' (X:61). Happiest therefore is a spontaneous social hierarchy in which all know, and integrate their sympathies with, their proper place.

[23] 'Une meilleure appréciation de l'ordre fondamental ennoblit donc notre résignation nécessaire, en la convertant en une soumission active. L'Humanité tend ainsi vers son attitude normale, comme suprême modératrice de l'économie naturelle, dont le sage perfectionnement devient le but continu de ses efforts providentiels, convenablement assisté par tous les agents, organiques et inorganiques, qui peuvent y concourir' (VIII:42–3).

result has been a gain in human power. But what impresses Comte is that through this step Humanity has also extended its affectionate essence to that part of the life-world whose active cooperation it has been able to secure. Dogs, horses etc. are not tamed only to be used. They become emotionally incorporated into the human milieu, both immediately and in a social sense. Solidarity extends to them, and in their dumb way *nos libres auxiliaires* reciprocate, and so elevate their own moral being (x:37).

The relation Comte sees as having been installed between humankind and domesticated animals, and thus more generally between it and the rest of the 'vital order', is founded on *attachement*, and brings into play the polyphonies of love.[24] It is a first step, then, towards the incorporation of the 'vital order' into Humanity itself. One effect is that Humanity expands. It comes to consist not only of the species bearing that name but of all animals who cooperate in the human endeavour.[25] The domestication of animals entails new forms of symbiosis, and introduces harmony into relations that would otherwise be indifferent or even antagonistic. All of which gave Comte warrant for thinking that the so-to-speak 'unsympathetic' conquest of the planet, as of fellow-humans by one another, was itself redeemable by the moral improvements on both sides of the relation it made possible.

Two further examples which belong to Comte's extravagant technological aspirations for the future, I have already mentioned. The first, through *l'utopie d'une fécondation spontanée*,[26] held out the prospect of modifying that part of *l'ordre vital* to which the human animal itself belongs. By separating propagation from the 'delirium and irresponsi-

---

[24] 'Relativement à nos auxiliaires, la sympathie humaine peut et doit suivre un meilleur cours, en perfectionnant, non-seulement leur situation, mais surtout leur nature, physique, intellectuelle, et morale, d'après le développement habituel de la vraie fraternité. Ceux qui sont herbivores se trouveront graduellement élévés, par le Grand-Être, à la dignité de carnivores, pour devenir à la fois plus actifs, plus intelligents, et même plus dévouées, en s'assimilant davantage aux serviteurs directs de l'Humanité' (x:358–9).

[25] 'On ne peut assez concevoir la constitution du Grand-Être qu'en combinant notre espèce avec toutes les races susceptibles d'adopter la commune devise des âmes supérieures: *Vivre pour l'autrui* . . . Le positivisme pouvait seul la systématiser, en incorporant au Grand-Être tous nos libres auxiliaires animaux, tandis qu'il en écarte d'indignes parasites humains' (x:37; emphasis in original). By this definition, the household pet is a part of Humanity, but not the incorrigible petty thief.

[26] The technical means Comte envisages are vague, and limited of course by current misconceptions about reproductive biology itself. He implies both artificial insemination, on which he is silent, and the artificial production of *le fluide vivifiant*. About the latter he only notes: 'On conçoit ainsi que, chez la plus noble espèce, ce liquide cesse d'être indispensable à l'éveil du germe, qui pourrait artificiellement résulter des plusieurs autres sources, mêmes matérielles, et surtout d'une meilleure réaction du système nerveux sur le système vasculaire' (x:276).

bility' of the current method, a 'systematic' approach could be taken to this 'most important of productions'. This would both facilitate population control (x:253) and make possible selective breeding ('hereditary transmission' would be 'reserved for its best organs') leading to a physiological improvement in the species as a whole (x:278). But again, as with the domestication of animals, there is a dimension of moral improvement. Indeed, that was the primary aim. By eliminating the need for sexual activity in human reproduction, we could create the biological conditions for universal celibacy. The ennoblement of marriage though chastity would mark an institutional advance equivalent to that which had previously led from polygamy to monogamy (ibid.). For women, whose desire for maternity was in any case greater than their purely sexual desire, this would be no effort. Motherhood itself, naturally, would remain – indeed, in the positively renewed image of *la Vierge-Mère*, it would be sanctified.[27] As for men, 'education and opinion would easily make prevail the need to conserve *le fluide vivifiant* for its normal destination' (x:277–8); this being to 'stimulate the blood' so as to 'strengthen all the vital operations' (x:276). The satirical possibilities of Comte's proposal, even without the religious trappings, are evident. (They have been deliciously explored in Vonnegut's short story 'Welcome to the Monkey House' (1968).) It may be noted, though, that Comte's preoccupation with virtue and saving women from sex at least deflected him from the growing Victorian flirtation with a purely racist eugenics.[28] The emphasis was on purifying the means of biological production at least as much as on enhancing the quality of results.

The last example is Comte's flight of fancy about improving the orbit of *la planète humaine*. The idea is alluded to in a passage of the *Catéchisme positiviste* where he is explaining his conception of 'modifiable fatality', and the mental attitude (resigned but active) which it implies. 'In proportion as the knowledge of the natural order extended', the priest tells his catechumen,

it was regarded as essentially modifiable, even by man . . . At present this idea extends even to the order of the heavens, its greater simplicity allowing us more easily to conceive improvements, with a view to correcting a spirit of blind

---

[27] Besides the inevitable *fête* with which the 'utopia' of *la Vierge-Mère* was associated, it was to hold a symbolically central place in Positive Religion, 'un résumé synthétique équivalent à celui que l'institution de l'Euchariste fournit au catholicisme' (x:279).

[28] In opposition to 'the irrational notion of races', Comte held to a Lamarckian theory (credited to 'a happy insight of Blainville') according to which 'les plus prononcées et fixes de ces différences vitales . . . paraissent dues à des influences locales, lentement accumulées par l'hérédité, jusqu'à produire le maximum correspondant de variation organique' (VIII:49). The frankly hypothetical nature of the theory is acknowledged, although it is still being prescribed for 'la saine philosophie . . . tant que les faits certains et nombreux ne le démentiront pas' (ibid.).

respect, though our weakness in regard to physical means for ever precludes our effecting them. (XI:54)

The idea is more specifically sketched out in the introduction to *Synthèse subjective*. It would be as if Earth itself 'could develop its physico-chemical activity so as to perfect the astronomical order by changing its own coefficients'. We are to imagine this occurring through a series of 'explosions like those that gave rise to the comets'. The effect would be to 'make the orbit of our planet less eccentric, and thenceforth more habitable' (XII:10).

Once more, what is striking is less the actual technology envisaged than its moral intent. Giving the planet a circular orbit would modify the climate. But why do it? Convenience and comfort are only part of the answer. In fact, as Comte makes clear (VIII:461), what is at stake with regard to all the technical measures that can be taken to correct for natural climatic conditions, from clothes and gas heating to the ultimate dream of orbital correction, is the cultural impact of geography on human difference.

Climate belongs to a larger list of 'sources of social modification' (VIII:443). These include the 'dynamic' *modifacteurs* associated with the role of individuals, and with the impact of (national) societies on one another, plus the 'fixed' ones of climate and genetic inheritance. Each represents an altering, but also alterable, aspect of the human milieu. Each is also destined to become progressively less influential as collective power grows, and as a fully developed harmony between organism and world comes to be established.[29] What diminishes the effect of 'dynamic' modifiers is both the global convergence towards industrialism and the growing importance of *continuité* in the 'normal' unity of the human ensemble.[30] In the case of climate and race, the stabilising and unifying effects of Humanity's 'ageing' are reinforced by the 'rise of civilisation' itself. Material advances which have enabled the species to spread out over the earth have increasingly smoothed out environmentally conditioned differences between group cultures. As the example of the lowered menstrual age in heated Russian cities seemed to show (VIII:461), technical compensations for natural differences in group conditions of life could even homogenise what were thought to be

---

[29] 'Quoique tous les modifacteurs deviennent de moins en moins intenses, la réaction du Grand-Être sur la fatalité qui le domine augmente sans cesse' (VIII:464).

[30] 'Il ne faut pas croire que cette source de croissante de régularité tienne seulement, ni même principalement, à l'heureuse transformation de notre activité collective, désormais industrielle au lieu de rester guerrière. Elle provient surtout de l'ascendant progressif que la continuité subjective acquiert nécessairement sur la solidarité objective. Devant cette prépondérance des morts, toutes les perturbations des vivants se dissipent de plus en plus' (VIII:463).

physiological differences between peoples. The overall effect of humanity's growing capacity to modify the 'involuntary' modifiers was to reverse, at the very summit of its social expression, the tendency of complex orders of reality to become ever more differentiated. If the 'law of increasing complication' operated unchecked in the human sphere, the question of social order, and with it that of morale as such, would have been insoluble. The correctives made possible by the growth of Humanity's modifying power were therefore crucial. They eliminate 'at first spontaneously, then more and more systematically', sources of disunity which stemmed from 'fundamental imperfections in the universal order' (VIII:459–60). The phrase is striking. An industrialism oriented to the self-perfecting moral unity of Humanity is drawn, 'more and more systematically', towards the 'improvement' of the *fatalité modifiable* of the Universe itself.

The ideal of an objectively perfected cosmos which Positivism subjectively installs at the heart of production is no doubt still human-centred. In the first instance, the measure of that outer perfection is the human perfection it would make possible. Beyond that, the ideal also transfers on to non-human reality, criteria of value – harmony, benevolence, unity – which first arose as ideals for humanity with regard to itself. However, an industrialism dedicated to such an end would certainly not be subordinating the appropriation of nature to egoistic motives such as greed, power-lust and vainglory. Nor, indeed, would it serve only to perfect the condition of the human species itself as a whole. For not only, in Comte's vision, does the Positively reconstructed project of industrialism assign to humanity *objectively* a cosmic mission to 'improve' on the pregiven material world, it does so *subjectively* as the most sublime expression of human love. That love – which Comte calls *l'amour universel* (VII:91) – is one that has become altruistic in the fullest possible sense. It is not just a love of each for all, of self for Self, of subject for Subject, but an affection which suffuses the whole world which humanity touches. It extends to the non-human Other. It even reaches beyond the world which is immediately and actively humanised. It moves outward to embrace, and benignly improve, not only everything in the range of the human senses, but the order of things as such.[31]

At the culminating stage, then, of the Positivist transformation, when

---

[31] 'Ainsi liée directement à l'ordre universel, l'Humanité se trouve pleinement dégagée de la tutelle fictive par laquelle son initiation dut spontanément suppléer l'absence de guide extérieur. Le Grand-Être inaugure irrévocablement sa providence universelle en appliquant l'ensemble des lois . . . à l'appréciation générale de son avenir et de la transition qu'il exige . . . Toutes les spéculations s'y tendent à consolider l'amour universel, seul capable de les systématiser, de les consacrer, et de les discipliner' (X:524–5).

Humanity has acquired the power to perfect the very order on which it depends, the human love for the human promises to transcend the collective *amour propre* that any humanism, however exalted, risks retaining as its limit. Cognitive humility was Bacon's first principle for a new science. For Comte, as for Bacon, this meant basing practice as well as theory on a recognition of the supremacy of immutable laws of nature. That recognition, however, clashed not only with the metaphysical inflation of individual reason, but also with the collective egoism that lordship over nature through positive science itself implied. Positivism's 'unanimous and continuous love' for 'the universal order' (VIII:368) resolved the antinomy. For it would entail not just grudgingly accepting, but cherishing and revering, the unsurpassable limitations which subordinate the Great Being of Humanity to the whole natural order – an order on which not just brute existence but even its 'modifying power' totally depend. With this moral step towards an affectively saturated humility, *le destin* itself (positively comprehended as 'the ensemble of known laws' (IV:191)) would be embraced.

Systematic fetishism and *l'amour universel*

The *amor fati* which crowns Comte's logico-historical account of the triumph of love in a curious way fulfills Saint-Simon's earlier gropings for a moral principle which would connect a scientific understanding of cosmic order to St Paul's dictum that God is love. Saint-Simon speculated that Newton's law of gravity, converted into a thesis of 'universal attraction', might provide the requisite link.[32] In similar fashion, the 'destiny' which Positive Religion enjoins and prepares us to love is conceived not just as a sobering corrective to human pride, but as Love itself writ large. Destiny soars on the wings of *la sympathie universelle*, both because *le destin* is imagined to be benevolent *towards* us and because *l'ordre universel* which it brings to perfection *through* us is an analogue of the moral Good to which Humanity historically tends.

However, Comte's conception of 'universal sympathy' departs from Saint-Simon's in two important respects. First, the benign character of the laws which rule the Comtean universe – its natural tendency towards the perfection of order – abstractly derives from the homeostatic properties of dynamic systems (I:602) rather than from the mutually attractive

---

[32] Saint-Simon's notion that the law of gravity might provide a 'law of laws' is outlined in his 1813 essay 'Sur la gravitation universelle', an extract from which is translated in Markham, 1952. For Comte, the law of gravity had an exemplary simplicity and generality, since it had 'radicalement liée toutes les notions célestes, à un degré dont la sociologie offre seule l'équivalent' (VII:512); but it otherwise held no special place in his system.

energetics of matter. Secondly, its scientific status in Comte's system is crucially different from the place it held in Saint-Simon's. For Comte, an absolute objective synthesis of the kind Saint-Simon sought as the axiomatic basis for a demythologised 'terrestrial morality' was ruled out of court. The Positivist synthesis was 'relative', and that meant relative to the standpoint, impulses and requirements of the evolving human observer. By the same token, it could only be 'subjective', both in the sense of aligning its founding principles with a frankly human standpoint and in being achievable only through, and in the form of, a certain blend of feeling and thinking. The sociolatric belief that universal sympathy without mirrored universal sympathy within was not given directly by reason, nor could it be justified by the strict operations of a phenomenal science.[33] It involved an attribution, inspired by faith, whose effects were moral and whose cognitive status was emphatically *fictif*.

It is in just this context that Comte undertakes his most startling manoeuvre: the proposed resuscitation of that elemental religious mode he called *fétichisme*. Not only, in fact, does he introduce it into his system as a necessary doctrinal supplement to the religion of Humanity, one that would complete *l'ordre légal* with *l'ordre volontaire* (XI:7), but in the *Logique positive* he begins to reconfigure Positivist worship itself into an updated and 'systematic' form of fetishism. The effect on his attempt to think the religious requirements of industrial society was to push the search for *une foi démontrable* to the point of complete contradiction. On the one hand, by securing, in an explicitly subjective mode, the final closure of his system, he risked reducing it to a social solipsism. On the other hand, by expanding the Positivist cult to include adoration of the whole 'universal order', he risked diminishing or even dethroning the divinised Humanity that was its focal object.

Comte, like Marx in the first chapter of *Capital*, took his conception of fetishism from contemporary writings on religion which hypothesised the animistic worship of material objects as its original form.[34] The

---

[33] Hence the order to be pursued by Positivist education, which would only initiate its pupils into the sciences by way of the subjectively synthesised seven sciences, and then only when preceded by a course in *la morale*. 'En effet, le dogme fondamentale de l'Humanité . . . ne caractérisent pleinement que les lois morales, sans pouvoir assez manifester les lois intellectuelles, et surtout les lois physiques. Il faut donc que celles-ci deviennent le principal objet de l'initiation abstraite, qui conduira graduellement à concevoir le Grand-Être comme le résumé nécessaire de l'ordre dont il constitue le meilleur élément' (X:193). To proceed directly into scientific education risked 'dessécher le coeur en détournant du but synthétique par des préoccupations analytiques' (X:192).

[34] According to Manuel (1962:186–7), the term fetishism, derived from Portuguese, was invented by Charles de Brosses in his *Culte des dieux fétiches*, and came to Comte via Benjamin Constant's use of it in *De la religion*.

'evidence' for this supposition was provided by imperial European contact with aboriginal cultures in North America, Africa and Polynesia. What were thought to be common elements in the religions of *les sauvages* were abstracted into an ideal type and projected back in time in order to complete the developmental sequence that could be traced from antiquity through medieval Christianity to the science and enlightenment of modern times.

Comte's re-evaluation of fetishism proceeds through a series of increasingly sympathetic refinements to the initial assessment he made of it in *Philosophie positive*. There, with the accent on the problem of knowledge, and against the background of a maturation model of cognitive development, he had balanced his epistemological critique of fetishism as an illusory form of knowing with a 'constructive' appreciation for its historically necessary role. On the first score, fetishism's hypothesis that entities were inhabited by spirits whose wilful activity (which we might influence through ritual or prayer) ruled the phenomenal world[35] was taken to be the matrix for every kind of 'theological' belief, up to and including the abstract essentialism of 'metaphysics' itself. On the other hand, and in opposition to the Enlightenment's (and Christianity's) purely negative judgment of primitive superstition, humanity's fetishist origins were not simply to be dismissed with 'smug disdain'. Both for individuals and for society as a whole, starting hypotheses, however fantastic, were essential if knowledge was to advance at all (v:50–1). Retrospectively considered, then, and even as we took pride in the distance humanity had travelled since this 'miserable original condition', we should accord fetishism – like childhood – the utmost respect as an indispensable and preparatory first step in the progress of the human mind (v:16).

But already this still somewhat condescending qualification was reinforced by an additional consideration. This was fetishism's role in the education of the (moral) sentiments. Besides providing a 'provisional' system of socially unifying belief, the specific hallmark of fetishism was that it combined a general preponderance of 'passions over reason' with a projection of such feelings into its personifications of the external world. To be sure, the ratio of feeling to intellect in *fétichisme* (as in those momentary fits of emotionalism which affect 'even the best minds') was excessive (v:37). This made impossible that freedom from dogma necessary for a field of phenomena to be investigable in a fact-oriented manner. Moreover, while commerce with spirits sustained an

---

[35] Fetishism always consisted of supposing 'les corps extérieurs, même les plus inertes, animés des passions et de volontés plus ou moins analogues aux impressions personnelles du spectateur' (v:29).

illusion of human power, and so stimulated 'the first rise of human activity', the fetishisation of 'most external bodies' interdicted 'all serious environmental modification', so that the development of that activity was extremely slow (v:56–7). Nevertheless, fetishist taboos had been responsible for moderating the destruction of fauna and flora and had paved the way for the domestication of animals (v:55). In its mimetic and imagistic forms of communication, fetishism had also developed a mode of representation that combined concept, percept and feeling (v:38). Overall, in fact, fetishism's 'spontaneous consecration' of *le dehors* had the singular merit of presenting the world as in 'perfect harmony with the spectator', a harmony which provided 'a full satisfaction' and which has never since been able to be retrieved.[36] This foreshadowed a subjective harmony of humanity and world which positivism alone would be able to recover and place on a scientific basis.

In *Politique positive*, this argument is taken still further. The fetishist peopling of sensuous reality with living beings evinced a venerative love towards *le dehors* which was essential for the rise of both knowledge and social life.[37] In this respect, indeed, and for all its intellectually untutored enthusiasm, fetishism was morally superior to the more advanced forms of 'theologism' which succeeded it. This was not to deny their own contributions. The rise of the gods had coincided with the rise of *civisme*, and the monotheist priesthood, at its Catholic best, had given a powerful impetus to the development of *altruisme*. However, the theological apotheosis of the divine absolute had alienated humankind from its most elevated sentiments in dealing with its own milieu. Fetishism imagined that all entities were moved by feeling and wilfully active. The Greek and Roman pantheons were still full of nature gods, though

---

[36] 'Tous les corps observables étant ainsi immédiatement personnifiés, et doués de passions ordinairement très puissantes, selon l'énergie de leur phénomènes, le monde extérieur se présente spontanément, envers le spectateur, dans une parfaite harmonie, qui n'a pu jamais retrouver ensuite au même degré, et qui doit produire en lui un sentiment spécial de pleine satisfaction, qui nous ne pouvons guère qualifier aujourd'hui convenablement, faute de pouvoir suffisament l'éprouver, même en nous reportant, par la méditation plus intense et la mieux dirigée, à ce berceau de l'humanité' (v:36–7).

[37] 'Pour qu'une telle conclusion acquière toute sa force sociologique, il faut la rattacher directement au principe universel de la logique positive: subordonner convenablement le subjectif à l'objectif, en construisant toujours la plus simple hypothèse qui puisse représenter l'ensemble des observations. Or cette soumission fondamentale de l'homme au monde se trouve instituée autant que possible par le fétichisme, puisqu'il la pousse jusqu'à l'adoration de la matière, d'après les affections et les volontés qu'il attribue au corps extérieurs' (IX:91–2).

[38] This had epistemological consequences as well. 'En renonçant ensuite à rien connaître au delà des lois réelles . . . on écarte ce rapprochement entre la mort et la vie, comme incompatible avec la régularité supérieure de l'ordre matériel. Mais la division fondamentale de la science physique en cosmologie et biologie maintient partout

limited in scope and power by a pitiless Ananke. Monotheism imagined the cosmos to be both dead and inert.[38] All wilful activity was reserved for a hidden God who sat outside phenomena and intervened (whether miraculously or as a continuing first cause of natural law) from a nether-world beyond the merely actual one given by our senses.

Here then was a reason not just to praise the historical contribution of our ancestors' first religion, but in some form or another to restore it. The fetishist imaginary offered a corrective to the withdrawal of affect from the natural world, a withdrawal which had become chronic even before the transitional epoch of metaphysics when an overweening intellect had rebelled against all fideistic restraint. For Comte this rebellion had been historically necessary. The monotheistic synthesis had to be intellectually overthrown for a better, science-based, one to arise. For that very reason, however, it had also become necessary to repair the subjective split between head and heart which that rebellion had made worse – a split which had produced such pathological outcomes as the inflation of signs over images and sentiments,[39] the reductive arrogance of *algébristes* (VII:471) and the inattention of revolutionary *légistes* to the subjective dimension of the society they would reform.

To achieve the requisite restoration of balance between intellect and sentiment it was immediately necessary to institute the religion of Humanity. But Comte's renewed appreciation for *fétichisme*, particularly in its difference from succeeding forms of theistic religion, had brought him to realise that this was insufficient if it terminated only in the reaffecting of the *human* milieu. Happily, the subjective and altruistic turn effected by the culmination of the scientific revolution in the moral science of man did not terminate there. Sociologising the episteme transformed all the other sciences, making it possible to reconceptualise their objects of knowledge as objects for us, and not merely in the instrumental sense. The domains of positive science, as reconceived from the vantage point of *la science finale*, become objects of affection,

---

l'activité spontanée, après l'élimination des attributs humains que le fétichisme y joignait. Sans une telle activité, seulement plus intense et variée chez les êtres vivants, l'ensemble de l'ordre naturel deviendrait inintelligible' (IX:88).

[39] An error compounded, for Comte, by a metaphysical theory of language which exaggerated the arbitrary character of conventional signs. 'Les vrais signes ne sont jamais arbitraires' (VIII:221). Needless to say, Comte's positive theory of language – which emphasised the function of language in 'fixing habitual links between the inside and the outside' – not only insisted on its socially produced character but also privileged the spoken over the written. 'Le langage visuel, qui d'abord prévalait, finit par devenir un simple auxiliaire du langage auditif' (VIII:230–1). One notes, though, that this is connected to a historical thesis according to which human language began through gestural imitation, and thus – unlike in romantic versions of phonocentrism (which stress the authenticity and originality of the voice) – was more visual than phonic in the 'primitive state'.

just as their human subject, no longer just a disembodied brain, becomes a socially implicated and subjectively coordinated centre of thinking, acting and feeling. With the establishment of such a doctrine, Positivism

directly combines the notion of the human order with that of the universal order, in representing the one as the necessary summary of the other. At the same time as this intimate connection procures for the artificial order the spontaneous consistency of the natural order, it makes us love the one as the basis for the other, in such a manner as to renew, under a better form, fetishist affections. (VIII:368)

But what was this 'better form'? And how could a renewal of 'fetishist affections' be achieved at all without violating scientific reason? The *Politique positive* had only posed these questions. It was not until publication of the *Logique positive* that Comte directly makes the case not just for 'appreciating' fetishism (for example in the memorial festivals devoted to it in the Positivist Calendar's seventh month) but for expanding Positive Religion – and its godhead – so as to incorporate elements of fetishism into the cult of Humanity itself.

Comtean sociology, as outlined in the *Politique positive*, had already indicated that the need to break from anthropomorphism and animist magic in scientific practice by no means eliminated the irreducible functions which these might play at another level – for example in the social production and reproduction of solidarity. To which, in the opening section of the *Système de logique positive*, he now added that even at the *cognitive* level the fictive explanations of fetishism would always have their place. The 'fundamental sciences' produced only formal, nomothetic, knowledge. As useful as this was for predicting and manipulating the external milieu, it could never fully satisfy our need for a unified understanding of *le dehors*, because formal knowledge only offered a limited handhold in grasping the always evanescent plenum of the real. 'In considering that each group of phenomena cannot ever be entirely fixed, one recognises that the immutability of natural laws cannot be squared with composite events, and remains limited to their irreducible elements' (XII:7). To imagine, then, that the complexity of events was benignly directed by phenomena themselves would enable us, beyond the limit of positive knowledge, to close the gap of explanation, while obviating any slide into resentment or despair that might otherwise be projected into this gap.

Nevertheless, archaic forms of fetishism could not just be wrenched from their socio-historical context and imported holus-bolus. If 'the domain of fiction' was to complement rather than contradict a positivised world-view, it had to 'become as systematic as that of demonstration, in order that their mutual harmony may conform to their respective destinations' (XII:12). In the most general terms, and following a schema in which the highest order of existence possessed not just 'life' but the attributes of thinking, acting and feeling, the universe could be imagined to consist of three orders of being. At the coordinating apex, *l'Humanité* alone was to be understood as possessing not just feeling and activity but an intelligent will. In a second category was the physical order of external reality, centred on *la planète humaine*. This order was not sentient. However, '[in] dissipating the theological prejudices which would represent matter as entirely inert, science tends to lend it the character of activity, which fetishism had spontaneously consecrated' (9). The 'final wisdom' of Positivism makes such consecration systematic, treating all activity 'as led by love towards universal harmony' (10). It thus 'conceives the world as aspiring to support man' – both in an everyday sense, but also through such fictions as orbital self-correction – 'in order to ameliorate the universal order under the impulsion of the Great Being' (X:12).

These first two orders grouped together all the concrete phenomena treated by the fundamental sciences. The first category included the domains of *la morale* and sociology; the second, that of physics (further divided into terrestrial and celestial). Biology was included in the first according to the 'dogmatical division' between cosmology and sociology and in the second according to the 'historical division' between external reality and the social and moral order. But there remained a third category consisting of the 'abstract' or 'fundamental' order in which were assembled those universal laws which pertained to 'the forms of existence common to all things'.[40] This was the domain of mathematics. It dealt with the most general laws of nature. It was also therefore the domain of the 'unmodifiable', and thus of that 'supreme fatality' which Positivism's reconstructed morale invested with all the majesty of a benign power standing over the universal order in the very process by which, through the actions of 'the Great Being', it was brought to perfection. This most abstract yet most fundamental dimension of being was to be conceived as pure sentiment. As the 'general milieu in which things accomplish themselves', it was 'animated only by universal sympathy, without action as without reflection' (XII:23).

The practical point of Comte's trichotomy was to bring within the orbit of an altruistic affection the entirety of the cosmos in which Humanity is placed. But this required that its principal elements not just be capable of being conceptualised as such. They needed to be rendered

---

[40] See Table B, 'Theoretical Hierarchy of Human Conceptions: or Synthetical View of the Universal Order', reproduced in the appendix to the English translation of the *Catéchisme positiviste* (Comte, 1973).

in a symbolic form through which they could be grasped by the sentiments as well as by the intellect. And, indeed, not just casually, but systematically, so that they could serve, and be affectively reinforced, as objects of worship. For this, evidently, not just the abstract language of science was needed but those forms of sentiment-laden representations which Comte called 'images'.

The iconic representation of Humanity itself presented no problem. With the image of Clotilde ever before his mind's eye, the individual 'servant' and 'agent' of Humanity could serve as a metonym for that larger whole which, in deference to the completeness of its existence, and to its aptness to stand in for the personal(ised) deity of the monotheists, Comte dubbed *Le* Grand-Être. In its greater amorphousness, the second term of the Positivist trinity was more difficult. To represent the physical, or 'cosmological', order *La Terre* was what humanly mattered. In the days before space photography, however, this Grand Fétiche could hardly be pictured, so Comte urged recourse to the poetic and artistic imagery that surrounded the idea of *le Monde* (XII:18). The real difficulty, however, concerned the third term in the series. It was wholly abstract and lacked a physical site. Comte's brilliant but eclectic solution was to fuse a western mathematical idea – the geometers' and logicians' 'space' – with the traditional Chinese worship of Heaven. The latter provided the signifying materials through which the purely ideational reality of the former could be symbolically invested with the spiritual force of *l'amour universel*. Space was not just emptiness, a universal container, but the generative medium in which we might imagine the most general laws of existence taking shape. 'In order that sympathy can be sufficiently developed, it is necessary to idealise not just the objective world, but also the subjective milieu in which we place all external phenomena' (X:23). Altogether, then, in the figure of a transcendent and fecund emptiness, the most abstract order of reality, its ordering as such is identified first with sentiment purified of activity and intelligence, then with fate, and finally with the logico-mathematical notion of an all-englobing *Espace*.

Not the least striking aspect of this third member of the trinity is that it brings Comte close to suggesting that nothingness is the ground of all being. Comte is drawn in that direction by a phenomenalism that had always regarded the category of being as suspect and insisted that events, not existences, were the proper topic for scientific inquiry. Unlike Nietzsche and Heidegger, however, through whom the negatively theological, or in the case of Mark Taylor (1984) the a/theological, implications of this thought have entered into contemporary postmodern discourse, Comte's rendition of it was firmly inscribed within a realism of the social. Priority is always given to what he takes to be the moral, reproductive, unifying and self-perfecting requirements of the social body. Thus his encounter with nothingness is never abyssal. The Space he would have us worship is filled with an edifying and harmonising content. Immediately following his enthusiastic proposal for the worship of Space, indeed, he further softens its potentially disturbing negativity. The 'full' properties of *l'Espace* – as the loving seat of *l'ordre universel* – are identified with those of the 'ether', which the popular astronomy of his day was wont to place in stellar space in consistency with the old dictum about nature abhorring a vacuum. 'Abridging the interval which the World, that is to say the Earth, fills between Space and Humanity, we can directly connect the two furthest elements of the supreme trinity, in attributing to *le fluide générale* the objectivity of the most abstract laws' (XII:25).

The categories of Positivism's expanded godhead in any case remained firmly *fictif*, and their ultimate justification was the greater human unity which they might make possible. From the beginning, indeed, Comte's synthesis had intended to provide the basis not only for harmonising individual minds. It aimed to be culturally ecumenical, both with regard to the past, so as to maximise its effects on social continuity, and internationally so as to maximise its potential for solidarising humanity on a global scale. Completing the 'Catholicism minus Christianity' of his scientific Humanism with the cultus of *le* Grand Fétiche and *le* Grand Milieu was conceived, *inter alia*, as a cross-cultural syncretism which would bring such unifying efforts to a climactic fulfilment. 'Rallying the elite of the white race with the majority of the yellow and the whole of the black, only the incorporation of fetishism into positivism can consolidate the universal religion' (XII:23).

Such arguments, however, in all the chimerical, not to say imperialising, guise in which they now appear, should not divert us from critically scrutinising the evolving socio-theology that remains at their core. Now that the main elements have been assembled, it is possible to consider that core more fully: not only as a response to the theoreticoideological requirements of the religious crisis Comte diagnosed, but also in the light they might throw more generally on the post-Nietzschean situation, and especially on the problems that arise when attempts are made to fill the nihilist void with divine or quasi-divine valuations of the human collectivity. I will turn to these questions in the next chapter.

For the present it will be enough to point out that Comte's final writings complicate any simple dismissal of his position as unthinkingly technological, or even as 'humanist' in the flatly anthropocentric sense criticised by Heidegger in his 'Letter on Humanism'.[41] This is not to say, however, that Comte's final position is completely unassailable in such terms. His supplemental injunction to worship *la Terre* sidesteps, rather than frontally addresses, the man/nature contradiction which Rousseau detected in the proto-industrial movement of modernity and which Marx envisaged as soluble, if at all, only through the abolition of private property. To worship *le Grand Fétiche*, while directing aggression away from warfare towards its useful exploitation, implies an aesthetic desecration at odds with sacralising the Earth. Comte avoids thinking about this by focussing on the 'universal love' implicit in the natural order itself, an order which is ultimately abstract and located beyond *la planète humaine* in any concrete and practical–sensuous sense.

Thus in the end Positivism only avoids an idolatry of Humanity by idolising order as such. The proposed cult of *l'Espace* makes evident that apotheosis of unity, and of the subordination of parts to the whole, of the ontic (beings) to the ontological (Being), which pervades every aspect of Comte's system. In making this move, moreover, the divine principle that begins to migrate in the *Synthèse subjective* from Humanity as such to a certain human idea of the cosmos becomes doctrinally lodged within subjectivity itself. On the face of it, this violates the defining principle of Positivism's *foi démontrable*, namely that *le dedans* should always subordinate itself to *le dehors*. In loving the universal order which the positivised soul projects into the universe, that faith remains wrapped up in its own subjectivity. Far from finding its *intellectum* in a fully scientific self-understanding, then, the faith that seeks it finds only itself. Indeed, if we question what Comte takes for granted – the identification of moral and physical perfection with one another in the idea of a perfectly harmonious formal system – the whole System dissolves into the arbitrary.

---

[41] '. . . the thinking in *Being and Time* is against humanism. But this opposition does not mean that such thinking aligns itself against the humane and advocates the inhuman, that it promotes the inhumane, and deprecates the dignity of man. Humanism is opposed because it does not set the *humanitas* of man high enough. Of course the essential worth of man does not consist in his being the substance of beings, as the 'Subject' among them, so that as the tyrant of Being he may deign to release the beingness of beings into an all too loudly bruited 'objectivity'. Man is rather 'thrown' from Being itself into the truth of Being, so that ek-sisting in this fashion he might appear in the light of Being as the beings they are . . . in accord with this destiny man as ek-sisting has to guard the truth of Being. Man is the shepherd of Being' (Heidegger, 1977b:210).

7 Humanity as '*le vrai* Grand-Être'

Comte's trinitarian formula for the Positivist godhead discloses the same general tension as appears throughout his system. A this-worldly, and antimetaphysical, demythologisation of the kind attempted more maximally by Nietzsche coexists with a remythologisation designed to buttress a new, and this time unassailable, foundation for reestablishing subjective unity in the face of the anarchy he feared was terminal. What resolves the tension is that the latter consideration is always given the upper hand. The 'sufficient incorporation of fetishism into positivism' (XI:7) leads neither to perspectivalism, nor to an unsettling infinitude, nor to a real plurality of gods. It produces a hierarchy in which *La Terre* and *l'Espace*, in their guise, respectively, of Grand Fétiche and Grand Milieu, are completely dependent for their religious meaning on the Grand-Être they make possible and whose worship heads the list.[1] If they are themselves to be regarded as sacred, it is only as a projective extension of *l'Humanité* or, more precisely, of the 'universal sympathy' engendered in and through us as its constituent agents and organs. The viability of the whole construct continues to hinge, then, on the move which in some sense made *l'Humanité* itself into a god.

[1] It should be cautioned that Comte's ideas on the Positivist godhead evolved considerably after he first introduced the worship of *le* Grand-Être, and were not fully worked out by the time he died. The categories of *le monde* and *l'espace* make their appearance in the last volume of *Politique positive* in a general discussion about positive education. To supplement its scientific side he proposes the establishment of *une poésie positiviste*, employing 'un nouvel ordre de moyens poétiques, que suscite la fusion normale de la fétichité dans la positivité . . . Par une telle incorporation, la maturité de l'art rentre en possession du monde extérieur . . . En développant ce domaine initial, la poésie positive devra l'étendre autant aux phénomènes qu'aux substances, d'après l'essor abstrait partout accompli depuis le fétichisme. Or, ce nouveau champ exige l'institution préalable des milieux subjectifs . . . [L]'éspace offre le premier exemple, et jusqu'ici le plus complèt, d'un tel artifice logique' (X:53). These hints grow into the full-scale trinity presented in the first chapter of the *Logique positive* two years later. This discussion is confined, though, to matters of theory and doctrine. The implications for worship and liturgy are left out of consideration. Given an already crowded, and multiply systematised, calendar of festivals, it is here, perhaps, that Comte might have been led to address the potential contradiction between his Sociolatry and a growing inclination to worship *l'ordre universel* as a whole.

What Comte sought – and thought he had found – was a god which, unlike the 'fictive beings' of the 'theological stage', would be intellectually in tune with the principles of positive science while still being able to play the authoritative and centring role for the individual and for society as a whole which 'God' had formerly played. I have tried to show how shaky the scaffolding was on which this whole edifice is built. However, as I have also argued, even as a flawed endeavour, Comte's attempt to replace God with *l'Humanité* is more worthy of examination than has usually been thought. The divinisation of humankind, whether explicit or not, goes to the heart of progressive, post-theistic attempts to rethink modernity's ideological situation, and the very contradictions by which Comte's positivist theology of the human are beset belong to what has long been problematic in that situation. Indeed, if we read Comte's oeuvre in this way it can acquire a fresh relevance to contemporary social thought, even as that thought grapples with the ethical and political implications of the groundlessness which it claims as its own, and which has swallowed up every kind of 'grand narrative' including that of the socio(-theo)logy that descends from Comte.

Faith after 'God'

Nietzsche wrote little directly about Comte. Yet from scattered comments and allusions it is evident that the discoverer of the Eternal Return considered the founder of Positivism one of the few modern thinkers of the first rank. In *Twilight of the Idols*, the rise of phenomenalism makes its appearance, after the long night of Greek and Christian metaphysical idealism, as 'day break – the first yawnings of reason' (1990:50). *Daybreak*, the book, places Comte himself at the summit of the scientific spirit's emancipatory movement. He is 'that great honest Frenchman beside whom, as embracer and conqueror of the strict sciences, the German and English of this century can place no rival' (1982:215).

At the same time, there was no question of following Comte into his religion of Humanity. Like others who found something to admire in the early Comte, Nietzsche thought that the *Grand-prêtre de l'Humanité*, with that self-identification, had gone off the rails. The chiding, though, is gentle. With the weariness of approaching old age, Comte, like Plato, had just stopped thinking. He had surrounded himself with acolytes through whom he sought only to monumentalise himself, and had infused the courageous and astringent 'work of his life' with 'enthusiasms, spices, poetic mists and mystic lights' (1982:215). Comte's decline into a rigid and lachrymose religiosity was in any case a secondary matter. It represented the extreme expression of a moralism which Nietzsche objected to fundamentally, and which, just as much as 'the embrace and conquest of the exact sciences', had been at the heart of Comte's project from the start.

Only in its exaggerations, moreover, was Comte's apotheosis of the social sentiments particularly idiosyncratic. Teachings about 'the sympathetic affects and of pity or the advantage to others as a principle of behaviour' were 'the moral undercurrent of the age'.[2] Such teachings 'have shot up with a mighty impetus everywhere', Nietzsche notes, and 'every socialist system has placed itself as if involuntarily' on their common ground. As for the French case, where the chasm between freethinking and an unreconstructed church was deepest:

The more one liberated oneself from dogmas, the more one sought as it were a *justification* of this liberation in a cult of philanthropy: not to fall short of the Christian ideal in this, but where possible to outdo it, was a secret spur with all French freethinkers from Voltaire to Auguste Comte: and the latter did in fact, with his moral formula *Vivre pour autrui*, outchristian Christianity. (1982:83)

Comte, then, was a Janus figure, his thought an arrow pointing backwards towards 'declining' values as well as forwards towards transvaluation. The error of his way had been to seek a synthesis between Christianity's 'moral residuum' and the scientific outlook – rather than, as Nietzsche himself attempted, to use the force of the latter to hammer the former to pieces.

Both Nietzsche and Comte claimed that their radically divergent positions were not only in tune with a scientific approach to human realities, but flowed directly from the rupture in thought which the adoption of such an approach entailed. In view of this, it is at first sight surprising that Nietzsche avoids an engagement with Comte's insistent linkage of the scientific to the moral via sociology and a science of Man. Pragmatically, perhaps, he felt no need to. In place of Comte's 'cerebral physiology' and 'sociology' he was simply operating with a different batch of special sciences – including classical philology, his own version of a corporeally based psychology, and a cultural hermeneutics historiographically extended into a 'genealogy of morals'. With these he pro-

---

[2] 'Today it seems *to do everyone good* when they hear that society is on the way to *adapting* the individual to general requirements, and that *happiness and at the same time the sacrifice of the individual* lies in feeling himself to be a useful member and instrument of the whole; except that one is at present very uncertain as to where this whole is to be sought, whether in an existing state or one still to be created, or in the nation, or in a brotherhood of peoples, or in new little economic communalities . . . but there is also a wonderful and far-sounding unanimity in the demand that the ego has to deny itself until, in the form of adaptation to the whole, it again acquires its firmly set circle of rights and duties' (Nietzsche, 1982:83).

ceeded to his own 'scientific' reading of the contemporary European 'moral' situation. It was left to others (above all Foucault), immersed in a further century of social-scientific development, to argue that Nietzsche's conception of the terrain covered by the *sciences humaines* – distributed among the vectors of life, language and labour (Foucault, 1970:351) – was more in line with the development these sciences came to mark out; and to argue, more importantly, that a scientific approach to the human precluded the very category of Man which emerged at the centre of Comte's construction as its transcendental referent and foundation.[3] Thus, we might say, a Nietzschean engagement with the 'anthropologism' underpinning Comte's moralism was (philosophically) possible, but (social-scientifically) postponed.

But we must also add: Nietzsche did not 'hear' Comte's argument for and about altruism in the first place, because there was no place in his thinking for its *sociological* register. It is not just that he rejected a hypostasised collective subject, as for example in the 'new idol' of the state (1961:75–8). For him, the movement of knowledge from the domain of individual strivings to the plane of social reality, however conceived, involved no shift in optic, no epistemological break. There was no specifically *social* reality to know.[4] All he could do, then, with Comte's 'outchristianing of Christianity', or indeed with the many senses the word 'social' acquired in nineteenth-century socialism, was to deconstruct it as the determinate expression of a reactive illusion.[5]

---

[3] 'To imagine for an instant what the world and thought would be if man did not exist, is considered to be merely engaging in paradox. This is because we are so blinded by the recent manifestation of man that we can no longer remember a time – and it is not so long ago – when the world, its order, and human beings existed, but man did not. It is easy to see why Nietzsche's thought should have had, and still has for us, such a disturbing power when it is introduced in the form of an imminent event, the Promise–Threat, the notion that man would soon be no more – but would be replaced by the superman; in a philosophy of the Return, this meant that man had long since disappeared and would continue to disappear, and that our modern thought about man, our concern for him, our humanism, were all sleeping serenely over the threatening rumble of his non-existence' (Foucault, 1970:322).

[4] With regard to Nietzsche's political thinking, Daniel Conway has challenged the conventional interpretation that he was a 'failed radical voluntarist', arguing that he was attempting to reopen the 'founding political question', that is, 'the justification of humankind itself, the warrant for its future as a viable, thriving species' (Conway, 1997). Conway does not challenge the view, though, that Nietzsche's thought was more generally assimilated to a paradigm which combines a voluntarist understanding of 'institutions' with a biologically framed understanding of 'peoples'. An investigation into Nietzsche's social categories, or lack of them, might start by looking precisely at his category of 'institution'. 'Our institutions are no longer fit for anything: everyone is unanimous about that. But the fault lies not in them but in *us*. Having lost all the instincts out of which institutions grow, we are losing the institutions themselves, because *we* are no longer fit for them' (Nietzsche, 1990:104).

[5] 'My objection to the whole of sociology in England and France is that it knows from

Nor, for the same reason, did Nietzsche have anything to say about the content of Comte's religious turn. Its content: not its weary tone of 'poetic mists and mystic lights', nor its punctilious prescriptions, but its precipitation, out of a sociologically transformed moralism, of a new deity. *Ecce Homo* (1969) concludes with the challenge: 'Have I been understood? – Dionysus vs the Crucified'. But if the Christian God was dead, was not the Crucified also? To which extent, as Nietzsche himself argued, the crucial fault line in the modern ideological field was no longer between Christianity (Reformed or Counter-Reformed) and everything he meant by Dionysus, but between the latter and Christianity's enlightened secular afterlife, including socialism in all its (not necessarily left-wing or even anticapitalist) forms.

Comte's contribution was to push the idea of the social all the way. Society was to be *worshipped* – not only because of the functional requirements of establishing industrial order, but because it is the genuine source of all that is sacred. Indeed, the 'Supreme Existence' constituted by humanity is now, as it latently was all along, *le vrai* Grand-Être (VII:354). It would have been more accurate, then, for Nietzsche's challenge to have been written: Dionysus vs Humanity. Such a divinity, however, was hard to recognise, even as a vital illusion, from a perspective that ruled out the possibility of any kind of transcending 'we'. When radical humanists lament that 'God is not yet dead because Man is not yet alive' (Gardavsky, 1973) latter-day Nietzscheans can only reply with a shrug. The small-'s' subject and the big-'S' Subject constitute one another (Althusser, 1971:170–7), the unitary 'we' and unitary 'I' are equally imagined in the image of a transcendental absolute, and if God is indeed dead, so too, his face in the sand erased by the sea, is Man (Foucault, 1970:387).

Even among those nineteenth-century thinkers who were sympathetic to the religio-moral dimension of Comte's project, there was a tendency to ignore, or explain away, the full force of what he came to affirm. Lévy-Bruhl, for example, whose *Philosophy of Auguste Comte* emphasised the underlying continuity between the *Cours* and the *Politique positive*, assumed that Comte's use of a theological vocabulary in reference to the subject–object of social science was only tactical. Positivism had always been a 'faith', and it remained one that was distinctive in being 'demonstrable'. As for the apparent contradiction in Comte's very notion of *une foi démontrable* (X:267), this 'lies merely on the surface'.

The number of men with sufficient leisure and enough culture to examine the conclusions and go into their proofs will always be small. The attitude of the

experience only the *decaying forms* of society and takes its own decaying instincts . . . as the *norm* of sociological value-judgment' (Nietzsche, 1990:103).

others must be one of submission and respect. But, differing on this point from the religious dogmas which humanity has known till now, the new faith will be 'demonstrated'. It will contain nothing which has not been established and controlled by scientific methods, nothing which goes beyond the domain of the relative, nothing which at any moment cannot be proved to a mind capable of following the demonstration. (Lévy-Bruhl, 1973:26–7)

Faith therefore signifies here not indeed a voluntary abdication of the intellect in the presence of a mystery which surpasses its power of comprehension, but a submission to fact, which in no way encroaches upon the rights of reason. (29–30)

The weakness of Lévy-Bruhl's gloss lies not so much in the distinction drawn between esoteric and exoteric doctrine – for which there is ample warrant in Comte's emphatically hierarchical conception of religious as of every other dimension of social organisation – as in his differential rendering of the word *foi*. In supernatural religion we have dogma and *foi révélatoire*, in Positivism *une foi démontrable*. Even the faith of the unlettered Positivist follower is of the latter type. In effect, however, this is to confuse two distinctions. One distinction is between the first-hand faith of those who know by some kind of immediate intuition, and that of those who accept, 'on faith', second-hand accounts of what is to be believed. The second – less self-evidently absolute than Lévy-Bruhl assumed – contrasts 'revelation' and 'demonstration' (based on 'fact') as alternative bases for religious faith. As a result of this conflation, 'revealed' religion is assumed to be wholly dogmatic and of the 'follower' type, Positivist followers are absolved of all credulousness, and at the summit, where faith and scientific knowledge supposedly converge, Comte's own faith is assumed – as pure 'submission to fact' – to be so far from the leaps and projections of revealed religion as to have nothing fideistic about it.

Quite aside from all the difficulties surrounding the identification (and construction) of factuality (if facts are always 'relative', how can they elicit 'submission'?), this understanding of Comte's credo relies on a reduced notion of religious faith: faith is just a species of strongly held opinion. In accordance with that, it depreciates the revealed quality of the old monotheism which rested, in its living core, not on dogma but on testimony (however mythic and distorted we may take it to be). It equally ignores the presence, at least after 1847, of a directly experienced quality in Comte's own religiosity, glossing over such things as his emphasis on (private) prayer.[6] The habit of prayer is enjoined not just for the Positivised masses, who must school themselves to obey, but for

---

[6] As a theoretical correlate, Lévy-Bruhl ignores the way that Comte, after 1847, modified his conception of Positivist faith so as to include a dimension of love. See chap. 1 of *Politique positive*'s second volume, especially VIII:7–59.

the whole Positivist priesthood. But why should scientists and positive philosophers *pray*? More to the point: to what or to whom? Not to address that question is to misconstrue the character, for Comte himself, of his 'demonstrable faith'.

To be sure, this 'faith' accorded with what Comte took to be scientific certitude (concerning, for example, the necessary moral and material dependence of the individual on Humanity as a whole). But it also proceeded from, and registered, a subjective encounter with the Great Being itself – an encounter which the prescribed devotions of Positive Religion were intended to reproduce as a continuing, and inspiring, experience. Nor could the objective and subjective dimensions of such a faith wholly coincide. The Great Being, *qua* the social dimension of humankind, might be 'real' in the Positivist view, but in its vastness and historicity it could never be a pure object of the senses. The subjective apprehension of Humanity was necessary as a complement to objective knowledge about it. At the same time, the effort to apprehend it imaginatively (with eyes closed) could not but overflow, sublimely, even a mind 'capable of following the demonstration'.

To insist that Comte's deificatory construal of Humanity be taken seriously, both as an idea and as an experience, is, in the first instance, an interpretative point. But an appraisal of Comte's religious move, and more particularly of the Grand-Être on which it pivots, also opens up questions with important practical ramifications concerning, first, the arising of a new religious *dispositif* – post-Christian and humanist – that Comte was among the first to explore, and secondly the place in this *dispositif* of the political. If it is historically correct to say that we still live 'amidst the dereliction of Nietzsche's idols',[7] it is also true that secularised moralism about the human, the social, the collective etc. continues to anchor, or at least animate, both discourses of state (and jurisprudential) legitimacy and discourses linked to projects of liberal or transformative reform. To this extent, even though Comte's particular theoretico-ideological assemblage may be irretrievably obsolete, critically reflecting on it may help to clarify some features of what such a commitment entails, at least in the thinking of those who would embrace what can be salvaged from the Enlightenment but are radically dissatisfied with the current historical drift. But in order to broach these questions we must first clarify Comte's anchoring category of *l'Humanité* itself. How, and how coherently, was it conceptualised? In what sense did Humanity have a divine character? And what – along the continuum, let us say, from the real to the fictive – was its status as an *existent*?

---

[7] The phrase is Philippa Berry's, from the preface to Berry and Wernick, 1993:ii.

The meaning(s) of 'l'Humanité'

One might imagine that the concept of 'Humanity', which serves multiply as the focal point, foundation and telos of Comte's system, is clear and distinct. In part because of this same multiplicity, however, it is a good deal less so than Comte himself imagined. 'By a happy ambiguity of language', he observes,

the same expression is used to designate the widest exercise of this highest affection [*l'humanité*] and also the race in whom it exists to the highest degree. And as in this fullest sense it is incompatible with any feeling of hatred towards other races, there is little inconvenience in using the term as the expression of the largest and most universal form of sympathy. The reader will therefore understand how, in my cerebral table, I was led to apply the name of Humanity . . . to the best type of vital unity, which, as the foregoing remarks will have shown, tends more and more towards dependence upon this instinct. (VII:703)

A happy ambiguity indeed. For it permits a conceptual slide from the human species considered generically as a type of higher primate, to the same considered collectively as a (developing) life-form in itself; and a further slide from this to 'the best type of vital unity', itself secured through the harmonising force of the highest form of (instinctual) sympathy which that totality comes to manifest the more it develops. Thus 'Humanity' is the highest love of which individual humans are capable, and which (replacing coercion) holds 'Humanity' emotionally together at the point at which it finally instantiates itself, in its fully mature stage, as 'Humanity'. Already we can identify at least four different senses of 'Humanity'. And, as we can also see, what enables Comte to read them all simultaneously, and without any sense of inconsistency, into the same word is not just a linguistic contingency but the coordinated relation they bear to one another within an entire conceptual apparatus.

For Comte, the key move in constituting this apparatus was to positivise the study of *l'homme* (a term which, to confuse things further, he replaced in later works with that of *l'humanité* (lower case) in referring generically to the species).[8] But Positivisation with a capital 'p' was not innocent. As Durkheim remarked, rather than begin with the patient assembly and careful comparison of social facts, as his method required, Comte proceeded straightaway to practical conclusions as though 'he

---

[8] After 1847 'la vague et irrationnelle notion de l'Homme', while continuing 'à servir l'unité zoologique' (VII:658), is generally dropped in favour of *l'humanité* (lower case) where its referent is biologically generic; *l'humanité*'s upper-casing (which had not appeared before 1847) denotes its explicitly religious usage as a term for *le vrai* Grand-Être.

already knew in advance the laws' that might connect them
(1964:19–20).

Comte's premature leap towards a completed knowledge of the
social gave itself an elaborate justification. In no branch of knowledge
was 'positive' science blindly inductive. Its consideration of 'relations
of resemblance and succession' always unfolded in the light of pre-
existing theory concerning both method and the nature of the object
field. Of course, if sociology was to be launched as *already* a positive
science, its initial, and initiating, body of theory would have to be
positivised in advance. But this operation belonged, in crucial part,
not to the science in question but to what the positive study of the
history of knowledge tells us about the relations between one basic
field of science and another. In the 'encyclopedic scale' (which
summarises the results of such study) each successively higher order
of knowledge bases itself on the one lower and (allowing for increasing complexity and restrictedness) adds additional laws of its
own. The taken-for-granted starting knowledge of sociology itself
could accordingly be *deduced* from its place in the scale, on the basis
of what could be *induced* from (1) the interrelation between the other
sciences combined with (2) what was (already) known about the
lower (and chronologically prior) branch of knowledge on which it
immediately rested.

Comte's primary assumption was that because of its historical and
logical place as the crown in the tree of knowledge, sociology had to be
a life science (its highest branch). As such, he further assumed, it not
merely complemented (human) biology by adding the social dimension
to our knowledge of the individual species member, but this social
dimension was itself to be understood as a form of life. And if this was
so, while *la société* had unique properties, which empirical investigation
would have to establish, we could be sure that the laws of life which
obtained in lower (less complex) species also applied to it. Prime
among these, at least according to contemporary biologists, and
particularly the Montpellier school from whose understanding of the
very distinction between life and non-life Comte took his cues (Canguilhem, 1994:237–9), was the axiom that the life of any organism
whatever depended on a 'vital consensus' between elements and functions. Without it the former would be inert and the latter would
evaporate.

To this there was an important corollary. While the non-life sciences
could proceed analytically, from the parts to the whole (the theory of
dynamic systems was the *last* branch of mathematical physics to be
developed), the life sciences had to proceed synthetically, from the

whole to the parts.[9] Without a prior consideration of the living organism to which they belonged, organs and tissues would be unintelligible from a biological point of view; and it was just the same for sociology. Paradoxically, then, as scientific knowledge advances, coming ever closer to the knowledge of human reality itself, the taken-for-granted pre-theory of the positive sciences does not diminish, as we might expect from a process which, at every step, has to dismantle 'anticipations of Nature' for scientific 'interpretation' to advance: it expands. What needs to be emphasised, though, is not simply the self-justifying circularity of Comte's importation of the bio-organismic metaphor into sociology, but that for Comte it was not metaphorical at all. The biological model was the linchpin of his whole construct. By way of the notion of 'vital consensus', it enabled him to conjoin a scientific understanding of the social–historical totality taken to comprise human life on the planet with a spiritual apprehension that Humanity – actually as well as ideally – subsists in love. If love is the essence of humanity, and if humanity embodies love to the highest possible degree, then the 'h' of humanity could be written, reverentially, in upper case.

In two respects however this bio-social construct still leaves the religiously elevated meaning of Humanity ambiguous. To be noted, first, is the stress it placed on the equation Comte wished to make between *humanité* (small 'h') as the widest exercise of altruism, and *Humanité* (big 'h') as the fully developed form of the organism bonded by it. The universal benevolence which provides *l'esprit de l'ensemble* in the special-ised scientific–industrial order that represents Humanity's final stage of self-development may be crucial to its harmonious wellbeing. But it is only one of three dimensions of such harmony, and could neither function nor persist independently of the other two. At both the individual and social level, the 'vital consensus' which 'normally' pre-vails in that perfected state entails not only harmony of sentiment ('sympathy') but harmony of intellect ('synthesis') and harmony of action ('synergy') as well (XII:9). That being so, 'the best type of vital unity' exceeds the moral–instinctual feeling Comte calls *l'humanité*, and cannot be straightforwardly named by it.

Lyotard, implicitly setting Comte against Comte, insists that if there are natural forces making for 'complexification, negative entropy, or more generally, development' in the dynamic equilibration of growing

---

[9] Not only did the general 'vital organisation' of an organism have to be theorised prior to that of its forms and functions, the whole 'series' of organic life needed to be established before scientific knowledge of particular life-forms was possible. *Leçon* 41 of the *Cours*, 'sur la philosophie anatomique' (III:384 et seq.), elaborates this point. One implication is that the completion, and sytematisation, of sociology is essential for that of biology as a whole.

systems, social or otherwise, these forces belong to the category of 'the inhuman' (1991:5–6).[10] Comte, in his final writings, went in exactly the opposite direction. He broadened the positivist godhead so as to *include* the inhuman under the forms of *le* Grand-Fétiche and (still more) *le* Grand Milieu. Into the latter, as we have seen, he projected the enlarged sense of unity proper to *le* Grand-Être in its final stage, by regarding *l'Espace* as the seat (*siège*) of natural propensities to harmonious development in all its dimensions. This allowed him to eat his cake and have it too. For while his broader theory of social unity, with its irreducible triplet of thought, action and sentiment, made it impossible to regard 'humanity' (the moral–instinctual *sentiment*) as the sole unifying essence of 'Humanity' (the realised bio-social entity), his fetishisation of *l'Espace* restored the former to ontological centrality by universalising it, at least *fictively*, as the benevolent principle that tends, throughout the cosmos, towards harmony as such.

If the first ambiguity surrounding the meaning of 'Humanity' concerns the (non)-identity between 'the largest and most universal form of sympathy' and 'the best type of vital unity' it helps constitute, the second concerns the social organism whose unity it is. To put it sharply: is the Humanity we are to acknowledge and worship as the Great Being the human species as such, taken throughout its history and considered at any one time in light of whatever condition of (dis)order, (dis)unity and (un)development it happens to be in? Or does it mean humankind only in its final, positive, pacific and truly globalised stage? If the latter, how could there have been 'serviteurs' of Humanity – all those saints in the Positivist Calendar, for example – before it came into being? If the former, what would be the qualitative difference between the 'vital consensus' proper to Humanity and the considerably less perfect forms of order that prevailed during the militarily based epoch of intertribal and then international warfare that preceded it? Or, again, is the divine referent a *virtual* Humanity, one scientifically reconstructed along the generalised and abstract lines recommended by Condorcet? But then how, except subjectively, could it be considered 'real'? (The same issue, we may note, does not arise as sharply from the vantage point of a humanism of the Feuerbachian type. There it is the generic essence of each individual human being – the infinite impulses to love, knowledge etc. within each and every one – which makes humankind godlike as a

---

[10] 'Since development is the very thing which takes away the hope of an alternative to the system from both analysis and practice . . . the question I am raising here is simply this: what else remains as politics except resistance to this "inhuman"? And what else is left to resist with but the debt which each soul has contracted with the miserable and admirable indetermination from which it was born and does not cease to be born? – which is to say with the other inhuman' (Lyotard, 1991:7).

species. But a humanism that holds that infinitude to be not just shared but a product of sharing, an emergent property of association as such, is confronted with more than one social totality, with regard to space–time and degree of virtuality, which might properly be sacralised in this way. Hence Nietzsche's comment that 'one is uncertain as to where this whole is to be sought' (1992:82)).

Comte did not, and could not, avoid the issue, though he was hampered (certainly in expression) by an insufficiency of terms for the various wholes in play. If we reserve the term *l'homme* for the species as it historically unfolds, and *l'Humanité* for its mature, final stage, then we could say that Comte's Great Being is not only the latter but also the former, but only in so far as it is grasped as always already tending to develop towards its maximal pole. Humanity, as the name of that Being, is the becoming-Humanity of Man – it being understood that, even in the Positive polity where the Great Being is finally acknowledged as the real and only god, Humanity, as the self-perfection of the human, is a limit condition asymptotically approached, but never fully reached.

The concept is undoubtedly teleological. Comte did not, however, think it through, still less try to validate it, by recourse to an explicit metaphysics of essence and realised potential. The becoming-Humanity of Man was analysed and explained in terms of sociological laws. We are already familiar with the story. Each expansion of 'society' – from families and tribal groups to national societies, all the way to a globally cooperative industrial order – creates a more differentiated order with a more developed basis of philosophical consensus. In so doing, it ratchets up both the level and modality of knowledge and the affective–instinctual base, all of which prepares the way for the next developmental leap. But where, in this narrative figure, is its central character?

In one sense *l'Humanité* can be located in the widening, universalising development of all affectively bonded social groups (*sociétés*), even the smallest.[11] From that angle, it transpires as a kind of (incipient) substance of which the social *qua* social consists. But it can also be identified with the objective social totality, taken in all its instances and

---

[11] Each 'partial association' could be considered to represent the Great Being, since it always at least partially instantiated its essential elements. 'Chacune d'elles, après avoir fourni le noyau, réel ou virtuel, de l'Humanité, restera toujours propre à faciliter sa notion spontanée. En effect, les deux attributs essentiels de l'existence collective, solidarité, continuité, retrouvent nécessairement dans ces moindres degrés, où, sans être aussi complets, ils deviennent mieux appréciables. Voilà comment la Famille et la Patrie ne cesseront jamais d'offrir, à l'esprit autant qu'au coeur, les préambules nécessaires de l'Humanité.' Indeed, stretching the same argument still further, and viewed in light of its ultimate bio-organisational potential, every animal species could be so regarded. 'Toute espèce animale constitue réellement un Grand-Être plus ou moins avorté, par un arrêt de développement dû, surtout, à la prépondérance humaine' (VIII:229).

dimensions, and considered from the perspective of this totality's histor-ical and geographical movement towards becoming a truly planetary society. Thus, underneath the first duality, between Humanity as actual and as potential totality, we discover a second (local/global) which itself articulates with a further difference between the 'physiology' (i.e. vital functioning) and 'morphology' (i.e. techno-institutional structure) of the particular *sociétés* of which the Great Being is composed. The duality of *l'Humanité* as a term referring both to the developing quality of the social tie and to that of society's general (i.e. technical, institutional, political, intellectual, religious etc.) form is reflected in the calendric organisation of Positivist worship.[12] Through one sequence of festivals, the faithful express gratitude for all the domestic, civic and humanity-wide ties and institutions, together with the rising scale of social sentiments on which these rely. Another sequence does the same for the overall march of civilisation from tribalism to modern industry. On each side, each step of progress, whether considered historically or in terms of its continuing (but rearranged) place in the culminating result, is 'appreciated' for what it prepares and contributes, until both series come together in the Feast of the Dead, and the annual round begins anew.

Three features of *le* Grand-Être, as Comte thus conceived it, are immediately apparent. (1) It is only at the scientific–industrial stage of actual development – with the establishment of a federated world society based on voluntary cooperation and universal altruism – that these variously distinguished senses of 'Humanity' begin to coincide. Until the positivisation process is complete, *l'Humanité* really *is* an ambiguous reality: instantiated *both* in the substance of affective associ-ation *and* in the structure and movement of the wider social totality within which that substance is embedded. (2) Diachrony inheres in the concept. What is sacralised as Humanity is not the (always imperfect) form assumed by the human collectivity at any developmental conjunc-ture, but the convergent movement towards Humanity (in both senses) to which it belongs. Humanity, that is to say, is not a static absolute, but the coming into being of a superior (way of) being. As such it is a process as much as a result. Indeed, the former is implicated in the latter, much as Hegel's *Weltgeist* included all the moments which logically preceded its realisation.[13] However, if Humanity's being in-

---

[12] As supplemented by the round of special festivals prescribed in the *Tableau sociolâtrique* (x:159).

[13] 'Notre Grand-Être n'est pas plus immobile qu'absolu; sa nature relative le rend développable: en un mot, il est le plus vivant des êtres connus. Il s'étend et se compose de plus en plus par la succession continue des générations humaines . . . De la conception normale du Grand-Être, nous passons donc à l'histoire de sa formation continue, dont l'ensemble résume tous les progrès quelconques' (VII:335).

cludes its becoming (and in this sense exists prior to its actual arrival as cooperative world society etc.), then (3) it can never be fully *present* in the phenomenalist way in which Comte wished to restrict the meaning of the 'real'.

It is just here that the *religion* of Humanity steps in to supplement what would otherwise be an ontic lack. If the Humanity to be worshipped could only exist subjectively – that is, as represented (and loved) by the mind that apprehends it – then a religion, as *par excellence* the manner of ensuring such subjectivity, was crucial. Comte's sociological analysis told him that religion, which secured the unity of group orientation and strengthened the altruistic impulses, was essential to the unity of every kind and level of society. Indeed, the wider the group and the more refined (i.e. higher but weaker) its affective ties, the more important religion was to its constitution and maintenance.[14] In the Positivist epoch, then, sustaining the representation of Humanity, through symbolism, ritual and the cultivation of collective memory, was indispensable, functionally, to the continuing existence of Humanity itself.

But this is not all. What was represented in the Great Being was itself, I have stressed, a becoming being. To grasp it as such at any point along the locus of its unfolding meant grasping that present (the 'statics' part of sociology) not as a monad but as including both its protensions (opening towards the telos that organises the optic) and retentions (the appreciatively grasped panorama of the human story up to now, with the present as its provisional result). To grasp the entire process of Humanity's becoming, then, is to grasp all its moments in their mutual connectivity. And if the private imagining of this is socially coordinated and maintained, such a connective grasp, in turn, constitutes that connectivity as a subjective social fact. Before the scientific–industrial revolution, when Humanity (in the various senses of social totality identified above) does not coincide with itself, establishing the subjective, as opposed to objective, *continuité* of Humanity is both impossible and unnecessary. But once the rise of positivity has shattered belief in the old gods, the situation changes. For at this point, because of the theoretico-ideological exigencies of the situation (which necessitated a new coordinating synthesis), the *objective* continuity of Humanity and thus its 'vital unity' as a living being come to depend on the self-conscious maintenance of its continuity at the *subjective* level. The practical implication

---

[14] Fetishism, lacking a priesthood, and worshipping 'specific bodies', was the least organised; Catholicism, with its independent priesthood, the most organised. The extrapolation into industrial society of this linearly regarded institutional development was already elaborated in Comte's 1826 essay 'Considérations sur le pouvoir spirituel' (x:176–215).

is evident: Positivism must be supplemented by an organised religion. But there is an implication for the self-consciousness that this implies which should be drawn out too. When the part and the whole finally come together (in 'that day', as the prophet put it, 'when we are all one, and His Name one') we discover that Humanity has objective being only to the extent to which it becomes – through the hearts and minds of its mutually conjoined individual members – a being for itself.

The collective subject

We are almost at the point where we can examine what it might mean to manoeuvre this construct into 'the God-shaped hole' (Fuentes) left by the departed (Christian) divinity. But, as I have just intimated, there is one last aspect of Comte's 'Humanity' that still requires comment: its relation to the modern category of 'the subject'.

In his study of modern social theory, John Milbank distinguishes between two broadly defined strategies for attempting to secure the (for him, crypto-theological) foundations of 'secular reason'.[15] Both involve appeals to an *immanent* transcendent. The first finds it in a providence reconfigured as scientifically knowable, and identified, in theories of progress, with the innate potential of natural materiality. The second, via notions of willed institution and *Homo faber*, finds it in the human subject, a subject which posits itself (as will and reason) as both its own author and the underlying sub-stance of all it knows and surveys. In the general movement of thought from early-modern political science (Machiavelli, Hobbes) to nineteenth-century sociology, Milbank argues, it is the first path which came to prevail. 'Thus "humanity's self-formation" gets gradually displaced by "the historical formation of humanity"' (1993:28).

So far, and in line with Comte's own *échelle encyclopédique*, I have been approaching his concept of Humanity from just that angle – that is, as a

---

[15] Milbank examines the 'secular reason' exhibited by political economy and sociology as a species of the 'secular theology' (of Galileo, Descartes, Newton, Hobbes and Leibniz) explored by Amos Funkenstein in *Theology and the Scientific Imagination* (1986). The first, for Milbank, continues the themes and methods of the second, though in a more disguised (but equally fallacious) fashion. 'The theme of the human construction of culture is . . . aporetically crossed in secular reason by the idea of the cultural construction of humanity. Where this moment is privileged, secular reason produces a privileged discourse about providence, which, unlike in medieval theology, violates the distinction between primary and secondary causes and invokes a final cause – "God" or "Nature" – to plug some supposed gap in immanent understanding. This kind of fusion of theological and scientific discourse has been proposed by Amos Funkenstein. However, he sees it as terminating with Kant. I see it as an element in political economy, and even as reinforced in the intellectual moves which generate "sociology"' (Milbank, 1993:4).

crowning reality that caps a cosmic movement of progress in order. In Comte's version, this transcendental guarantor of meaning and value is at once the positivised knowledge object of social science, and a kind of super-organism which evolves to the point where, with Positivisation itself, it becomes a self-conscious and self-transformative force for perfecting what (for itself) is the 'universal order'. Put this way, however, it is clear that Comte's thematisation of Humanity participated at once in both strategies identified by Milbank.[16] The 'Humanity' which replaces the Christian, Jewish and Islamic God in Comte's religious imaginary is an immanent product of the non-human. But in this very replacement its destiny is to double over as a (reflexively knowing) subject, to take charge of itself and its world, and thence to humanise, actively, everything on which it depends. When we try to pin down, then, what exalts Humanity – objectively in nature, subjectively for (each of) us – we can see that it acquires its paramount and anchoring status by way of the second foundational route. On this side, Humanity is identified with the thinking, willing and, finally, self-autonomizing human subject – which, at least in left and liberal thought, and until the last few decades, has been secular reason's main line of march.

The effect of projecting Humanity into the conceptual space of the Cartesian (and post-Cartesian) ego was not just to positivise this latter category, but to collectivise it. Where German philosophy developed an ever more abstruse philosophy of the individual subject (as thought reflecting both on itself and on the ego it presupposed), Comte, following Condorcet, insisted on a historical sociology of human thought which regarded it, and its expressions, as the collective result of a collective process. The development of the *ego cogitans* towards self-consciousness was likewise translated into a socio-historical positivity: the destined emergence of a Humanity which (through the triumph of Positivism) comprehends itself as that.

The epistemological implications of rethinking what was attributed to the individual subject of knowledge in terms of collective mentalities whose determinate development is traced out by the empirical history of the sciences were a centrepiece of *Philosophie positive*. Key, in this rethinking, was the self-limiting relativisation of knowledge claims, which referred the meaning of 'truth' to the actually developing proto-

---

[16] In giving Comte a 'providentialist' reading, Milbank emphasises Comte's relationship with de Bonald, whose social ontology Comte 'inverts', and the dependence of de Bonald on Malebranche's occasionalism. All this, for Milbank, served to import into French sociology a conception of social being which systematically confounded the difference between the transcendent and the finite. See Milbank 1993:51–61.

cols of the specialised sciences on the one side, and to the felt/understood pressures of human needs on the other. But while this move generally placed Comte on the side of Kant's 'Copernican revolution in thought' (the human subject as the inescapable centre of knowing, valuing and acting in a world which objectively had no centre), Comte did not examine the relation of his own deabsolutising turn to that elaborated in Kantian critique. He was content, without getting caught in the coils of critical metareflection, to have subsumed traditional epistemology into the terms of a sociology of knowledge, with its law of three stages, encyclopedic scale and theory of uneven development. In the event, it was Charles Renouvier and his circle, grouped around the antipositivist *Revue de Métaphysique et de Morale*, who introduced Kantian themes into moderate French Republican discussion about moral reconstruction, and so prepared for Durkheim's compromise (Wallwork, 1972:9–16; Giddens, 1971:65). This compromise saw Comte's socio-historical relativisation of the practical *a priori* as a crucial improvement over Kant; and it saw Kant's liberal preoccupation with the autonomous rational individual as an equally crucial corrective which needed to be introduced into some better sociological account of the reconstructive requirements of post-Revolutionary France.

The question to be pursued here, however, concerns the ontological implications of Comte's collectivisation of the subject. If Humanity as a whole is to be conceived not only as a kind of organism but as a (self-)productive, and increasingly self-aware, agent of thought feeling, and action, how are we to understand its nature and functioning as such? How is this collective subject constituted vis-à-vis the individual subject? In what sense can it be conceived, in its collective manner of being, as *a* (singular) subject at all? Comte's answer is forthright, though easy to misread. Society may be an organism, but it is one like no other. On the one hand, the individual human beings that make it up are only ever, whatever their achievements and self-understandings, *organs* of that larger being. Yet at the same time those individuals are 'the only active elements'.[17] Thus the collective subject only exists as such, i.e. as a consciously acting agent vis-à-vis its milieu, to the extent that it functions as a coordinated network of individuals. Structurally considered, then, 'the fundamental bond of sociality consists of a permanent conciliation between combination and independence' (x:34). In early phases of social development this bond is restricted by particularisms, and is coercive in the face of egoistically dominated thought and conduct. The collectivity comprising humankind as a whole at this stage

---

[17] 'Partout c'est vraiment le Grand-Être qui produit, mais toujours par les organes individuels' (VII:421).

is, correspondingly, only virtual. But even in the final state, when Humanity is instituted, religiously, politically, industrially, scientifically, *as* a collectivity, the unity with which it functions is an always problematic resultant of the voluntary cooperation of the independently thinking (and self-abnegating) individuals who make it up.

Such cooperation could not be just the product of isolated individuals. It presupposes that there is already, in some sense, a group. But if we then ask what primordially constitutes this group, and especially in a sociological sense, i.e. as something more than the sum of individual inclinations, the puzzle only deepens. For despite ontologising the social ('Humanity can never be decomposed into individuals') and endowing it with life, there is no pregiven and integral 'we', whether at the level of consciousness or even of sentiments. For Comte, once we are beyond the intimate 'union' of the family, the affective basis of intra-individual cooperation – *altruisme* – bonds the human group only indirectly; that is, by virtue of the way in which it connects each individual member to a connecting Third. In *Philosophie positive* this 'other' is conceived intellectually as a body of commonly held ideas. In *Politique positive*, it is *l'Humanité* apprehended subjectively. Which means: through the orienting and affectively charged image which each has internalised of the totality which, by virtue of this sharing, they together compose. If we employ the typology developed by Sartre in *Critique of Dialectical Reason*, then we can say that Comte's *société*, even in its most collective form, never surpasses seriality. Just as the members of a crowd at a bus stop are connected with one another only through their individual relation to the same externality, the collectivity comprised by Comte's Humanity consists in the last analysis in a concurrence of individual attachments. At most, i.e. as unified by religious adherence, it takes the form of a pledge group[18] whose self-representation as an organism is itself designed – consciously – to 'conciliate' its contradictory and inessential unity as *un être composé*. And this remains the case throughout the history of social development; albeit that in its final stage the mechanism

---

[18] For Sartre, pledge-groups, in which all represent the group to, and over against, one another, are a special case of the series. The latter is constituted as a group only incidentally, through the mediation of an external 'common object' (1960:385). The 'organicity' of a group, which may form a 'common object' which all are pledged to represent, is 'avant tout l'apparence, illusoire et immédiat, du groupe quand il se produit dans le champ practico-inerte et contre ce champ' (381). While Sartre extends the notion of a pledge group to the kind of instituted organicity Comte wishes to restore and perfect, he particularly emphasises, at the limit of group survival, the mobilisation of fear. 'La réinvention fondamentale, au coeur du serment, c'est le projet de substituer une peur réelle, produit du groupe soi-même, à la peur externe . . . Et cette peur comme libre produit du groupe et comme action corrective de la liberté contre la dissolution sérielle . . . c'est la Terreur' (448).

becomes sociologically transparent, and the mediating Other through which this unity is achieved comes to be redefined as *le vrai* Grand-Être, i.e. as the Positively apprehended idea of the ensemble thus constituted.

For all his insistently social critique, then, of the essentially private character of Catholic spirituality, with its moral psychodrama of individual salvation, the subjectivity to be fashioned by Positive Religion is cast in a similar form. This accords, no doubt, with Comte's own formative religious experience – the post-mortem extrapolation of his *amour désintéressé* for Clotilde[19] – and thus, too, with his deepest sense of what it would mean to become pervasively social. But the implication is striking. In contrast with Durkheim's theory of 'collective effervescence' (1968b:226) as the (ritually repeated) founding experience of modern-rational *civisme*, as of every other kind of socially established ideal,[20] the divine reality unveiled as Humanity is encountered not as the ego's emptying out into a 'we' but as a transcending symbol conjured up in the imagination of each adherent. Neither in the theory nor the practice nor the experience of Positive religiosity is there any ecstasy of the social.[21]

This is not necessarily to Comte's discredit. The notion that a fusional communality is essential to social bonding and is the essence of the

---

[19] 'Auguste Comte n'a jamais mieux aimé l'Humanité comme il aime Clotilde: il faut donc aimer l'humanité comme il aime Clotilde. L'expérience a une valeur universelle: elle présent le parfait modèle du don que tout homme doit faire à l'Humanité' (Gouhier, 1965:210). Unfortunately, Gouhier undermines the force of this precise characterisation of Comte's (1846–7) religious experience by also asserting: 'L'unité humaine est une communion. Aimer l'Humanité, c'est sentir cette unité et participer joyeusement à cette communion' (ibid.). Communion (implying *present* others) is a misleading term for what was always, for Comte, a solitary experience of a harmony within.

[20] 'It is in fact at such moments of collective ferment that are born the ideals upon which civilisation rests. The periods of creation or renewal occur when for various reasons individuals are led into a closer relationship with each other, when reunions and assemblies are most frequent, relationships better maintained, and the exchange of ideas most active. Such was the movement of collective enthusiasm which . . . gave birth to Scholasticism . . . the Reformation and Renaissance, the revolutionary epoch, and the socialist upheavals of the nineteenth century. At such moments this higher life is lived with such exclusiveness and intensity that it monopolizes all minds to the more or less complete exclusion of egoism and the commonplace. At such times the ideal tends to become one with the real, and for this reason men have the impression that the time is close when the ideal will in fact be realized and the kingdom of God expressed on earth. This illusion can never last because the illusion cannot maintain itself at such a pitch . . . All that was said, done and thought in this period of fecund upheaval survives only as a memory . . . It exists as an idea or rather as a composition of ideas' (Durkheim, 1965:91–2).

[21] Compare Durkheim: 'Of course it is only natural that the moral forces (that religious images) express should be unable to affect the human mind powerfully without pulling it outside itself and without plunging it into a state that may be called *ecstatic*, provided that the word be taken in its etymological sense (ek-stasy)' (1968b:227).

social itself – its magmatic form – can produce an even more repressive collectivism while falling further into the organicist temptation. But there is a highly consequential rider. The 'we' of the Humanity to which we each belong in Comte's scenario is not intrinsic to our being, nor a humbling discovery of being with others in the world. It is first and foremost a representation which, if it is to be felt and regarded as transcendent to the individual at all, has first to be subjectively produced. The religious practices of Positivism were bound, then, to involve an immense and continuous labour, beginning with the daily labour of memory and prayer.

The divine status of Humanity

What does it mean, though, for Comte to speak of Humanity as 'a new god' (VII:342) and, indeed, as *le vrai* Grand-Être? What attributes read into the category I have been seeking to elucidate could justify its designation as *divine*? It must be said at once that Comte's use of god-language reflects a linguistic exigency. If the religious dimension of social life is irreducible, but theistic religion has historically monopolised the way in which that dimension is mapped, a certain amount of terminological borrowing is hard to avoid. How else than by appealing to such terms as *le* Grand-Être (capitalised) could he have designated a reality which, while 'having nothing mystical about it', was destined to occupy (as he saw it) the same place in the psychic and social life of industrial society as 'God' did before?

Yet the theistic designation was also precisely intended. In what Comte took to be intrinsic and crucial respects, the new god was continuous with the old not just in its psycho-social function but in some of its substantive characteristics. 'Humanity' inspired and incarnated the highest form of selfless love. It was the ultimate source of moral authority. If not omniscient, it was both the subject and the limiting horizon of all knowledge about the world (as of ourselves). Like the old god, it was both transcendent and immanent (transcendent to the individual; immanent to the social as its highest possibility, and immanent to the individual as the potential for altruistic attachment). It was also a 'jealous god' and would brook 'no other masters among its servants' (VII:397). Finally, Humanity not only *had* being, it *was* one, in point of harmony and beneficence the most perfect there is. The wondrous and majestic secret of that being similarly revealed itself to us in the fullness of time, both objectively as an essence made apparent in its existence, and subjectively as a matter of inner individual experience.

In other respects, however, the two beings – God and Humanity –

were not at all equivalent. The biblical deity may make itself manifest here below, but its throne was infinitely distant in the above and beyond. *L'Humanité*, by contrast, was not in the least a supersensible entity. However virtual before the positivist transformation, and however imbricated in subjectivity after it, it was wholly in the world. Nor, whatever the necessity of its guiding presence in the subjectivity of the scientifically knowing mind, was it a Creator, or any kind of First Cause. At his most extravagant Comte speaks of the Great Being as the head of the terrestrial biosphere, the 'chief' of an 'immense league, with animals as voluntary agents and plants as material instruments', to which even 'inorganic forces join themselves as blind auxiliaries, to the extent that they have been conquered' (VII:617). This is a god for us, even for 'our' fellow-creatures, but it is not a god over everything in nature. It is Lord of the Earth perhaps, but not King of the Universe. What *L'Humanité* gained in 'realism' over the old god it therefore lost in eminence. In effect, *l'Humanité* lacked all traditional attributes of divinity except those related to morality and the setting of human ends. And even in this domain it was deprived of the supreme motivating power exercised over the individual by a deity who could redeem from death, being able to provide the individual with only the solace, and moral incentive, which might be wrung from expecting a 'subjective' prolongation of life as a respected, or treasured, private or public, memory.

By the same token, if the Great Being was mighty, it was not omnipotent. Its modifying power extended only to its immediate external and internal milieu, and only then within the limits of modifiability proper to the lower, but more fundamental, orders of being of which that milieu consisted. Unlike the old god, its existence was 'subordinated to immutable laws' and 'carried no absolute satisfaction, nor even security' (VII:354). Its knowledge, likewise, was limited by the finite powers and fixed location of the human knower. Its immanence and transcendence to the individual, finally, had nothing ineffable about it, but were just an effect of the individual's location in society as a condition of its own material and psychological existence. In short, if Comte's Humanity replaces the God in whom a scientific age is no longer able to believe, and whose most active partisans, even, no longer worship in good faith,[22] it does so not as 'that than which nothing greater can be conceived' (Anselm)[23] but as the only 'living' reality in

---

[22] 'Les plus actives théologistes, monarchiques, aristocratiques, ou même démagogiques, manquent, depuis longtemps, de bonne foi. Leur Dieu est devenu le chef nominal d'une conspiration hypocritique, désormais ridicule d'odieuse . . .' (VII:397–8).

[23] For a straightforward discussion of Anselm's ontological proof, see Coppleston, 1962:183 et seq.

the sensory world which is more elevated than our individual selves, and upon which, at the same time, we are each naturally and inescapably dependent.

So far, we might say, with all secular, i.e. 'this-sided', forms of humanism. In whatever register – whether ethical or political, collectivist or individualist, radical or conservative, democratic or hierarchical, communitarian or anarchist, bio-social or cast in terms of rights or freedoms – any commitment which consciously places humankind at the fixed centre of the Good and the Ought bears the same ambiguous relation to theistic faith properly so-called. Ideological balance here is not easy to maintain. A humanism which stresses too much its discontinuity with the old faith would forget the eminence attributed to its own central term. At the limit of such forgetfulness it would shade into lack of faith, and cease to be a humanism at all. A humanism which did the reverse, however, and thought itself just to have found a better god, would forget the more overwhelming sense of eminence which has to be forgone when we switch allegiance from the one deity (but can we still use this word?) to the other. In Heidegger's terms: for nihilism (i.e. the *Destruktion* of the metaphysical idols) to complete itself through a transvaluation, the place of God must remain empty.[24] To fill that place with Humanity is not just ungodly – 'never can Man put himself in the realm of God, because the essence of Man never reaches the essential realm of God' (1977a:100). It would also restrict what counts for human value by imprisoning consciousness within the walls of a new Absolute wherein questions not grounded in its (assumed) facticity and functional demands are ruled out of court.

Comte, though, does not trouble himself with this. Precisely because of his sociological decoding of all gods as anthropomorphic, and of all religion as intrinsic to society's 'vital unity', he took it for granted that the place held by God in prepositivist thought was not only fraudulently occupied but misconceived. The Christian God was a contradictory mixture of absolute power, wisdom and goodness[25] which reflected an

---

[24] 'Thought metaphysically, the place that is peculiar to God is the place of the causative bringing about of whatever is, as something created. That place of God can remain empty. Instead of it, another, i.e. a place corresponding metaphysically, can loom on the horizon – a place that is identical neither with the realm belonging essentially to God nor with that of Man, but with which Man comes once more into a distinctive relationship' (1977a:100).

[25] 'Cette complète autocratie rendait la conception de Dieu profondément contradictoire, et par suite temporaire. Car un examen approfondi nous interdit de concilier une telle toute-puissance, soit avec une intelligence sans bornes, soit avec une bonté infinite . . . Si nous pouvions toujours nous placer dans les circonstances les plus favorables à nos recherches, nous n'aurions aucun besoin d'intelligence . . . L'omnipotence exclut donc l'omniscience. Son incompatibilité avec une parfaite bonté est encore plus évidente . . .

increasingly strained attempt to sustain an 'absolute' synthesis in the face of advancing positivity and its own intrinsic impossibility as a project (VII:17). The primary error of theology – an unavoidable, and even in its time useful effect of limited scientific and technical knowledge – had been to confuse God as that which names our highest value with God as ultimate cause. The cognitive focus of this insight, however, leads Comte to denigrate (as 'mysticism') whatever sense of awe, sublimity and infinitude associated with the idea (and experience) of divinity for believers can *not* be reduced to the pure, but morally practical, benevolence of which the real Great Being consists.[26] To this extent Comte falls under the Heideggerian stricture. By imagining that his 'Humanity', with all its pious trappings, could fully substitute in human consciousness for the deity it was designed, according to the best available principles of social engineering, to replace, he blinded himself to what horizons and senses of being such a restricted sense of transcendence might disallow from entering in.

Such a critique, however, has its own limits. As Wyschogrod has pointed out,[27] Heidegger's concern to unconceal the 'question of Being' takes for granted the indefinite continuation of that aspect of the life world which is constituted by human association, which is precisely what, in his concern for the disruption of *continuité* in *la grande crise*, Comte problematises. Not to see this might lead us to overlook what was in fact the most striking aspect of the new deity whose worship Comte sought to establish. If *l'Humanité* was 'real' and non-fictive, if it therefore had, so to speak, more being than the old god, it was also highly fragile. Unlike the eternal God of monotheistic religion, *l'Humanité* was finite not just in space but in time. Its place in the sequence of natural history was at the very end. Nor, more important, was the 'security' of its existence guaranteed (VII:354). Once born, it could fall apart and die. It was that very prospect, the threat of social dissolution, which propelled Comte into action in the first place. That threat itself, furthermore, was not just a matter of chance, beyond our control. The

Les volontés d'un être qui serait vraiment tout-puissant se réduiraient donc à de purs caprices' (VII:408–9)

[26] As religious 'aberrations' typical of monotheism, quietism and mysticism are often coupled together. Comte never evinces any interest in the content of such experience, simply dismissing all such preoccupation as an egoistic and morally useless indulgence, '[une] dégénération affective qui dispose à négliger les oeuvres pour ne cultiver que les inspirations' (X:93).

[27] Wyschogrod's argument is developed in the last two chapters of *Spirit in Ashes* (1983). These deal, respectively, with Heidegger's concepts of *Dasein* and (modern) technology. The latter, she argues, in its mass-death-producing form, undermines the 'everydayness' presupposed in Heidegger's account of 'authenticity' in the face of individual dying.

objective and subjective existence of Humanity actually depends – both as the necessary completion of its becoming and as the condition for its *continuité* – on its being interiorised as the venerated object of belief. The persistence of this belief required, in turn, a vast social effort.

Real love does not stop at welcoming the good, it impels us to realise it as much as possible. Prescribing the study and celebration of Humanity is not just for the sake of the sweet satisfactions this would inherently bring. The overall aim is to make us better serve the Supreme Being, whose conservation and improvement exacts a *continuous activity*. (VII:362; my emphasis)

From religion to politics

The point is vital. Comte's positivised conception of religion, his insistence that Humanity should rightly occupy, socially and psychologically, the place previously filled by the monotheistic deity (just as 'God' had replaced the gods of polytheism, and those the spirits of fetishism), was not simply a transfer of divinity on to a new term. The substitution simultaneously reorganised the space into which the new term was inserted. Comte's manner of deifying Humanity, together with his bio-social understanding of that category, redefined the transcendental signified at the centre of belief – i.e. of affect-laden cognition – by converting it into a phenomenally presenting Real which could only be that if those who 'believed in it' *practically accomplished its being*.

This amounted to the claim that under modern conditions the sphere of religion comes into a new relation with the practice of politics. With the rise of *l'esprit positif*, religion comes to know what it was, though till now confusedly, from the start. That is: a body of practices which on the one hand maintains social unity (the objective being of Humanity), and on the other inspires progress (the realisation of Humanity as a global condition). Religion discovers itself, then, to be political through and through. And the converse is also the case. Politics, conceived by Comte, as by Marx, on the model of artifactual production, i.e. as the practice of producing and reproducing social relations, discovers itself to be inextricably bound up with religion. This was not just because 'religion' provides the ethical foundation for praxis, gives it ends; but because with the socio-historically reflexive demystification of 'God' the realisation dawns that such a Transcendent, even if brought down to earth, is only ever real, or real in its effects, as the outcome of a work. Thus the highest aim of political practice is theogenic – to make the god. That theogeny was indeed indispensable. In its absence it would be impossible either to secure any stable orientation for political practice (without which politics would degenerate into the mere play of self-interest) or to secure its real ground, i.e. society as the site on which praxis occurs.

A comparable perspective is outlined by Marx in the 'Theses on Feuerbach'. There the 'social humanity' presupposed, in the 'new materialism', as the goal and touchstone of 'critico-revolutionary practice' is radically distinguished from the utopian horizon of idealist thought by the truth criterion in terms of which its propriety to serve as the guiding norm of political practice is claimed. 'Man must prove the truth, i.e. the reality and power, the "this-sidedness" of his thinking in practice' (Marx and Engels, 1947:197). The category of 'social humanity', in other words, is capable of validation, but not absolutely, not as the product of an ontotheology. Its validity is demonstrated – or not – entirely at the level of practice, i.e. to the extent it is actualised in the course of political action driven (and striving) to bring it about. Comte's religion of Humanity shares with Marx's antireligion of social humanity the praxological inscription of his founding category. In this respect, however, Comte goes one step further. The regime of voluntary cooperation destined (through the political intervention of workers and women led by Humanity's scientific and ideological vanguard) to prevail in Humanity's realised state by no means simply springs into being when we break the fetters which impede it. Nor, once in existence, and leaving aside Comte's different understanding of what these fetters consist in, can the maintenance of Humanity as such be left to chance. The 'social humanity' or 'voluntary cooperation' that would spring forth once industrial society had been properly reorganised has to be reproduced at every moment. And this, above all, because it rests on an (unnatural) preponderance of 'sociability over personality' and on a subjective consensus of mind, heart and body which likewise requires a reproductive – in Comte's terminology, 'rebinding', i.e. religious – practice.

Comte places his thesis concerning the (Positive) convergence of religion and politics in the context of a set of assumptions which are all open to challenge: that 'God' is a fiction, and now an impossible one; that I and we need to be attached to an (updated) equivalent in order to obviate the mental and emotional anarchy which would otherwise ensue; and that the requisite substitute actually exists, ready to hand – it was indeed the real and rational core of what were called the gods all along. Regardless of whether we accept these propositions, in Comte's very insistence on the need for a religious – *and therefore pan-political* – humanism, his representation of Humanity as divine, or quasi-divine, sharply illuminates some of the difficulties that arise when we try to think through the implications of founding secular political thought on any such basis.

Viewed from within the Enlightenment critique of (theistic) religion, i.e. the tradition summarised and criticised by Marx in *The Holy Family* and other early works (Marx and Engels, 1955:47–50, 59–68), for humankind to make humanity its highest value was to attempt an end to religious self-alienation by way of a profound shift in attitude. At its most joyous and affirmative it appeared to those who first proclaimed it – in the century between the French Revolution and the Victorians – as a mental home-coming, an end to exile. It was an act of self-affirmation, in which an enlightened humanity recognises itself in its gods and draws the appropriate conclusions. 'Criticism', noted Marx approvingly in 1843, 'has plucked the imaginary flowers from the chain not so that man will wear the chain without any fantasy or consolation but so that he will shake off the chain and cull the living flower . . . Religion is only the illusory sun which revolves round man as long as he does not revolve round himself' (Marx and Engels, 1955:42). Whence a *first* dilemma. If this collective self-affirmation merely ratified, or sanctified, the actually existing social totality, then humanism (as the name for this over-turning) would fall prey to an idolatry that was all the worse for being both socially conservative and self-enclosed in currently prevailing thought and imagination. On the other hand, if Humanity is elevated not as what it happens currently to be, but as an essence behind the appearance, or as an ideal to be realised, then we risk worshipping an abstraction. And such abstractions, if rendered into moral–political absolutes, can be manipulated, in the name of 'mending' what Gillian Rose (1992) calls 'the broken middle', to serve all manner of authoritarianisms.

Comte's developmental ontology aimed to resolve the contradiction. But this resolution – which defined Humanity *qua* the highest value as both actual and ideal through the mediating term of a humankind which (in the static and dynamic laws which regulate it) is always a becoming-Humanity – meant that the god's existence was reliant, and in the final stage of the Positive Polity, consciously so, on a social practice that involved each and every one of us. That involvement was immense, not to say heroic. To be sure, the final realisation of Humanity, replete with all the practices which constituted it as society's sacred centre, was not a creation *ex nihilo*. For Comte, the Great Being had always existed in an objective (if immaturely developed) sense. The shift required by scientific and industrial progress concerned the need to complement its objective being with subjective being. This itself was unthinkable without a long historical preparation – for Comte, one that had taken half a millennium. Nevertheless, and not only as an inaugurating act, to make Humanity into a transcending figure that would provide the motivating basis for the voluntary cooperation which the objective being of Humanity would then become, required a massive injection of human agency, unprecedented in scope and extent.

Through the installation of a Positive Polity, Comte envisaged the systematic institution of a new form of practice: *politique positive*. If the immediate aim of this practice was to cure the current social pathology, its long-term aim was to maintain the good health of society ever after. In the positive state, politics would at last be systematically subordinated to *la morale*. It would be bound, that is, in the service of Humanity, a service whose aim, above all, was to provide 'artificial support' for the Great Being's 'naturally accomplished' functions of progress and order.[28] Thus conceived, the religion of Humanity becomes identical with the politics of social reproduction, itself regarded as the ongoing maintenance of *socialité* as such. Given the moral and material dependence of individual being on collective being, such care presents itself to Comte – and, he insists, should present itself to all – as a historical imperative. Care for the social must become, now and forever, the paramount and overriding human concern.

This, however, leads to a *second* dilemma. Humanism, whether Comte's or Feuerbach's, begins with a postulate of human self-affirmation. In some sense or other, 'we' are taken to be our own highest value. However, if we escape the first dilemma (the actual versus the ideal we) by casting that commitment in essentially political terms, and if we further assert, with Comte, that the sustenance of Humanity (objectively or subjectively) cannot be spontaneously guaranteed, then this affirmation turns against those who make it. For in affirming the paramountcy of care for the social we must deny, or at least thoroughly subordinate, the needs and desires of the individual self. This is not just, as in John Stuart Mill's principles of utilitarianism, a moral constraint on the latter wherever my rights to satisfaction collide with those of others. It is a continual subordination of ego to *l'autrui* in the daily economy of human life. Collective self-affirmation thus turns into individual self-sacrifice, whose unhappy implications Comte is only able to cover up by a theory of instincts according to which altruism corresponds to an organismic need that can, with suitable education and moral training, subordinate all other needs to it. Marx obviated the same problem, but in a different way. In the *Economic and Philosophic Manuscripts*, he

---

[28] 'C'est uniquement ainsi que la politique peut enfin se subordonner réellement à la morale, suivant l'admirable programme du moyen âge. Le catholicisme ne put que poser vaguement cette immense question sociale . . . Pour y parvenir, il fait consister la politique à servir l'Humanité, c'est-à-dire à seconder artificiellement les diverses fonctions, d'ordre ou de progrès, que le Grand-Être accomplit naturellement' (VII:361–2).

asserted that the disalienation of labour through the complete abolition of private property, class domination and the forced division of labour could in itself create the conditions for a permanent resolution of the contradiction between the individual and society (1964:44–7). With the negation (of the conditions for human self-actualisation) negated, the collective would cease to be hypostasised in the form of an objectified and coercive state. Then, with relative as well as absolute deprivation overcome through the all-round development of the productive forces, 'the free development of each would be the condition for the free development of all' (Feuer, 1959:29).

We may grant Marx's deeper understanding of what, in industrial capitalism, stood in the way of achieving a real community of interests. But even if we withhold the Freudian objection about the limits of culturation given the perversity of individual desire, the sociological consideration raised by Comte challenges any simple-minded under-standing of what such a project might entail. If it is correct to argue that, from the most intimate sphere of association to the widest and most public, both a collectivist ethic and the community sustained by it require a continual practice of symbolic, ritual, intellectual and political maintenance, then it is hard to see how, even with the reduction in the working day, there could be the *leisure* (Pieper, 1952) for refounding human culture, beyond the 'realm of necessity', on the freedom of each and all. So shifting humanity's sacred centre from an external absolute to itself as its own relative absolute is by no means as straightforwardly emancipatory as it might seem. If it frees us from one set of hetero-nomous commitments, it draws us to take up others which promise to be even more onerous. We are saddled with the duty of perpetual involvement in that political activity (political even when it takes cultural or religious forms) which is needed to foster collectivity and, at the limit, to keep that collectivity socially, and psychologically, alive.

Sociolatry and the death of the social

Comte's faith in Humanity, I have been suggesting, has the peculiar structure of a belief in which the existence of that to which loyalty is given depends not simply on the belief itself (this was the cultural circularity of the old gods) but also on the activity of Humanity-making which that belief inspires and underwrites. Not just a *fides quaerens intellectum*, it was a *fides quaerens agendum* (a faith seeking to be enacted). Politics, of the socially reproductive yet historically developmental kind which Comte encapsulated as 'order and progress', was necessary to close his system.

The irreducibly political, and thus indeterminate, character of Comte's social theory is at variance with its claims to a strict positivity. Its closure was not only 'outside the text' but also *in the future* and thus outside any presentable reality to which evidential appeal might be made. It has its own coherence, however, and critical theorists in the tradition of Horkheimer and the Frankfurt School may find in this very inconsistency a welcome recognition of the essential difference between knowledge in the human and in the natural sciences which makes a pure scientism in the former both theoretically inadequate and practically undesirable. Furthermore, while Comte's 'scientific' stress on the requirements of order in the transformed dispensation is certainly more in tune with what Ernst Bloch called the 'cold current' of socialist thinking than with the 'warm one',[29] the politics which, for Comte, is not only necessary to reach the historical summit from which the speculative gap between theory and reality is finally closed, but continues to be necessary, more than ever, once it is attained, is not incompatible with a certain (Gramscian) politics of the left. It is not only those whom Habermas has dubbed 'neo-conservative postmodernists'[30] who have recognised that social relations need to be worked on if they are to last, let alone to improve.

Yet in the frantically organised and supervised 'circle of rights and duties' surrounding the individual in the Positive Polity there is still something symptomatically excessive. It is as if, despite Comte's insistence on the irreducibly social character of human life, and on the inexorable movement towards the perfection of that sociability, his faith had a hollow centre.

On one point Comte is explicit. He had no confidence whatever in the possibility that the cross-national and even intranational social ties necessary to cement the highly differentiated and specialised activity of industrial society would spontaneously emerge, even after the requisite institutional and intellectual reforms had eliminated the contradictions of transition between it and survivals from the *ancien régime*. But there is also a corollary, discussed earlier, which is both unstated and more startling. In the religious reform which Comte proposed to ensure the

[29] 'The 'unmasking of ideologies . . . and a disenchantment of metaphysics belongs to the most useful *cold stream* of Marxism. To the *warm stream* of Marxism, however, belong liberating intention and [a] materialistically humane, humanely materialistic real tendency, towards whose goal all these disenchantments are undertaken' (Bloch, 1995:209).
[30] Pre-eminently Daniel Bell. In his essay 'Modernity – An Unfinished Project', Habermas distinguishes between the 'antimodernism of young conservatives' (Bataille, Derrida, Foucault), 'the premodernism of old conservatives (a dying breed)', and 'the postmodernism of neo-conservatives' (Foster, 1983:14).

existence, and persistence, of those social ties, what is to be installed, in the first instance, is a drastically impoverished mode of association. In the Positivist Church, what holds together the body of adherents is the serial sociality of individuals joined together only by the coincidence of their beliefs in, and devotions to, *l'Humanité*. Of course this limited sociality is not seen as complete in itself. It was to provide just the subjective basis for voluntary cooperation, outside the sphere of religion, between role-divided individuals. It is that cooperation itself which Comte identifies – under the rubric of *l'esprit d'ensemble* – with the vital unity proper to industrialism. Nevertheless, and even with the added effects of *synergie* among the 'cerebral functions' of intelligence, sentiment and action (x:56–60), the mere fact of such cooperation is granted no power, not even a weak power, to sustain itself without the constant interventions of organised humanist religion.

Durkheim, who detected a contradiction within Comte's thesis concerning the need to complete the differentiating process while at the same time enlarging and homogenising the institutional sphere of morality and religion, suspected here a fundamental defect in Comte's understanding of the affective dimension of the social tie. That is why his rethinking of Comte's diagnosis of industrialism's problem of order in *The Division of Labour* begins with a discussion of Aristotle's distinction between two kinds of friendship (1968a:54–6). One kind of friendship is the bonding that occurs between those who are alike; another (Durkheim had just married) is the bonding between those who are complementarily different.[31] Comte had certainly seen the division of labour 'as something other than a purely economic phenomenon' (Durkheim, 1968a:62), but he had not sufficiently grasped the strong emotive, and solidarising, bonds to which it could give rise. Thus the 'mechanical solidarity' held up by Comte as more crucial than ever in modern times was actually much less so than he had thought.

It is understandable, though, that Durkheim never repeated his argument concerning the affective dimension of 'organic solidarity' in his subsequent work. For it makes an illicit jump from the zone of the face-to-face to that of the more impersonal solidarity that binds the social across distances of space and time. From a Comtean standpoint it

[31] For marriage as a paradigm case of organic solidarity, see Durkheim, 1968a:56–63. His overall argument is that 'the sexual division of labour is the source of conjugal solidarity' (56), that 'the state of marriage in societies where the two sexes are only weakly differentiated thus evinces conjugal solidarity which is itself very weak' (59), and that sexual differentiation has advanced considerably in industrial society, so that 'one of the sexes takes care of the affective functions and the other of intellectual functions' (60), with the overall result that 'today conjugal solidarity makes its action felt at each moment and in all the details of life' (61).

was impossible to think the latter as an extension of any kind of interpersonal *attachement*. Thus it was quite irrelevant to a theory of solidarity at the societal, let alone global, level whether the poles between which such particularistic affect flowed were 'like with like' or 'like with unlike'. Comte's sentiment of 'benevolence', on which these more extended ties depended, had nothing personal about it. It connected individuals with one another (as Durkheim's more consistent theory about the 'cult of the individual' *qua* moral personality recognised (1968a:407))[32] only indirectly and morally. That is: only in so far as individuals represented agents or organs of Humanity for one another, with all such attachments being mediated by each individual's subjective attachment to Humanity itself.

If this is so, however, then the paradox of Comte's asocial conception of the solution to early industrialism's 'social crisis' extends all the way into his conception, in principle, of the social tie. In his religious discourse, the quality of being social is linked to a category to which are attributed the characteristics of a living being, and which, on the analogy of a kind of super-individual, simultaneously constitutes itself as a unitary subject 'which alone produces' (VII:421). In his speculative sociological analysis of this entity in its 'final state', the inner unity which makes Humanity 'vital' resolves into *un concours* of individual states of mind and soul. Whether viewed ontologically, then, or from a perspective that would insist on the need to incorporate in any definition of the social a dimension, however abstract or attenuated, of intersubjectivity, we are forced to conclude that the care for the social which is to become, now, our paramount duty, does not directly orient its praxis towards the social at all. Or rather, to put it as strongly as I dare: it is motivated by a devotion which has already and from the start abandoned the ground on which it claims to stand.

Two related features of Comte's program for resolving the 'crisis' of his times can be elucidated in just such terms. The first is the blurred relation, within Comte's conception of the praxis requisite for establishment and maintenance of social order, between what, following

---

[32] Durkheim's analysis of moral individualism as the cultic centre of the contemporary *conscience collective* is further developed in his essay 'L'individualisme et les intellectuels' (*Reveue Bleue*, vol. 10, 1898), written in the context of the Dreyfus affair. The contemporary form assumed by religion, he asserts, 'is precisely this religion of humanity whose rational expression is the individualist morality . . . One is thus gradually proceeding towards a state of affairs, now almost attained, in which the members of a single social group will no longer have anything in common other than their humanity, that is, the characteristics which constitute the human person in general . . . This is why man has become a god for man and why he can no longer turn to other gods without becoming untrue to himself' (cited in Giddens, 1972:23). The synthesis of Kant with Comte in this formulation is striking.

Althusser (1971:121 et seq.), I have been calling the moments of production and reproduction. There is a parallel here with the loose use of the term 'socialisation' in popularised sociological discussion, for example when enduring patterns of gender or ethno-cultural difference and hierarchy are accounted for in such terms. What is left unexplained is why, or how, the social relations which become culturally embedded and institutionalised exist in the first place. Comte's recurrent notion of 'order' raises the same question. For Comte, once the political has been duly subordinated to the moral, its role is to back up (*seconder*) 'artificially' the order in progress which the Great Being achieves 'naturally' (VII:362). But this 'naturally' requires its 'artificial' supplement. Indeed, as Comte argues in the following volume of *Politique positive*, the institution of religion and the achievement of social unity are indissociable (VIII:7–8). One way of glossing this would be to say that the religious *rebinding* of society into a unity is not distinct from its *binding*. Yet what can that mean? For it implies that *la société* has no organic existence as such independent of its being reproduced – in which case we may wonder whether anything is being reproduced at all.

This brings us to a second feature: the element of artificiality (his own term) in the form of association which Comte's program was intended to establish. This lies not merely in the technological spirit with which *politique positive* is conceived, as a designed social blueprint. The deeper artificiality lies in what that design aims to bring about. I have already noted that the supplementary social bonding instituted by the practices of Positive Religion is extrinsic to the otherwise non-integral and 'composite existence' into which it has to be introduced. This bonding is also social in only the most superficial of senses, that is, by virtue of the simultaneity of individual attachments to a similar idea of the whole. But if we then go on to ask what the existential status of this whole is, and more to the point, of that more 'objective' yet englobing whole which this supplementary bonding was itself supposed to achieve – Humanity as unified and unitary social being – a curious weightlessness in the entire chain of reasoning begins to be apparent. For that redeemed totality only replicates an idea of the social which itself purports to be induced from scientific study. But there was no study, because the idea of the social in question was introduced *a priori* into the very definition of the sociological field.

In terms of the immediate lines of intellectual influence, we may say that Comte's organic–holistic concept of *société* passed into Comte's thinking from the ritualised Catholicism of his youth, from the Christian idea of the 'mystical body of Christ', from the *Imitatio*, above all from the justificatory proto-sociology of the Catholic conservatives (de Bonald, de Maistre and Chateaubriand) whose ontology he sought to combine with the progressivist historicism of the *philosophes*. For Comte himself it could be legitimately inferred from the historical development of the sciences. But either way, his model of the social was only that. It is not just that in realised form a fully social society had never before existed. Even in the *société* depicted in *Politique positive*, it does not exist either, except as an assemblage of suitably motivated individuals institutionally decked out and arranged so as to resemble it. 'Morally envisaged', Comte declares, 'positive society constitutes an objective representation of the Great Being. Its elements should thus arrange themselves according to their aptness for representing Humanity, that is according to their more or less sympathetic nature' (x:62). In sum, just as the social ties reproduced in the religion of Humanity collapse into the process of their reproduction, the associative bonds thereby 'produced' are not the social as such, but a simulation of it. Like the audio-visual studio products discussed by Benjamin in the context of art (1969:218–20), Comte's 'positive state of society' was a copy for which there was no original – a simulacrum which, with its realist rhetoric, obscured the extent of the absence for which its own implementation was designed to compensate.

To see Comte in this way is to place his conservative preoccupation with order in a new light. Of course that pre-occupation cannot be denied. Stability, unity, harmony in the face of tendencies towards what he perceived and experienced as social disintegration were uppermost among his concerns. In analysing these tendencies, what he foregrounded was the crisis of transition, and the intellectual and affective anarchy he thought was being exacerbated by the failure (before Positivism) to go beyond a purely negative and critical orientation towards the ideology and institutions of the old regime. Nor was this the only source of the order problem. In addition to transitional conflicts among theological, meta-physical and positive world-views, he also detected (though these were early days) an inherent difficulty facing the task of establishing the vital unity of the new industrial, work-based and above all increasingly task-specialised form of society towards which reconstructive efforts needed to be directed. If industrial society offered the possibility of realising the most harmonious form of social order – one based on the voluntary cooperation of altruistically motivated individuals – it also left us with no choice but to pursue that immensely difficult path. The price of failure, moreover, would be dire. The very differentiation that distinguished industrialism and established the conditions for the most complete and universal form of society was itself incipiently disintegrative. *L'esprit de détail*, with its narrowed horizons and emphasis on individual achieve-ment, militated precisely in that direction unless checked by counter-vailing measures, perspectives, sentiments and institutions. As too, we must add, did the corrosive effects of new social conflicts stemming from pathologies, as Comte saw it, in the management of class relations arising from industrialism's *overall* division of social labour.

If we put all this together, we can see the multitude of threats to the continuing integrity and vitality of the social with which Comte imagined himself as having to deal. Hence, we may say, the exaggerated, surplus repressive, program he thought was needed to cope with it. It would be tempting to leave the matter at that. In the context of multiplying threats to the stability and harmony of social life, Comte just succumbed to a misty-eyed nostalgia. What he sought, in effect, was a phantasmatic restoration, *mutatis mutandis*, of medieval socio-cultural forms in an industrial techno-scientific context.

No doubt some such vision was indeed driving him on. But if so, he also crosses the line from that problematic – with its echoes of the hankering after *Gemeinschaft* that became a floodtide in similar social theorising in Germany – to another that was more drastic. His system aimed at being and claimed to be pervasively social. But it secretes at its contradictory core a theory of the impossibility of the social. His program of reform is similarly out of kilter. Far from aiming to realise the most harmonious and developed form of human association conceivable, it advocates the institutionalisation of a simulated social body to mitigate the effects of modernising forces which render such a body in any more authentic sense impossible to sustain. Comte's society–god would seem, then, to be utterly insubstantial. Its worship as supreme reality is a desperate attempt to fabricate the effects of sociality in the face of actual desocialisation, just as the sociolatric religion surrounding the moral absolutisation of this imagined totality substitutes an alienated and self-sacrificial regime for any less minimal sense of the social that we might be able to imagine and hope for (for example: a community of passional mortals held together, across the web of an always fractured, conflictual and opaque interactivity, by flows of authentic mutual sympathy and support).

On this reading, Comte, *par excellence*, the thinker of Humanity in place of God, manifests in the contradictory depths of his 'positive' thinking an anxiety that is heightened precisely by the substitution he sought to bring about. Unwittingly, then, the founder of sociology, and the founder of it as a *science sacrée*, is also the first thinker of what contemporary theory, via Baudrillard (1983b), has come to call 'the end of the social'. If the old god has culturally expired, the new one is stillborn. 'Humanity', as the reconstructed foundation of knowledge, sentiments and action in industrial society, and taken to be such because it is identified with the integral vitality of that society's very being, as indeed of every other, is dead on arrival.

8 Socio-theology after Comte

The second death of God

In retracing the steps which led Comte from positive philosophy to positive politics, and thence to the primacy of the sentiments, subjective synthesis and the 'direct institution' of Positive Religion, we have seen that Comte's attempt to reconcile (humanist) faith and (positivised) reason not only rested on false closures, but it failed, even in its own terms, to establish either the coherence or the positivity of its posited transcendental signified. Whether considered in terms of continuity, memory and *l'Humanité*'s diachronic dimension, or of solidarity and the synchronic dimension of its 'vital consensus', Comte's fashioning of the Positivist *intellectum* led him to adopt a contradictory social ontology such that the transcendent and integral being with which he wanted to couple the actuality of the social not only did not, but could not, exist in the sense desired. Indeed, as programmatically envisaged, it could only realise itself as a simulation of what it claimed to be.

Thus Comte's *foi démontrable* undermines itself. His endless system-building, together with the rhetoric of certitude in which it is clothed, protected him against that realisation. However, suppose it had not. Or rather: suppose that we let the foreknowledge of the project's impossibility enter into a consciousness grappling with the same overall problem. Then the absence of a focalising centre for thought, feeling and action would present itself (at least for a mind 'seeking God') more sharply than ever. Indeed, it would recur with redoubled pain, since the cultural supersession of the Christian deity in the elevation of Society and Humanity was not just a cognitive move, but entailed a reinvestment of (so to speak) orientational eros in the substituted term. We can even imagine a further stage in which faith in faith itself collapsed – leading, through all the phases of mourning, to an acceptance that the intellectual and cultural situation had irrevocably changed so that no centring and foundational orientation, *modo theologico*, could ever again be restored; and that this, henceforth, was the place from which thinking had to begin.

In the figure one can unfold from such a reflection on Comte's project, it is as if a *first* death of God – the death which Positivism claimed to have made good[1] – is followed by a *second* one. Only this time it is Society, History, Humanity etc. which reveals itself to have been (all along) a phantasm without any other status than that on the plane of phenomenal actuality; a plane which has itself, with the first death of God, become identical with the only meaningful sense in which there is reality at all.

We might say that this second death still belongs to the first. Christianity, Jean-Luc Nancy reminds us, has had two ('antithetical') ideas of the divine: *deus absconditus* and *deus communis*.[2] If Comte ditched the first it was only by elevating the second. Even in its own terms, besides, Positive Religion was at variance with its own principles. Behind the abstractions of Humanity and Society, especially when endowed with the capacity to think, feel and act, lies an anthropomorphism no less projective because projected on to human material. The very notion of an integral subject is predicated on an *a priori* idea of the ego or 'society' which has been rendered suspect by the advance of the human sciences. Its manoeuvring into the vacated place of God falls apart with the movement of critique,[3] including (in his multi-impulse notion of subjectivity, and implicitly serialised conception of *société*) Comte's. At root, indeed, there was an incompleteness in Positivism's rupture with Platonism. If there is no 'real world' beyond the actual one, then the actual one is not (in the Parmenidean sense) 'real' either.[4] So much, then, for any identification of the social with the firm ground of the real.

Nietzsche's embrace of becoming, which pushed him towards 'transvaluation' and his 'most abyssal thought' of the Eternal Return, set itself up as a 'noble' and 'free-spirited' alternative to all ontologising. But in such matters, as Nietzsche was the first to acknowledge, there is no one way.[5] Comte's formulation of the 'God question', no less than

---

[1] 'La supériorité nécessaire de la morale démontrée sur la morale révélée se résume donc par la substitution finale de l'amour de l'Humanité à l'amour de Dieu' (VII:356). For the 'décadence de Dieu', see IX:507–11.

[2] 'Christianity has had only two dimensions, antithetical to one another: that of the *deus absconditus*, in which the Western disappearance of the divine is still engulfed, and that of the god-man, *deus communis*, brother of mankind, invention of a familial immanence of humanity, then of history as the immanence of salvation' (1991:10).

[3] According to Heidegger, we may add, Nietzsche's own 'will-to-power' is ultimately trapped in the same metaphysic.

[4] 'We have abolished the real world: what world is left? – the apparent world perhaps? . . . But no! *With the real world we have also abolished the apparent world!*' (Nietzsche, 1990:51; italics in original). See also Lefebvre's critique of 'le nouvel éléatisme', which he particularly identifies with the rise of structuralism (Lefebvre, 1971:262–78).

[5] 'This – is now *my* way: where is yours? Thus I answered those who asked me "the way". For *the* way – does not exist!' (1961:213).

Nietzsche's, emerges out of the idiosyncrasies of his deepest impulses, as deployed within the field of its available possibilities. In that regard we can make an obvious historical point. The stressfully abandoned theism with which Nietzsche was wrestling was 'reformed', Lutheran, individualist. Comte's was Catholic, and the product of the Counter-Reformation. Hence, just as the Protestant emphasis on the 'innerness' of Spirit migrates, in Nietzsche's atheism, to Dionysus and the will-to-power, so Comte's own break from transcendental religion bore with it a socially realist concept of institution, ceremony and symbolism, itself tied to an organicist and hierarchical social paradigm inherited from the medievals.

In France after the Revolution, the transposition of these elements into this-wordly sociological terms was also politically induced. Besides its initial attraction for proto-socialist reformers, Comte's fashioning of Positivism responded to the unstable post-Revolutionary state's need for an ideological alternative to Catholicism in a country still saturated with its culture. In the Third Republic, established after the disastrous defeat by Prussia in 1870–1, and following the bloody suppression of the Paris Commune, this need became pressing. A context was provided by the reforms in the 1880s which wrested control of primary education from the church. This was vigorously followed up, after the menacing rise of a racist and revanchist right during the Boulangist agitation and Dreyfus Affair in the 1890s, by attempts to introduce a Republican version of civic and moral education into the school curriculum. Thus, while the eccentricities and extreme anti-individualism of Comte's own system had doomed it to marginality, a generation later the stage was set for the official reception of a suitably softened and liberalised version. With an admixture of Kant (revived in France during the Second Empire by Renouvier and Boutroux), it was precisely this which Durkheim and his school were able to provide.[6]

Overall, then, it is hardly surprising that the pursuit of a post-theistic

---

[6] A vivid (but hostile) indication of the politico-moral fervour that inspired Durkheim after he was appointed to the Sorbonne (in 1902, to teach education) is given by Nizan in *The Watchdogs*. After mentioning the ascendant administrative role, particularly in professorial hiring, that Durkheim came to play in Paris after the education minister, Liard, had rescued him from provincial obscurity at the University of Bordeaux, Nizan adds: 'The introduction of Sociology into the curriculum of the *écoles normales* sealed the official triumph of this official morality. Over a period of a few years, Durkheim with extraordinary perseverance and great authoritarian rigor, constructed his system of thought and carried his teachings far and wide; and he dressed this system in the venerable trappings of science. In the name of this science, our schoolteachers now teach French pupils to respect the French Fatherland, to justify collaboration between the classes, to accept everything they see, and to commune in the cult of the Flag and Bourgeois Democracy' (Nizan, 1971:109).

philosophy in France should take a long detour through a sacralisation of the social.[7] Nor that it should take a simultaneously political, religio-moral and sociological form. That same detour, moreover – which attempted to meet the anomic challenge of materialist unbelief through the positivistic appropriation of the Counter-Revolutionary Catholic critique of individualistic rationalism – provides a key for understanding later developments. It explains why modern French thought, having been the privileged site for the rise of the social as a 'scientific' category, has also been the site for that category's most thorough dismantling. It more especially explains why that occurrence – the effect both of an ideological disintegration and of an intellectual discrediting – had quasi-religious overtones, as an anti-humanist reprise of Nietzsche's 'death of God'.

It would require another study to show how, in the wake of attempts first to salvage Comte's system, then to face the void at its centre, this disturbing thematic came to assert itself in French social theory – to the point, indeed, where it became, in the third quarter of the twentieth century, not just a proclaimed but an *affirmed* intellectual event. Most proximately, as Descombes (1980) has chronicled, and Derrida attests (1982:114–15), the theoretical demise of humanism in post-1945 France begins with the publication of Heidegger's 'Letter on Humanism', itself written in response to questions put to him about Sartre's *Existentialism and Humanism*.[8] The far-reaching consequences of the humanism con-troversy, whose deconstructive noise has scarcely yet died down, can be understood against the background of several accompanying features of the postwar intellectual landscape. These included the gathering influ-ence of Kojève's Nietzschean and Marxist rereading of Hegel, the rise of structuralism out of ethnography and Saussurian linguistics, and a confrontation of the anti-historicist objectivism of the latter with both neo-Hegelian philosophies of the subject and newly imported Husser-lian and Heideggerian phenomenology.[9] And through it all have been the successive receptions and reinterpretations of Nietzsche, first

---

[7] This pursuit went across the political spectrum. The proto-fascism that began to form in the 1890s, spearheaded by Charles Maurras, was drawn to its own – nationalist and anti-Christian – version of a religion of the social. For the influence of Comte on Maurras, see Nolte, 1965:52. For Maurras's conception of *Déesse France*, see ibid.:143.

[8] For the immediate circumstances of Heidegger's 'Letter on Humanism', see Heidegger, 1977b:190–2. For a commentary on it as a strategic (self-rehabilitating) intervention, see Bordieu, 1991:90 et seq.

[9] For a clear but critical account of 'modern French philosophy', including the formative role of Kojève, and the (post)structuralist reaction against Sartre, see Descombes, 1980. For the confrontation between Marxism and structuralism, see Sebag (1964); and for the interrelation among Nietzsche, Heidegger and Derrida, see Behler, 1991 (esp. 107–58).

through Kojève and Bataille, then in the context of existentialism, then –
spurred by the French publication of Heidegger's pre-war commentaries
– through those for whom Nietzsche was the forerunner of antifounda-
tionalism in its various contemporary forms (Allison, 1985).

But this is only to take stock of the immediate context. A fuller
understanding of what underlies and frames all those poststructuralist
'deaths' (of the subject, Man, history, the author, referentiality etc.)
which were announced in the 1960s by Foucault, Barthes,[10] Derrida
and others, would have to take account of the longer-term vicissitudes of
French sociology itself since its classical period. These would include
the way in which Durkheimian sociology critically appropriated and
relaunched Comte's larger social and religious project,[11] its falling apart
and disillusionment after 1914,[12] the emergence, with Lévi-Strauss, of a
desubjectified and dehistoricised structural anthropology,[13] and the way
in which, through Bataille's appropriation of Mauss's essay on gift
exchange (Mauss, 1967) and (with Hubert) sacrifice (1964), a revised
conception of the social, influenced by reflections on the 'primitive',
broke from the integralist model of society, reconceived the truth of
religion, and provided a new bridge to Nietzsche and Marx (Bataille,
1985:69–70, 120 et seq.).

This complex development had its inner logic.[14] But it also responded
to the shocks of real history. The subjective dissolution of the Society-
god had already begun on the killing fields of 1914–18. Nizan (1971) has
chronicled the subsequent revolt by a new generation at the Sorbonne
against the lingering influence of Durkheim and the other pre-war
watchdogs of bourgeois *morale*. Weakened by fresh polarisations, the
Third Republic that had sponsored them disintegrated, to be replaced
by the Vichy regime after the German invasion. The horrors of the

[10] In literary theory the death of Man takes the form of the 'death of the author' (the key
essay is included in Barthes, 1977). See Biriotti and Miller, 1993:1–52.

[11] I have discussed Durkheim in these terms in Fekete, 1984:139–43. Durkheim's most
forthright acknowledgment of his (corrective) relation to Comte came in the course of a
polemical exchange with the Thomist Simon Deploige (Giddens, 1971:71). Durkheim
had good reason, at this stage, to stress the Comtean provenance of his sociology, since
Deploige accused him of being an intellectual agent of German philosophy and social
theory, a most damaging charge in the period leading up to the First World War, and
one no doubt with anti-Semitic undertones.

[12] For Durkheim's own melancholic descent, especially after his son was killed in the
Balkans in 1915, see Henri Peyre's foreword to the essays on Montesquieu and
Rousseau (Durkheim, 1965a:xii).

[13] See especially Lévi-Strauss's introduction to Mauss's *Essai sur le don*, published in
English as the first chapter of *Structural Anthropology* (1967).

[14] In his 1968 essay 'The Ends of Man', Derrida (1982:114–22) relates this logic to the
'decentring' effects of linguistics and ethnology and to contradictions (an inconsistent
Heideggerianism) in the presiding influence of Sartre.

thirties and forties completed the work of the Great War in discrediting the grand narratives of reason and progress.

After 1945, among the new inheritors of French thought there was a further resurgence of oppositional thinking, including a revival of Marxism informed by a rediscovery of Marx's early writings.[15] This was spurred on by the Algerian war, the nuclear arms race, anticolonial struggles in South-East Asia, and the crystallisation of a dissident bohemianism as the alienated flip-side of the candy-floss corporatism which accompanied the long postwar economic boom. It was in this radicalising context that the battles among existentialists, phenomenologists and new-wave structuralists broke out, and when what Foucault and others called 'anthropologism' was pronounced by some at an end. Finally, in the disillusioned aftermath of 1968, and with the total discrediting of the 'socialist' camp (*inter alia* through the writings of Solzhenitsyn on the Gulag), the detotalising animus that had first been directed against the residues of Catholicism and sociologism was increasingly directed – despite the (mostly continuing) *gauchisme* of the deconstructionist cohort[16] – against Marxism itself.

Even so brief a sketch may serve to make one thing clear. Whatever the ideological ambiguities in which French socio-theology was born, and however we interpret the postmodern swerve, the dissolution of its sacred categories has been, in the widest sense,[17] a left-wing occurrence. From Bataille to Nancy, the dismantling of Society/Humanity has been linked on the one hand to ideology–critique (transmuted into an immanent critique of metaphysics), and on the other to demythifying the actual travails of social being. It also gives rise to a new, and radical, challenge: how, if at all, and without any foundationalist metaphysics of the subject, History, or Society, to conceive forms of sociality that point beyond capitalism altogether.

One may readily conclude from the collapse of Comte's and Durkheim's classic attempt to construct a 'positive' socio-theology that what they attempted could not be done, in *any* form, without invoking a

---

[15] Publication of Marx's early (1845 and earlier) writings began with the edition of Lanshut and Mayer in 1931. For a discussion of this edition and its French translation, see Althusser, 1969:50–3.

[16] Foucault and Deleuze, for example, were sympathisers in the 1970s of *Gauche Prolétarienne*.

[17] Derrida, who was a friend of Althusser's, has always identified himself as sympathetic to the left; Lyotard was a member of the *Socialisme ou Barbarisme* tendency till the mid sixties; Foucault and Deleuze worked together on the prison reform project in the 1970s, which was close to *Gauche Prolétarienne*; and Barthes's early work is openly Marxist. Harder to characterise are Bataille (in the 1930s, an ultra-leftist fascinated by the symbolic aspects of fascism) and Blanchot, whose political sympathies were similar to Bataille's.

metaphysic of collective being which was at variance with the intended positivity of the project. However, as Bataille's Dionysian conjuring with 'expenditure' and the ecstatic aspect of sacrifice (1985:130–6) suggests, one may conceive the social as harbouring an immanent transcendent without in any way essentialising or hypostasising society, or any version of the human collectivity. The same point can be made, then, about the 'second death of God' as about the first. Just as theism, of a kind, can survive even a sympathetic encounter with Nietzsche,[18] so can 'God-seeking' reflections on the social. It is possible to endorse – even push to the limit – the demise of Comte's and Durkheim's hypostasised concept of 'Society' while still seeking, through a fundamental reflection on the social element of human being, to give an account of what can, or does, draw us forward and beyond our finite selves. Even in the midst of a hyper-critical 'suspicion towards all metanarratives' there might be other ways to continue what was necessarily unaccomplished in French sociology.

To illustrate how this might be done, I want to conclude by examining three contrasting responses that have been made in recent decades to questions still resonating in French social theory from amidst the ruins of the Comtean project. The first is Louis Althusser's intra-Marxist polemic against 'theoretical humanism'. The second is Jean Baudrillard's proclaimed 'end of the social'. The third is Jean-Luc Nancy's reflection on 'inoperative community'. At first sight the differences of approach among these thinkers are so stark as to obscure the thematics they all engage. Althusser, in the name of Marx, undertakes a partial reconstruction of the Comtean matrix. Baudrillard, bespeaking a capitalism gone viral and hyper-real, pronounces an end to any conceivable version of sociology or its object. Nancy, in an ethicised dialogue with Nietzsche, Heidegger and Bataille, essays a primordial rethinking of community. Besides their ideological differences – Althusser an avowed Leninist, Baudrillard ironically disengaged, Nancy a non-theistic non-Marxist love-oriented communitarian – their positions crystallised in three different decades, the 1960s, 70s and 80s, by whose moods and horizons they are also marked. At the same time, however, each manifests a similar preoccupation with the fundamental nature of social

---

[18] For a self-consciously postmodern discussion about the place of Nietzsche in 'theology at the end of the century', see Scharlemann, 1990. Of the interlocutors, Mark Taylor's position is the most open to Nietzsche, welcoming him indeed with almost open arms: 'The end of theology is apocalyptic – inevitably apocalyptic. The death of God is the death of theology. This end is simultaneously the consummation and the dissolution of the history of the Christian West. To appreciate the difficulties and the opportunities for thinking at the end of theology, it is necessary to consider the end that guides the historical process from the beginning' (50).

(as opposed to, if also in relation with, individual) being. Each is concerned to find, through such inquiry, a transcending principle for progressive praxis which, if not apodictic, is in some sense compelling. All three, finally, differ from classical French sociology in that they accept *both* the Marxist critique of its elided socio-economic categories *and* the poststructuralist critique of philosophical anthropology, absolute historicism and self-realising theories of the human subject (including the expression of these in Marxist form).

Within this general frame, the positions which Althusser, Baudrillard and Nancy stake out certainly clash. Nevertheless we might think of them as pointing towards *complementary* sites of inquiry regarding the locus of a transcending social principle – a principle which, in their different ways, they are all concerned to uncover, even as they exorcise the social–ontological ghosts of Comte and Durkheim.

Althusser: Humanism without Humanity

In a polemical 1972 essay, André Glucksmann described Louis Althusser's controversial rereading of Marx as a 'ventriloquist structuralism'.[19] At several points in this study I have suggested that, at a deeper level, Althusser's 'intervention for Marx' was in fact influenced by Comte. More particularly, I have suggested that it was guided by the idea that Marx could be understood as having accomplished, in his 'immense theoretical revolution' (Althusser, 1970:182), what Comte himself, in the vocabulary of Positivism, claimed to have achieved. Just as Comte insisted that positivising knowledge in the social–human domain facilitated and necessitated a wider epistemic change, so Althusser insisted that Marx's departure from left-Hegelianism, and the humanist idealisms of his youth, entailed a double 'epistemological break'. Inaugurating the 'science of history' (historical materialism) transformed philosophy – 'the Theoretical' – by inaugurating the 'theory of the history of theoretical formations' (the materialist dialectic).[20]

---

[19] The title of Glucksmann's contribution to *New Left Review* 72, a special issue on Althusser. Other notable contributions were by Ernest Mandel and Norman Geras. None of the significant commentaries on Althusser in English (e.g. Resch, 1992; Benton, 1984; M. Glucksmann, 1974; Eliot, 1987; Thompson, 1978) seem to have placed much weight on the importance of Comte.

[20] 'This "epistemological break" concerns conjointly two distinct theoretical disciplines. By founding the theory of history (dialectical materialism), Marx simultaneously broke with his erstwhile ideological philosophy and established a new philosophy (dialectical materialism). I am deliberately[!] using the traditionally accepted terminology . . . to designate this double double foundation in a single break' (Althusser, 1970:33). For an elaboration, see especially the introduction and the essays 'Contradiction and Over-determination' and 'On the Materialist Dialectic' in *For Marx* (Althusser, 1969).

This is not to say that Althusser's Marx is simply Comte in disguise. The container of what Comte called positive sociology is filled, in Althusser's Marxist replacement, with concepts which are incompatible not only with the Hegelian and 'economist' problematics which are their stated target, but with any version, even 'inverted', of Comte's holistic theory of socio-history. There is no *société*, no 'order and progress'. Althusser's 'social formation' is an 'overdetermined' structure of structures. Each mode of practice is quasi-autonomous and determined in its 'index of effectivity', and 'in the last instance' by the economic.[21] History is the heterogeneous site of multiple temporalities (1970:132–5). Althusser's Marx, indeed, is credited not only with 'opening up' the 'new continent of History' (1969:14), but also with that overcoming of ('essentialist') metaphysics usually associated with Nietzsche, Heidegger and the linguistic turn (Macksey and Donato, 1972:249). Nevertheless, in *For Marx* and *Reading Capital*, the 'Marxist philosophy' that Althusser claims is buried but 'active' in Marx's 'mature' work (1969:14), and which Althusser sets himself to disengage through a 'symptomatic reading' of Marx's texts (1970:32–3), is formulated in strikingly Comtean terms.[22]

By drawing on Comte's positivist understanding of philosophy as the science of science, Althusser aimed both to repudiate the Engels/Stalin notion of dialectical materialism as a general theory of nature, and also to rescue the philosophical enterprise from the immediate or 'lingering' death (as an 'evanescent critical consciousness') to which Marx himself would have consigned it (1969:34). Althusser was forced, on pain of losing his Marxist credentials, to disavow this conception of Marxist theory as 'theoreticist'.[23] In 'Lenin and Philosophy' he substituted a

---

[21] '[I]n History, these instances, the superstructures, etc., are never seen to step respectfully aside when their work is done or, when the Time comes, as his pure phenomena, to scatter before His Majesty the Economy as he strides along the royal road of the dialectic. From the first moment to the last, the lonely hour of the "last instance" never comes' (Althusser, 1969:113).

[22] One single footnote in *Reading Capital* acknowledges the provenance. After quoting from the opening volume of *Philosophie positive* on the founding of modern physics, Althusser notes: 'Bacon, Descartes and Galileo thus determine the transition of physics to positivity, and at the same time the beginning of the general preponderance of the positive state. With his double articulation of the sciences and the law of the three states, Comte is the most rigorous thinker so far of this general theoretical problem: how the distinct practices which constitute a "division of labour" are articulated together, and how this articulation varies with the mutation in these practices' (1970:205–6n4).

[23] Althusser signals his retreat in his foreword to the 1970 (Italian) edition *Lire le Capital*, repeated in the English edition of that same year. '[O]ne of the theses I advanced as to the *nature of philosophy* did express a certain "theoreticist" tendency . . . To define philosophy in a unilateral way as the Theory of theoretical practices (and in consequence a theory of the differences between the practices) is a formulation that

revised notion according to which (Marxist) philosophy is 'the class struggle in theory' (1971:22).[24] But it is the early Althusser (1959–68) which concerns me here, and especially the less-visible reworking of Comte which Althusser appears to be engaged upon, in this same period, with respect to a neighbouring problem: the implications of 'the general preponderance of the positive state' (1970:205) for the Marxist theory of ideology. Consider, in that light, the following passage from *Reading Capital*.

This 'break' between the old religions, or ideologies, even the 'organic' ones, and Marxism, *which is a science*, and which must become the 'organic' ideology of human history by producing a *new* form of ideology in the masses (an ideology which will depend on a science this time – *which has never been the case before*) – this break was not really reflected by Gramsci, and, absorbed as he was by the necessity and the practical conditions for the penetration of the 'philosophy of praxis' into real history, he neglected the theoretical significance of this break and its theoretical and practical consequences. (1970:131; emphasis in original)

The coherence of Althusser's comment relies on the dual value given to 'ideology'. On the one hand it is an epistemological category, on the other hand an irreducible social reality. As the former, ideology is a non-scientific mode of cognition, a circular and subjectively centred discourse which only 'knows' what the subject has already projected into it. As the latter, ideology consists of all the actively embedded 'systems of representations' through which individuals live their relation to the social relations in which they are implicated, and in terms of which they identify, as functioning 'subjects', with what and where they are. Gramsci, says Althusser, understood 'ideology' only in the latter sense, i.e. as subjective orientation. This enabled him, correctly, to understand Marxism as having the capacity, even the mission, of becoming, in its historical turn, an 'organic' ideology. The 'philosophy of praxis' would replace both the liberalism of the market and the traditional forms of religion as the 'ideological cement' binding together postcapitalist society and motivating its further advance. But, since Gramsci collapsed historical and dialectical materialism together – failing to appreciate the transformed 'Theoretical' represented by Marxist philosophy – he ignored the epistemological sense of 'ideology'. He thus glossed over the

could not help but induce either "speculative" or "positivist" theoretical effects and echoes' (1970:8; emphasis in original).

[24] See also the title essay of *Lenin and Philosophy*, especially 49 et seq. After disengaging the appropriate formulations about partisanship, idealism versus materialism etc. from some texts of Lenin's, Althusser concludes by noting that 'what is new in Marxism's contribution to philosophy is a new *practice of philosophy. Marxism is not a (new) philosophy of practice, but a new practice of philosophy*' (1971:67; emphasis in original).

break between all preceding 'organic' ideologies and this one. In effect, he missed the difference between ideologies based on ideology (the case hitherto) and 'Marxism, which is a science' and is destined to produce 'a *new* form of ideology in the masses . . . which will depend on a science this time'.

It is precisely in such terms, of course, that Comte understood the status and mission of *philosophie positive*. If Althusser's formula – an ideology that depends on a science – seems more paradoxical, this was because of his (*marxisant*) use of the term ideology itself. For Althusser, the term covers not only what Comte, in his theory of knowledge, called theology and metaphysics,[25] it also covers what Comte came to call *la morale*, thought of as the entire 'subjective' dimension of *la société*.

But the Comtean echo in Althusser is not confined to that of Comte's first synthesis. Althusser's criticism of Gramsci refers not just to the theoretical consequences of Gramsci's failure to recognise the (scientifically) ruptural character of the 'philosophy of praxis', but also to the 'practical consequences' – consequences which extend, in fact, to the whole field of politics. Now, this field Marxism has transformed in a scientific direction too. First: through its general theory (for example, the centrality it accords to the class struggle); secondly: because it strategises action by way of a comprehension of political practice as always intervening on, and from within, the specific complexity of a 'conjuncture' (Althusser, 1969:175–82). For that same reason however (here Althusser is following Gramsci) the politics of class struggle should not be understood in too narrow a sense. More is involved than the struggle for state power. Theory has a politics, and so does ideology itself. The epistemological break effected by Marxism has implications for aesthetics, education and the sciences, with ramifications in turn for the formation of social alliances and the overall relations of force. It also implies, as illustrated (we infer) by Althusser's own 'intervention', a scientifically informed politics of that same philosophico-ideological break.[26]

A general framework for conceptualising a 'scientific policy towards ideology' is sketched out in Althusser's celebrated essay 'Ideology and Ideological State-Apparatuses' (1969:121–76). As a social reality, ideology is defined as the set of instituted practices within and through which individuals are 'interpellated' as subjects (1971:162). On its subjective side, it mediates between (unconscious) desire and social

[25] Durkheim used the term 'ideology' in just this sense (1964:14).
[26] For Althusser's application of this formula to his own 'intervention' ('for Marx'), see 1969:21–31.

identification to constitute a continually reproduced imaginary[27] within which social relations (and their conflicts) are 'lived "spontaneously"'(1971:160). On its objective side, ideology operates through 'ritual practices' directed by 'state ideological apparatuses'. These, in turn, are to be distinguished from the coercive apparatus of the state as operating mainly 'by ideology' rather than 'by violence' (1971:138). But, finally, state ideological apparatuses also operate alongside the state's repressive ones in the process wherein the dominant nexus of social relations is reproduced. All that is missing, though it is developed elsewhere,[28] is a theory of political practice itself as the production and reproduction of social relations, and, as a region within that, a theory of ideological politics conceived as acting upon the (re)production of ideology through struggles over its codes and practices.

Althusser presents these theses in a highly schematic way. The historical reference is vague, though the essay does contain an illustrative comment on the state education system ('The School'). This, he argues, has replaced the church in capitalist society as 'the dominant state ideological apparatus', both through its transmission of bourgeois myth and through its sorting and socialisation of individuals into the differentiated pyramid of 'social posts' (1971:146–9). Althusser (who was himself a teacher at the École Normale de la rue d'Ulm)[29] thus affirms an emphasis on education that was prominent for both Comte and Durkheim, though with the Marxist qualification that ideological institutions are secondary (if essential, and quasi-autonomous),[30] and that the school's current role is to reproduce *capitalist* social relations rather than those of 'society' as such.[31] But as Althusser's remarks on Gramsci

---

[27] Althusser presents as his 'central thesis' that 'Ideology is a "representation" of the imaginary relationship of individuals to their real conditions of existence' (1971:152).

[28] Althusser sketched out a theory of 'Marxist political practice' (e.g. 1969:175–82), but it was Poulantzas (1970) who developed Althusser's notions about power, the state, and class politics into a full-scale system.

[29] One of the post-Revolutionary elite *Grandes Écoles* and specialising in the humanities, its graduates filled university posts throughout France (Bourdieu, 1988:252–5). It was thus an institution which produced teachers to teach teachers. Durkheim, like Althusser, had been a graduate (*normalien*).

[30] The strategic role of 'the school' in reproducing capitalist social relations nonetheless means that 'the unprecedentedly deep crisis which is now [1968–70] shaking the education system of so many states across the globe, often in conjunction with a crisis shaking the family system, takes on a political meaning' (1971:149).

[31] Althusser's thesis about the dominance of the school (or 'the School–Family couple' (1971:49)) might be sustainable for earlier phases of capitalist development. However, the rise of the mass media, consumer culture and the 'society of the spectacle' have rendered the claim increasingly dubious, even if a rigorous meaning could be given to the 'dominance' of an ideological institution in the first place. The case, moreover, of an ideological institution like advertising, which is economically determined and which functions as an *internal* element of the accumulation process, implies the need for a

suggest, it is not the *currently dominant* ideological institutions which really interest him. His main concern is to clarify the nature of *socialist* ideology, considered in its oppositional function, but still more as the nascent, but finally dominant, discourse of a postcapitalist order. What, though, does establishing this 'new ideology' entail? What rituals and 'state-ideological apparatuses' are to be deployed for the task? What, indeed, at the level of 'systems of representations', is to be its *ideological* (as opposed to scientific) *content?*

Althusser rarely addresses these questions directly, but in one of the essays in *For Marx*, 'Marxism and Humanism', we get at least the inkling of an answer. 'Today', he tells us, 'Socialist "Humanism" is on the agenda.' Why? Because 'as it enters the period which will lead it from socialism (to each according to his labour) to communism (to each according to his needs), the Soviet Union has proclaimed the slogan: All for Man, and introduced new themes: the freedom of the individual, respect for legality, the dignity of the person' (1969:221).

A generation later we may smile, but Althusser's argument about the humanist slogans that appear in the Communist Party of the Soviet Union program of 1963 is worth tracing out. He meditates on 'the significance of this historical event' along two tracks. Along the one, he stresses the theoretical peril of any recourse to slogans about 'Man'. The term humanism, unlike the term socialism, has 'no scientific value'. To overlook this, and then justify it by reading humanism back into Marx, would compound the error. It would misunderstand, above all, the 'scientific' character of the break Marx made from any such perspective: a break indicated, in the 'Theses on Feuerbach', by Marx's insistence that to grasp human history in its 'practical-sensuous' actuality we must stop contemplating the human essence and study instead 'the ensemble of social relations' (1969:242–3).

Along the other track, Althusser defends the Soviet slogans. Ideology, he insists, is irreducible, even in a classless society. It is in a different register from knowledge, serving to motivate, ethicise, inspire etc., and on this level the capital-'h' Humanist language of the Soviet party program is to be endorsed. Here too, though, there are perils. Humanism is a labile 'ideologeme'. Its precise political meaning depends on the inflection given it and the context in which it is advanced. Above all, we must distinguish between socialist and bourgeois humanism. The latter, still dominant in the French education system, misconstrues a class-divided 'society' as essentially unifiable on the basis of what its

further theoretical development of the whole notion of ideology and its related practices which Althusser does not even begin to undertake. For a structural account of a hypothesised 'post-Fordist' shift in 'the regime of signification', see Lash, 1990:4–5.

(exploited/exploiting) members humanly share.[32] Socialist humanism avoids the error by eschewing such universalism. In a capitalist context it can only be a 'class humanism', expressed as partisanship for the working class, in the name of the community-without-classes its victory would make possible. This continues right into the period of socialist transition, when classes, residually, still exist, and the threat of capitalist restoration is still present. But, it transpires, a new epoch is now upon us. Class antagonisms in the leading socialist society have been overcome. Henceforth, socialist humanism comes to have two different forms: 'class humanism, where the dictatorship of the proletariat is still in force (China etc.), and (socialist) personal humanism, where it has been superseded (the U.S.S.R.)'. These correspond to 'two necessary phases. In "personal" humanism, "class" humanism contemplates its own future, realised' (1969:222).

Admittedly, adds Althusser, there is something situationally specific about all this. In the still-resonant aftermath of Krushchev's 'secret' speech, 'All for Man' coupled with calls for 'legality', 'respect for the person' etc. are the slogans of destalinisation. In capitalist democracies these same slogans have a second function as well. Holding out the prospect of a 'peaceful road' to socialism, they aid in the formation of a united front. They provide ground for 'a dialogue between Communists and Social-Democrats, or even a wider exchange with those "men of good will" who are opposed to war and poverty. Today', Althusser opines, 'even the high road of Humanism seems to lead to socialism' (221).

However, there is something in the Soviet ideological turn which also goes beyond the political moment. During the long period of transition, 'socialist humanism [in 'personal' form] . . . can see itself not only as a critique of the contradictions of bourgeois humanism, but also and above all as the distillation of the latter's "noblest" aspirations'. Across that entire epoch, it points to a form of human community from which market relations have been expunged. And as that limit is approached, its own character as ideology changes. Ceasing to have any connection with class hegemony (even working-class), it becomes, instead, 'the relay whereby, and the element in which, the relation between men [sic] and their conditions of existence is lived to the profit of all men' (1969:236).

---

[32] '[T]he score of the Ideology of the current ruling class integrates into its music the great themes of the Humanism of the Great Forefathers, who produced the Greek Miracle even before Christianity, and afterwards the Glory of Rome, the Eternal City, and the themes of Interest, particular and general, etc., nationalism, moralism and economism' (1971:146).

That Althusser's *whole* argument functions – 'conjuncturally' – as an apologetic for the mid-1960s Soviet party line, is self-evident. Controlled destalinisation at home, the parliamentary road abroad, 'peaceful competition' with the capitalist West internationally, the litany is (or was) familiar. Althusser makes no bones about it. He writes as a faithful, if intellectually embattled, militant of the French Communist Party,[33] a party whose loyalty, indeed subservience, to Moscow was, and remained, notorious. For this allegiance Althusser came under fire even from supporters,[34] especially after the PCF's contribution to defeating the insurgency of 1968. His adhesion to the PCF coexisted uneasily with his stated aim of demolishing the Stalinist deformation of Marxism and Leninism *from the left*.

The political *furore* occasioned by Althusser's stubborn partisanship focussed on this point. But that partisanship also had a deeper significance in relation to his project. A Catholic activist in his youth, he had joined a new, and better, church. In his work of theoretical 'clarification' and 'correction', he was reworking that church's official doctrine, above all to provide a ground for its (would-be) scientifically based faith. Like Comte's Humanism, Althusser's Communist conviction is a *fides quaerens intellectum*. And like Comte's, too, it is not just *theoretically* Positivist. Althusser's Marxist version of *une foi démontrable* is linked to the equivalent of a Positive *politics*. It is so, moreover, not only as an instrumentalism, through Marxism's 'scientifically' based strategy and tactics, but in Althusser's insistence that such a faith (any faith) can only be subjectively sustained through a set of 'mainly ritual practices' (1971:158–62); practices which, in the final stage of human development, have likewise to be deliberately set up and maintained.

In sum, Althusser rethinks the ideological program he takes (from Gramsci) to be intrinsic to the process of socialist transformation, by rendering it in the terms of Comte's *religion positive*. This leads him, correlatively, to think Lenin's 'vanguard party' – the locus of fusion between intellectuals and militants, theory and practice, science and politics – into the space of Comte's revamped *pouvoir spirituel*.

For Althusser, then, the church-like ethos of the Communist Party, which he parodies in his style, is to be taken seriously. Whatever its strategy-determining functions, the Party (linked to the (capital letters) World Communist Movement) is also an 'ideological apparatus'. As

---

[33] Which he joined in 1948 and quit only in 1981, in order, as he later puts it, 'to spare the Party further embarrassment' after he killed his wife. For Althusser's reflections on his experience with the PCF, see 1993:227–54.

[34] Notably Rancière, though in his memoir (1993:236) Althusser claimed that most stuck with him, even those who left or were expelled from the Party.

such it has the same functions as were ascribed to organised religion by Comte: as a centre for doctrinal development and dissemination, as an organiser of ritual practices (rallies, demonstrations, memorials, May Day, etc.) and as keeper of the Communist flame. To be sure, Althusser's (and the post-Stalin CPSU's) version of Positive religiosity is far less strenuous and totalistic than Comte's. There is no hyper-organised calendar of worship, no *Culte de la Femme*. Its ethical content – a collectivism qualified by respect for the human person, individual rights etc. – derives more from Durkheim's liberal correction of Comte's program in *The Division of Labour* than from the *Catéchisme positive*. In short, the Party, as Althusser sees it, supervises *le dogme* and *le culte* but not *le régime*. On the other hand, Althusser is more Comtean than Durkheimian in subscribing to the (Leninist) idea of an ideological apparatus which is (in principle) independent of the (socialist) state. He also reverts to Comte in advancing 'Humanism' itself as the largest ideological envelope within which Communism as a 'system of representations' is to be expressed.

Mutatis mutandis, the fit indeed would seem to be perfect. Except for one small detail. History, for Althusser, is 'a process without a subject' (1969:95–7). The social formation which replaces the non-scientific category of *société* is a 'complex and over-determined' structure of structures (210–11). The diachronic dimension cannot be understood as the unfolding essence of Man, nor the synchronic as an integral and transcending super-being. For that same reason – the decentring displacement that, for Althusser, made Marx a *Marxist* (1969:24–7) – humanism, as a system of belief in, and worship of, 'Humanity', is scientifically *empty*. Neither in reality, nor for knowledge, is there, can there be, any such object. Humanity may be a supreme value, but it is not a something which can be known, narrated, intervened in or strategised on behalf of. The same (Althusser turns here to Lacan) goes for the 'human person'. Given the repression that fissures the oedipal subject inscribed within the order of the symbolic (1971:189–90), what is benign, even mandatory, as a progressive civic totem is also (in theory as well as in fact) an ideological construct that must be dismantled before knowledge of 'the human' can begin. In short, by locating social scientificity in (the later) Marx rather than in the sociology of Comte and Durkheim, and then by reading that scientificity in the anti-essentialist light of (post)structuralism, the Humanism that Althusser endorses *ideologically* is firmly tied to a 'theoretical anti-humanism'.

Now, on one level, as against Comte's own Positivism, this is a real gain. Althusser's humanism without Humanity releases the system from the Comtean bind. If positivised faith does not have to be organised around a single transcending point, if that point does not have to be phenomenally 'real', if the referent of *l'Humanité* is itself declared '*fictif*' – while still serving as a (necessary) symbol through which to express 'our noblest aspirations' – then Positivism's false, and forced, closure does not have to be made. This leaves the 'open discourse' of (social) science free to go on its way without having to collapse into the (socialist) ideology it scientifically and philosophically supports.[35] Furthermore, Althusser's Marxist distinction between the social relations to be reproduced (internal to the 'mode of production') and the politico-ideological process wherein this occurs (the 'order of reproduction') also releases Comte's analysis from the catastrophist sense of terminal crisis that comes from their conflation. Althusser's version of Positive Religion is not burdened with the task of continually recreating 'Humanity', at the price of otherwise letting the human collectivity as such completely dissolve.

However, Althusser's emendation of Comte raises problems of its own. In the first place, any ideological system that distinguishes between an exoteric understanding of its doctrine – humanist slogans taken at face value, for example – and an esoteric understanding, in which these same slogans are comprehended 'scientifically', implies a social hierarchy at variance with what 'socialist humanism' would seem to imply. For Comte, as for Counter-Reformation Catholicism, this was not itself an objection. Perhaps not for Althusser either.[36] For his Christian or Positivist predecessors, in any case, the disjuncture between lay and expert levels of doctrinal understanding was not absolute. The eminent term – God or Humanity – was taken, however understood, to be both singular and 'real'. So the split in subjectivity between doctrinal leaders and ideological followers was mitigated by the shared indubitability of *both* what is deemed to be sacred *and* the deeming itself. For Althusser, by contrast, there is no such common focus for faith and knowledge.

[35] For Althusser's discussion of the 'openness' of scientific discourse, and his deployment of the circle and the mirror as figures for the 'ideological' formulation of the 'classical problem of knowledge', see 1970:52–6. The passage concludes: 'The mere substitution of the question of the *mechanism* of the cognitive appropriation of the real object by means of the object of knowledge, for the ideological question of *guarantees* of the possibility of knowledge, contains in it that mutation of the problematic which rescues us from the closed space of ideology to the open space of the philosophical theory we are seeking.'

[36] 'In the strict sense, an *egalitarian conception of practice* – and I say this with the deep respect every Marxist owes to the experience and sacrifices of the men whose labour, sufferings, and struggles still nourish and sustain our whole present and future, all our arguments and hope – *an egalitarian conception of practice* is to dialectical materialism what egalitarian communism is to scientific communism: a conception to be criticized and superseded in order to establish a scientific conception of practice exactly in its place' (1970:58; emphasis in original).

Indeed, there is no focalising object at all. The 'humanity' of socialist humanism is neither thematised nor thematisable. For Althusser, moreover, the scientific understanding of humanist discourse is in an entirely different register from humanism itself as an ideological system of representations. Whence a serious difficulty. In the absence of a common hinge, it is hard to see how, except instrumentally and from *le dehors* (in a 'scientific policy' *towards* ideology), the two planes – Marxist science and socialist ideology – could be *ideologically* articulated together at all.

This raises a frontal difficulty for Althusser's justificatory theory of the Party. Why, in the first place, 'Communism'? Why, other than that we do, should we *believe* in the socialist struggle? If the Party of Humanity has no reply to these questions other than in an ideological language which it knows to be no more (though no less) than that, it would be open to a serious charge: that it subsists in bad faith. Various escapes are possible. One would be to recast the notion of Communist faith itself. We might take nothingness, or *différance*, as the 'groundless ground' of both democratic community and the engagement it inspires.[37] Alternatively, we might take our stand from within the given subjectivity of movements in struggle, for example on *justice*. However, unless that notion (on which there is an entire literature) is examined further, and if the thirst for justice is taken to be its own justification, the motives associated with it may relax into a self-convinced moralism that is vulnerable to the soundings of Nietzsche's hammer. That was just the suspicion voiced by an anonymous French critic who detected only guilt and rage in the 'moral and ideological reason' which Althusser (in a talk to students) endorsed as the proper spirit of the political militant.[38]

There is need, in any case, for a deeper ideological reflexivity than Althusser offers. Althusser's enterprise of 'theoretical ideology', and more particularly that aspect of it which concerns the socialist equivalent (or non-equivalent) of theism's principle of transcendence, may have established some conceptual parameters. As a clarification in substance, however, Althusser only provides the most tentative of starting points. In the absence of a solution – and how could ideological theory *ever* be apodictic? – the site of such inquiry must be kept open. This would be a

---

[37] 'It [the 'finite being' 'shared' in 'community'] is a groundless "ground", less in the sense that it opens up the gaping chasm of an abyss than that it is made up only of the network, the inter-weaving, and the sharing of singularities' (Nancy, 1991:27). See also the discussions by Horowitz ('Groundless Democracy') and Cupitt ('Unsystematic Ethics') in Berry and Wernick 1993.

[38] 'Voici la formule chimique du militant: *le ressentiment de l'ouvrier, plus la mauvaise conscience de l'intellectuel:* quel horrible mélange!' (*Recherches*, 1974:22; emphasis in original).

salutary recognition, but it would have disturbing implications for any Leninist theory of the Party. Against all doctrinalism, it would imply that the tension between 'communist', or left-humanist, faith and its 'scientific' (self-)understanding should be acknowledged, even deliberately maintained. From which we might conclude that for the political left to assume the role and temper of a church in the first place is illicit and counterproductive.

Althusser's unremitting effort to justify that idea in the tough-minded terms of an anti-humanist humanism is unconvincing. Perhaps he knew that a Leninist closure and the results of his striving to fashion an orthodoxy for it were as artificial and unsustainable as Comte's. (The fantasy element did not escape him. In his autobiographical memoir he confesses, throughout his political and intellectual life, a recurrent desire to be 'the master's master' (1993:167).) Regardless, the key questions to which his position might lead if we pushed it to give a better account of its underpinnings and presuppositions are simply unasked. How, for example, in line with a socialist humanism linked to a 'theoretical anti-humanism' are we to think its horizon of community? How can we do so non-teleologically, or without recourse to a notion of Humanity or Society as an integral metabeing? In what register, indeed, are we to couch such a commitment? What is the meaning of the ethical, or the sacred, if the social to which such categories and dimensions are referred is to be conceived as a non-expressive non-totality? Again, if 'I' and 'we' are asymmetrical non-unities, what would it mean to speak of 'our' noblest aspirations, or 'my' dignity as a person? How, if at all, are we to think freedom, justice, happiness in the medium of a deontologised subjectivity?

We are, it seems, back to first principles, yet blocked by a mixture of sociologism and dogmatism from pushing such questions along. For all of Althusser's efforts, then, to clarify the ideological element of the movement from and for which he speaks, that element remains finally opaque. At the place where his thought stops, everything is still to play for.

Baudrillard: the end of the social

By Marxifying Comte and then applying an anti-essentialist correction, Althusser would refigure Leninist orthodoxy. If we dispense with his Party loyalty, his 'intervention' might be given a more heterodox interpretation. It opens the way for us to imagine ourselves within an invisible Church of the Left (for example Derrida's 'New International' (1994)) grappling with the mysteries of a faith that has neither a 'real' subject nor a 'real' object, and whose cultural reproduction is as necessary for sustaining it as its ideological forms of expression are inadequate for that faith's 'scientific' self-comprehension. Either way, Althusser's humanism without Humanity is, in a Comtean sense, *reconstructive*.

The position developed by Jean Baudrillard – an ex-Nanterre ex-sociologist who became, 'after the orgy' of the 1960s, 'France's leading philosopher of postmodernism' and 'the lone ranger of the postmarxist left' (to cite the hype)[39] – could hardly present a sharper contrast. Where Althusser, like Comte and Durkheim, aimed to synthesise and rectify, Baudrillard is anarchic and 'pataphysical'.[40] Baudrillard's pronouncements about the 'end of the social' (1983b) pronounce an end not only to any treatment of that category as divine, but to any project of transforming, improving or reviving the social at all. The end of the social is not even apocalyptic. It bespeaks, as the ultimate disillusioning of both radical and liberal teleology, 'the end of the end'.[41]

At first sight, Baudrillard's significance for the tradition of thinking which sought a post-theistic principle of transcendence in the actuality or ideality of human society lies simply here. With his insistence that the movement of history, or rather the movement of capital, has rendered 'the social' unthinkable, the socio-theological project, whether in Positivist or Marxist form, is definitively brought to a close.[42] There would, indeed, be little more to say were it not that Baudrillard's negation proceeds as an immanent critique – both on its Marxist side, where Marxist categories are themselves unmasked as the 'mirror of produc-

---

39 The last two phrases are from the publisher's blurbs for *America* and *Cool Memories*. The phrase 'after the orgy' is Baudrillard's own (1993:3–13).

40 The term 'pataphysics', taken from Jarry, is 'a science of imaginary situations, a science of the simulation or hypersimulation of an exact, true, objective world, with its universal laws, including the delirium of those who interpret it according to these laws' (Baudrillard, 1983b:33–4).

41 Citing Canetti on 'the dead point' (Baudrillard, 1990:14–15) and Virillio on the paradoxes of speed-up and lived time, Baudrillard advances a particularly sweeping (and chronologically specific!) version of the idea that history has ended. 'At some point in the 1980s, history took a turn in the opposite direction. Once the apogee of time, the summit of the curve of evolution, the solstice of history has been passed, the downward slope of events began and things began to run in reverse. It seems that like cosmic space, historical space-time is also curved . . . This is the problem: is the course of modernity reversible, and is that reversibility itself reversible? How far can this retrospective form go, this end-of-millennium dream? Is there not a "history barrier", analogous to the sound or speed barrier, beyond which, in its palinodical movement, it could not pass?' (1995:10, 13).

42 Baudrillard's obsequies for 'the social' conclude: 'Nevertheless, let us tenderly recall the unbelievable naivety of social and socialist thinkers, for thus having been able to reify as universal and elevate as ideal of transparency such a totally ambiguous and contradictory – worse, such a residual or imaginary – worse, such an already abolished in its simulation – "reality": the social' (1983b:86).

tion' (1985), and on its sociological side, where the 'social' is given a 'sociological' death. Concerning the former, the force of the negative does not wholly disappear, though where it migrates to only becomes clear when we explore the meaning of the latter. As for that, it is a question of taking Baudrillard at his word. While acknowledging (in an interview with Sylvère Lottringer) that 'My point of view is completely metaphysical', he immediately adds: 'The only "sociological" work I can claim is my effort to put an end to the social, to the concept of the social' (Gane, 1993:106).

Indeed, that work is 'sociological' (in the French manner) in two respects. First, because the 'end of the social' is itself presented as a moment in the unfolding of social being; and secondly because, as an echo of what 'the social' meant in classic French social theory, a religious aura envelops its very disappearance into the Baudrillardian black hole of 'general exchange', 'the masses' and 'third-order simulation'. To be sure, unlike those who used to worry about the 'moral crisis' of industrialism, or who worry today about capitalist restructuring and the 'tearing of the social fabric', Baudrillard's response is one of neither panic nor regret. But neither is it as flatly cynical as some critics have supposed. Later in the same interview he goes on to remark that his deepest aim is to 'bring theory into a state of grace'. This would mean, he adds, continuing 'the game of appearance and disappearance' by making 'the real', and even 'god or the gods', appear once more (Gane, 1993:122). All of which would suggest not only that ending the social is a religiously tinged event, but that Baudrillard's obsequies are another, and not just the final, chapter in the thought adventure which opens with Comte.[43]

Shifts in terminology, as well as perspective, have made it difficult to interpret the logic of Baudrillard's writings.[44] His abandonment of discursive theory after *For a Critique of The Political Economy of the Sign* (first published in 1972) creates further hazards. Still, a thread of sorts is provided by his summary self-characterisation in *The Ecstasy of Communication*. Thematically, he tells us (1988:11), he had always focussed on the fate of 'the object', understanding by that the object in

[43] Among Anglophone commentators, Mike Gane is notable in his stress on Baudrillard's relation with French sociology, and especially its concept of religion and the sacred (1991:9).

[44] The problem of interpretation has not been helped by tendencies among both supporters (Kroker and Cook, 1988) and critics (Kellner, 1989) to identify Baudrillard's thought with a culturally substantialised 'postmodernism', a term Baudrillard refused. Besides Gane, 1991, good recent commentaries include Levin, 1996, and Genosko, 1994.

commodity form both in its development as a form, and in its pervasively reifying effects on social life. In these terms, what characterises the movement of Baudrillard's thought is the way in which a Frankfurtian pessimism about the prospects of resistance by the human subject gives way to a perverse championing of the object itself.[45] This shift in perspective takes him, in Mike Gane's phrase, 'from critical to fatal theory' (1991).

Baudrillard's earlier work[46] can be read as an extension of Adorno's and Marcuse's analysis of advanced capitalism as a one-dimensional and totally administered society. His initial move was to incorporate Debord's play with Benjamin's analysis of 'mechanical reproduction' ('All that was lived has passed over into a representation' (Debord, 1977:2)) to seal fatally the sense of historical impasse. From there the analysis takes off, highlighting, in its admitted extremism, the direst tendencies in the mediatised ultra-capitalism it seeks to describe. Thus, claims Baudrillard, the fusion of sign and commodity in what Debord called 'the society of the spectacle' has led to a form of exchange (of meanings in culture, of commodities in the market) more enclosed and reified than anything imagined by Marx (Baudrillard, 1981:143–63). With this same shift, moreover, the Promethean and 'revolutionary' epoch of production is itself over. 'We have passed from the commodity law of value to the structural law of value, and this coincides with the obliteration of the social form known as production' (1995:10). Not only, with the rise of mass production, mass marketing, and the culture industry, has the industrial capitalist primacy of production over circulation and exchange been reversed. What has collapsed with this primacy is something still more fundamental: the plausibility of conceiving the social according to the same model, i.e. as the space for the deployment of purposive action and critico-revolutionary practice, and thus also as the scene of production in a theatrical sense as well (1983b:82–4).

The panoptical gaze and display of mass media amplifies the effect. Horkheimer and Adorno had already noted that 'real life is becoming indistinguishable from the movies'.[47] Baudrillard adds that where every-

---

[45] 'The only strategy possible is that of the object. We should understand by this, not the "alienated" object in the process of disalienation, the enslaved object claiming its autonomy as a subject, but the object such as it challenges the subject, and pushes it back on its own impossible position' (1990:113).

[46] *Le système des objets* (1968) and *La société de consommation* (1970). The former has been translated (London: Verso, 1996). Extracts from the latter can be found in Poster, 1988, chap. 1.

[47] 1989:126. The comment is preceded by one even more reminiscent of Baudrillard's hyper-reality: 'The whole world is made to pass through the filter of the culture industry. The old experience of the movie-goer, who sees the world outside as an extension of the film he has just left (because the latter is intent on reproducing the

thing is a 'scene' (Greek: stage) there is no backstage, a condition which, following the same etymology, is precisely 'ob-scene' (Foster, 1983:130). So the line is erased, and not only in the mediatised arts, between what presents itself and what is represented. In the 'third order of simulation', it has become objectively impossible to distinguish between concept and referent, map and territory, the real and its model (1983a:1–2). An unresponsive hyper-reality has dissolved the stage into a screen,[48] while capital has vaporised into the electronic circulation it stimulates. Thus, at the peak of the transformation descried by the Frankfurt thinkers, and announced, in different tones, by McLuhan,[49] capitalism has both imploded and gone into hyperspace. Under the circumstances, there is not only no exit through purposive social change, but the 'cognitive mapping' (Jameson, 1984:90–2) aimed at in such projects has become a fruitless and groundless endeavour.

It follows, of course, that sociology in the old 'scientific' sense has become impossible. If Baudrillard's analysis is nonetheless 'sociological', this is not, then, because of its method or epistemology, but because of a (perverse) continuity with the classics at the level of its themes. To see this we must look more closely at the terms in which his argument about the 'end of the social' is actually couched. In his key essay on that theme (1983b:65–94), Baudrillard advances three 'possible hypotheses':

1. *The social has basically never existed.* There has never been any 'social relation'. Nothing has ever functioned socially. On this inescapable basis of challenge, seduction and death there has never been anything but *simulation* of the social and the social relation. (1983b:70–1)

2. *The social has really existed, it exists even more and more*, it invests everything; it alone exists. Far from being volatilised it is the social which triumphs; the reality of the social is imposed everywhere. But contrary to an antiquated idea which

world of everyday perceptions), is now the producer's guideline. The more intensely and flawlessly his techniques duplicate empirical objects, the easier it is today for the illusion to prevail that the outside world is the straightforward continuation of that presented on the screen' (ibid.). In contemporary retail complexes, 'English pubs' and recycled vernacular architecture, the feeling of being in a movie set is no longer an illusion on the side of the movie-habituated subject. The studio-modelling of the built environment (cities as theme parks) erases the line between real and hyper-real, and inaugurates Baudrillard's world of 'third-order' simulation.

48 'Television is still the most direct prefiguration of this. But today it is the very space of habitation that is conceived as both receiver and distributor, as the space of both reception and operations, the control screen and terminal which as such may be endowed with telematic power' (Foster, 1983:128). In *Seduction* (1979) Baudrillard introduces a fourth order of simulation, 'the digital', where the control screen becomes actualised in the personal computer.

49 The paradigm shift to the 'electric age' is proclaimed in *Understanding Media* (1965) in such phrases as 'field awareness', 'the reversal of the overheated medium' and the rise of the 'audio-tactile'. For Baudrillard's (partly sympathetic) critique, see 1981: 172 et seq.

makes the social into an objective progress of mankind, it is possible to envisage that *the social itself is only residue* . . . Litter piling up from the symbolic order as it blows around, it is the social as remainder which has assumed real force and which is soon to be universal . . . (72)

3. *The social has well and truly existed, but does not exist any more.* It has existed as coherent space, as reality principle . . . The social has not always been a delusion as in the first hypothesis, nor remainder, as in the second. But precisely it has only had an end in view, a meaning as power, as work, as capital, from the perspective space of an ideal convergence, which is also that of production – in short, in the narrow gap of second-order simulacra, and, absorbed into third-order simulacra, it is dying. (82; italics in original)

At first sight the points are inconsistent. (1) and (2) contradict one another, and the 'middle' view advanced in (3) is at variance with the two preceding. The epochs and movements of social being which are alluded to have a fuzzy, and multiple, historical reference. When was 'the social'? When was it not? The argument begins to come into focus when we realise that Baudrillard is not only conducting a Frankfurtian, Situationist and McLuhanite rampage through Marx. He is doing so from a position that has already taken its bearings from Mauss's and Bataille's reconsideration of the 'primitive', centred on potlatch and the dynamics of the gift, and from the critique this makes possible of the Durkheimian (and behind that, Comtean) sociology, with whose conception of the *primordially* social it marked a break.

From this vantage point, Baudrillard draws a trenchant conclusion. The social, such as sociology imagined it – the glue holding together an integral group, sublime and auto-affected, producer and product, instantiated in the institutions it gives itself, and through which it and they are reproduced – was not originary. As Sahlins (1972) and Clastres (1987) had shown, 'there were societies without the social' (1983b:67). To call these still 'societies' would itself be dubious. Perhaps, then – Baudrillard's first hypothesis – *the social was only ever a mirage*, a changing agglomeration of visible rules, customs and ceremonies, which was all along operated by a symbolic process it futilely sought to master, and to conjure away.

Baudrillard's second hypothesis, the social as remainder, both proposes how the mirage of the social came to have substance – as the undischarged accumulation of the practico-inert – and points to a secondary mechanism in which those excluded from the pseudo-social which arises on its basis are themselves reincorporated into it. In a spiralling movement, the social, as the remainder of the remainder it continually excretes, finally consumes its own corpse. Sociology, which would benignly socialise everything, proclaims the last rites. However, with the onset of industrial modernity, collective life acquires the energy and cognitive perspective for project and intent. And in that 'narrow gap' the illusions of sociology in thinking itself able to map the social – as action, as ends in view, as institution and reinstitution – acquire some real foundation. Here, at least, and in conceptualising as 'objective' a simulation model which it was itself actively recycling back into the world, French sociology may have been illusory, but it had 'effects of truth'. (As, too, in nineteenth-century context, had Marx's preoccupation with transforming 'social relations'.)

However, continues hypothesis (3), it has these no longer. With the collapse of the referent into the sign, of the social into its own code, both the object of sociology's gaze, and the 'perspectival space' from which it might be viewed, have gone. And gone too, Baudrillard suggests – in a footnoted hypothesis (4) – is the very dynamism of the social: i.e. that clash of forces, and energy to act and plan, which derived ultimately from a vast deterritorialisation, and from which sociology itself drew strength. In the era of media, rule-by-polling, and capital-become-viral, 'the social has imploded into the masses' (1983b:91n12). Where it was, if it was at all, is now *le masse* – a black hole of densely networked communication which resists meaning, cannot be worked on, and, as the object of no possible knowledge, can be neither encountered nor rigorously conceived.[50] Thus, for Baudrillard, the social today is triply dead. As a phantom, it was never alive. As a reality, it was only ever a corpse artificially given life. And finally, as a vampire, it has given up the ghost, a dead death, an abyss of indifference, sucking the life out of the symbolic itself.

Two features of this construct should be emphasised.

The first is that Baudrillard posits his farewell to the social, and the necessity of its disappearance, on the basis of a change taken to have occurred, for what are ultimately technological and socio-economic reasons, in the character of social existence. Thus, for all his double move out of Durkheimianism – by recourse to the symbolic as the primordial–social on the one side, and to the late-capitalist implosion of the social on the other – he stays within the orbit of the ontological question (what is the being of the social?) around which it was discursively organised. The simulated social projected by sociology turns out to have been merely an episode (conceptual, but also real) in the history of a more inclusive 'social' that cannot any longer be thought of under that name. This enveloping reality is itself a *composite* social, which

---

[50] Cf. Benjamin: 'The mass is a matrix from which all traditional behaviour towards works of art issues today in a new form. Quantity has been transmuted into quality. The greatly increased mass of participants has produced a change in the mode of participation' (1969:239).

includes not only (Comte and Durkheim's) *société* but also the economic order of exchange and the more primal order of the gift and the symbolic, not to mention the 'social' that still piles up as remainder, as well, in current mode, as the black hole into which all these others have now disappeared.

This is not to say that Baudrillard ontologises the social in the same manner as classical French sociology. Given the disparate modes of the 'social' it would inscribe, the englobing and historically changing reality he (namelessly) gestures towards in his genealogical sketch-plan has a contradictory complexity. It is an assemblage without essence, and not to be conceived as either entity or substance. Nevertheless, the conceptual space within which Baudrillard's narrative unfolds still maintains, at the most abstract level of its patterning, a basic sociological presumption: that somewhere in the zone of what he is trying to speak of there is a break in the continuity of being which permits us to speak of the associative/interactive element of the human as irreducible, exhibiting a character, and range of possibility (including 'disappearance'), all of its own. If he is to be criticised in this respect, indeed, it is for not being sociological enough. By not attempting to conceptualise the complex social ontology he deploys, he conveniently elides the multiple meanings of the 'social' whose end he hypothesises. This simplification, in turn, authorises him to overstate the extremity of the late-capitalist situation in line with the 'metaphysical' concerns which, all along, underlie his account. Not the least charm of Baudrillard's position is that this itself – as a challenge designed to awaken the force of the gift – can be construed as a deliberate stratagem.

The second noteworthy feature of Baudrillard's 'hypotheses' concerns the transformed meaning he gives to their central motif. 'The end of the social' had been a central concern for Comte and Durkheim, too. For them, however, it had been linked to anxiety about a primal social dissolution. Failure to sustain 'humanity' or 'society' as religiously experienced transcendents risked an ideological catastrophe in which, dissolved by cynicism, impulse and egoism, the integration and reproducibility of the group as such were at risk. The paradox of Baudrillard's formulation is that it enables him to say, on the one hand, that the nihilism feared by classical sociology has triumphed. It has done so, indeed, immanently: in the medium, and through the metamorphosis, of the social itself. On the other hand, since the social was nothing in the first place, precisely nothing has dissolved. With its passage into sidereal circulation, simulation and 'the mass', the nothing has nothinged itself. To which extent, the 'end of the social' is not a cause for lamentation. It brings the fall of an illusion, and bespeaks a fatality to embrace.

Nothing, perhaps, has given Baudrillard's critics greater difficulty than this embrace. It would, in fact, be unintelligible if we missed on the one hand its contestatively mocking tone, and on the other its Nietzschean resonance. Here, though, we must be careful. If the 'end of the social' evokes the 'death of God', it must also be understood in the context of Baudrillard's parallel account of the rise of simulation. The translation is startling. The eclipse of the real – and of the 'social' – by the hyper-real in the 'third order of the simulacrum'[51] realises, in material form, the culminating stage of Nietzsche's account of how the 'real world' at last became a myth. ('What? There is no real world? Then there is no apparent one either.')

I have already suggested that the death of Man, Society etc. in postmodern French theory has amounted (and self-consciously) to a second deicide. But Baudrillard goes one better. His sociological refor-matting, in light of late-capitalist development, of Nietzsche's story about the rise and fall of the (ultimately) 'real' inverts the meaning not only of classical sociology's anxiety about social disintegration, but also the meaning which Nietzsche gave to that story's outcome. In Baudril-lard's end-play, the scene of action, and the locus of the collapsed line between the real and apparent, has shifted from that of the *subject* (western consciousness from Platonism to 'the free spirits') to that of the *object* (1990:111 et seq.). Through the reifying effects of commodifi-cation and semiosis, the social itself has become object. Indeed, it has done so not just as another object among many, perhaps to be mastered once more, but in a ghostly way: it loses itself in the more general 'objectality' of the world, as that world metamorphosises from artefact to simulacrum, ever more radiant with effects of the 'real'. Under the circumstances, the Nietzschean daybreak – the emergence of a self-affirmative will-to-power – has become impossible, even unthinkable. Thus, if the end of the social recapitulates the death of God, it is also worse. It is the 'end of the end', the deadening of power, the declension of the will.

But there is something more. If the social passes over to the object, and if the object has a metastatically excessive 'will' of its own, then an

---

[51] Baudrillard summarises the 'three orders of simulacra' as follows: '*Counterfeit* is the dominant scheme of the "classical" period, from the Renaissance to the industrial revolution; *Production* is the dominant scheme of the industrial era; *Simulation* is the reigning scheme of the current phase that is controlled by the code. The first order of simulacra is based on the natural law of value, that of the second order on the commercial law of value, that of the third order on the structural law of value' (1983a:83). The third order combines two features, whose relation he assumes to be intrinsic: (a) the universalisation of 'economic' exchange (beyond even the zone of commodities and the money economy) and (b) a mode of representation – the hyper-real – in which sign objects are simulacra without original (1995:72–4).

evil power is installed at the heart of what a residual incarnationist religiosity might still like to think of as the source and horizon of the Good. In the Baudrillardian theatre, all works as if the social – the objectal social, the social that finally makes the social as simulacrum dissolve – is possessed by an evil genie.[52] We are far from Dionysus, but even further from the Crucified. So what, then, is Baudrillard's faith? We may suspect a diabolism, or at least a heretical version of Benjamin's chess automaton: an anti-God that is programmed to 'win every time'. But Baudrillard's heresy is, as he insists, 'Manichean' – which is to say dualistic.[53] Just as in any Manichean construct, then, there is also, but elsewhere, and not for Baudrillard lodged in any kind of 'subject', a counterprinciple to the 'God' who rules appearances and would reconcile (and finalise) the world. This other is *the symbolic*: that element of the social (in the widest sense) which – as 'reversibility' incarnate – resists being defined, and mastered, at all.

It is just here, in fact, that Baudrillard takes up his position. The power that capital has become is irresponsive. What is called for – at first apocalyptically, but then more mysteriously – is a change of terrain:

We will not destroy the system by a direct, dialectical revolution of the economic or political infrastructure . . . We will never defeat the system on the plane of the real . . . We must therefore displace everything onto the sphere of the symbolic where challenge, reversal, and overbidding are the law. (1995:36–7)

The wager is that despite the ever more pervasive effects of an accumulation and exchange process that has gone 'into orbit', that prevents the exigencies of the symbolic from asserting themselves, and that, as dead labour consuming the living, is social death itself, the symbolic is none the less inextinguishable. But how can the symbolic be brought back to life? How can it topple its rival? The answer is given by the question.

---

[52] The idea is developed in *Fatal Strategies*. 'There is no reality principle, nor one of pleasure. There is only a final principle of reconciliation, and an infinite one of evil and seduction.' Hence 'beyond the ecstasy of the social, of sex, of the body, of information', there are three 'ironic' strategies. These are identified with 'the evil genie of the social, of the object, and of passion' (1990:72).

[53] 'There are in fact two principles at stake: on the one hand . . . the fundamental attempt to rationalize the world, and on the other hand there is the inverse principle . . . adopted by the "heretics" all the way throughout the history of Christianity. This is the principle of evil itself. What the heretics posited was that the very creation of the world, hence the reality of the world, was the result of the existence of the evil demon. The function of God, then, was really to try to repudiate this evil phantom – that was the real reason God had to exist at all . . . It is once again the principle of seduction that needs to be involved in this situation: according to Manichaeism, the reality of the world is a total illusion; it is something which has been tainted from the very beginning . . . seduced by a sort of *ir*real principle since time immemorial. In this case, what one has to invoke is precisely this power of illusion' (Gane, 1993:139). This theme is developed throughout Baudrillard's later work, but see especially 'Whatever Happened to Evil?' (Baudrillard, 1993:81–8).

What would be required is a challenge beyond the limit, a reverse extermination, in short a countergift which capital cannot top. '*We can respond to death only by a superior death . . . defying the system with a gift to which it cannot respond save by its own collapse and death*' (ibid.; emphasis in original).

This challenge can be conceived in various ways, as *défi*, gaming, countergift, fatal strategy. But it does not yield a politics, at least not in any rational, calculative, sense. The social (but what can this now mean?) is to be seduced – magicalised into being – rather than produced yet again. Nor is 'seduction' to be thought voluntaristically. It proceeds *from* the object, from the 'sacred horizon of appearances' (1979:75), and it returns *back* to the object only as an elicited response. Thus the challenge Baudrillard speaks of is already within the charmed circle it would explode. Capital itself 'challenges' the social: both by turning everything into use-value and sign–economic exchange and, in the form of wage labour, by offering a 'gift without the possibility of counter-gift' (1995:37). It is in these terms that Baudrillard discusses (and seems to endorse) the wave of hostage-taking and bombings by *gauchistes* in the early 1970s – the countergift of a 'violent death' in response to 'the slow death capital offers its workers' (39). The companion essay to 'the death of the social' finds similar reasons to approve of electoral apathy and of mass trends towards a refusal of meaning (1983b:48). The same consideration can even inspire 'theory' itself. This too, through a provocatively abject and excessive miming of the object, can offer a challenge. Against exponents of a tedious political didacticism, Baudrillard writes: 'Better a despairing analysis in felicitous language than an optimistic analysis in an infelicitous language . . . That is where true depressive thought is to be found, among those who speak only of the transcending and transforming of the world, when they are incapable of transforming their own language' (1996:103). This leads him, in the same essay, to an almost Kantian maxim: 'The absolute rule of thought is to give back more than you were given. Never less, always more. The absolute rule of thought is to give back the world as it was given to us – unintelligible. And if possible to render it a little more unintelligible' (105).

Nancy: community without communion

Althusser's Marxist transposition of Comte affirms humanism (with appropriate class correction) as an ideological position. But it does so only on condition that Humanity is dismantled as an ontological category, and that its moral force as the end of ends is replaced by that of a 'communist commitment' which is itself only negatively defined.[54] For Baudrillard, the movement of social being (whose theorising he *abandons*) has both rendered 'the Revolution' illusory, and also undercut the appeal to a language of social relations in terms of which, from the Marxist side, any notion of the social as an integral and transcending totality might itself be criticised, or for that matter advanced (1983b:66–7). At the same time, the rise and fall of the 'social' ushers in a world whose hyper-real excesses paradoxically secrete, in the irrepressible destructive/creative dynamics of the 'symbolic', something more primal than the social, and more apt to be described as an immanent force for the divine.

Baudrillard's shift in ground dispenses with all recourse to teleology, communist or otherwise. But it still leaves us with a question he does not ask: what the reawakened symbolic might itself engender. It has been tempting to read into this silence an idealisation of the primitive, though Baudrillard's writings are as hostile to nostalgia as to utopia. Whatever might lie beyond 'the vanishing point' (1986:5 et seq.), the horizon that beckons is left obscure. For Comte, this horizon was the object of a master science, and the ground of reality itself. Taking one prudential step back, Althusser affirmed that there *was* a horizon, but all that could be rigorously said about it is that it designates a social formation based on a mode of production which precludes class domination. Its ideal element – which Blanchot called the 'exigency of community' (1986:3–4) – was a purely ideological figure, and so neither the object nor the basis of any knowledge. Baudrillard simply refuses to contemplate any such exigency – whether as a site for reflecting on sociality, or a site for reflecting on the vanished god which Positivist or socialist humanism had projected onto it. In the end, then, if Althusser has only banalities to offer about the form of sociality which might lie on the other side of 'the river' (1993:224), Baudrillard, by ensconcing theory itself in his own other of the symbolic, has nothing to say about it at all.

Nevertheless, from a left perspective, and even amidst the 'dereliction of the idols', the question about how we might think – or rather rethink –

---

[54] 'The communism to which the Soviet Union is committed is a world without economic exploitation, without violence, without discrimination – a world . . . that can do without shadows or tragedies' (Althusser, 1969:238). See also the more personal statement in the mémoir (1993:223 et seq.). 'I believe the only possible definition of communism – if one day it were to exist in the world – is *the absence of relationships based on the market*, that is to say of exploitative class relations and the domination of the State' (ibid.:225). Such negative definition is consistent, of course, both with a 'materialist' refusal to engage in utopian speculation and with a form of negative theology.

the question of 'community' still remains. How: both with regard to what it *is*, as a fundamental trait of social being (if we eschew the model of a fusional social superimposed on a Hobbesian egoism, how might the *in common* of social life be conceived?); but also ideologically, as the touchstone of political value, and as the desirable itself. And here, if we are to conceive community not as a pure ideal (perhaps as a lost paradise to which we long to return), might we not build on what is disclosed by pursuing the first question? If so, this would be a matter neither of nostalgia nor of utopia. It would mean affirming, welcoming, giving maximal (or at least optimal) play to a feature of our collective life which is already, and always, however precariously, present.

This is just the approach taken by Jean-Luc Nancy in his reflections on the 'inoperative community' (*la communauté désoeuvrée*) (1991:1–42). It should be said at once that Nancy's engagement with the shaping themes of French sociology is nothing like as direct as in the two previous cases. If he evinces an interest in the fundamental character of social being, he does so from a vantage point which rejects in principle the objectifying style that is the hallmark of that tradition (even for Baudrillard). He writes rather as a philosopher; and more particularly as that kind of philosopher for whom western philosophy as traditionally developed (from Plato to Hegel) has exhausted its possibilities. The tradition has not only said everything that could be said within it; by enclosing its thought-objects in concepts which erase their alterity, it has ever more completely forgotten the question of being that initially set the tradition in motion. For Nancy, as for Derrida, as for Heidegger who provided a prototype for both, philosophy is left with the task of meditating on its own closure, with the aim thereby of reopening thought to that phenomenological inquiry into the Being of beings that Heidegger called 'thinking' (1977b:341 et seq.).

Not that Nancy is a pure or uncritical Heideggerian. His *Experience of Freedom* (1993) is concerned with resuscitating a category – freedom – which is indispensable in the formulation of any kind of emancipatory politics, and which had been central to German philosophy before Heidegger. The inquiry proceeds by locating the place in the movement of Heidegger's thought, from *Sein und Zeit* to the later work on poetics and technology, in which the grounding of (human) being in freedom has been abandoned. It is a similar gesture, with but also against Heidegger, that guides Nancy's meditation on the meaning of 'community'; a meditation which he undertakes by thinking through, to places Heidegger would or could not go, the meaning of that associative aspect of *Dasein* Heidegger termed *Mitsein*, 'being with'. Heidegger's enthusiasm for the 'national–social revolution' indicated 'a vision of a people and a destiny conceived in part at least as a subject' (Nancy, 1991:14). For Nancy, this rationale[55] was not just an aberration. It indicated that Heidegger had never wholly broken from the philosophy of the subject, an incompleteness already evident (in *Sein und Zeit*) in Heidegger's failure to understand how '*Dasein*'s "being-towards death" was . . . radically implicated in its being-with – in *Mitsein*' (ibid.).

But if Nancy conducts his inquiry into the nature of community as a critical development out of Heideggerian ontology, in three respects it still belongs to the discursive field I am trying to describe.

First is the question itself, of 'community'. This question both harkens back to a formative concern of classical French sociology (the fundamental constitution of *société*) and is couched (this was 1983) as a critical reflection on a key orienting idea of the left. Acknowledging both the 'history of betrayals' and the collapse of existing socialisms before the triumphal march of capital, Nancy accepts, but only in 'a sense quite foreign to Sartre's intentions', that 'communism is the unsurpassable horizon of our time'. What concerns him particularly is the 'emblematic' meaning of that term, an emblem 'which no doubt amounted to something other than a concept, and even something other than the *meaning* of a word' (1991:1). 'Communism' expressed (past tense, because 'this emblem is no longer in circulation except in a belated way for a few') two desires. On the one hand, 'the desire to discover or rediscover a place of community at once beyond social divisions and beyond subordination to technopolitical dominion'; and on the other, 'a place from which to surmount the unraveling that occurs with the death of each of one of us – that death that, when no longer anything other than the death of the individual, carries an unbearable burden and collapses into insignificance' (ibid.). The problem for Nancy is that the idea of community has generally been confounded with that of *communion*. The latter, which would swallow up individual finitude in the 'absolute immanence' of a transcending 'we', is actually the death of 'community' as that which would respond to this double desire. The confusion has been abetted, moreover, by an insistence that community be thought of as 'a community of *human* beings', understood as a mode of collectivity that would accomplish, integrally and in the manner of a produced work, 'the essence of humanness' (3).

Nancy's (theoretical) antihumanism, a version of which we have already encountered in Althusser, brings us to a *second* respect in which his rethinking of community relates to the themes of contemporary

---

[55] Elaborated, classically, in Heidegger's address in 1993 as the incoming Rector of Freiburg. For a detailed account of the address and its context, see Farias, 1989:96–112.

socio-theology. It is post–'death of God' and preoccupied with the implications for social theory of the antimetaphysical Nietzschean aftershock. The main implication, for Nancy, is shatteringly clear. It amounts to an imperative: even in the midst of what might be conceived as a redemptive project, 'God' must in no wise be smuggled back in. The essay which closes *The Inoperative Community* – 'Of Divine Places' – is implacable on this point. A 'sickening traffic', he notes, 'has grown up around a so-called return of the spiritual and of the religious'. But '[f]orgetting the death of God, when not politically or commercially motivated, is tantamount to forgetting thought' (1991:122).

Nancy aims to dislodge not only whatever derivatively theistic associations still hover around an essentialism of the 'human', but also any negative theology that might be coaxed out of the divine disappearance itself.

The death of God called for and brought forth a mode of thought that ventures out where God no longer guarantees either being or the subject of the world. At these extremes, over these abysses or amid this drifting no god could possibly return . . . [and] there is no reason why the divine should lend its name to what thought explores or confronts in its withdrawal. (ibid.)

The stricture extends to those who would make the *Abgrund* of Being, or, *différance* or, in historical mode, a profound sense of cultural desolation in which 'the god no longer speaks', themselves into signs of deity. But if reviving the deity through the idea of its (unrecoverable) absence is illusory, filling the vacuum with a sacralised idea of the social is worse. It is positively dangerous. To see this we must avoid a misrecognition. In the biblical notion of a covenanted community, or of community as the mystical body of Christ, 'God is for the community – and a community . . . is what it is only before the face of the gods' (1991:142). Such a community does not entail, as we might imagine, a communion type of bonding at all. All of its members face what they each experience as 'my God', and do not find 'within the community itself the presence of what binds it together'. The converse is the case where the gods are absent. Then the integrally unified community 'is capable of becoming horrifying, massive, destructive of its members and itself, a society burned at the stake by its Church, its Myth, or its Spirit'. The nightmare is a community which 'thinks it is God, thinks it is the devastating presence of God' when it is 'no longer placed facing him and his absolute remoteness' (143).

A *third* feature of Nancy's account of community relates him to modern French social theory more directly. This is the special status he accords Bataille, as the one 'who has gone furthest into the crucial experience of the modern destiny of community' (1991:16). Nancy's essay proceeds principally, in fact, as a commentary on Bataille's *own* (re)thinking of community, examined as the history of a ground-breaking, but finally unsuccessful, attempt.

This history, with its successive efforts to square Marx with Mauss, Freud, de Sade and Nietzsche, and with its evolving dichotomies of general versus restricted economy, heterology versus homogeneity, excess versus utility etc., had its ratiocinative side. But it was also, Nancy insists, the history of an experience (ibid.) – in the first instance a political experience, ignited, in the age of Hitler and Stalin, by a fervid activism; but at the same time too, a literary, artistic and even 'personal' one. What drew it along was a quest: for a kind of community that Bataille was not in the end able to find, except for fleeting moments, or to elucidate to his own satisfaction.[56]

Bataille's quest took him through a variety of experimental groups – from the Surrealist 'community of artists' and the street-fighting Contre-Attaque, to Acéphale, whose secret face was turned to finding within itself an exemplary human sacrifice – just as it also took him, during the isolation of the war years, into the private intensity of friend-ships and 'the community of lovers'.[57] What Bataille was trying to discover (and live) was a mode of association that was (against the right) free and egalitarian, but also imbued with a transgressive intensity precluded in the prevailing socialist vision. In opposition to the 'fascist orgy', the ecstatic quality of its being together would come, not from the extinction, but from the heightening to the limit of 'clear consciousness'. It was a heightening, therefore, that had nothing to do with the unity of all in One, nor even with a dialectic of recognition (the discovery of self in the other and the other in the self). It came, rather, from the *interruption* of any such identificatory desire. Community of that kind would have to satisfy three desiderata: that it not be structured in dominance; that the being together of those it related not be subordi-nated to the 'restricted economy' of work and production (whether material or cultural);[58] and that the group not set itself up as a Sovereign over its members. The first requirement barred the door to fascism, which, with respect to the second, held a certain fascination (Nancy, 1991:16–17). The third barred the way as well not only to the nation-

---

[56] An index of that failure, for Nancy, was that Bataille did not publish his sociology of religion, and was not able to complete his master work *On Sovereignty* (Nancy, 1991:21).

[57] In a sympathetic counterpoint to Nancy's reflection, written and published between the first and second essays of Nancy's book, Blanchot's *La communauté inavouable* amplified the meaning of these successive moments (1986). See also Stoekl's introduction to the collection of Bataille's writings in *Visions of Excess* (1985:ix–xxiii).

[58] For a more-or-less systematic account of the distinction between 'restricted' and 'general economy', see Bataille 1988.

alism and neo-medieval hankering for organicity of the traditional right, but also, in combination with the second, to the collectivism espoused by social democracy or (Stalinised) Bolshevism.

Suspended, as Nancy puts it, 'between the two poles of ecstasy and community' (1991:20), and stimulated by his encounter with the work of Mauss and Hubert, Bataille's guiding insight was that the secret of a community which took the form of communion was 'the operative and resurrectional truth of death' (1991:17). At first, indeed, this was just the form in which he was drawn to pursue it. Hence his growing fascination with blood sacrifice, both among archaic societies and as a renewed historical possibility in his own. But he equally recognised that a community founded in sacrifice had no logical place to stop. Rushing 'headlong into immanence', it points towards the 'horror' and 'total absurdity . . . of the death work, of death considered as the work of common life'. And the same was true even of the inauthentic version, in which the sacrificial production of 'immanent being' was only 'simulated'. Here too the work of death

> was still accomplished, at least to a relative degree, in the form of the domination, oppression, extermination, and exploitation to which all socio-political systems finally lead . . . It was not only the Sun King who mixed the enslavement of the State with radiant bursts of sacred glory; this is true of all royalty that has always already distorted the sovereignty it exhibits into a means of domination and extortion. (1991:17–18)

In such terms, says Nancy, Bataille came to realise the aberrance of what he characterised as his own 'paradoxical nostalgia' for 'the royal and religious edifice of the past'. This nostalgia was aberrant not just because it was impossible to go back, or even because the desideratum was a community *without* class domination. It was so, rather, because 'the effort to which [it] corresponded was an immense failure' and 'something essential was missing from the world in which it collapsed'.[59] Hence, eventually, Bataille's complete turning away from community as a political project (he seeks his model in the isolated community of artists or lovers). Hence also, in the experimental groups in which he participated from the late 1920s till 1939, his concern to explore what might be entailed by a 'negative community' – a 'community of those who have no community'[60] because, in the sovereign excesses of its members, the sovereignty of the group itself has been sacrificed.

In retracing Bataille's adventure, Nancy's main concern is to address,

---

[59] Bataille, *Oeuvres complètes*, 8:275, cited in Nancy, 1991:18.
[60] This phrase of Bataille's is Blanchot's epigraph for part 1 of *The Unavowable Community*, on 'negative community' (1986:1–28) and is extensively commented on throughout.

or at least formulate, the problems that, in his view, Bataille's attempts to think the relation between ecstasy and community on some model other than that of communion were never able to surmount. At the limit of Bataille's thinking, where Nancy sets himself to begin, these problems stemmed from 'the paradox of a thinking magnetically attracted toward community and yet governed by the theme of the sovereignty of a *subject*' (Nancy, 1991:23). The furthest that Bataille had been able to go was in conceiving community as connecting ecstatic beings through the sharing of an ego-nihilating desire – his capitalised NOTHING. But this sharing was still conceived as a communing between subjects, which posited, on the one side, a shared third term which embodied the essence of that communing, and on the other, a kind of individual subject, as the place where this sharing became transparent to itself.[61]

For Nancy, Bataille's crucial insight had been that community, regarded as something other than the 'night of immanence', was not a being, still less a super-being, but an experience of being in common that occurs when we each, in 'clear consciousness' (and not therefore in the effusions of an ego that would lose itself in the experience of being fused into a communal self), exist outside ourselves, ec-statically. But to convert that insight into a clear thought, we must do what Bataille would not: let go of the communion model of community entirely. This in turn might make it possible to better understand the relation not only between community and ecstasy, but between both of these and death, which for Nancy as for Bataille is their linking term.

Nancy proceeds from an existential consideration. The anticipated death which is each our 'ownmost' always has an outside wherein it (and I) appears in the world as the finitude of the other for an other. In this sense, and against Heidegger, we could say that the ecstatic character of *Dasein* derives not simply from its *own* thrownness and being-unto-death, but from the relational implication of that finitude as something shared in our being-with others. My singularity as a mortal being is not something self-enclosed, to be cultivated, suffered or asserted. It is the effect of a continual 'ex-posure', of each as a singular and finite other for each, such that the singularity of *Dasein* is even constituted by the field of finitudes in which it 'co-appears' (*com-parait*).[62] In the 'community of lovers' – which for Nancy as for Bataille served as a paradigm

---

61 '[I]n his writings from the period of *la Souveraineté* . . . it is as though the communication of each being with NOTHING were beginning to prevail over the communication between beings, or as if it were necessary to give up trying to show that in both cases it was a question of *the same thing*' (Nancy, 1991:22).

62 'Finitude *co-appears* or *compears* (*com-paraît*) and can only *compear*: in this formulation we would need to hear that finite being always presents itself "together", hence severally: for finitude always presents itself at a *hearing* and before the judgment of the

(1991:24–6) – it is in this sharing/dividing (*partager*) of finitude, rather than in the lovers' suicide pact (which only exemplifies communion as a death work), that the unbreakable link between love and death is to be found. At the ecstatic zenith of consciousness – wordlessly, perhaps, with passions unleashed, in the mutual contact of skin with skin – I find myself not to be a sovereign over others, or even a sovereign among others, but a singularity which exists as such in being shared. Community, then, is not that to which we 'belong', but simply the 'spacing of this dislocation'. It is the place where, as finite other for finite other, we are always outside ourselves. And likewise for any communing practice we might think of as making community 'happen'. 'What "there is" in place of communication is neither the subject nor the object of communal being, but community and sharing' (1991:25).

Thus, 'community' in the sense which Nancy strives to identify is not something to be built, produced or brought into being. It is as opposed, in fact, to anything which might be the object of a project, or the result of a work, as to community conceived of as communion. In fact it is manifest in, and as, the *unworking* of all the instrumentalities which make organised social life – ever more intensively – what it has become. Hence the qualifier, which borrows a term from Blanchot, *désœuvrée*. Still less, at the same time, is *la communauté désœuvrée* some kind of prelapsarian condition – oral culture, the intimacy of the face-to-face etc. – which has been tragically negated in the giddy but disintegrative progress of a technologised and globalising capitalism, and which it would be good, or salvific, to recover. The 'inoperative community' is the originary 'being-with' that is the precondition for any sociation whatever. (This, Nancy suggests, had been Rousseau's thought in the *Second Discourse*: he had posited a sociality in the 'state of nature' that preceded 'society', and that preceded, therefore, both the unity and division to which the institution of 'society' gave rise.[63]) Community, then, as 'that which communicates in community, and [as] what community communicates', always exists (ibid.). And it will continue to exist – even at that extreme limit of totalitarianism where the 'compearance of singularity' threatens to be destroyed (or where sharing

---

law of community; or, more originarily, before the judgment of community as law' (1991:28).

[63] 'In [Rousseau's] thinking, society comes about as the bond *and* as the separation between those who, in "the state of nature", being without any bond, are nonetheless not separated or isolated. The "societal" state exposes them to separation, but this is how it exposes "man", and how it exposes him to the judgment of his fellows. Rousseau is indeed in every sense the thinker par excellence of compearance' (Nancy, 1991:29–30).

'threatens to destroy what is shared') – so long as mortal beings live among, and beside, one another at all.

At this point, however, we may wonder if Nancy's answer is strictly in line with Bataille's question. For if the 'unheard experience' of community that he seeks to elicit from Bataille is to be disengaged through a meditation on *Mitsein*, has he not detached it from the very considerations that propelled Bataille's own interest? By opposing the inoperative community to the communion concept from which, Nancy argues, Bataille never quite freed himself, the equation of community with the sacred (even a Dionysian experience of the sacred, on the edge of sacrifice) is snapped. At the same time, the rethinking of ecstasy in relation to death and community which Nancy's move entails, converts community into an eternally recurrent feature of existence. At which point it is hard to see what remains of its *political* significance, whether as a critical reference point for analysing/denouncing the deficiencies of capitalist sociality, or as a programmatic goal, the 'real' community which we might aspire to bring into being.

Yet the fruit has not fallen so far from the tree as it might seem. First, concerning its religious dimension, while Nancy carries forward Bataille's critique of the Society–God even against Bataille's own hankerings for the sacred, yet, in a different sense, Nancy's 'inoperative community' itself has a transcendent quality. After noting that even in the extermination camp, which is 'in essence, the will to destroy community', 'community never entirely ceases to resist this will', Nancy adds:

Community is, in a sense, resistance itself: namely, resistance to immanence. Consequently, community is transcendence: but 'transcendence' which no longer has any 'sacred' meaning, signifying precisely a resistance to immanence (resistance to the communion of everyone or to the exclusive passion of one or several: to all forms and all the violences of subjectivity). (1991:35)

This is not the transcendence of a deity, either with respect to a commanding will or majesty, or with respect to an immortality, in whose perfection and infinitude we might lose and save ourselves. Nor is the goodness in such a figure to be thought of incarnationally. Nevertheless, something of the divine is still manifest in it. Nancy's community is a real force, dwelling in the human world, which unceasingly 'acts' (though not as an agent) to resist the supreme evil of 'immanence'.

Nor, by the same token, is the 'inoperative community' an entirely apolitical notion. If it dispels the idea of community as 'a work to be done or produced', it refigures community as 'a gift to be renewed and communicated'. It points, then, to an 'infinite task' ('a task and a struggle that Marx grasped and Bataille understood') 'at the heart of finitude' (1991:35). On this interpretation, the standpoint of 'community' would certainly imply a politics; though it would also imply both an end to means-and-ends thinking (and thus to politics as strategy and tactics) and to Promethean activism as its emancipatory mode. Instead, '[i]f the political is not dissolved in the socio-technical element of forces and needs (in which . . . it seems to be dissolving before our eyes), it must inscribe the sharing of community'. Thus '"political" would mean a community ordering itself to the unworking of its communication . . . consciously undergoing the experience of its sharing' (40). And the defining feature of such a politics would be communication itself – 'as when Lyotard, for example, speaks of the "absolute wrong" done . . . to the one who does not even have the language in which to express the wrong done to him' (35–6).

Several objections may be lodged against this view. One is that Nancy's politics of community merges too readily into a contemporary politics of 'voice'. By moving from the terrain of struggle against the conditions which produce the 'wrong' to that of its (mere) representation, do we not leave these conditions unchallenged? By insisting on the absolute opposition between community and communion, warrant may also be given for an even more adaptive move. This would be to see something hopeful in the unworking of collective work, and of the collectivity as the product of its own work, by the 'techno-economic exigencies' of capital itself.[64] It may be said that the *Communist Manifesto*'s modernist paean for the cultural dynamic of capitalism, in which 'all that is solid melts into air' (Feuer, 1959:10), points in a similar direction. But if Marx and Engels endorsed the break-up of precapitalist institutions and traditions, what made this liberating was the prospect of new forms of solidarity, and of communal institution, which capitalist development, against itself, would also bring about. Where no such dialectic can be presumed, such a position, for all its benign intention, is hard to distinguish from mere complacency towards the culturally dissolvent force of the market. A politics defined, finally, as 'the communication of community' is a politics without mediations. It would not be unfair to say, indeed, that it is the very purism of Nancy's position – his disinclination to consider as the proper site of the political that messy middle ground between community and communion, between making happen and letting be, between task and work – which accounts for the liberal gloss it can be given.

Whatever the validity of these objections, they do not negate the overall interpretative point. Nancy is operating – in however altered and attenuated a form – within the same implicitly 'socio-theological' pro-

---

[64] For a forthright adoption of this position, see Agamben, 1993.

blematic as we have seen in the cases of Althusser and Baudrillard, a problematic which he too, in his way, seeks to deconstruct. No doubt, in continuing to posit a transcendental dimension to the social, Nancy goes as far as possible to deny both divinity and substantiality to that dimension. It is the very force of his denial which gives his position, against all tendencies towards 'communion', its critical edge. We might say, however, that it is this which also limits him politically. Despite Nancy's wish to thematise the 'inoperative community' almost constitutively as that which leaves the vacated place of God empty (and especially sociology's secularised version of the *deus communis*), the emphatically anti-absolutist and anti-totalising movement of 'communication' is accorded an absolute moral value such that (by relegating all else to demonic immanence and fallen instrumentality) it commands the political field. In such terms, the second-order practices indispensable to any transformist horizon – i.e. those which would work on the mediating structures of social life – become unthinkable.

Politics, transcendence and the social

If I may risk a summarising formula that is perhaps unavoidably fuzzy, since all its terms and relations are precisely at issue in the problem field whose emergence I have been trying to describe, what links the otherwise disparate reflections of Althusser on 'socialist humanism', Baudrillard on the 'death of the social' and Nancy on the 'inoperative community' both with one another, and, through Durkheim, with Comte's earlier attempt to launch a Positive religion, is this: that – from the midst of an intellectual culture which continues to affirm the Enlightenment break with any otherworldly metaphysics – they are part of a common effort to develop an orientation towards politics, social life and what (for lack of a better word) I will call the transcendent; and to do so in a way that links these moments indissociably *together*.

Politically, such thinking relates itself to a practice of human improvement, however conceived. Its character as *social* theory stems from conceiving that practice, even if the pure production model is disavowed, as acting upon the conditions, relations or constitutive character of social life, which is itself regarded as a *sui generis* reality. And its *transcendent* dimension lies in the commitment to, and effort to secure, an ideological reference point that calls or commands such practice *from infinitely beyond* what is immediately given in the mundane play of prevailing interests and needs. What closes the loop, and defines the 'family resemblance' between positions, is that (in some sense) the social itself, rather than any transmundane reality, is taken to be the site or source of the beyond that calls. It is this idea which gives (what I will term, for short) the 'French' tradition of modern social theory both its paradoxical character and, in combination with its derivatively Catholic ontological approach to the social, its distinctiveness.

Marx's revolutionary atheism was no doubt inscribed within the same general field of thought. For him, however, the (left Hegelian) project of realising the Absolute was assimilated without remainder into the always incipiently transformist politics of the class struggle. The independent conceptualisation or even representation of the 'social humanity or human society' which was the highest orienting value for revolutionary praxis was therefore unnecessary. Operating on consciousness at all, as for example in Feuerbach's critique of religious self-alienation, was an idealist diversion that could lead to class collaborationist politics. To realise the ideal and emancipatory aims of German philosophy, we must enter instead into the actual conflicts of the world.

If Marxism, and the tradition of revolutionary socialism, continued nonetheless to harbour a theology of the social ('communism as the riddle of history solved'), that theology remained, as Benjamin put it, 'wizened and out of sight'. For Comte, on the other hand, in the aftermath of a revolution that had actually occurred, and in a country where the Reformation had not, it was a matter of rethinking and reinstituting, rather than just practically translating, what was phantasmatically occluded in the old religion. In that context, where the spirit of an unreconstructed Christianity was cornered by reaction, and political discourse was haunted by nihilism (at the limit, de Sade's 'republic of crime'), constructing a new principle of transcendence could plausibly present itself as an essential component of social reform.

In line with a social moralism forged in the Revolution itself, and taken to its furthest extent, Comte's Positivist move was to identify the requisite principle of transcendence with what it took to be a wholly this-sided but nonetheless morally eminent reality: the developing social totality constituted by the species as a whole. This totality, *l'Humanité*, was at once *le* Grand-Être and the proper object of a science. Given this duality, completing the scientific revolution by founding 'sociology' was not just a gain for knowledge. It would also transform all the other sciences by linking them up in a philosophical system endowed with a worshipful attitude towards this eminent object, an object whose inner development was represented by the rise of those same sciences. Positive science, from being the enemy of religion, would thus achieve the unachieved ambitions of Christianity to unite knowledge and faith in a truly systematic theology – albeit one in which the supernatural *Dieu* was replaced by a 'relative' absolute which was located firmly in the world, which changed through time, and which was subject to all the laws of nature. Within the system, sociology (capping the 'objective' synthesis) and *la morale* (capping the 'subjective' synthesis) would provide a positive knowledge of what a scientific understanding revealed to be *le vrai Dieu*.

A crucial weakness of Comte's solution lay in the *a priori* concepts of 'society' and 'Humanity' introduced analogically into his social 'science' from contemporary biology. These relied on an organicist and developmental metaphorics vulnerable to the scepticism of a phenomenally based conception of science which Positivism itself methodologically endorsed. In effect, there was a gap between the real and ideal objects of sociology that was covered over in the way its knowledge object was conceptually constructed. The practical impossibility of the Positivist solution flowed from the same gap, which could only be closed on the plane of the real by actually instituting Humanity as a transcendent force within individual subjectivity. In the face of capitalist industrialisation, whose techno-economic dynamic a bio-organismic conception of the social could not begin to grasp, such an attempt, through establishing a fully articulated and punctiliously ritualised Religion of Humanity, was doomed to sectarian marginality.

Durkheim's amendment of the Comtean program to some degree addressed these weaknesses. On the historical side, he ditched the 'law of three stages' and de-emphasised memory work as a key component of the subjective maintenance of the transcendent reality to be constituted out of *société*. With regard to the new *morale* required by industrialism he privileged ritual over belief, and insisted that the *conscience collective*, as a homogenising force for social unity, was necessarily reduced in role and scope. He also abandoned the philosophical unification of the sciences as a key component of that *morale*'s supporting intellectual framework, which sociology alone would provide. He further amended the Comtean program by identifying *la société* with Kant's kingdom of ends, but shorn of its formalism by the way in which these ends themselves evolved together with the structure of *la société*. In place, then, of Comte's wholesale creation of a religion of Humanity, Durkheim's sociology would underwrite a solidary civic religion focussed on the universal element of (each national) society. This civic religion was itself expressed, given the highly differentiated structure of industrial society, in a socially and morally responsible individualism which respected the sanctity and autonomy of the person.

The rallying power of this elevated liberalism against the proto-fascist forces mobilised in the Dreyfus affair cannot be discounted. However, the semi-official status that Durkheimian sociology and sociolatry subsequently achieved also indicated a slackening of Positivism's transcendent element. In shifting to a *civisme* that made fewer practical demands, Durkheim had done more than just abandon Comte's authoritarian and baroque blueprint for the new order. He had also reduced the distance and tension between *l'Humanité* and present conditions, such that, in the Durkheimian translation, the contemporary form of the transcendent element of the social, the liberal–conservative logos articulated by the *conscience collective*, was all too readily identifiable with the ideal which actually existing industrial capitalist society gave itself. At the same time, Durkheim persisted in regarding *la société*, whether in 'mechanical' or 'organic' mode, as an integrated supra-individual entity. Not only was this to retain a suspect bio-organismic model of the social, it also continued in the Comtean track of figuring the transcendent call of the social in the mirror of a God which had itself been figured in the mirror of a perfectly harmonious and unified community. What I have called the 'second death of God' in post-Durkheimian French social theory has been the history of the collapse and disavowal of this idea.

Comte's inadequate account of the relation between social being and the 'social tie', his conflation of the social with its reproduction, and his failure to produce an idea of Humanity's actualisation other than as reliant on a vast and self-abnegating effort to create and keep it going *as* an idea, already pointed to this collapse. *Le* Grand-Être, and the unfolding *société* it subjectively represented, were simulacra whose hollowness was hidden only by the convoluted rationalisations of his faith. The same anxieties about the fragility of Society as a socially constructed transcendent haunted Durkheim's revised espousal of a morally individualist civic religion; and these similarly pushed to the background questions about that category's conceptual underpinnings (Marxist or Rousseauian ones, for example, about the alienated constitution of the *conscience collective*) which it would have been dissolvent to pursue. But how could faith in Humanity or Society be disavowed if its sacral object *practically* anchored the Good? Or if sustaining that faith was all that stood in the way of *actual* social dissolution? For disavowal of the Society–god to be something other than a despairing move, it was not enough just to let the imaginary goose out of the imaginary bottle. It required more indeed than radicalising the analysis so as to disentangle questions concerning the destiny of society under the techno-economic conditions of capitalism from that of society as such, though this was a necessary step. To affirm the death of the Society–god while still affirming a political commitment oriented towards the transcendent dimension of the social would necessitate, as well, a reconceptualisation both of social being and of what might be regarded as transcendent 'within' it. It would require, in effect, the sociological equivalent of Nietzsche's 'transvaluation'.

Negatively, this would mean sweeping aside a conception of the primordially social as a fused totality which behaved as a collective subject and which presented itself transcendentally in the image either of monarchical Authority or of a common body in which all were lovingly conjoined. Bataille's critique of 'sovereignty', and his corresponding quest for an acephalic community (1985:178–81), pointed trenchantly in this direction. It implied a critique not only of medieval corporatism and its One True God, but also of classical sociology's vision of a solidary *société industrielle*. Not to mention nationalisms of every stripe, and all nostalgia for pre-industrial *Gemeinschaft* (the paradise that never existed) as well. A similar breadth of target is discernible in Althusser's critique of social essentialism. His general model of ideology – a 'specular' structure in which the small-'s' subject is 'interpellated' by the projective big-'s' Subject – is illustrated by simultaneous reference to the Catholic mass and to the swelling themes of a universalist bourgeois humanism propounded in French state schools.

For Althusser, though, ideology in some such form was functionally indispensable, both for individual formation and for social reproduction. Indeed, it was so not only in class societies, but in all social formations whatsoever. This in turn provided sociological warrant for halting the demolition of Comtean and Durkheimian socio-theology halfway. Althusser adopted, in effect, a compromise position. He insisted on the ideological necessity of a (socialist) humanism that was – without reconsidering the kind of community at which socialists aimed – rigorously underwritten both by a 'theoretical antihumanism' and by a critique of Society as an 'expressive' totality. There was no such compromise for Bataille. Meditating ceaselessly, and experimentally, on the cruel secret that underlies any unitary idea of society, he wrestled forthrightly with the disturbing implication which demolishing any social ontology of that kind held *substantively* for the left. This was the suspicion it brought towards the 'community' of commun-ism itself, whether as a feasible or even desirable emancipatory goal.

From Bataille, at the same time, derive two possible ways in which, from a radical perspective, the relation between the social and the divine might be *affirmatively reconceived*. One, building on gift, sacrifice and 'general economy', would be a sociologically inflected Dionysianism which – in Baudrillard's *défi* – places its chips on the potential for 'reversibility' of 'symbolic exchange'. A second, highlighted by Nancy, would be to rethink 'community' in terms other than, indeed in categorical opposition to, those of 'communion'. For Bataille no doubt

these ways were not distinct. Even as differentially developed we might
see in them only a complementary distinction between the dynamic and
static dimensions of Comte's god, respectively rendered into the spirits
that attend (for Baudrillard) metamorphosis and (for Nancy) communication as the freedom to exist.

Regardless of their relations and differences, what is noteworthy
about these two pathways is the similarity of their lines of flight. In
relation to the deification of the social they each aim to overcome, theirs
is an *anti-immanentist immanentism*. This is not as contradictory as it
sounds. Baudrillard's 'symbolic' and Nancy's 'inoperative' community
beckon to us from *beyond* the confines of a social world that always
threatens to close in on itself. Yet against any such closure, they exercise
a force, of a resistance and of an attraction, from *within* the very nature
of social life itself. On the one hand, that is to say, both Baudrillard and
Nancy repudiate, as hell on earth, any idealised figure of a *socius* that
would present itself as a god to those bonded together by and within it.
On the other hand, both are nonetheless immanentist with respect to
their own, drastically revised, understandings of what inextricably
belongs to the nature of social being. To this there is an equally
important corollary. If, for Baudrillard and Nancy, adopting the perspective of 'general economy' and/or 'the between' shifts the social site
of immanence, it also changes the meaning of the transcendent which
might be represented as 'being' there. In contrast to the society–god of
classical socio-theology, the equivalent category in *postmodern* socio-
theology is to be conceived as neither an essence nor an entity, nor
indeed as something lodged, as it was for Comte, in human subjectivity.
Nor, at the same time, can it be regarded as just another name for God.
What Baudrillard affirms is a transformative fire which might permit the
gods to 'appear'; for Nancy, it is the liberating air of a communing exposition which opens us to that empty infinitude into which the abandoned and abandoning gods have definitively disappeared. In both
cases, if such metaphors can be used this way at all, we have divinity of
process rather than divinity of being.

It may easily be said that the efforts by Nancy and Baudrillard to
preserve a non-theistic space for the transcendent in social theory come
at the price of depoliticising it; just as, by contrast, Althusser's Marxified
Comte elevates political categories at the expense of being able to think
the transcendental element from which the ideological dimension of
that politics beckons. Thus neither Baudrillard's reflections on the
altered social being of advanced (post-Fordist) capitalism, nor Nancy's
rethinking of Bataille's 'community', nor Althusser's reflections on
(socialist) humanism are sufficient in themselves. None give an adequate

account of the relation between politics, social being and the 'god' that attends the secular left. Nevertheless, each of these thinkers puts in play a set of considerations which are as absent from one another's thinking as they were from the pre-postmodern socio-theology of Comte and Durkheim. Given their incompatibilities, a synthesis would be hard to imagine. Taken as a whole, I would simply say, their thought gives us a field of questions, issues and dimensions that cannot be avoided by those who might wish, from a resolutely 'this-worldly' perspective, to clarify the transcending ideological element within the project of an emancipatory social transformation, such as it might be conceived today.

As for the religious status of such thinking, whether Althusser, Baudrillard and Nancy continue not only the classical nineteenth-century attempt to replace theology with sociology, but also ('a/theologi-cally') the project of theology itself, may be debated. I am inclined to argue yes to the first and no to the second, in order to highlight the radical nature of the breach with any form of otherworldliness which classical sociology attempted but was not able to make complete. To define this whole thought-adventure from the baseline of traditional theology (as does John Milbank) is doubtless illuminating. But it runs the risk of a reduction in which the religious preoccupations of secular reason are seen only as flawed, aberrant or shamefaced versions of the real (theological) thing. In an age when, in common opposition to both religious fundamentalisms and the closed horizons of late-capitalist culture, a new dialogue is developing between 'believers' and 'non-believers' on the ground of contemporary theory (Blond, 1998), what we need to develop, perhaps, is a more agnostic vocabulary, the sense of a discursive field that includes theology *and* all its post-theological continuations. This would make it easier to engage substantive religio-political issues across the theistic divide.

All that is clear is that the 'French' project is not over, and that efforts to provide a conceptually adequate *intellectum* for a redemptive but politically embedded faith in collective human possibilities will retain their currency, and continue to press for better questions and better answers, so long as some such faith continues to be generated out of the socio-historical process itself.

References

Primary sources

Comte, A., 1853, *Positive Philosophy*, translated and abridged by H. Martineau, 2 vols., Chapman, London. [This edition was authorised by Comte.]

1963, *Discours sur l'esprit positif*, Union Générale des Editions, Paris.

1970, *Oeuvres d'Auguste Comte*, ed. Sylvain Pérignon, 12 vols., Éditions Anthropos, Paris. (Vols. I–VI: *Système de philosophie positive*; vols. VII–X: *Système de politique positive*; appendix to vol. X: the 6 *opuscules*; vol. XI: *Catéchisme positiviste*; appendix to vol. XI: *Appel aux conservateurs* and *Discours sur l'esprit positif*; vol. XII: *Synthèse subjective, tome I, Logique positive*.) [References in the text are to vol. and page number unless otherwise indicated. 'xa' and 'xIa' refer to the appendices of those volumes.]

1973, *The Catechism of Positive Religion*, trans. R. Congreve, August Kelley, Clifton, N.J.

Secondary sources

Agamben, G., 1993, *The Coming Community*, University of Minnesota Press, Minneapolis.

Allison, D., 1985 ed., *The New Nietzsche: Contemporary Styles of Interpretation*, MIT Press, Cambridge, Mass.

Althusser, L., 1969, *For Marx*, Allen Lane Penguin, London.

1970, *Reading Capital*, New Left Books, London.

1971, *Lenin and Philosophy and Other Essays*, New Left Books, London.

1974, *Éléments d'auto-critique*, Hachette, Paris.

1993, *The Future Lasts Forever: A Memoir*, New Press, New York.

Ariès, P., 1981, *The Hour of Our Death*, Knopf, New York.

Aristotle, 1962, *The Politics*, Penguin, Harmondsworth.

1970, *Ethics*, trans. and ed. J. A. K. Thomson, Penguin, Harmondsworth.

Bacon, F., 1901, *The Advancement of Learning*, Collier, New York.

1960, *The New Organon*, Bobbs-Merrill, Indianapolis, Ind.

Barthes, R., 1977, *Music, Image, Text*, Hill and Wang, New York.

Bataille, G., 1985, *Visions of Excess: Selected Writings 1927–1939*, University of Minnesota Press, Minneapolis.

1988, *The Accursed Share: An Essay on General Economy*, Zone, New York.

Baudrillard, J., 1979, *De la séduction*, Éditions Galilée, Paris.

1981, *For a Critique of the Political Economy of the Sign*, Telos, St Louis.

1983a, *Simulations*, Semiotext(e), New York.

1983b, *In the Shadow of the Silent Majorities*, Semiotext(e), New York.

1985, *Le miroir de la production: ou l'illusion critique du matérialisme historique*, Éditions Galilée, Paris.

1986, *Amérique*, Grasset, Paris.

1988, *The Ecstasy of Communication*, Semiotext(e), New York.

1990, *Fatal Strategies: Crystal Revenge*, Semiotext(e), New York, Pluto, and London.

1993, *The Transparency of Evil*, Verso, London.

1994, *The Illusion of the End*, Stanford University Press, Stanford.

1995, *Symbolic Exchange and Death*, Sage, London.

1996, *The Perfect Crime*, Verso, London.

Becker, C., 1932, *The Heavenly City of the Eighteenth Century Philosophers*, Yale University Press, New Haven.

Behler, E., 1991, *Confrontations: Derrida/Heidegger/Nietzsche*, Stanford University Press, Stanford.

Benjamin, W., 1969, *Illuminations*, Schocken, New York.

Bentham, J., 1995, *The Panopticon Writings*, ed and intro. M. Bozovic, Verso, London.

Benton, T., 1984, *The Rise and Fall of Structural Marxism: Althusser and His Influence*, Macmillan, London.

Bernal, M., 1987, *Black Athena: The Afro-Asiatic Roots of Classical Civilisation*, Free Association Books, London.

Bernstein, E., 1961, *Evolutionary Socialism: A Criticism and Affirmation*, Schocken, New York.

Berry, P., and A. Wernick, 1993 ed., *Shadow of Spirit: Religion and Postmodernism*, Routledge, London and New York.

Biriotti, M., and N. Miller, 1993, *What Is an Author?*, Manchester University Press, Manchester.

Blanchot, M., 1986, *The Unavowable Community*, Station Hill Press, Barrytown, N.Y.

Bloch, E., 1995, *The Principle of Hope*, vol. I, MIT Press, Cambridge, Mass.

Blond, P., 1998, *Beyond Secular Philosophy*, Routledge, London.

Bloom, H., 1993, *The American Religion*, Simon and Schuster, New York.

Blumenberg, H., 1985, *The Legitimacy of the Modern Age*, MIT Press, Cambridge, Mass.

Bottomore, T., and M. Rubel, 1963 eds., *Karl Marx: Selected Writings in Sociology and Social Philosophy*, Penguin, Harmondsworth.

Bordieu, P., 1988, *Homo Academicus*, Polity Press in association with Blackwell, Cambridge.

1991, *The Political Ontology of Martin Heidegger*, Stanford University Press, Stanford.

Bourgeois, L., 1896, *La solidarité*, La Nouvelle Revue, Paris.

Burke, E., 1965, *Reflections on the Revolution in France*, Holt, Rinehart and Winston, New York.

Bury, J., 1960, *The Idea of Progress: An Inquiry into Its Origin and Growth*, Dover, New York.

Caird, E., 1885, *The Social Philosophy and Religion of Auguste Comte*, John Maclehose, Glasgow.

Canguilhem, G., 1991, *The Normal and the Pathological*, Zone, New York.

1994, *A Vital Rationalist: Selected Writings from Georges Canguilhem*, ed. F. Delaporte, Zone, New York.

Clastres, P., 1987, *Society vs. the State: Essays in Political Anthropology*, Zone, New York.

Cobban, A., 1982, *A History of Modern France*, vol I: *1715–1799*, Penguin, Harmondsworth.

Cohn, N., 1971, *The Pursuit of the Millennium: Revolutionary Millenarians and Mystical Anarchists of the Middle Ages*, Oxford University Press, New York.

Colletti, L., 1972, *From Rousseau to Lenin: Studies in Ideology and Society*, New Left Books, London.

Conway, D., 1997. *Nietzsche and the Political*, Routledge, London.

Coppleston, F., 1962, *A History of Philosophy*, vol. II: *Medieval Philosophy*, part I: *Augustine to Bonaventure*, Doubleday, Garden City, N.Y.

Davies, I., 1995, *Cultural Studies and Beyond: Fragments of Empire*, Routledge, New York.

Debord, G., 1977, *The Society of the Spectacle*, Black and Red, Detroit.

Derrida, J., 1974, *Of Grammatology*, Johns Hopkins University Press, Baltimore.

1982, *Margins of Philosophy*, University of Chicago Press, Chicago.

1994, *Specters of Marx: The State of the Debt, the Work of Mourning, and the New International*, Routledge, London.

Descombes, V., 1980, *Modern French Philosophy*, Cambridge University Press, Cambridge.

Devall, B., and G. Sessions, 1985, *Deep Ecology*, Peregrine Smith, Salt Lake City.

de Maistre, J., 1971, *The Works of Joseph de Maistre*, trans. and ed. J. Lively, Schocken, New York.

Durkheim, E., 1951, *Suicide*, Macmillan/Free Press, New York.

1962, *Socialism*, Collier-Macmillan, New York.

1964, *The Rules of Sociological Method*, Collier-Macmillan, New York.

1965a, *Montesquieu and Rousseau: Forerunners of Sociology*, University of Michigan Press, Ann Arbor.

1965b, *Sociology and Philosophy*, Cohen and West, London

1968a, *The Division of Labour in Society*, Collier-Macmillan, New York.

1968b, *The Elementary Forms of the Religious Life*, Allen and Unwin, London.

1972, *Selected Writings*, ed. A. Giddens, Cambridge University Press, Cambridge.

Easthope, A., 1991, *British Post-Structuralism since 1968*, Routledge, London.

Eliot, G., 1987, *Althusser: The Detour of Theory*, Verso, London.

Farias, V., 1989, *Heidegger and Nazism*, Temple University Press, Philadelphia.

Fekete, J., 1984 ed., *The Structural Allegory*, University of Minnesota Press, Minneapolis.

Feuer, L., 1959 ed., *Karl Marx and Friedrich Engels: Basic Writings on Politics and Philosophy*, Doubleday, Garden City, N.Y.

Feuerbach, L., 1957, *The Essence of Christianity*, Harper and Row, New York.

Foster, H., 1983 ed., *The Anti-Aesthetic: Essays on Postmodern Culture*, Bay Press, Port Townsend, Wash.

Foucault, M., 1970, *The Order of Things: An Archaeology of the Human Sciences*, Tavistock, London.

Freud, S., 1949, *Civilisation and Its Discontents*, Hogarth, London.

1950, *The Ego and the Id*, Hogarth, London.

1990, *The Origins of Religion: Moses and Monotheism, Totem and Taboo, and Other Works*, Penguin, London.

Fukuyama, F., 1992, *The End of History and the Last Man*, Free Press, New York, and Maxwell Macmillan, Toronto.

Funkenstein, A., 1986, *Theology and the Scientific Imagination from the Middle Ages to the Seventeenth Century*, Princeton University Press, Princeton.

Gane, M., 1991, *Baudrillard: Critical and Fatal Theory*, Routledge, London.

1993 ed., *Baudrillard Live: Selected Interviews*, Routledge, London.

Gardavsky, V., 1973, *God Is Not Yet Dead*, Penguin, Harmondsworth.

Genosko, G., 1994, *Baudrillard and Signs: Signification Ablaze*, Routledge, London.

Gerth, H., and C. Wright Mills, 1958, *From Max Weber: Essays in Sociology*, Oxford University Press, New York.

Giddens, A., 1971, *Capitalism and Modern Social Theory: An Analysis of the Writings of Marx, Durkheim and Weber*, Cambridge University Press, Cambridge.

1972 ed., *Emile Durkheim: Selected Writings*, Cambridge University Press, Cambridge.

1993, *New Rules for Sociological Method*, Stanford University Press, Stanford.

1994, *Beyond Left and Right: The Future of Radical Politics*, Stanford University Press, Stanford.

Girard, R., 1972, *Violence and the Sacred*, Johns Hopkins University Press, Baltimore.

1987, *Things Hidden since the Foundation of the World*, Stanford University Press, Stanford.

Glucksmann, A., 1972, 'A Ventriloquist Structuralism', *New Left Review*, 72.

Glucksmann, M., 1974, *Structuralist Analysis in Contemporary Social Thought: A Comparison of the Theories of Claude Lévi-Strauss and Louis Althusser*, Routledge and Kegan Paul, London.

Gouhier, H., 1933–41, *La jeunesse d'Auguste Comte*, 3 vols., Vrin, Paris.

1965, *La vie d'Auguste Comte*, Vrin, Paris.

Guillory, J., 1993, *Cultural Capital: The Problem of Literary Canon Formation*, University of Chicago Press, Chicago.

Habermas, J., 1987, *The Theory of Communicative Rationality*, 2 vols., Polity, Cambridge.

Hall, S., 1984, *The Politics of Thatcherism*, Open University Press, in association with *Marxism Today*, Milton Keynes.

Harrison, F., 1975, *Order and Progress: Thoughts on Government: Studies of Political Crises*, ed. and intro. M. S. Vogeler, Harvester, Hassocks, Sussex.

Hayek, F., 1953, *The Counter-Revolution of Science*, Free Press, New York.

Hegel, G. W. F., 1953, *Reason in History*, Bobbs-Merrill, Ind.

1967, *Phenomenology of Mind*, Harper and Row, New York.

Heidegger, M., 1977a, *The Question concerning Technology, and Other Essays*, Harper and Row, New York.

1977b, *Basic Writings*, ed. D. Krell, HarperCollins, San Francisco.

Hirst, P., 1975, *Durkheim, Bernard and Epistemology*, Routledge and Kegan Paul, London.

Horkheimer, M., 1972, *Critical Theory: Selected Essays*, Seabury Press, New York.

Horkheimer, M., and T. Adorno, 1989, *Dialectic of Enlightenment*, Continuum, New York.

Horowitz, G., 1977, *Repression: Basic and Surplus Repression in Psychoanalytic Theory: Freud, Reich and Marcuse*, University of Toronto Press, Toronto.

Hubert, H., and M. Mauss, 1964, *Sacrifice: Its Nature and Function*, Cohen and West, London.

Huntington, S., 1996, *The Clash of Civilizations and the Remaking of World Order*, Simon and Schuster, New York.

Husserl, E., 1965, *Phenomenology and the Crisis of Philosophy*, Harper and Row, New York.

Innis, H., 1982, *The Bias of Communications*, University of Toronto Press, Toronto.

Jameson, F., 1984, 'Postmodernism, or the Cultural Logic of Capital', *New Left Review*, 146: 55–92.

Kaufmann, W., 1966, *Hegel: A Reinterpretation*, Doubleday, Garden City, N.Y.

Kellner, D., 1989, *Jean Baudrillard: From Marxism to Postmodernism and Beyond*, Polity, Cambridge.

Kofman, S., 1978, *Aberrations: le devenir-femme d'Auguste Comte*, Aubier-Flammarion, Paris.

Krémer-Marietti, A., 1980, *Le projet anthropologique d'Auguste Comte*, Société d'Édition d'Enseignement Supérieur, Paris.

1982, *Entre le signe et l'histoire: l'anthropologie positiviste d'Auguste Comte*, Klincksieck, Paris.

Kroker, A., and D. Cook, 1988, *The Postmodern Scene: Excremental Culture and Hyper-Aesthetics*, Macmillan, London.

Laclau, E., and C. Mouffe, 1985, *Hegemony and Socialist Strategy: Towards a Radical Democratic Politics*, Verso, London.

Laing, R. D., 1969, *The Divided Self*, Penguin, London.

Lasch, C., 1991, *The True and Only Heaven: Progress and Its Critics*, Norton, New York.

Lash, S., 1990, *The Sociology of Postmodernism*, Routledge, London.

Lefebvre, H., 1971, *Au-delà du structuralisme*, Éditions Anthropos, Paris.

Leiss, W., 1972, *The Domination of Nature*, Braziller, New York.

Lerner, D., 1996, *The Politics of Meaning*, Addison-Wesley, Reading, Mass.

Levin, C., 1996, *Jean Baudrillard: A Study in Cultural Metaphysics*, Prentice Hall and Harvester, London.

Levinas, E., 1969, *Totality and Infinity*, Duquesne University Press, Pittsburgh.

Lévi-Strauss, C., 1967, *Structural Anthropology*, Basic, New York.

Lévy-Bruhl, L., 1973, *The Philosophy of Auguste Comte*, Putnam, New York.

Littré, É.,1845, *Auguste Comte et la philosophie positive*, Hachette, Paris.

1864, *De la philosophie positive*, Hachette, Paris.

Lovelock, J., 1979, *Gaia: A New Look at Life on Earth*, Oxford University Press, Oxford.

K. Löwith, 1949, *Meaning in History: The Theological Implications of the Philosophy of History*, University of Chicago Press, Chicago.

1967, *From Hegel to Nietzsche: The Revolution in Nineteenth Century Thought*, Doubleday, Garden City, N.Y.

Lukacs, G., 1971, *History and Class Consciousness*, Merlin, London.

Lukes, S., 1972, *Emile Durkheim, His Life and Works: A Historical and Critical Study*, Harper and Row, New York.

Lyotard, J.-F., 1984, *The Postmodern Condition: A Report on Knowledge*, University of Manchester Press, Manchester.

1991, *The Inhuman: Reflections on Time*, Stanford University Press, Stanford.

1992, *The Postmodern Explained to Children: Correspondence 1982–1985*, Turnaround, London.

Macherey, P., 1989, *Comte: la philosophie et les sciences*, Presses Universitaires de France, Paris.

Macksey, R., and E. Donato, 1972 eds., *The Structuralist Controversy*, Johns Hopkins University Press, Baltimore.

Manuel, F., 1962, *Prophets of Paris*, Harvard University Press, Cambridge, Mass.

Marcuse, H., 1955, *Eros and Civilization: A Philosophical Enquiry into Freud*, Beacon, Boston.

1960, *Reason and Revolution: Hegel and the Rise of Social Theory*, Beacon, Boston.

1966, *One Dimensional Man*, Beacon, Boston.

Markham, F., 1952, ed. and trans., *Saint-Simon: Selected Writings*, Oxford University Press, Oxford.

Martineau, H., 1853 ed. and trans., *The Positive Philosophy of Auguste Comte*, 2 vols., Chapman, London.

Marx, K., 1964, *The Economic and Philosophic Manuscripts of 1844*, International Publishers, New York.

Marx, K., and F. Engels, 1947, *The German Ideology*, International Publishers, New York.

1955, *Marx and Engels on Religion*, Foreign Languages Publishing House, Moscow.

Mauss, M., 1967, *The Gift: Forms and Functions of Exchange in Archaic Societies*, Norton, New York.

McLuhan, M., 1965, *Understanding Media*, McGraw-Hill, New York.

Milbank, J., 1993, *Theology and Social Theory: Beyond Secular Reason*, Blackwell, Oxford.

Mill, J. S., 1961, *Auguste Comte and Positivism*, University of Michigan Press, Ann Arbor.

Nancy, J.-L., 1991, *The Inoperative Community*, University of Minnesota Press, Minneapolis.

1993, *The Experience of Freedom*, Stanford University Press, Stanford.

Nietzsche, F., 1961, *Thus Spake Zarathustra*, Penguin, London.

1968, *The Will to Power*, Random House, New York.

1969, *On the Genealogy of Morals* (includes *Ecce Homo*), Random House, New York.

1982, *Daybreak: Thoughts on the Prejudices of Morality*, Cambridge University Press, Cambridge.

1990, *The Twilight of the Idols/The Anti-Christ*, Penguin, London.

1997, *Untimely Meditations*, Cambridge University Press, Cambridge.

Nisbet, R., 1965, *Emile Durkheim*, Prentice-Hall, Englewood Cliffs, N.J.

1973, *The Social Philosophers: Community and Conflict in Western Thought*, Crowell, New York.

Nizan, P., 1971, *The Watchdogs: Philosophers of the Established Order*, Monthly Review Press, New York.

Nolte, E., 1969, *The Three Faces of Fascism: Action Française, Italian Fascism, National Socialism*, New American Library, New York.

Norris, C., 1991, *Spinoza and the Origins of Modern Critical Theory*, Blackwell, Oxford.

Parsons, T., 1968, *The Structure of Social Action*, 2 vols., Free Press, New York, and Collier-Macmillan, London.

Pickering, M., 1993, *Auguste Comte: An Intellectual Biography*, vol. 1, Cambridge University Press, Cambridge.

Pieper, J., 1952, *Leisure: The Basis of Culture*, Pantheon, New York.

1960, *Scholasticism: Personalities and Problems of Medieval Philosophy*, Pantheon, New York.

Poster, M., 1988 ed., *Jean Baudrillard: Selected Writings*, Polity, Cambridge.

Poulantzas, N., 1970, *Pouvoir politique et classes sociales*, Maspero, Paris.

Recherches, 1974, no. 12 (unsigned): *Généalogie du Capital: l'idéal historique*, CERFI, Paris.

Resch, R., 1992, *Althusser and the Renewal of Marxist Social Theory*, University of California Press, Berkeley and Los Angeles.

Rose, G., 1992, *The Broken Middle: Out of Our Ancient Society*, Blackwell, Oxford.

Rousseau, J.-J., 1963, *The Social Contract and Discourses*, Dutton, New York.

Sahlins, M., 1972, *Stone Age Economics*, University of Chicago Press, Chicago.

Sartre, J.-P., 1960, *Critique de la raison dialectique*, Gallimard, Paris.

Scharff, R., 1995, *Comte after Positivism*, Cambridge University Press, Cambridge.

Scharlemann, R., 1990 ed., *Theology at the End of the Century: A Dialogue on the Postmodern with Thomas J. Altizer, Mark C. Taylor, Charles E. Winquist, Robert P. Scharlemann*, University Press of Virginia, Charlottesville.

Sebag, L., 1964, *Marxisme et structuralisme*, Payot, Paris.

Simpson, G., 1969, *Auguste Comte: Sire of Sociology*, Crowell, New York.

Smart, B., 1993, *Postmodernity*, Routledge, London.

Starr, P., 1995, *Logics of Failed Revolt: French Theory after May '68*, Stanford University Press, Stanford.

Taylor, M., 1987, *Altarity*, University of Chicago Press, Chicago.

Thompson, E. P., 1978, *The Poverty of Theory and Other Essays*, Merlin, London.

Vonnegut, K., 1968, *Welcome to the Monkey House: A Collection of Short Works*, Delacorte Press, New York.

Wallwork, E., 1972, *Durkheim: Morality and Milieu*, Harvard University Press, Cambridge, Mass.

Weber, M., 1958, *The Protestant Ethic and the Spirit of Capitalism*, Scribner, New York.

White, F., 1981, *Famous Utopias*, Hendricks House, Putney.

Woolhouse, R., 1993, *Descartes, Spinoza, Leibnitz: The Concept of Substance in Seventeenth Century Metaphysics*, Routledge, London.

World Commission on Environment and Development, 1987, *Our Common Future*, Oxford University Press, Oxford.

Wright, T., 1986, *The Religion of Humanity: The Impact of Comtean Positivism on Victorian Britain*, Cambridge University Press, Cambridge.

Wyschogrod, E., 1985, *Spirit in Ashes: Hegel, Heidegger, and Man-Made Mass Death*, Yale University Press, Newhaven.

Index